Voice and Context in Eighteenth-Century Verse

Voice and Context in Eighteenth-Century Verse

Order in Variety

Edited by

Joanna Fowler
Loughborough University, UK

and

Allan Ingram
Professor of English, University of Northumbria, UK

Selection, introduction and editorial matter © Joanna Fowler and Allan Ingram 2015
Individual chapters © Contributors 2015

All rights reserved. No reproduction, copy or transmission of this publication may be made without written permission.

No portion of this publication may be reproduced, copied or transmitted save with written permission or in accordance with the provisions of the Copyright, Designs and Patents Act 1988, or under the terms of any licence permitting limited copying issued by the Copyright Licensing Agency, Saffron House, 6–10 Kirby Street, London EC1N 8TS.

Any person who does any unauthorized act in relation to this publication may be liable to criminal prosecution and civil claims for damages.

The authors have asserted their rights to be identified as the authors of this work in accordance with the Copyright, Designs and Patents Act 1988.

First published 2015 by
PALGRAVE MACMILLAN

Palgrave Macmillan in the UK is an imprint of Macmillan Publishers Limited, registered in England, company number 785998, of Houndmills, Basingstoke, Hampshire RG21 6XS.

Palgrave Macmillan in the US is a division of St Martin's Press LLC,
175 Fifth Avenue, New York, NY 10010.

Palgrave Macmillan is the global academic imprint of the above companies and has companies and representatives throughout the world.

Palgrave® and Macmillan® are registered trademarks in the United States, the United Kingdom, Europe and other countries.

ISBN 978–1–137–48762–9

This book is printed on paper suitable for recycling and made from fully managed and sustained forest sources. Logging, pulping and manufacturing processes are expected to conform to the environmental regulations of the country of origin.

A catalogue record for this book is available from the British Library.

A catalog record for this book is available from the Library of Congress.

Typeset by MPS Limited, Chennai, India.

This volume is dedicated to the memory of Bill Overton

Contents

List of Figures ix

Acknowledgements x

Notes on Contributors xi

Professor Bill Overton, 1946–2012: A Personal Memoir xv
Hermann Josef Real

Introduction 1
Allan Ingram and Joanna Fowler

Part I Form and Influence

1 Pope's Horatian Voice 11
   Nigel Wood

2 Celebrating *Universal Beauty*: Henry Brooke's
   In-between Poetics 29
   John Baker

3 Argumentative Emphases in Pope's *An Essay on Man* 47
   Tom Jones

4 'Stricken Deer and Digressive Diplomacy': The Influence of
   Matthew Prior upon William Cowper 64
   Conrad Brunström

Part II Science and Nature

5 'When Universal Nature I Survey':
   Philosophical Poetry Before 1750 83
   Megan Kitching

6 Metering Mineral Resources: Verse Jewels on Earth's Treasures 101
   Kevin L. Cope

7 Deserted Village and Animated Nature: An Ecocritical
   Approach to Oliver Goldsmith 117
   Brycchan Carey

8 Footnotes to a Nation: Richard Llwyd's
   Beaumaris Bay (1800) 133
   Elizabeth Edwards

Part III Women's Verse and Genres

9 'I wish the child, I call my own': [Pro]Creative Experience in the Poetry of Jane Cave Winscom 155
Ashleigh Blackwood

10 Figs and Fame: Envisioning the Future in Women's Poetry 173
Mascha Hansen

11 Women Poets and the Mock-Heroic Elegy 191
Joanna Fowler

Part IV Self and Others

12 Getting Personal: Swift's Non-Public Poetry 211
Allan Ingram

13 Blind Woman on the Rampage: Priscilla Pointon's Grand Tour of the Midlands and the Question of the Legitimacy of Sources for Biography 230
Chris Mounsey

14 'What a Creature is Man': The Melancholia, Literary Ambition and Manly Fortitude of Robert Burns 248
Leigh Wetherall Dickson

Bibliography 267

Index 282

List of Figures

8.1 R. LLwyd (1800) *Beaumaris Bay, A Poem; with Notes, Descriptive and Explanatory* (Chester: J. Fletcher), p. 1   134

8.2 Llwyd, *Beaumaris Bay*, p. 23   135

Acknowledgements

The editors would like to express our thanks to the Department of English, Drama and Publishing at Loughborough University, and to its administrative staff, for hosting the Bill Overton Memorial Conference on Eighteenth-Century Poetry in September 2013. This volume arises out of papers given there. We should also like to record our appreciation and gratitude to all those who spoke at the conference, particularly to our three plenary speakers, John Lucas, Christine Gerrard and Jim McLaverty, and to those who attended and gave it their support.

The images of *Beaumaris Bay* have been reproduced by permission of Llyfrgell *Genedlaethol Cymru/The National Library of Wales*

Notes on Contributors

John Baker is Maître de conférences (Senior Lecturer) in English in the Languages Department of the Université Paris 1 Panthéon-Sorbonne. He has published in English and French on various aspects of eighteenth-century poetry, on themes such as the night, originality, theodicy, sensibility and melancholy. He contributed to the co-authored volume *Melancholy Experience in the Literature of the Long Eighteenth Century*, published by Palgrave/Macmillan in 2011. His research interests include poetry and the history of ideas in the long eighteenth century.

Ashleigh Blackwood is a Postgraduate Research Student at the University of Northumbria. Her research operates alongside the Leverhulme Trust project 'Fashionable Diseases: Medicine, Literature and Culture, 1660–1832'. She specializes in connections between eighteenth-century literary narratives and reproductive medical discourses. Her thesis is entitled 'Managing Maternity in Eighteenth-Century Literature'. Her other interests include early modern medicine, the history of medical publishing and public engagement. Ashleigh has acted as a research consultant and curating assistant on two public engagement projects: the Lottery Heritage funded 'The Good Humour Club', and 'Shandy's Physicians', a public exhibition for the Royal Society of Medicine, London. Her current research focuses on representations of abortion in late eighteenth-century women's writing and medical interpretations of eighteenth-century reading practices.

Conrad Brunström is a Lecturer in English Literature at Maynooth University, Ireland. He is the author of *William Cowper: Religion, Satire, Society* (2004) and *Thomas Sheridan's Career and Influence: An Actor in Earnest* (2011). He has published articles on eighteenth-century figures as diverse as Samuel Johnson, Frances Burney, Charles Churchill and James Beattie. He is a committee member of the Eighteenth-Century Ireland Society and is currently working on a full length study of the poetry and crafted rhetorical personality of Matthew Prior. His broader eighteenth-century research interests include theatre history, poetry, religion, queer studies, oratory and nationalism.

Brycchan Carey is a Professor of English Literature at Kingston University, London. He is the author of *From Peace to Freedom: Quaker*

Rhetoric and the Birth of American Antislavery, 1658–1761 (2012) and *British Abolitionism and the Rhetoric of Sensibility: Writing, Sentiment, and Slavery, 1760–1807* (Palgrave, 2005). His most recent collection, *Quakers and Abolition*, co-edited with Geoffrey Plank, was published by University of Illinois Press in 2014. He is currently writing a book about the intersection of natural history and antislavery in the long eighteenth century as well as co-editing books on *Early Caribbean Literary Histories* (with Nicole Aljoe and Tom Krise) and *Birds in Eighteenth-Century Literature* (with Sayre Greenfield and Anne Milne).

Kevin L. Cope is Professor of English and of Comparative Literature at Louisiana State University. The author of *Criteria of Certainty: Truth and Judgment in the English Enlightenment, John Locke Revisited* and *In and After the Beginning: Inaugural Moments and Literary Institutions in the Long Eighteenth Century*, Cope is the editor of the annual journal *1650–1850: Ideas, Aesthetics, and Inquiries in the Early Modern Era* and also the editor of the review and bibliographical annual *ECCB: The Eighteenth-Century Current Bibliography*. The author of over 75 journal articles and of multitudinous reviews, Cope is active in university governance and has written on topics in higher education such as the statewide articulation of courses and the development of block transfer programmes. He frequently appears on syndicated talk radio and television news programmes. Cope's current research deals with the subterranean side of the Enlightenment, whether earthquakes and mining or hermits and their grottos.

Elizabeth Edwards is a Research Fellow at the University of Wales Centre for Advanced Welsh and Celtic Studies, Aberystwyth. Her publications include *English-Language Poetry from Wales 1789–1806* (2013). Her edition of the poetry of the labouring-class writer Richard Llwyd will be published in 2015.

Joanna Fowler completed her PhD under the supervision of Professor Bill Overton. She taught on both poetry and eighteenth-century modules at Loughborough University for seven years, and has previously published articles on the prose fiction of Eliza Haywood and Aphra Behn.

Mascha Hansen is Lecturer in English Literature at the EMA University of Greifswald. Her research interests are centred on, or centred by, eighteenth-century women, with a focus on women writers such as Frances Burney and the bluestockings. She has published on women's involvement in, and views on, science, the *Bildungsroman*, house-owning, futurity and depression, and has recently co-edited a volume on *Swift and his Contemporaries* (2013).

Allan Ingram is Professor of English at the University of Northumbria. He has published widely on eighteenth-century topics, including work on James Boswell, Swift and Pope and on aspects of insanity. He was Director of the Leverhulme Research Project, 'Before Depression, 1660–1800' (www.beforedepression.com), and is Co-Director of a second Leverhulme project, 'Fashionable Diseases in the Long Eighteenth Century' (www.fashionablediseases.info). His most recent works include the co-edited four-volume collection *Depression and Melancholy 1660–1800* (2012) and the Broadview Press edition of *Gulliver's Travels* (2012).

Tom Jones works on poetry, poetics and eighteenth-century intellectual hitstory in the School of English, University of St Andrews. Publications include *Pope and Berkeley: The Language of Poetry and Philosophy* (Palgrave, 2005), and *Poetic Language: Theory and Practice from the Renaissance to the Present* (2012). His edition of Pope's *Essay on Man* is scheduled for publication in 2015. He is also working on a biography of George Berkeley.

Megan Kitching is a final-year PhD candidate in the Department of English, Queen Mary, University of London. Her research interests lie in literature and science, and the literature and culture of the long eighteenth century, and her current research examines natural-philosophical poetry published in Britain between 1709 and 1809. Her work has appeared in *Eighteenth-Century Fiction* and the *Journal of New Zealand Literature*.

Chris Mounsey worked for several years in theatre before an accident and four months immobility, in which reading was the only possible occupation, led to an academic career. Degrees in philosophy, comparative literature and English from the University of Warwick followed, and a doctorate on Blake founded an interest in the literature of the eighteenth century. He now teaches at the University of Winchester, is author of *Christopher Smart: Clown of God* and editor of *Presenting Gender, Queer People, Developments in the Histories of Sexualities,* and *The Idea of Disability in the Eighteenth Century*. He is also author of *Understanding the Poetry of William Blake through a Dialectic of Contraries* (2011), and *Being the Body of Christ* (2012).

Hermann Josef Real is Emeritus Professor of English and Director of the Ehrenpreis Centre for Swift Studies at the Westfälische Wilhelms-Universität, Münster. He is editor of Swift's *The Battle of the Books* (1978) and co-editor of *Swift and his Contexts* (1989). He has convened six Münster symposia on Jonathan Swift since 1984, and edited and co-edited their transactions (as *Proceedings* and *Reading Swift*). He has also co-authored a monograph on *Gulliver's Travels* (1984), co-translated and annotated the *Travels* into German (1987; 4th ed., 2011) and annotated a new translation of *A Tale of a Tub* in German (1994). He has edited the annual *Swift Studies* since its inception (1986). Other book publications include three anthologies of edited essays on Swift. The latest volume of *Reading Swift* was published in 2013, and his Index to David Woolley's edition of *The Correspondence of Jonathan Swift* (1999–2007), with Dirk F. Passmann, in 2014. For the past five years, he has been working as co-editor on a new old-spelling critical edition of the Prose Works of Jonathan Swift (http://www.anglistik.uni-muenster.de/Swift/online.swift/index.html).

Leigh Wetherall Dickson is Senior Lecturer in eighteenth- and nineteenth-century literature at Northumbria University and began her career there as a post-doctoral Research Associate on the Leverhulme-funded 'Before Depression 1660-1800' project (www.beforedepression.com). She has written and published extensively upon the experience of presumed mental disease, and was the co-general editor and volume editor for *Depression and Melancholy 1600–1800*, 4 Volumes (2012). She is now one of the directors of 'Fashionable Diseases: Medicine, Literature and Culture, ca. 1660–1832', also funded by the Leverhulme Trust for three years (http://www.fashionablediseases.info). Her current research focuses upon the relationship between fashion, fame and illness in the long eighteenth century, and is particularly interested in how the pursuit of fame was viewed as a type of contagious disease.

Nigel Wood is Professor of Literature at Loughborough University. He is also an Honorary Senior Research Associate of the Shakespeare Institute at Stratford-Upon-Avon (University of Birmingham), and has written extensively on both Shakespeare and, among his eighteenth-century work, he has edited the OUP World's Classics volume on *She Stoops to Conquer and other Eighteenth-Century Comedies* (also including plays by Fielding, Garrick, Colman and O'Keeffe), and *Dr Johnson and Fanny Burney*, a selection of Burney's journal and diary entries on the associations between her and Johnson and the Thrales; he is completing an edition of Evelyn Waugh's *Put Out More Flags* plus a study of Alexander Pope's allusiveness.

Professor Bill Overton, 1946–2012: A Personal Memoir

Hermann Josef Real

FAREWEL, too little and too lately known.
John Dryden, *To the Memory of Mr. Oldham*

I first met Bill Overton at one of those legendary Paris colloques, initiated by our late friend, Professor Paul-Gabriel Boucé, at the Sorbonne Nouvelle, and subsequently organized and run by Professors Suzy Halimi and Serge Soupel. I can no longer remember exactly what year, but it was relatively late in our lives. I do recall that for the occasion I had teamed up with Dirk Passmann, and together we held forth on 'Barbarism, Witchcraft, and Devil Worship: Cock-and-Bull Stories from Several Remote Nations of the World'.[1] To our surprise, Bill came to the podium after this wildly mad talk and said to us with a smile: 'Thank you for an enjoyable paper.' Then he paused in mid-sentence and repeated: 'Thank you for a *most* enjoyable paper', emphasizing 'most'. My immediate reaction was, 'What a kind thing to say; I will take to this man.' Later in the afternoon, Bill gave his own talk, and, predictably, he spoke about what mattered to him most, seventeenth- and eighteenth-century poetry, and how to read it: punctuation, he rightly pointed out, affecting intonation and voice, and voice and intonation being meaning. One of the passages he had selected for discussion was from *Paradise Lost*, also one of my favourite poems, and, in the very amicable discussion afterwards, we embarked on Milton's compositors. Was the poet himself responsible for the punctuation of his immortal poem or were the compositors, we asked ourselves? Back home, the discussion led to an epistolary exchange about hermeneutics and 'correct' readings, and we started sending each other offprints of scholarly articles.

After Paul-Gabriel Boucé died, Dirk Passmann and I decided to convene a 'Colloque in memoriam Paul-Gabriel Boucé' in Münster in February 2010. Bill happily accepted our invitation, suggesting a very sexy title, 'Sex and Gender in the Augustan Heroic Epistle', and expressing his delight about the forthcoming event. He loved being in Germany, he told us, having family in Cologne. A heavy burden of administrative work and paper-marking notwithstanding, Elaine came with him not to read a paper herself but to listen to Bill's and to spend as much time with him as possible. What I had found most striking about the two from the beginning was the deep love they both felt for, and showed to, each other. What they had not realized, however, was that Münster held a sore trial of that love in store for them. Let me explain: the conference facilities were new and modern, clean and functional, breakfasts and lunches were excellent, the lecture theatre fully equipped with all sorts of technical gadgets and the beautiful Gothic Überwasserkirche (Our Lady over the Water) and the Romanesque Paulus Dom (St Paul's Cathedral) in view of the locality (forgive me for blowing my own trumpet), but there is always a But in life. At one stage, I had to tell Bill that the conference facilities had been converted from a former Catholic seminary, and all the bedrooms were single, strictly single, and no exceptions permitted. I still treasure the letter Bill wrote in a kind of comic despair when I broke the news. For a moment, I feared that he might cancel the reservation, though in the end, manfully, he did not. I do hope that meanwhile, in the kindness of heart that was so characteristic of him, he has forgiven me.

We met again in the following year at Mascha Hansen and Jürgen Klein's splendid sequel at Greifswald in 2011. Erika and I had come by car, Bill came by plane and train, respectively, and we went to collect him from the station. I remember the heart-warming smile he flashed at us when alighting from the train. On that occasion, Bill spoke about Lord Hervey, and if I had not already known what a superb scholar he was, that paper, since published in the conveners' *Great Expectations*, would have told me.[2] In our private conversations during coffee breaks and at the dinner table, he confessed to suffering from some unspecified and undiagnosed back pain. In his Christmas letter that year, he told us about his imminent retirement and his joy at the prospect of completing his edition of Lord Hervey's poems, finishing on the coda, 'Elaine and I hope you and yours have the best of Christmases and New Years. Very warmest and most affectionate best wishes from us both.' A month later, on 18 January 2012, we received a piece of devastating news, which at first we refused to believe: 'The back trouble I have turns out not to come from the back at all but from a tumour in my pancreas.' Although Bill was clearly in an emotional turmoil at this moment, he never lost his outward calm for a second, pointing out reasons for hope at the same time. For one, he assured us, he was in good medical hands, in fact, in the hands of a world authority on pancreatic cancer, and, for another, he went on in great excitement, Elaine had decided to receive him into her even more loving and caring hands for ever: they were getting married on 28 January.

Erika and I have a blow-by-blow account of the wedding (if that is the appropriate metaphor). 'It was a most joyous occasion', Bill wrote *post festum*. 'We had a very simple ceremony, with a strict interdiction on such items – and you know Elaine can be very strict – as confetti, overly smart dressing, presents and verbal chastisement of small children. The weather obliged, too: we had plenty of sunshine, and mild temperatures.' This report was accompanied by a link to the website set up by Elaine's favourite niece, which showed us photos of all 19 guests at the party. We were so happy to be allowed a share in Elaine and Bill's happiness.

In May 2012, Erika and I drove to Leeds in order to attend a reception in honour of the dedicatee of a Festschrift to which I had been invited to contribute. On the way home, we passed by Loughborough, seeing it signposted on the motorway. We dithered for a moment whether to surprise Bill and Elaine and drop by, but since we could not be sure whether we were welcome under the circumstances, we decided not to. Back home, we told Bill that we had been thinking of him and had sent him warmest telepathic greetings from the motorway, which, we pointed out, should have made his ears tingle. Bill responded on 10 June in what turned out to be his last letter to us, and it confirmed that our decision had been the right one. As always, Bill was charming (indulging in parody of eighteenth-century sublime style here and there): 'I fear that my telepathic powers did not extend to detecting your recent proximity, but both of you are often in my thoughts, and it would indeed be very good to see you again. I also fear, though, that an unannounced visit might find me out or in less good shape than I would like, so you made the right choice in not calling by, much though I would otherwise have appreciated a visit.' At the time of writing, there was still hope that our friend Jürgen Klein would be able to pull off another colloque in Hamburg in December of 2012. (That never materialized, alas, for all sorts of reasons.) If it were to materialize, Bill continued, 'I shall be delighted, and I would do my very best to be there.' As we all know by now, that was not to be the case: Erika and I never saw Bill again. So we have to take comfort in his very last sentence to us: 'Elaine joins me embracing you over the ether and sending you our love and very best wishes.' Once more, dear friend, hail and farewell. *Terraque sit super ossa levis.*

Notes

1. Published in (2008) *Swift Studies*, 23, 94–110.
2. (2012) 'Lord Hervey, Death and Futurity' in M. Hansen and J. Klein (eds) *Great Expectations: Futurity in the Long Eighteenth Century* (Frankfurt am Main: Peter Lang), pp. 141–60.

Introduction

Allan Ingram and Joanna Fowler

This volume arises from the Bill Overton Memorial Conference on 'Eighteenth-Century Poetry' convened in September 2013 by Dr Joanna Fowler, Professor Elaine Hobby and Professor Allan Ingram. The subject of the conference was chosen because of Bill's career-long enthusiasm for and engagement with eighteenth-century verse, most evident in his work on the poetry of the 'Anonymous Lady', on the verse epistle and in the edition of the poetry of Lord Hervey on which he was working when he died in September 2012.

The intention behind the conference was to revisit the poetry of the eighteenth century, particularly in light of recent critical approaches and the opening up over the last decades of the range of verse now regularly discussed and studied. We hoped to recover something of the richness and excitement of what was then a form of writing practised by both professionals and amateurs, by the highly and the scarcely educated, those heavily influenced by past traditions and those more interested in expressing something important to them in the best way they could. In particular, we wished to show that, significant and influential though the poetic giants of the period were, other voices were continually being heard, arising from a variety of impulses and dealing with a variety of contexts and concerns through their work. The present collection, which comprises a selection of papers, reworked as academic chapters, is intended as a reassessment of the importance of verse as a medium in the period, and as an invitation for readers to explore many of the less familiar figures dealt with, alongside the received names of the standard criticism of the period. Contributors, from the United States, France, Germany and Ireland, as well as the United Kingdom, include both established names and current postgraduate students, reflecting the lively interest there now is in this field. The volume, we believe, is likely both to open new areas of research for fellow academics and to help revitalize the study of eighteenth-century verse for a student readership. Above all, if it plays a part in stripping this period form of the accretions of solid respectability it acquired during earlier centuries and allows it to speak to current readers with some of the directness of the original texts, then it will have performed a valuable service.

The key works for contemporary study of eighteenth-century poetry were the twin volumes edited by Roger Lonsdale some 30 years ago – *The New Oxford Book of Eighteenth-Century Verse* (1984) and *Eighteenth-Century Women Poets: An Oxford Anthology* (1989). These collections overturned the received view of the verse of the period as dominated by a small number of elite male poets and made clear that writing and reading poetry were activities entered into at all levels of society, and that the poetic voice was freely adopted for all kinds of topic, from the serious and public to the highly personal or the utterly trivial. These anthologies were followed up with ones by David Fairer and Christine Gerrard (*Eighteenth-Century Poetry: An Annotated Anthology*, 1999), Joyce Fullard (*British Women Poets, 1660–1800: An Anthology*, 1990) and Paula R. Backscheider and Catherine E. Ingrassia (*British Women Poets of the Long Eighteenth Century*, 2009). Works since then have developed the vitality and range of poetry, without losing sight of the significance and achievement of those figures previously held as dominant. Publications covering the whole of the field include those by John Sitter (*The Cambridge Companion to Eighteenth-Century Poetry*, 2001, and *The Cambridge Introduction to Eighteenth-Century Poetry*, 2011), David Fairer (*English Poetry of the Eighteenth Century, 1700–1789*, 2003) and by Christine Gerrard (*A Companion to Eighteenth-Century Poetry*, 2006). These are vital texts for the field, building on Lonsdale and serving as excellent introductions for students and general readers. More selective, but still taking a wide perspective, is Patricia Meyer Spacks' *Reading Eighteenth-Century Poetry* (2009), which emphasizes the distinctiveness and urgency of much of the poetry of the period. The present volume is not intended to compete with these, but to enter the same market, dealing as it does with specific aspects and figures of the period, poetry that was part of what is now recognized as a vital medium of thought, of expression and communication. The study of the verse of the eighteenth century, so often in the past dwarfed by the Romantics, is now a significant and exciting field with excellent scholarship appearing all the time. This book, we hope, will be part of that movement, gaining from its momentum and contributing to it through its study of previously overlooked writers and forms, and its re-examination of more major figures within that context. To repeat Lonsdale's 'conviction', it will demonstrate that 'the world of eighteenth-century poetry is at once less predictable and more familiar than we have been led to believe'.[1]

Our title, *Voice and Context*, is intended to throw the emphasis of the volume on both the individual and the time and place in which he or she was writing. If in 'voice' we are interested in what made a poet distinctive, or even to lack distinctiveness, we also recognize the importance of those many aspects of circumstance – biographical, social, political and cultural – that gave impetus to the adoption and development of a way of writing poetry. The subtitle, of course, is from the beginning of Pope's 1713 hymn to Britain and its royal inheritance – shortly, as Pope was aware, to pass to a Hanoverian incumbent:

> Here Hills and Vales, the Woodland and the Plain,
> Here Earth and Water seem to strive again,
> Not *Chaos*-like together crush'd and bruis'd,
> But as the World, harmoniously confus'd:
> Where Order in Variety we see,
> And where, tho' all Things differ, all agree.[2]

Pope's 'Order in Variety' is a statement of the potential for recapturing something of man's prelapsarian condition within a politics – that of Stuart Britain – and a landscape that reflect the best of all possible worlds. It is an ideal brought down to earth, not with a bump but with realistic and reasonable expectations of what is possible: productive coexistence is, and beauty is and, obviously, poetry is. Indeed, the form of Pope's poetry acts as a demonstration that potentially discordant elements, 'Earth and Water', upland and downland, natural growth and cultivation, are capable of being incorporated within a formal celebration of 'Order' in spite of their intrinsic 'Variety'. That is the best that fallen mankind can hope for.

Our intention, in picking this quotation, was less grandiose. Rather, we were interested in explorations of the ways in which poets, from professionals like Pope himself, to amateurs like most of the other writers covered in the volume, made coherent and formal sense from the many and various kinds of context that led to the desire for expression – the natural world, for example, relations with other people or with oneself, issues of gender, particularly of femininity within a masculine society or even admiration for or influence by a poetic master or predecessor. Hence the four divisions within the collection – though in doing this we were well aware that many other possible divisions might have been chosen.

Part I of this volume is entitled 'Form and Influence'. Trying to define 'eighteenth-century verse' is a difficult task, because, as Lonsdale points out, many poets' work can be classified as 'very much of their period' and 'a variety of interesting individual voices' can be found in both print and manuscript, writing in a range of genres and forms.[3] Despite the seeming dominance of the pentameter couplet and then blank verse, the period saw much experimentation with prosody. In terms of influence, while the earlier Augustans drew on classical models and forms, 'Gray and his generation', Lonsdale notes, went 'back to the native tradition of Spenser, Shakespeare, and Milton, or further afield to the Orient, Scandanavia, [and] the Middle Ages', and inspiration continued to come from diverse sources throughout the long eighteenth century.[4] In the opening chapter, 'Pope's Horatian Voice', Nigel Wood explores the author's *Imitations of Horace* and how, even though Pope 'adopt[ed] Horace's example – stylistically and philosophically' to engage in literary debates and explorations, the interaction between the two authors' works often represents a dialectic rather than a simple out-and-out affiliation. John Baker, in 'Celebrating *Universal Beauty*: Henry Brooke's In-between Poetics', similarly, explores the complex nature of influence and how this 1735 philosophical poem exhibits a 'between-ness' both in a formal sense (mixing verse with extensive footnotes), its style, and its poetic influences, 'occupy[ing] a middle ground' between Pope's *An Essay on Man* (1733–4) and James Thomson's *The Seasons* (1730; 1746). This Pope poem is also the subject of Tom Jones's work, 'Argumentative Emphases in Pope's *An Essay on Man*', but the focus switches to how Pope continually self-edited his work, exploring how grammatical and typographical changes to the poem can influence its interpretation and argument. In the final chapter of the Part, '"Stricken Deer and Digressive Diplomacy": The Influence of Matthew Prior upon William Cowper', Conrad Brunström revisits the topic of William Cowper's main influences which, he writes, 'could be conveniently abbreviated to just two: John Milton and Matthew Prior'. However, Brunström complicates the idea that the former impacts on Cowper's serious verse and the latter his lighter compositions, analysing different examples of Cowper's and Prior's poems. He concludes his argument by entering the discussion about a possible tripartite connection between Prior–Cowper–Wordsworth.

When one thinks of eighteenth-century verse and representations of nature, the pastoral will inevitably come to mind. David Fairer declares that, 'Its malleability, as a mode rather than a genre, offered opportunities for poetic experiment [in the period], and the widespread familiarity of its codes allowed for considerable ingenuity and playfulness.'[5] Part II of the volume on 'Science and Nature', while looking at pastoral poems (albeit in new ways), also explores scientific-philosophical verse and poems that explore topography, both above and below the ground. According to Clark Lawlor, 'The "New Science" of the previous century, which stressed the role of the human body as a machine and the universe as a great watch mechanism, encouraged or even forced eighteenth-century poets [...] to contemplate deeply their place in the great scheme of things or "Chain of Being".'[6] Megan Kitching's essay, '"When Universal Nature I Survey": Philosophical Poetry Before 1750', the first of this Part, presents a review of philosophical poems from the opening half of the century, exploring the tensions between this type of verse and satire, and how these poems 'turn questions raised by natural philosophy towards their moral and theological implications'. From didactic philosophical verse to poems that can be seen to teach readers about the earth's underground, Kevin Cope, in 'Metering Mineral Resources: Verse Jewels on Earth's Treasures', explores different examples of 'gem verse' or works that present 'versified geology'. Infusing often recondite diction into metrical compositions, these poems explore and celebrate the 'subterranean' like pastorals survey the countryside. Brycchan Carey's 'Deserted Village and Animated Nature: An Ecocritical Approach to Oliver Goldsmith' broaches the question of the location of the village of Auburn depicted in this well-known pastoral in a different way. Carey presents an ecocritical view of the poem, reading its descriptions of the landscape against Goldsmith's *History of the Earth and Animated Nature* to 'aid our understanding of the text's ecological significance as much as its social and cultural importance'. To conclude Part II, Elizabeth Edwards, in 'Footnotes to a Nation: Richard Llwyd's *Beaumaris Bay* (1800)', explores the polyvalence of this place poem that presents a 'topographical tour' that also 'highlight[s] the existence of a Welsh-language literary past'. The poem has to share its pages with bounteous footnotes and Edwards examines how the reading of the poem differs if you consider or ignore the peritext and the political implications of this.

In the 'Introduction' to his anthology, *Eighteenth-Century Women Poets*, Lonsdale acknowledges 'the risk of seeming to segregate [...] [women poets] from the literary mainstream, which would be misleading. Yet, although they shared some problems of acceptability with their less privileged male contemporaries, it is not unreasonable to consider them in some aspects as a special case, given their educational insecurities and the constricted notions of the properly "feminine" in social and literary behaviour they faced.'[7] Part III of the volume, on 'Women's Verse and Genres', considers women poets' responses to birth, death and life and one's literary legacy, addressing genres and topics that could be seen as, traditionally, male dominated as well as those specific to female experience. In '"I wish the child, I call my own": [Pro]Creative Experience in the Poetry of Jane Cave Winscom', Ashleigh Blackwood identifies six 'birth poems' by the author and argues that these can be read collectively as a group to 'capture a strong sense of the importance of reproduction as a cultural concept' in the period. They can be read alongside non-fictional medical texts, like midwifery manuals, to help us understand the fears faced by expectant mothers as well as their hopes for their children. Mascha Hansen's 'Figs and Fame: Envisioning the Future in Women's Poetry' looks at the symbolism of 'figs' for female voices, linking them to hope and ambitions. The chapter analyses how women poets throughout the long eighteenth century addressed the notions of time, fame and futurity. Finally, Joanna Fowler, in 'Women Poets and the Mock-Heroic Elegy', considers how three female poets produce this kind of verse for a dual purpose: they explore the human/animal bond while 'adopt[ing] a mode often used to disparage women, and, with origins that can be traced back to Ovid and Catullus, to make a point about women as poets'.

It seems appropriate that a volume entitled 'Voice and Context' ends with a Part entitled 'Self and Others'. Backscheider and Ingrassia start their 'Introduction' to their anthology with the statement that 'During the time period [...] people read poetry for entertainment, news, and self-improvement' and discuss its public/private dimension. They continue: the 'public function of reading and writing poetry [during the century] should not suggest that poets failed to aspire to the highest aesthetic achievements or that the poetry of the period lacks emotion and fails to draw on personal experience'.[8] Part IV of this volume looks at both the personal side of a poet becoming a public figure and the private cost of a public reputation. Allan Ingram's chapter entitled 'Getting Personal: Swift's Non-Public Poetry' inspects the 'fluidity of the private/public borderline in Swift's poetry', looking at, for example, some of Stella's 'Birthday Poems' and the 'Market Hill' poems and how Swift presents personal friends and experiences for 'semi-public' entertainment. In 'Blind Woman on the Rampage: Priscilla Pointon's Grand Tour of the Midlands and the Question of the Legitimacy of Sources for Biography', Chris Mounsey interrogates how useful and reliable published poems, such as verse epistles, based on supposedly private events, journeys and relationships, are when trying to recover biographical information about a blind female poet and her experiences as a disabled woman and writer. The final chapter, Leigh Wetherall Dickson's '"What a Creature is Man": The Melancholia, Literary Ambition and Manly Fortitude of Robert Burns', looks at how Burns turned to his favourite sentimental verse to understand his emotions and thoughts, and examines extracts from his letters, commonplace book and poems to consider how the man and his melancholia were explored in his private, semi-private and public documents.

Verse quotations are presented in two different ways in this volume: if a poem comes from a collection or anthology that provides line numbers then these are used; however, if the texts are without lineation then page numbers have been employed.

Notes

1. (2003) 'Introduction' in *The New Oxford Book of Eighteenth-Century Verse* (Oxford: Oxford University Press), pp. xxxiii–xli (p. xxxix).
2. (1963) *Windsor Forest* in J. Butt (ed.) *The Poems of Alexander Pope* (London: Methuen), pp. 195–210, lines 11–16.
3. 'Introduction' in *The New Oxford Book of Eigtheenth-Century Verse*, p. xxxiii.
4. 'Introduction' in *The New Oxford Book of Eighteenth-Century Verse*, p. xxxiv.
5. (2003) *English Poetry of the Eighteenth Century, 1700–1789* (London: Longman), p. 79.
6. (2006) 'Poetry and Science' in C. Gerrard (ed.) *A Companion to Eighteenth-Century Poetry* (Oxford: Blackwell), pp. 38–52 (p. 39).
7. (1990) 'Introduction' in *Eighteenth-Century Women Poets: An Oxford Anthology* (Oxford: Oxford University Press), pp. xxi–xlvii (p. xliii).
8. (2009) 'Introduction' in *British Women Poets of the Long Eighteenth Century: An Anthology* (Baltimore: Johns Hopkins University Press), pp. xxiii–xxxviii (p. xxiii).

Part I
Form and Influence

1
Pope's Horatian Voice

Nigel Wood

There is a reassuring motive for choosing to translate a famous author in that you are servant to the master voice, relaying as innocently and accurately as you can past sentiments and tropes. In the wake of this irreproachable impulse, on the other hand, one might discover less obedient traces, not quite *graffiti*, but – because not announced – perhaps more insidious projections of the self; the 'strong' authors need to be misprized in order that their complex literariness might survive, but also that the imitator is no plagiarist. Interpretation has to intervene and not only at the micro level, but also in constructing the wider perspective, where the source text *does not* fit and, issuing from that dissonance, a cross-cultural dialogue emerges. In Wolfgang Iser's phrase, 'translatability is motivated by the need to cope with a crisis that can no longer be alleviated by the mere assimilation or appropriation of other cultures'. This gesture could be a form of 'therapy for a growing awareness of cultural pathology'.[1] The spectrum of cross-cultural adherence embraces imitation as well as academic translation, and the effect of 'coping' and negotiating is only a difference of degree. Pope's *Imitations of Horace* offer us some material for reassurance in that the ethics of retirement and its apparently apolitical consequences are very much part of what is overt about the very form of the literary choice: the inclusion of the Horace text interleaved with Pope's own and the adoption of Horace's own conversational register. It is homage of an intricate kind, and the refusal to represent his own voice as standing alone is perhaps evidence of such intricacy; it might not do, however, to rest on the assumption that the later author was simply in thrall to the earlier, and this chapter will explore the consequences of focusing on the moment of Pope's imitating: its immediacy and synchronic position as well as its more universal significance.

This is also part of the developing debate about the literary imitation in the period: the extent to which it was quasi-translation, substantially motivated by the aim of rendering the source, yet demonstrating one's own reading in the process, or, more radically, a display of enfranchisement where a familiar source was defaced or eventually left behind. Horace's example exhibited both varieties, using Lucilius's outspokenness as sanction for his own temerity or the liberal attacks of Old Comedy as a template for a 'low' vocabulary and dramatic alternations of tone. On the other hand, these models were unartful, even if effective, as he ventures in *Satires, I.iv.*38–62 and *I.x.*1–24.[2] This contest between art and direct truth-telling is embedded in two established modes of regarding satire itself: is it principally strategic, always using the contemporary for vivid examples but only to point to recurrent faults and a transcendent ethics, or is it really motivated by the need to name names and expose vice in particular? For analysts of the genre, there is a similar oscillation between a formalist approach, where particulars are merely elements in a larger scheme, and a historical focus, where the satiric fiction is wielded only to denounce real villains and temporizers.[3] Pope's Horace *Imitations* are variously examined as a series of neo-classical gestures, returning the reader from the Augustan precedent to a carefully cultivated self-image, and yet this puts in the shade a number of personal anxieties and political nuances that were also prime motives.

I

In the second volume of Pope's 1735 *Works*, the idea of adopting Horace's example – stylistically and philosophically – grew to maturity. In the 'Advertisement' to the Horatian pieces, Pope provides his own context for turning to the poet: '*The Occasion of publishing these* Imitations *was the Clamour raised on some of my* Epistles. *An Answer from* Horace *was both more full, and of more Dignity, than any I cou'd have made in my own person*'.[4] There then follows as 'Satire 1', his version of *Satire, II.i*, and then, as 'Satire 2', *Satire, II.ii*. The section is rounded off with imitations of the second and fourth of John Donne's own *Satires*, although Horace's preoccupation with courtly pretension shines through in both.[5] Both Horace satires had appeared before: *Satire, II.i* in 1733, and *Satire, II.ii* in 1734. Donne's *Satire IV* had appeared in 1733 as *The Impertinent; Or a Visit to the Court. A Satyr. By an Eminent Hand*. As the 'Advertisement' makes clear, the gesture of collecting together his two appropriations of Horace – with two satires of Donne – is a form of defence and redress. In his *Of Taste*, the early title for his *Epistle To The Right Honourable Richard Earl of Burlington*, published in a prepossessing 16 page folio in December 1731, there seemed to some an inappropriate allusion, in his portrait of the *arriviste* Timon, to the sudden wealth of James Brydges, the first Duke of Chandos, and the *'Clamour'* refers to this unfortunate – and probably opportunistic – mischief-making.[6] In the third edition of the poem, now entitled *Of The False Taste* (January 1732), Pope included an exculpatory letter, where he confesses to the *'pain'* that this *'Clamour'* had caused him: *'This way of Satire is dangerous, as long as Slander rais'd by Fools of the lowest Rank, can find any Countenance from those of a Higher.'*[7] The dignity of the Horatian voice was thus part of a rather localized debate about the place of satire in the Hanoverian regime; Pope felt that his own *ethos* had been questioned, and – for the second volume of his 1739 *Works* – the 'Advertisement' to the *Imitations* concludes with a tag from Horace's own *Satire, II.i* (line 70), capitalized in the parallel Latin text of the 1735 edition: 'Uni aequus Virtuti atque ejus Amicis' ('kindly only to virtue and her friends'), and rendered at line 121 of Pope's poem as 'TO VIRTUE ONLY, and HER FRIENDS, A FRIEND'.[8] That same volume commences with a full version of his *An Essay on Man* (pp. 1–58), a formal grouping of the 'Ethic Epistles' followed by various 'Epistles', and then the 'Satires of Horace Imitated, with Satires of Dr Donne Versify'd by the Same Hand' (pp. 109–61). As a statement in its own right, this volume merits a close eye on its immediate context and its codes.

II

It is tempting to regard Pope's adoption of Horace's example as somehow inevitable. For Reuben Brower, the process of these *Imitations* was not simply one of 'mimicking' a style: 'Both poets disclaimed interest or influence in affairs of state, although their friendship with the "great" made their role and their poetry seem politically significant to others.'[9] The equivalence of his architecturally restrained Twickenham villa with Horace's Sabine Farm also signals themes of rural retirement and its non-aligned virtues and clear-sighted perspective, and it establishes a distance between those who owe their artistic prominence to the favour of those in power, on the one hand, and intrinsic poetic qualities on the other.[10]

However, there was not complete agreement as to just what Horace's example actually might mean. We get no direct colouring on this from what we know of the Horace volumes that Pope possessed: the Heinsius Elzevir (1629) and Desprez *Opera* (1695) were standard editions, and are unannotated in the Hartlebury Castle copies; Alexander Cunningham's *Poemata* (1721) and the Ben Jonson translation of *The Art of Poetry* (1640) simply show an interest in, and deep engagement with, the original.[11] As Frank Stack has shown, Horace could be the theorist of poetic effect (due in the main to his *Art of Poetry*) and also the proud individualist, freed from party and consistent allegiance, yet also a politically aligned commentator and sometimes a writer constantly searching for the authentic self, outside of personae and the republic of letters.[12] This elusiveness could be tactical (and rhetorically astute) or, eventually, a hindrance for a satirist.

That Horace failed to stir John Dryden is explicable on two counts; first, there was a lack of heroic aspiration – follies were identified and corrected but rarely excoriated – and also the severity and incisiveness of attack was muted by an inevitable servility. Horace educates and this is no negligible virtue, for 'Satire is of the nature of moral philosophy, as being instructive', and he is 'more copious' than Juvenal 'and profitable in his instructions of human life'.[13] His verse is, however, of a 'low' style, fit often for his subject, yet still pedestrian.[14] Dryden, though, in terms that would have resounded with the dedicatee of his 'Discourse Concerning the Original and Progress of Satire' (1692; title-page – 1693), Charles Sackville, sixth Earl of Dorset, identified him as a 'temporizing poet, a well-mannered court slave [...] ever decent, because he is naturally servile'.[15] Indeed, these are the sentiments of Persius's first Satire that Dryden imitated in his *Satires of Decimus Junius Juvenalis* (1693). The comparison with his mentor, Lucilius, is unflattering:

> Unlike in method, with concealed design,
> Did crafty Horace his low numbers join;
> And with a sly insinuating grace
> Laughed at his friend, and looked him in the face[.][16]

Lucilius – as did Juvenal – could lash the vices of court and city, whereas Horace went more indirectly to work and was the lesser satirist for it.

At best, Horace was correct and instructive; at worst, 'temporizing' and timorous. When Dryden had chosen to translate Horace, in the *Sylvae* (1685), it was the poet of contented retirement that emerged:

> How happy in his low degree,
> How rich in humble poverty is he,
> Who leads a quiet country life![17]

For Pope, this perspective obviously held attractions; his Twickenham retreat offered a privileged perspective on the transitory possessions of Whitehall glory. What was for Dryden a certain obsequiousness could be proof of recognition by an enlightened authority for Horace. In the letter to Arbuthnot that Pope revised for publication in the 1735 edition, Horace figures prominently in what can only be described as Pope's apology for satire. The original letter of 2 August 1734 (in response to that of Arbuthnot's of 17 July 1734) takes up the invitation to protect himself by reforming rather than chastising in his satire by noting how ineffective this might render the poetry:

> General Satire in Times of General Vice has no force, & is no Punishment: People have ceas'd to be ashamed of it when so many are joind with them; and tis only by hunting One or two from the Herd that any Examples can be made[.][18]

The expanded, retrospective 'letter' takes on this decidedly Juvenalian tone, and rebuts the charge that Horace was servile by claiming that 'much freer Satyrists' than he were protected by influential patrons:

> Augustus and Mecœnas made Horace their companion, tho' he had been in arms on the side of Brutus; and allow me to remark it was out of the suff'ring Party too, that they favour'd and distinguish'd Virgil. You will not suspect me of comparing my self with Virgil and Horace, nor even with another Court-favourite, Boileau: I have always been too modest to imagine my Panegyricks were Incense worthy of a Court[.][19]

In a muted way, then, Pope fashions an opposition platform for Horace and himself: given the times in which Horace wrote, it was appropriate for satirists to be 'protected and caress'd'.[20] If confronted with the vice and lawlessness of the rule of a Nero or Domitian, then the role of the writer is altered – and he remembers the execution of Lucan and the exile of Juvenal as evidence of less enlightened times.

As Howard Weinbrot has reminded us, the sense that Pope wrote in an 'Augustan Age' does not direct our reading as securely as it seems.[21] Horace may, indeed, have been protected by powerful patrons, yet that still does not protect him from the charge that he negotiated with a dubious apparatus of power. Pope's projected 'Epitaph on one who would not be buried in Westminster Abbey' (1738) tells its own story:

> HEROES and KINGS! Your distance keep:
> In peace let one poor Poet sleep,
> Who never flatter'd Folks like you:
> Let Horace blush, and Virgil too.[22]

Published by Pope himself in the 1738 *Works* (Vol. II.ii), the epitaph gathers its force from the author's own exiled status – by religion, politics and choice. For Horace and Virgil, the decision to support a possibly unethical regime was a reasonable tactic to allow their thoughts some level of public recognition; Pope's position was less secure. Indeed, by 1738 and his first dialogue for an 'Epilogue to the Satires', originally entitled *One Thousand Seven Hundred and Thirty Eight*, Dryden's very phrasing (out of Persius, see above) for Horace's strategies finds its way into his attempt to break free of Horace's influence:

> But Horace, Sir, was delicate, was nice;
> Bubo observes, he lash'd no sort of Vice:
> [...]
> His sly, insinuating stile
> Could please at Court, and make AUGUSTUS smile:
> An artful Manager, that crept between
> His Friend and Shame, and was a kind of Screen.[23]

Cunning and indirection are, one should note, merely the other side of the coin of Horace's celebrated virtues of control and careful judgement. Pope himself goes out of his way to allow the reader to trace a line of influence from Persius via his own note to these lines, wherein he quotes the Latin for lines 116–17 of 'Satire I', and uses Dryden's own phrasing.

One should not forget that Horace's slyness is introduced by Pope's *adversarius* in the dialogue, yet even if distanced in dramatic terms from an apparently more authentic personal accent, 'he' does not qualify the charge of Horace's compliance in the poem; indeed, in his immediate determination to address Walpole as the 'Great Man' – as 'Pope' – the Prime Minister's craft in 'screening' his private financial dealings from public view is directly indicated: 'Come, come, at all I laugh He laughs, no doubt, / The only diff'rence is, I dare laugh out', an implicit dig also at Horace's complaisance.²⁴ The assumption of a Horatian persona is thus multivalent, and Pope knew this. Samuel Johnson's verdict from his 'Life of Pope' is faint praise for this technique, for his *Imitations* were 'relaxations of his genius':

> The employment became his favourite by its facility; the plan was ready to his hand, and nothing was required but to accommodate as he could the sentiments of an old author to recent facts or familiar images; but what is easy is seldom excellent; such imitations cannot give pleasure to common readers [...]. Between Roman images and English manners there will be an irreconcilable dissimilitude, and the work will be generally uncouth and party-coloured[.]²⁵

The notion that a reader was merely to bring the source text alongside the adapted sentiments is much as Pope himself encouraged; the increased annotation and interleaving of the Horace original with his own phrases throughout the textual history of his Horatian *Imitations* is testament to a certain scholastic interest that he wished to share with the literate reader, but there are three basic questions that remain once we inspect the 'borrowed' material in Pope's texts. First, how Horatian are his apparent allusions to the earlier examples? Second, there may be a significant journey taken from his straightforward compliment to Horace in the 1711 *An Essay on Criticism* (where he 'charms with graceful Negligence, / And without Method talks us into Sense') to the exasperation at his divagations and equanimity by 1738: why did Pope change tack so completely, and what takes its place?²⁶ Last, how do we therefore read the *Imitations* – as Johnson understood the desired approach, or with an eye on more sophisticated theories about imitation and adaptation that Pope himself understood and promoted?

III

Both the Horatian Satires chosen for inclusion in the *Works* have at least two faces: outward-facing, involving the projection of an aesthetics and/or politics of retirement wherein Pope is deeply aware that suburban existence might offer little actual protection, and, on the other hand, a less easily discerned private dimension wherein the personal accountability of the satirist is explored and his ethos (tentatively) established. This latter analysis is not to be confused with the persona created as part of the poetic strategy, as a rhetorically necessary means to the greater end, but rather as a contribution to Pope's own display of doubt and a compensatory discourse. In 'Satire 1', the dialogue with Fortescue circles around whether a writer ought to note the legal curbs that might limit satiric freedoms; 'Satire 2', for the most part praise of Hugh Bethel, celebrates the virtues of a simplified life wherein hospitality and genuine fellowship might flower. William Fortescue is not quite chosen to confirm the same qualities as Bethel; as Private Secretary to Walpole from 1715 to 1727, he did, indeed, introduce the poet to the Prime Minister probably in 1725.[27] Bethel was a less prominent friend; now retired from front-line politics (no longer an MP since 1722), and one who had by then no connection with Whitehall temporizing. As 'blameless Bethel' he stands as one who escapes any undue passionate fixations in *An Essay on Man*.[28] It should not, however, escape our notice that he is also introduced to exemplify how even the most deserving cannot suspend natural law:

> Shall burning Ætna, if a sage requires,
> Forget to thunder, and recall her fires?
> On air or sea new motions be imprest,
> Oh blameless Bethel! to relieve thy breast?
> When the loose mountain trembles from on high,
> Shall gravitation cease, if you go by?[29]

Both poems, in their own way, wonder whether social and class 'gravitation' can ever 'cease', and whether even the most boldly righteous can go quietly to their graves if governments require compromise and acquiescence. Etna consumed Empedocles because he believed that, if he jumped into the volcano, he might return alive reincarnated as a God. Horace, in the climax of his *Ars Poetica*, regarded this hubristic act as evidence that one cannot save even the most earnest of souls from foolishness: '[...] sit ius liceatque perire poetis; / invitam qui servat, idem facit occidenti' ('Let poets enjoy the right to die at their own hands; he who saves a man against his will could be said to murder him').[30] Poets are not Gods and are not immortal.

They are, therefore, open to political force and coercion, satirists especially. 'Fortescue' advises a certain discretion, and directs the poet to safe eulogies whereby 'a Knighthood, or the Bays' might be the aim, or lyric vapidity, where a 'softer Art' reigns – or, with the Epistles to Burlington and Bathurst in mind, less specific references: 'A hundred smart in Timon and in Balaam: / The fewer still you name, you wound the more'.[31] Fortescue's status as mediator is complimented by the equivalence with Gaius Trebatius Testa, Horace's original addressee. There is, however, a certain tentativeness in this parallel; Pope did not readily credit the prefix 'F.' as indicating any particular character, leaving the reader to imagine that it might be some generic Friend. It was not until Warburton collected the 1751 *Works* that the subtitle 'To Mr. FORTESCUE' was included. The more we inspect Pope's comments to Fortescue on the first drafting of the 'Satire' on 18 February 1732-3 the more ambiguous it appears; wishing him the best in his candidature as Judge of Common Pleas, Pope also foresees a time when he may 'sleep and be quiet; *ut in otia tuta recedes*' but with the rider that this might be *'otium cum dignatate'*, Cicero's hope for the great and good of Rome, the Optimates who advised the state from retirement.[32] It is then that he introduces the fact that he might be figured in the poem:

> I fancy it will make you smile; but though, when first I began it, I thought of you; before I came to end it, I considered it might be too ludicrous, to a man of your situation and grave acquaintance, to make you Trebatius, who was yet one of the most considerable lawyers of his time, and a particular friend of a poet.[33]

Pope cannot have believed that Fortescue would be anything other than a reluctant supporter of any opposition to the Walpole administration.

The dialectic of the poem is, thus, less Socratic than might be supposed. Having – even if advertently – run up against influential patrician opinion in the Chandos affair, Pope was genuinely weighing in the balance how satire might attain its mark in the early 1730s. The poem does have the friend in, or near, power ultimately admit the Poet's case: 'The Case is alter'd', especially if any 'Plaintiff' (154-5) were to take issue with the 'grave Epistles' (151) he is in the process of writing. Edmund Plowden's coining of the phrase had become proverbial, yet its initial motive had become dislodged from a context that would not have been lost on Pope: as a celebrated Catholic recusant lawyer (yet one who was still approached by Elizabeth in 1578 to be Lord Chancellor), who refused higher office on account of growing religious persecution, the allusion reveals one public range of meanings – clustered around an obviously threadbare sense that Walpole and George II could come to know true worth when they saw it and at least one that is private – Pope's prevalent realization that there would be added temerity for a Catholic to speak out. The full text of the saying runs, 'The case is altered. No Priest, no Mass', referring to Plowden's defence, in a trial for heresy, that it was in fact a layman conducting the Mass, not a priest, and that the service had been a put-up job to supply evidence against those who had attended.[34]

The clarion call for the rights of the satirist is rightly praised (105–42); the clouds part, and the Poet emerges as 'arm'd for Virtue when I point the Pen' (105), commencing an expanded version of Horace's lines 39 to 60. Stack's perception that this passage moves towards darker hues in both poets is generally accurate, yet there are significant detours in Pope's journey.[35] Horace's satiric weapon, the 'stilus', means both a pen and a dagger, and it is a resource principally of self-defence:

> [...] sed hic stilus haud petet ultro
> quemquam animantem et me veluti custodiet ensis
> vagina tectus; quem cur destringere coner
> tutus ab infestis latronibus?[36]
> (But this pen and dagger will never voluntarily attack any
> man alive but will rather come from robbers' attacks?)

Pope could not so securely believe himself protected from the 'shameless, guilty Men' (106) of his age, and, in a greatly expanded imitation of Horace's section on the human propensity to use whatever weapons lie to hand, Pope's version leaps off into a description of how the truth-value of satire might be its own shield, just as both Boileau and Dryden discovered (111–14), and also how a sense of the moral duty of the satirist, a friend only to Virtue, prompts her/him to 'strip the Gilding off a Knave' (115) with little provocation. It is also a slight – but still significant – alteration from the source that while Horace cites his major literary influence, Lucilius, as the devoted friend to Virtue, Pope assumes that role for himself, and what seems like homage in the Horace becomes self-proclamation in the Pope. Indeed, Horace's more oblique proceeding is largely ignored by Pope.

A similar tactic forms the centrepiece of *Satire, II.ii*'s grasp of the simple life that closes Pope's version, for the rugged and unspoiled Ofellus, who could only rent his own homestead – translated as Bethel, is granted his own accents in the Horace; in the Pope, his 'Ofellus' gives way to the poet before placing Swift alongside as precariously master of himself, 'let Lands and Houses have what Lords they will'.[37] There is charity here, constructed out of simple hospitality and generous ownership. For Ofellus, as for Horace, dispossession could occur all too easily, as the events of 41 BC testified; the new owner, Umbrenus, will still have to face the forces of mortality and transience, and the immediate reality is that the rights of use, short of ownership, *ususfructus*, is, indeed, kin to the realities of use and occupation, now granted to Ofellus, even if leased.

The depth of this reassurance and the vivid details of the simple board is, on the other hand, a compensation for abstract possession and could be viewed as built upon loss, just as 'Satire 1' implies that the bravery of the satirist could be snatched away by others' legal might. The opening promise, that the poem will turn upon the 'Virtue and the Art / To live on little with a chearful heart' (1–2) is, we learn, in the next line '(A Doctrine sage, but truly none of mine)', a more forceful abnegation than in the Horace, where the precept results from the converse of Ofellus, his own *sermo*.[38] This is not the Virtue of the Schools, and it is, like the protection for the satirist, explored in 'Satire 1', an active talent, but Pope in both poems is not completely assured of his Stoicism. Just as he shared Horace with Swift, he also understood Bolingbroke's particular nuanced use of 'Virtue', a quality of the physical constitution as well as the effect of correct moral choice – but it is produced by exile – however self-imposed – and dispossession.

IV

To get a comprehensive sense of what was available for Pope in Horace it is necessary to regard the assumption of a Horatian voice as tactical and as wedded to an immediate cultural context; in other words, Pope was well aware of the contradictory associations offered by Horatian allusion, yet produced a distinctive sense of self-assertion by this means, a rhetoric that – for those who cared to – might project an accent specifically applied to his life and immediate circle. Horace supplied an honoured – and honourable – screen for self-excuse. Thomas Creech's translation steered clear of most of the conversational 'lowness', for – contrary to Quintilian's opinion that the *Satires*' aim to correct vice might involve impolite means – the contemporary poet was to confront the vulnerability of our 'Common Schools' wherein 'all is permitted to every Eye, and laid open to the dullest sight by the most shameful Notes that can be pen'd'. On the contrary, Horace is, in any case, a safer model, as he 'laughs men out of their Vices, and doth not lance or cauterize the sores, but tickles till He heals' and should be kept like that.[39] The basic rediscovery that the etymological root for the term, 'satire', implied variety rather than vituperation, tracing it to *lanx satura* (a bowl containing varied fruit) rather than a satyr (*satyros* – a hairy woodland creature known for frank speech), allowed several novel emphases in the satirist's art, principally an attempt at smoothness of style and controlled detachment, an overview of folly distinct from a challenge to individual vice.[40] Joseph Addison was clear in his position on this: 'A Satyr should expose nothing but what is corrigible'.[41] This clarity of purpose is often at a stand with Horace whose discursive charm and poised sincerity came over as too low-key and conversational to inspire reform and 'lance' the blemishes of vice. It could also provide a defensive camouflage, as André Dacier noted about his work: 'Horace is a true Proteus, that takes a thousand different Forms, they have often lost him, and not knowing where to find him, have grapled him as well as they could; they have palm'd upon him in several Places, not only Opinions, which he had not, but even those which he directly refutes.'[42] Indeed, it was this 'Delicacy', according to René Rapin, in his 'Reflections on Aristotle's Treatise on Poesie', that marked Horace out: 'for it was only by the way of Jest and Meriment that he exercis'd his Censure'.[43] For some, Horace was the temporizer, jesting where he should be arraigning; for others, he was the satiric craftsman, deploying his insinuating and oblique style to effect real reformation. This pragmatism was not often praised at this time, and Dryden was not alone in prizing the otherwise limited Persius as the more steadfast thinker: 'There is a spirit of sincerity in all he says. You may easily discern that he is in earnest, and is persuaded of that truth which he inculcates', whereas Horace is 'sometimes an Epicurean, sometimes a Stoic, sometimes an Eclectic; as his present humour leads him'.[44]

This variegated style was undoubtedly a boon to Pope; the conversational delivery allowed an enactment of friendship, freed of a search for mercenary advantage.[45] On one level, it helped him deal with the Chandos affair and its escalating notoriety; on another, it provided a discourse where the very virtues of genuine friendship projected an ideal of public resonance, and which stood as an implicit rebuke to cronyism. It did not, however, serve him as well once issues of straightforward moral choice were necessary.

This thread of private association joined to public virtue is strong in the 1735 collection, and becomes insistent in the scabrously ironic *The First Epistle of the Second Book of Horace, Imitated* (1737), where George II is no Augustus, and therefore Pope's apparently straight translation from Horace carries irony to the same degree that a clear difference is noted.[46] This Augustan Age is devoid of any patrons like Maecenas, symptomatic of his own hard road, but also of the relatively cushioned *gradus* for which Horace was so grateful; as Stack notes, the satire could be at his expense, too, for while it allows for 'the fine detachment and ironic astringency which are so evident in Horace's text', it, at the same time, is clear-sighted about Horace as the flatterer of his Emperor.⁴⁷ In 1735, Pope had not so obviously broken cover. Gaining friends is now an act of freedom and political choice.

This is most evident in his oft-stated reverence for Bolingbroke, whose role for Pope at this time might be best illustrated by the close to *An Essay on Man*, where his guide and friend resembles another: Horace:

> Teach me, like thee, in various nature wise,
> To fall with dignity, with temper rise;
> Form'd by thy converse, happily to steer
> From grave to gay, from lively to severe.⁴⁸

The concept of 'Virtue' in its more technical sense is explored in Bolingbroke's work in passages where the comment on corrupt government is at its most insistent. Calling for a Patriot King in 1740 (in Pope's edition), he made it clear that assessing personal ethical choice was not complete until the individual had taken into account a public impact for good (however defined). This outward-facing 'introspection' on a micro level fostered 'the Preservation of Liberty', where 'Virtue' and 'Publick Spirit' enjoyed free – and directed – rein. The Patriot (non-Hanoverian) King was to regard 'Publick Virtue' as the 'sole Means of acquiring any degree of Power or Profit in the State'.⁴⁹ As has been often noted, the tone is veering to the Utopian.⁵⁰ In a final French exile, his sense of how limited this hope might be permeates the 'Idea'. In 1735, however, and his *Dissertation upon Parties*, not all was futile; in an almost Horatian exile at Dawley, he specifically associated 'friendship' with an oppositional stance, in contrast to the 'Friends to the Government' who provide a 'prostituted' association:

> Such Men are really incapable of Friendship; for real Friendship can never exist among Those, who have banish'd Virtue and Truth. They have no Affection to any but Themselves; no Regard to any Interest, except their own.⁵¹

It is thus that a party interest is unpatriotic. The constitution is frequently severed from government throughout history, and its resumption and survival stems from those who have 'Virtue enough [...] how unprofitable soever it may be at all times, and how unpopular soever at some'. What raised the ire of the government was the assumption that – by definition – this virtuous quality derived from 'our Forefathers, in the Cause of Liberty', and could not be evident in the present political arrangement. Rome (and Cato, especially) provided a beacon of steadfast adherence to a few simple principles that promoted an imperial 'Grandeur' 'but when Luxury grew to favour Corruption, and Corruption to nourish Luxury; then Rome grew venal'.[52] As David Morse has made clear, this civic sense of 'virtue' carried many contemporary associations: of a distrust of Walpole, to be sure, but also a positive emphasis on what was taken to be a classical perspective wherein retreat meant clarity, and egotistical display gave way to a spirit of negotiation and compromise.[53] Horace is neither heard – nor exploited – by Pope in an unequivocal way. The sense that he needed the dignity of a Horatian persona, and that he tapped into the skilful urbanity of his sources throughout is only partially correct: Pope has no Maecenas to provide him with a carriage and he only hopes that the rights of possession will be honoured by the new Augustus. The basic question posed by a close examination of the allusive associations raised by this comparison is one of, as Iser notes, how any translator copes with a sense of crisis when he or she reaches into the past. Pope needed more than just 'dignity' in 1735, and the camouflage of speaking as if participating in an academic exercise; he needed to exceed Horace, in recognizing that the virtues of detachment and rational perception were only part of the story.

Notes

1. W. Iser (1996) 'The Emergence of a Cross-Cultural Discourse' in S. Budick and W. Iser (eds) *The Translatability of Cultures: Figurations of the Space Between* (Stanford, CA: Stanford University Press), pp. 245–64 (p. 248).
2. Horace (1929) *Satire, I.iv* and *Satire, I.x* in H. R. Fairclough (ed.) *Horace: Satires, Epistles, Ars Poetica* (Cambridge, MA: Harvard University Press), pp. 48–61, pp. 112–23. For a detailed treatment of this use of Lucilius's example, and its exploitation in *Satires, II.i*, see N. Rudd (1982, c.1966) *The 'Satires' of Horace* (Bristol: Bristol Classical Press), pp. 86–131.
3. This is succinctly summarized in D. Griffin (1994) *Satire: A Critical Reintroduction* (Lexington: University Press of Kentucky), pp. 115–32.
4. (1735) 'Advertisement' in *The Works of Alexander Pope, Esq; Vol. II* (London: L. Gilliver), p. 108.
5. These satires are headed by a Horatian epigraph, taken from *Satires, I.x*, lines 56–9, where Horace wonders whether it was personal to Lucilius that his verses lacked an easy flow – perhaps an inability to do otherwise – or whether it was the rough nature of his subject matter. Certainly, Pope draws out the Horatian accents from Donne, stressing the importunity of court witlings (*Satire IV*) and the untrustworthiness of lawyers and their impatience with plain sense (*Satire II*):

> Thus much I've said, I trust without offence;
> Let no Court-Sycophant pervert my sense,
> Nor sly Informer watch these words to draw
> Within the reach of Treason, or the Law.

See Pope (1953) *Satire IV* and *Satire II* in J. Butt (ed.) *The Twickenham Edition of the Poems of Alexander Pope, Vol. IV* (London: Methuen), pp. 23–49 and pp. 129–45, lines 125–8.

6. The identification could, unfortunately for Pope, be quite apposite: the Duke had done well out of his position as Paymaster of the Forces from 1707–12, and he had been ennobled by George I. His profuse and self-regarding use of riches is exactly the vice and weakness that Pope was making an example of in the 'Ethic Epistles' (now more normally known as the four *Moral Essays*) that were first grouped as such in the second volume of the 1735 *Works*. Chandos's huge and prominent Cannons was situated in Little Stanmore, a rapidly growing suburb to the north-west of London; completed in 1724, it had taken over ten years to build, and cost around £200,000.
7. (1951) 'Argument of the Use of Riches' in F. W. Bateson (ed.) *Twickenham Edition [...], Vol. III.ii*, 3rd edn (London: Methuen), pp. 127–9 (p. 128).
8. (1739) 'Satires of Horace' in *The Works of Alexander Pope, Esq.; Vol. II. Containing his Epistles, &c.* (London: Robert Dodsley), pp. 5–14, Book II, Satire I, line 121.
9. (1959) *Alexander Pope: The Poetry of Allusion* (Oxford: Clarendon Press), p. 284.
10. The positive qualities inherent in this intertextual play are best summed up in M. Mack (1969) *The Garden and the City: Retirement and Politics in the Later Poetry of Pope, 1731–1743* (Toronto and London: University of Toronto Press), pp. 163–87, and P. Martin (1984) *Pursuing Innocent Pleasures: The Gardening World of Alexander Pope* (Hamden, CT: Archon Books), pp. 39–61.
11. Maynard Mack does note though the Latin inscription on the third flyleaf of the Heinsius item the rather Horatian gesture of celebrating friendship: 'amicitiae causa/caste posuit' (in [1982] *Collected in Himself: Essays Critical, Biographical, and Bibliographical on Pope and Some of his Contemporaries* [Newark, NJ: University of Delaware Press], p. 419).
12. (1985) *Pope and Horace: Studies in Imitation* (Cambridge: Cambridge University Press), pp. 3–17.
13. J. Dryden (2000a) 'Discourse Concerning the Origin and Progress of Satire' in P. Hammond and D. Hopkins (eds) *The Poems of John Dryden, Vol. 3, 1686–1693* (Harlow: Longman), pp. 310–450 (p. 400).
14. Dryden, 'Discourse Concerning', pp. 404, 413 and 420.
15. Dryden, 'Discourse Concerning', p. 415.
16. Dryden (2000b) 'The First Satire of Persius. In Dialogue Betwixt the Poet and his Friend, or Monitor' in P. Hammond and D. Hopkins (eds) *Poems [...], Vol. 4, 1693–1696* (Harlow: Longman), pp. 139–52, lines 227–30.
17. (1995) 'The Second Epode of Horace' in P. Hammond (ed.) *Poems [...], Vol. 2, 1682–1685* (London: Longman), pp. 378–85, lines 1–3.
18. (1956b) '17 July 1734' and '2 August 1734' in G. Sherburn (ed.) *The Correspondence of Alexander Pope, Vol. III, 1729–1735* (Oxford: Clarendon Press), pp. 416–17 and p. 423.

19. '26 July 1734' in *Correspondence, Vol. III*, p. 420.
20. '26 July 1734', p. 420.
21. (1978) *Augustus Caesar in Augustan England: The Decline of a Classical Norm* (Princeton, NJ: Princeton University Press), pp. 68–85.
22. (1964) in N. Ault and J. Butt (eds) *Twickenham Edition [...], Vol. VI*, 1st edn reprinted with minor corrections (London: Methuen), p. 376.
23. (1953) in *Twickenham Edition [...], Vol. IV*, 2nd edn, pp. 295–309, lines 11–12 and 19–22.
24. 'Epilogue', lines 26 and 34–5.
25. (2006) *The Lives of the Most Eminent English Poets; With Critical Observations on their Works*, R. Lonsdale (ed.), 4 vols (Oxford: Clarendon Press), IV, p. 78.
26. (1939) *An Essay on Criticism* in E. Audra and A. Williams (eds) *Twickenham Edition [...], Vol. I* (London: Methuen), pp. 233–326, lines 653–4.
27. See (1956a) Pope's letter to Fortescue '10 May, 1725 (?)' in G. Sherburn (ed.) *Correspondence [...], Vol. 2, 1719–1728* (Oxford: Clarendon Press). The gesture of thanks in this letter also includes a first reference to what will emerge writ large in the satire: a determination not to be bought by any promise of future preferment: 'I have more esteem for him, & will stay till he is out of Power (according to my Custome) before I say what I think of him' (p. 294).
28. (1950) in M. Mack (ed.) *Twickenham Edition [...], Vol. III.i* (London: Methuen), IV.126.
29. IV.123–8.
30. In *Horace: Satires, Epistles, Ars Poetica*, pp. 450–89, lines 466–7.
31. Pope, 'Satire 1' in *Twickenham Edition [...], Vol. IV*, pp. 1–21, line 22 and 29 and lines 42–3. Further references are by line number to this edition and are placed in parentheses following the quotation.
32. 'Letter XXXII to William Fortescue' in *Correspondence [...], Vol. III*, p. 351. See Cicero (1958) 'Pro Sestio' in R. Gardner (trans.) *Orations: Pro Sestio, In Vatinium* (Cambridge, MA: Loeb), pp. 96–8. Horace's fullest description of this desirable state can be found in *Odes, II.xvi* (see Horace [rev. ed. 1927] *The Odes and Epodes*, C. E. Bennett [trans.] [Cambridge, MA: Loeb], pp. 148–51).
33. 'Letter XXXII', p. 351. What is more, the early editions include further obfuscation, in having the prefix as '*L*' (1733–5).
34. See J. Ray (1737) *A Compleat Collection of English Proverbs* (London: J. Hughs), p. 175. Howard D. Weinbrot has outlined the range of adverse comment on the poem, and identifies two alternative answers (depending on one's reading) to this closing agreement: the one stung by Pope's close association (among the close-knit circle of friends) with Bolingbroke and therefore regarding the otherwise neutral references to ethically sound friendship as cover for partisanship and a Patriot cause; the other, wondering how strong and bold that apparently climactic last part-phrase of Pope's might actually be. If all he can safely attempt is verse 'such as Sir *Robert* would approve' ('Satire 1', line 153), then it might be the case that Fortescue's initial premise had been carried ([1979] 'Such as Sir Robert Would Approve? Answers to Pope's Answer from Horace', *Modern Language Studies*, 9, 5–14).
35. See *Pope and Horace*, pp. 43–54 (and his inclusion of Bolingbroke's understanding of Senecan retreat in this regard out of *The Idea of a Patriot King*, pp. 54–5).
36. *Satire, I.i* in *Horace: Satires, Epistles, Ars Poetica*, pp. 4–15, lines 39–42.

37. Horace, *Satire, II.ii* in *Horace: Satires, Epistles, Ars Poetica*, pp. 136–47, lines 112–36; Pope, 'Satire 2' in *Twickenham Edition [...], Vol. IV*, pp. 51–69, lines 129–60 and 179–80. Further references are by line number to this edition and are placed in parentheses following the quotation.
38. *Satire, II.ii*, lines 2–3.
39. (1684) 'Preface' in *The Odes, Satyrs, and Epistles of Horace Done into English*, T. Creech (trans.) (London: Jacob Tonson), pp. v–vi. Pope, though, was well aware of Horace's occasional coarseness: see J. Spence (1966) *Observations, Anecdotes, and Characters of Books and Men*, J. M. Osborn (ed.), 2 vols (Oxford: Clarendon Press), I, p. 227.
40. This is lucidly summarized by A. Marshall (2013) *The Practice of Satire in England, 1658–1770* (Baltimore: Johns Hopkins University Press), pp. 40–69, and Griffin, *Satire*, pp. 12–34.
41. (1965) 'No. 209. 30 October, 1711' in D. F. Bond (ed.) *The Spectator*, 5 vols (Oxford: Clarendon Press), II, pp. 320–2 (p. 321).
42. (1692) 'The Preface of M. Dacier' in *Miscellany Poems upon Several Occasions* (London: Peter Buck), p. xxviii.
43. (1706) *The Whole Critical Works of Monsieur Rapin in Two Volumes* (London: H. Bonwicke, T. Goodwin, M. Wotton, B. Tooke and S. Manship), II, p. 228.
44. Dryden, *Discourse Concerning*, p. 402. This elusiveness, and its possible aims, was not often relished, as Stack points out; there is, however, at the same time an endemic politics in this, appearing the stronger as he got older, as Shaftesbury noticed (see *Pope and Horace*, pp. 6–11).
45. On his death-bed, Pope confessed to Hooke that 'There is nothing that is meritorious but virtue and friendship, and indeed friendship itself is only a part of virtue' ([1956c] '19–29 May, 1744' in G. Sherburn [ed.] *Correspondence [...], Vol. IV, 1736–44* [London: Methuen], p. 526). Bolingbroke concurred, claiming it to be '"the whole duty of man"' (Spence, *Observations*, I, p. 269). For a lucid account of Bolingbroke's reasons for investing so much in this type of 'friendship', see E. D. Jones (2013) *Friendship and Allegiance in Eighteenth-Century Literature: The Politics of Private Virtue in the Age of Walpole* (Basingstoke: Palgrave Macmillan), pp. 83–106.
46. In the 'Advertisement', Pope brings to the reader's attention his addition of 'one or two of those Virtues which contribute to the Happiness of a Free People', and reminds George (as apparently Horace reminded Augustus) that the 'decent Freedom' exploited by the skilled poet 'under due Regulations' could be of use to the state, and ensure his repute – on which he 'must depend, for his Fame with Posterity' (pp. 191–2). The amalgam of support for a court and an (elected) monarch with the threat that this is not to be enjoyed unconditionally is not in the original.
47. *Pope and Horace*, p. 157.
48. IV.377–80.
49. H. St John Bolingbroke (1740) *The Idea of a Patriot King: With respect to the Constitution of Great Britain. By a person of quality* (London: 'T.C.'), pp. 8, 63.
50. See B. Hammond (1984) *Pope and Bolingbroke: A Study of Friendship and Influence* (Columbia: University of Missouri Press), pp. 138–42.
51. Bolingbroke (1735) *A Dissertation upon Parties; in several letters to Caleb D'Anvers, Esq; dedicated to the Right Honourable Sir Robert Walpole* (London: G. Faulkner), p. 109. This equivalence of the suburban farm with oppositional

politics is basic. See Martin, *Pursuing Innocent Pleasures*, pp. 119–44, and B. Lauren (1975) 'Pope's Epistle to Bolingbroke: Satire from the Vantage of Retirement', *SEL*, 15, 419–30.
52. Bolingbroke, *A Dissertation*, pp. 113, 145, 213.
53. (2000) *The Age of Virtue: British Culture from the Restoration to Romanticism* (New York: St. Martin's Press), pp. 47–109 (a corrective to Pope's more optimistic line on benevolism is detailed at pp. 96–107).

2
Celebrating *Universal Beauty*
Henry Brooke's In-between Poetics
John Baker

Preamble

Behind the philosophical poems published in the early decades of the eighteenth century lies the principle of an active, informing and benevolent deity that is perceptible in the manifestations of the natural world in all their diversity and ingenuity; it is a unifying principle, but one ultimately beyond the grasp of human understanding. The contours of this deity, more impersonal than personal, and thus less Christian than deistic, are shifting and vague; they vary from poem to poem and remain, inevitably, elusive at best. They gesture towards or intimate rather than delineate. The authors of these poems, ambitiously trying their hand, deploy various linguistic strategies that test the limits of language to express the attributes of their God and to celebrate the beauties and harmony of the created world, and the sense of wonder it inspires. At times, they also express a profound sense of disquiet concerning the role and place of man in the scheme of things.

Alexander Pope, in the course of the opening passage of Epistle II of *An Essay on Man*, was to present the human condition as subject to division and discord, and man as a creature prone to excess, indecision and conflicting instincts and desires – a divided being in a world of 'elemental strife'.[1] This 'middle state' (II.3) paradoxically means not only that man 'hangs between; in doubt to act or rest, / In doubt to deem himself a God, or Beast' (II.7–8), but also provides an incitement to seek refuge and cultivate a middle ground in ethics, a possible haven of moderation and security in, from and for one's own self. The concluding couplet of the passage, itself a verdict on man, echoing the thoughts and words of Blaise Pascal, is clearly a cause for concern rather than a source of reassurance: 'Sole judge of Truth, in endless Error hurl'd: / The glory, jest, and riddle of the world!' (II.17–18). This moral and existential 'betweenness', and the notion of betweenness in general, can usefully be displaced and employed to explore the nature of a poem by the young protégé of Pope (and of Swift), Henry Brooke (1703?–83). This chapter will suggest that Brooke's *Universal Beauty* (1735) can be read as being in between not only the two major philosophical poems of the period, James Thomson's *The Seasons* (1730; 1746) and Pope's *An Essay on Man* (1733–4), but is also in between in its own right, in other respects, such as the poet's choice and treatment of material and his poetic vision.

After several periods living in London during which he at first, from 1724, pursued his law studies at the Temple but also embarked upon a literary career with Pope's help and encouragement, Brooke was to leave the capital for the last time and return to his native Ireland following the controversy generated by the announcement of forthcoming performances of his play *Gustavus Vasa: The Deliverer of his Country* (1739) at Drury Lane, and its banning by the Lord Chancellor. The play, in rehearsal at the time, was judged to purvey a political message hostile to Sir Robert Walpole and his government.[2] Four years previously, Brooke had published the six parts that make up his poem *Universal Beauty*.[3] He appears to have left London in some haste and wrote to Pope, probably in November 1739: 'I was much concerned that I had not an opportunity of taking leave of you when I came for Ireland. I earnestly wished to see you, because I feared it was for the last time, and I wanted to thank you once for all, for much good you have done me, and more particularly for revising and passing your friendly judgment upon some lines of mine that, indeed, were scarcely worth your reading.' Brooke continues with fulsome praise for his mentor, putting Pope on a par with Virgil ('equal pleasure') and Homer ('equal warmth'), but below Shakespeare, who procures 'greater rapture', and Milton, who procures 'more astonishment'.[4] That Brooke was guided and influenced by Pope is clear, and the use of heroic couplets as the chosen verse form for his poem was predictable. In many ways, however, the poem is closer in its optimism, its generosity, its visionary qualities and its descriptions of the natural world to Thomson's blank verse poem, *The Seasons*. Maynard Mack writes in the third section of the introduction to his edition of *An Essay on Man*, 'The *Essay* as a Poem': 'Almost all the philosophical materials in the *Essay* can be paralleled in Thomson's *Seasons*, yet two poems could hardly be less alike.'[5] Brooke's poem is not a synthesis of the two, but in several respects it does appear to occupy a middle ground in the sense that it incorporates elements from both. Arguably, however, at times its visionary passages go beyond what even Thomson expresses, or are at least akin to the final lines of *Winter* and the crowning and concluding 'A Hymn' in their celebratory tone.

While *Universal Beauty* is, unsurprisingly, very much a poem of its time, and blends into and builds on and from the spate of philosophical poems that characterize the early eighteenth century, several features mark it out. One concerns the margins of the poem: the elements that make up the peritext. Other poets, such as Pope and Thomson, do supplement their poems with prefaces, summaries of contents and arguments (as in *An Essay on Man* and *The Seasons*), and Pope parodied and exaggerated to farcical proportions the whole practice and vogue of providing prefatory material and scholarly, explanatory footnotes in his 1729 *The Dunciad, Variorum. With the Prolegomena of Martin Scriblerus*. The added material he provides takes the form of appendices, testimonies of authors, errata and copious 'remarks' (footnotes). The first of the footnotes, on the spelling and etymology of the title word 'Dunciad', gets the reader well and truly bogged down, crowding out the opening lines of the poem itself, and making the enterprise entertainingly and absurdly lopsided and bottom-heavy. However, Brooke's numerous footnotes (more than 200 in all), sometimes short and succinct, at times dense and elaborate, have a serious function. They are there to fulfil a didactic purpose, and are an integral part of the poem. They constitute a studious and unlikely contrast and complement to an often enthusiastic poem. This is one form of Brookian betweenness: there is a visible contrast on the pages of the poem between the heroic couplets, the fervent, even ecstatic, passages and his footnotes, which indicate Brooke's desire to make his poem accessible and clearly understood, and to bestow on it a 'scientific' authority and legitimacy. He writes in his Preface to Part I (a preface that is mind-boggling in its scope and ambition): 'the technical terms are as few, and the whole explained and made as easy and obvious as possible'.

Within the poem itself, Brooke is an in-between poet first and foremost because he is at once a metaphysician and a rhapsodist. Here again he is not alone: he can be aligned with Anthony Ashley Cooper, third Earl of Shaftesbury (though the latter wrote no poetry, his prose style, as in *The Moralists*, is often rhapsodic and energetic), and with Thomson in whose *Seasons*, natural philosophy, descriptions of natural phenomena, moral reflection and the expression of wonder and elation at the beauty and variety of the world are interwoven. James Sambrook in the introduction to his edition of *The Seasons* identifies a number of different themes and trends in Thomson's poem – devotional, georgic, scientific, descriptive, subjective and so on, while acknowledging that the list itself remains incomplete.⁶ If stylistically, formally and instinctively, Brooke's writing occupies a space somewhere between Thomson and Pope, one can suppose that as a young, promising poet he was seeking to make the best of both worlds. *Universal Beauty* is Brooke's first and only major poetic work, though he was to become an accomplished man of letters, playwright, translator, essayist and novelist.

The world he describes, fashions and puts into poetry is one that is itself, at times, both in between *and* hybrid, as is manifest in some of his descriptions of the phenomenal world of nature, and in the choice of his illustrations, as with, in Part V, the snail (both house and inhabitant) (V.89–106) and the modest earthworm (V.73–88), and, in Part III, creepers, of which more will be said later (III.271–96). Similarly, Brooke expresses a penchant for the sticky and viscous, such as juices and slime, which are substances halfway between liquid and solid. The poem can be labelled as in between, also, because Brooke's descriptions and celebration of nature can be perceived as the contrary of an anthropomorphic vision, as though he was giving a bee's-eye, or a snail's-eye view (or vision) of the world, although this is patently not the case but is rather a mirror effect. He perceives in the natural order creative and constructive qualities and accomplishments, a harmonious purpose, that he approves of and admires and that, he claims, mankind seeks only to destroy. But the human eye empathizing with bees, or snails, or animalcules or streams, remains just that: a human eye and vision, an anthropomorphic projection and construct.

Brooke unceasingly portrays and proposes an idealized view of the natural world and its workings, holding it up as the model for human behaviour. 'Oh why can't people be more like bees, or beavers, or streams, or the air, or creepers!', he seems to be saying. There, where physico- and astro-theologians like John Ray and William Derham saw and laid bare evidence of God's wisdom and handiwork in all aspects of creation, Brooke also sees nature as informed and infused by God's creating sense and soul and as endowed with 'wisdom'. He also detects and extols in the works of nature a 'social' and benign purpose that man lacks but should copy and emulate. While Pope and Thomson make clear their awareness of the imperfections of the natural world and overtly address the question of theodicy, as well as the shortcomings and 'inhumanity' of man, Brooke paints an unremittingly bright and hopeful, at times ecstatic, vision of the natural world as in these lines from Part I, which portray a world of consummate delight, both catalogue and vision:

Unspeakable! their Landskip Hill, and Dale,
The lowly Sweetness of the Flow'ry Vale,
The Mount elate, that rises in Delight,
The flying Lawns, that wanton from the Sight,
The florid Theatres, Romantick Scenes,
The steepy Mountains, and luxuriant Plains,
Delicious Regions! Plants, Woods, Waters, Glades,
Grotts, Arbours, Flow'rets, Downs, and rural Shades,
The Brooks, that sportive wind the ecchoing Hills,
The pearly Founts, smooth Lakes, and murmuring Rills —
Myriads of *Edens!* Blissful! Blissful Seats!
Arcadian Groves, sweet *Tempe*'s blest Retreats,
Delightful *Enna*'s and *Hesperian* Isles,
And round, and round throughout, *Elysium* smiles —
Consummate; Joy, Peace, Pleasure without End,
Thro' Mansions numberless their *Guests* attend,
Nor long inanimate[.] (I.133–49)

The words fall over each other in their desire to express the 'unspeakable' beauty and variety of the world. Brooke delights in multiplying, in accumulating, in simply naming and listing. Man, however, is singled out as a blot on this ideal landscape at several points in the poem. The human being, on his or her rare appearances, is a shadowy, insubstantial figure, constantly found wanting and is spoken of in disparaging terms in the following apostrophes:

"Ah Nature! thou hadst scap'd thy only Blot,
"Cou'd Man but cease to be — or hitherto were not;
"Ay, there's the Task, the Labour of our Song,
"To prove that All is right — tho' Man be wrong." (III.88–91)

And later in the same book, he continues:

"O *Nature!* whom the Song aspires to scan,
"O *Beauty!* trod by proud insulting Man,
"This boasted Tyrant of thy wondrous Ball,
"This mighty, haughty — little Lord of All;
"This King o'er Reason — but this Slave to Sense,
"Of Wisdom careless — but of Whim immense;
"Tow'rds *Thee!* incurious, ignorant, profane,
"But of his own — dear — strange — Productions vain."
(III.325–31)

There is an unmistakably Popean symmetry and use of antithesis evident here not only in the sentiments and the scorn expressed, but also in the formulation, where the oxymoronic 'Wisdom careless' slides and blends into the no less oxymoronic 'Whim immense', where 'Wisdom' shrinks and is compacted into mere 'Whim'. There is similarly an exact echo of Pope's triumphant last lines (and line) of Epistle I of his *An Essay on Man*, with the expression of a moral ontology which proclaims that everything is as it should be, and man should learn to accept the limits of his nature and his understanding:

> All Nature is but Art, unknown to thee;
> All Chance, Direction, which thou canst not see;
> All Discord, Harmony, not understood;
> All partial Evil, universal Good:
> And, spite of Pride, in erring Reason's spite,
> One truth is clear, "Whatever IS, is RIGHT." (I.289–94)

Pope achieves at the end of Epistle I an act of bravado where he wholeheartedly, with as much craftsmanship as gusto, denounces man's pretensions and pride, and yet takes stock of the situation, and explains why God has created the world as it is, and why man should content himself with things as they are. Pope thus appears, even if he does not actually have access to any understanding beyond the limits ordained by his human state, at least to be a knowledgeable and well-informed border guard. Establishing man's limits and limitations is not a central preoccupation for Brooke. Taken as a whole, *Universal Beauty* is far less didactic and moral in scope than Pope's *An Essay on Man*, far more absorbed in describing the natural world.

Three beginnings

I would like to set the opening of *Universal Beauty* beside the opening lines of two other similar poems that are exactly contemporary, Pope's *An Essay on Man* (1733–4) and John Arbuthnot's *Gnothi Seauton: Know Your Self* (1734), before going on to consider some aspects of Brooke's poetics. That the poems came in a cluster and the fact that the writers were, or so one can surmise, aware of each other's projects, suggests some degree of friendly emulation. The three works can be broadly grouped under the rubric of philosophical or wisdom poems in that they undertake wide-ranging enquiries into human identity and purpose, man's place in and relation to the world and universe, and the origin and nature of that universe. They are poems of metaphysical and ethical quest and questioning, voicing doubts as well as convictions. Arbuthnot's poem, an unexpected and precious piece, is much shorter than the other two (137 lines), and its scope is correspondingly more limited. Brooke's stands apart, as has been said, in its celebratory tone and focus on the natural world. Helen Margaret Scurr, in her still useful and informative monograph on Brooke (1922), recalls that there is internal and external evidence, as quoted above (n.3), of Pope's influence and aid; several lines and echoes in the poem, as we will see, testify to the internal evidence. The three poems are written in heroic couplets, though Scurr regrets this in Brooke's case:

> Brooke, like Pope, used the couplet; he would probably have done better if, like his fellow versifiers of philosophy, Thomson, Cooper, and Akenside, he had followed Shaftesbury's advice, and employed blank verse, in which he would have found a vehicle more appropriate to his theme.[7] The restrictions of the rimed couplet are out of harmony with the contemplation of infinity.[8]

The opinion that blank verse is associated with freedom, a generous and progressive poetics and visions of the infinite, while the heroic couplet is consciously limited in its outlook and scope, conservative and prudent, seeking symmetry, balance and decorum, no doubt has some truth in it, but remains true in part only. Brooke, while not attaining Pope's mastery in the use of the rhyming couplet (who did?), uses the couplet form to express an enthusiasm and vigour, and an optimism that in Pope is deliberately and carefully channelled and tempered. Scurr criticizes Brooke's use of iambic pentameter rhyming couplets, then, as somehow a wrong choice, ill adapted to his purpose:

> His massing of detail and expansion of ideas often prevent him from coming to a period within twenty couplets. Pope's couplets are easily detachable for quotation; each flashes with a splendid polish, and the effect of the whole is that of a brilliant mosaic fashioned from a thousand glittering fragments. It is difficult to find in Brooke one quotable couplet. Few are even detachable.[9]

This detachability and the quotable quality of the couplets were not Brooke's prime concern (nor were they Pope's) but Brooke does make a varied use of the heroic couplet, at times perfectly symmetrical and harmonious, at others, urgent, breathless and disjointed to good effect. The rhyming couplet does not appear to shackle his poetic enthusiasm and vision.

The metaphor that opens Epistle I of Pope's *An Essay on Man* is that of a battue, with the seeker after truth portrayed as a country gentleman, beating the ground to flush out what is hidden, to make it break cover and to see what moral truths the poet can bag. Any inclination to develop a lofty vision of humankind is immediately and effortlessly laid to rest in the perfectly delivered first lines. Here is Pope's breezy, relaxed, inclusive, almost chatty opening:

> AWAKE, my St. JOHN! leave all meaner things
> To low ambition, and the pride of Kings.
> Let us (since Life can little more supply
> Than just to look about us and to die)
> Expatiate free o'er all this scene of Man;
> A mighty maze! but not without a plan;
> A Wild, where weeds and flow'rs promiscuous shoot,
> Or Garden, tempting with forbidden fruit.
> Together let us beat this ample field,
> Try what the open, what the covert yield;
> The latent tracts, the giddy heights explore
> Of all who blindly creep, or sightless soar;
> Eye Nature's walks, shoot Folly as it flies,
> And catch the Manners living as they rise;
> Laugh where we must, be candid where we can;
> But vindicate the ways of God to Man. (I.1–16)

One has the impression that human existence affords little time or opportunity to analyse or grasp quite what is going on, that life is an aside, put, as it is, between brackets: '(since Life can little more supply / Than just to look about us and to die)'. This offhand, reader-friendly overture packs in a remarkable amount, in the antitheses, the allusions and with the modals and imperatives nudging us in the right direction. There is no grandiose invocation here, no lavish apostrophe to the muses or a statement that Pope intends to go to regions that no poet has ever been to before. There are no flights of fancy. This poet's feet are firmly planted on the ground. The mean and low, like the giddy, are eschewed, as are the pejorative 'sightless' and 'blind'. Pope magisterially stakes out his territory – his own middle ground. He is ambitiously and implacably cautious.

Though it is, in its own way and on its own terms, a clearly signalled sequel to Milton's epic, the theodicy proposed is, again, markedly and succinctly urbane and modest rather than of epic proportions. The Garden of Eden, the backdrop and dramatic setting for much of *Paradise Lost*, is here slipped in in passing. If you blink you may miss it. The double negation 'not without a plan', even coming after 'A mighty maze!' with its attendant exclamation mark, is itself a token of almost ironic caution: God's grand design is 'not without a plan' (not much rhapsody or poetic hubris there). A clear, if discreet and undramatic, echo of Milton there may be, then, but a theodicy nonetheless. However, the gap between the two, Milton and Pope, marks a sea change visible for all.

Here is how John Arbuthnot (bap. 1667, d. 1735) commences his own more uneasy and personal enquiry that appears to be taking up the gauntlet-cum-injunction thrown down and intoned by Pope at the beginning of Epistle II: 'Know then thyself, presume not God to scan; / The proper study of Mankind is Man':

> What am I? how produc'd? and for what End?
> Whence drew I Being? to what Period tend?
> Am I th' abandon'd Orphan of blind Chance;
> Dropt by wild Atoms in disorder'd Dance?
> Or from an endless Chain of Causes wrought?
> And of unthinking Substance, born with Thought?
> By Motion which began without a Cause,
> Supremely wise, without Design, or Laws.
> Am I but what I seem, mere Flesh and Blood;
> A branching Channel, with a mazy Flood?[10]

'What am I?' and not 'Who am I?' asks Arbuthnot, taking an objective, rather than a subjective stance, in this dramatic and studied opening sequence of questions. The questions, seven in the first five lines alone, while not actually colliding like Lucretian atoms (God forbid!), do convey an anxious haste and urgency. The paradoxes and irony, typical of Pope's poetry and neo-classical poetics as a whole – 'unthinking Substance, born with Thought', 'Supremely wise, without Design, or Laws' – indicate that Arbuthnot takes such purportedly Epicurean propositions to be absurd. Such was the overwhelming consensus of the day even though, ironically, Lucretius's *De Rerum Natura* (c.55 BC) remained *the* reference and model (and counter-model) for the 'universe' poems of the period. The physician Arbuthnot, seconding the metaphysician, is on hand to remind us that our body is not our 'self', and he seems to be picking up on one of the questions raised in Locke's inquiry into identity in *An Essay Concerning Human Understanding*.[11] He moves on only to find himself back where he started, despite the unceasing transformation and renewal of the body:

> New Matter still the mould'ring Mass sustains,
> The Mansion changed, the Tenant still remains;
> And from the fleeting Stream repair'd by Food,
> Distinct, as is the Swimmer from the Flood.
> What am I then? (p. 2)

Pope, having discounted the possibility of 'knowing' God in Epistle I of the *Essay*, states that Man (or human nature) is all we can aspire to know, or try to know. The quest for self-knowledge, in the rest of Pope's poem, shows a self-doubting being, buffeted by conflicting desires and aspirations. For Arbuthnot too, man is a divided, contradictory being: 'Essence divine, with lifeless Clay allay'd, / By double Nature, double Instinct sway'd' (p. 2). Christianity alone, he concludes, can provide solace and hope of sorts.

Brooke, however, starts the first of his six books in a much grander, more epic style, with an exuberant invocation in the form of apostrophes to pagan, classical divinities, Tritonia (Minerva, descending from the heavens) and Venus Urania (rising out of chaos). There is no unease, no doubt to cloud the horizon, at least for the moment. In Part I, the world is presented as a vast and beautiful canvas, which is harmonious, exquisitely conceived and designed, and a masterpiece of divine art from a, indeed *the*, supreme artist – the author of what Brooke later refers to as 'the World's great Poem' (III.2). Yet immediately after the invocations he goes on, in a passage that recalls Arbuthnot, to fire a series of questions in quick succession that seem to ricochet off in all directions but are meticulously contrived:

> O say, while yet, nor *Time*, nor *Place* was found,
> And Space immense, in its own Depth was drown'd;
> If *Nothing* was, or *Something* yet was not,
> Or tho' *to be*, e'erwhile was *Unbegot*;
> If caus'd, then how? — if causeless, why Effect?
> (No Hand to form, nor Model to direct)
> Why ever made?— so soon! — or why so late?
> What Chance, what Will, what Freedom, or what Fate? —

> Matter, and Spirit, Fire, Air, Ocean, Earth!
> All Nature born! — nor conscious of its Birth —
> Alike unconscious did the *Womb* disclose,
> And *Nothing* wonder'd whence this *Something* rose—
> Then by what *Pow'r*? — or what such *Pow'r* could move?
> Wisdom, or Chance? — Necessity, or Love?
> [...]
> Whence are your Attributes of *Time* and *Place*
> Won from *Eternity* and boundless *Space*?
> Motion from Rest? just Order from Misrule?
> A World from Nought? — *All Empty*, now *all Full*,
> From Silence Harmony? from Darkness Light?
> And beamy Day, from everlasting Night?
> Light, Matter, Motion, Musick, Order, Laws!
> And silent dark Nonentity the Cause? (I.25–38; 43–50)

There is a fine compactness of argument here. The tumbling questions and the sifting through the options, objections, paradoxes and inconsistencies, with the use of accumulation or listing (epitrochasm) in lines 33 and 49, keep the movement going and spur on the poem. The density of expression and the sustained poetic energy deployed in these lines make them a choice example of several aspects of Brooke's in-between and hybrid poetics – a rhapsodic neo-classicism is, here, a rhapsody of doubt.

There are 21 question marks in the passage (I.25–50), without taking into account the implicit, or the multiple or cluster questions. Brooke does not lapse into a facile rejection of Lucretius (though he does reject pantheistic and Epicurean atheistic positions later in the poem), but in his questioning explores the paradoxes and the insoluble nature of the problem of origins. The unfathomable character of the enigma is conveyed in the impossible image or adynaton of line 26: 'And Space immense, in its own Depth was drown'd'.

The opening passage, with its references to time and place, and above all the dispute between 'Something' and 'Nothing', also recalls John Wilmot, the Earl of Rochester's 'Upon Nothing' and Pope's own 'take' on the theme: 'In Imitation of the Earl of Rochester: On Silence' (1712; 1736). The passage is philosophical not only in the nature of the questions raised, but also in the quality and process of the close reasoning at work. The staccato delivery, expressing something between astonishment, incredulity and apprehension, reinforces the way the questions mount up in a cumulative manner, each one appearing before the previous one has had time to be resolved. Relentless in their 'sequent toil', this measured breathlessness, and economy and density of expression, translate at once a sense of urgency and perplexity in Brooke's attempt to get at the truth. The opening ontological question is as vast as it is simple. How can anything at once 'be' and come into being? It is only through language that the impossibility of the matter becomes apparent (or even exists), and can be articulated.

The poetic portrait of moral, self-questioning, self-doubting man, sketched out by Arbuthnot is, like that of his friend, literary accomplice and fellow Scriblerian, Pope, a mixture of paradox, contradiction and balance. It is a personal poem, less deistic than Christian, addressing as it does a personal God. It is also a poem of limitation and a proficient exercise in restraint: a pocket-sized philosophical poem, providing an outline of what man is, arguing how far and to what he can aspire. Brooke, too, exploits this probing, interrogative vein even if it is far less prominent than the visionary and descriptive, more Thomsonian, passages and vignettes in *Universal Beauty*.

This is not to say that there is no celebration in Pope's *An Essay on Man*. There is, and more than is sometimes acknowledged. A. D. Nuttall quotes, in his study of the *Essay*, the famous passage at the end of Epistle I, beginning with the lines: 'All are but parts of one stupendous whole, / Whose body Nature is, and God the soul' (I.267–8), which contains Pope's poetic profession of faith, a paean to things as they are and an acceptance of the world and the human position in that world. Pope does not dwell on or describe in detail particular phenomena, as Brooke and Thomson do, but the balance and harmony in the lines acknowledge and celebrate the divine presence in the created world with unparalleled skill. Thus 'God the soul':

> Warms in the sun, refreshes in the breeze,
> Glows in the stars, and blossoms in the trees,
> Lives thro' all life, extends thro' all extent,
> Spreads undivided, operates unspent[.] (271–4)

Nuttall comments on the passage as a whole (I.267–80): 'The eighteenth century is conventionally despised for want of strong religious feeling connected with natural beauty. But it is hard to think of a living writer who could match the cumulative impetus of these lines. Pope himself remains for once magnificently unironic, almost rapt.'[12] The passage is not far in tone and thought from Thomson's lines in *Spring*:

> What is this *mighty Breath*, ye Curious, say,
> That, in a powerful Language, felt not heard,
> Instructs the Fowls of Heaven; and thro' their Breast
> These Arts of Love diffuses? What, but God?
> Inspiring God! who boundless Spirit all,
> And unremitting Energy, pervades,
> Adjusts, sustains, and agitates the Whole.[13]

But Pope's avowed purpose is to observe and take the measure of moral man. Where Brooke can be aligned with those whom Samuel Johnson was to refer to condescendingly as the 'brethren of the blank song' (with David Mallet and Thomson in particular, and later Mark Akenside), rather than with the practitioners of the heroic couplet, is in his close interest in the natural world, in insects, animals, plants, and trees, indeed all natural phenomena.[14] No other poem at the time, apart from Thomson's *The Seasons* and Mallet's *The Excursion* (1728), celebrates the natural world in all its diversity and profusion, with so little restraint, with so much enthusiasm and attention to detail as Brooke's *Universal Beauty*.

James Thomson writes in his preface to the second edition of his *Winter* in 1726:

> I know no Subject more elevating, more amusing; more ready to awake the poetical Enthusiasm, the philosophical Reflection, and the moral Sentiment, than the *Works of Nature*. Where can we meet with such Variety, such Beauty, such Magnificence? All that enlarges, and transports, the Soul? What more inspiring than a calm, wide, Survey of Them? In every Dress *Nature* is greatly charming!

He goes on to succinctly map out the programme of what would become the 1730 poem *The Seasons*:

> How gay looks the *Spring!* how glorious the *Summer!* how pleasing the *Autumn!* and how venerable the *Winter!*—But there is no thinking of these Things without breaking out into POETRY; which is, by the bye, a plain, and undeniable, Argument of their superior Excellence.[15]

Brooke shares this fervour and follows Thomson's lead in his *Universal Beauty*, giving nature and the natural world the central role in his poetic quest and celebration. As Scurr has suggested, he may well be taking up, also, the invitation in the 1728 edition of Henry Needler's writings where William Duncombe writes in his Advertisement: 'The Essay on the Beauty of the Universe *is but a* Sketch *(as Mr. Needler himself owns)* […]. *I wish it may incite some* able Hand *to treat more amply so useful and entertaining a subject.*'16 Brooke is singularly receptive and sensitive to the beauty of the world, and sees in the manifestations of Nature, in its all-pervasive aesthetic quality, ethical lessons and messages that man should listen to, model himself on and live by.

A poetic celebration of the in-between

Among the elements of the natural world that Brooke singles out for notice, the small and insignificant have their place quite naturally alongside the large and the inanimate. All creation appears to be endowed with a soul and enjoys its rightful and 'fit' place in nature. Brooke will not insist, as Pope was to, at least in part, on the pecking order, nor on the ladder or chain of being. Certainly, everything is in its 'due' and 'appointed' place (words that appear regularly in Pope and Brooke), though Brooke's is a horizontal rather than a vertical order. In turn, he marvels at the intricacies of the mechanics and the profusion of this creation, and the lessons to be drawn from all God's creatures, great and small. One, the description of the creeper, of trailing and climbing plants, illustrates Brooke's inclusive bent and his sympathy for the in-between and overlooked. It is an unexpected choice, which gives him the opportunity to deploy elements of that rich, elaborate, scientific language that some eighteenth-century poets, including Thomson, delighted in using.

Brooke introduces the creeper following a description of a forest, as an example of how nature, as though purposeful and attentive, 'intervenes' in creation to establish a balance between opposites. The 'mighty Fabric' (III.248) of the forest trees is offset and balanced by the existence of other, more humble vegetation. This is the opportunity for the poet to develop the theme of harmony and interdependence, what he calls mutuality and reciprocity, as creepers need trees, plants or rocks to latch on to, just to be and to endure. They cannot exist in isolation. Crossing over, naming, separating and mingling are the stamp of Brooke's poetics. Brooke succeeds even in blending the plant and the animal realms, seeing in the creeper a 'plantal Reptile' (273):

> Thus mantling snug beneath a verdant Veil,
> The *Creepers* draw their horizontal Trail,
> Wide o'er the Bank the *plantal Reptile* bends;

> Adown *its Stem*, the rooty Fringe depends,
> The *feeble Boughs* with anch'ring Safety binds,
> Nor leaves precarious to insulting Winds.
> The *Tendrils* next of slender, helpless Size,
> Ascendant thro' luxuriant pamp'ring rise;
> Kind Nature sooths their Innocence of Pride,
> While buoy'd aloft the flowering Wantons ride;
> With fond Adhesion round the Cedar cling,
> And wreathing, circulate their am'rous Ring,
> Sublime, with winding Maturation grow,
> And clench'd retentive, gripe the topmost Bough;
> Here climb direct, the ministerial Rock,
> And clasping firm, its steepy Fragments lock;
> Or various, with agglutinating Guile,
> Cement tenacious to some neighb'ring Pile;
> Investing green, some Fabric here ascend,
> And clustring, o'er its Pinacles depend.
>
> Defective, where contiguous Props evade,
> Collateral *they* spring with mutual Aid;
> Officious, brace their amicable Band,
> And by reciprocal Communion stand;
> Bless'd Model! (by Humanity expell'd)
> The Whole upholding Each — the Whole by Each upheld.
> (III.271–96)

The passage is full of present participles, participial adjectives ('mantling', 'anch'ring', 'insulting', 'pamp'ring', 'flowering', 'agglutinating' and so on), and a glut of verbs that express motion and attachment ('bend', 'depend', 'bind', 'rise', 'ride', 'cling', 'cement', 'spring', 'ascend', for example).[17] The impeccable alexandrine with its central caesura that closes the passage ('The Whole upholding Each — the Whole by Each upheld') encapsulates the poetic symmetry of the world that Brooke wishes to convey with its rich, phonic harmony and its syntactic and grammatical balance and variation.[18] It completes the passage summed up in the word 'officious' (293) which the *OED* gives as '(*arch*.) eager to render services or help to others' and which Samuel Johnson glosses as 'kind: doing good offices'.[19] The terms employed in the concluding lines all converge to form a semantic alliance: 'contiguous', 'collateral', 'mutual Aid', 'officious', and 'reciprocal Communion'. This 'Bless'd Model' is there again to contrast with, and damn, human failings and pride, and the inhumanity that Brooke refers to regularly throughout the poem: 'And man's proud science is alone to spoil' (VI.86). Nature, it would seem, can do no wrong.

Throughout *Universal Beauty* Brooke develops a generous and eclectic poetics. Lionel Stevenson saw in Brooke a precursor of Blake: 'a mystic isolated in an age of reason'.[20] Scurr too insists on the influence of Jacob Boehme not only in *Universal Beauty*, but also, and indeed more so, in the later Christian poem *Redemption: A Poem* (1772). This marks him out as a poet somehow stranded and alienated in his century, which he clearly is not. He can be said to be a visionary in the sense that the mixture of close observation and intuitive insight, as well as the marriage of the physical and the metaphysical, give a particularly intense colouring to the poem. His is an all-embracing, expansive and yet exact imagination. Even in the dense, scientific passages, cumbersome at times, *Universal Beauty* is a celebration of language. It is the work of a writer with a real feel for language, unafraid, who had a way with words and a gift for surprise, and it is a poem fuelled by a desire to celebrate the world and to celebrate poetry itself.

Notes

1. (1993) *An Essay on Man* in M. Mack (ed.) *The Twickenham Edition of the Poems of Alexander Pope, Vol. III.i* (London and New York: Routledge), I.169. Further references are by Epistle and line number to this edition and are placed in parentheses following the quotation.
   Henry Brooke employs the phrase 'elemental strife' twice in *Universal Beauty*; first, at the end of Part I (lines 361–3) where he sings the praises of air, its benefits for life and the continuous process of renewal:

   > By *This*, the Quadrupeds, the Reptiles breath;
   > *This gives* the Bloom of vegetative Life;
   > *Corrects* the Seeds of elemental Strife[.]

   The second reference appears in Part IV, line 25. See H. Brooke (1735) *Universal Beauty. A Poem* (London: J. Wilcox). Further references are by part and line number to this edition and are placed in parentheses following the quotation.

2. This incident unites Pope, Thomson and Brooke in a common cause: the Patriot opposition to Walpole. Christine Gerrard writes that 'The summer of 1738 was one of Pope's happiest and busiest on the Patriots' behalf. He spent much of his time with Bolingbroke editing the manuscripts of Thomson, Mallet, Hill, and Brooke's Patriot dramas, planned for an onslaught on the London theatres' winter season. Twickenham became a meeting-place for the disaffected[.]' See C. Gerrard (1994) *The Patriot Opposition to Walpole: Politics, Poetry, and National Myth, 1725–42* (Oxford: Clarendon Press), p. 88.

3. Helen Margaret Scurr writes that *Universal Beauty* 'was written between 1727 and 1735, during and after the time of his second trip to London. External and internal evidence indicate that it was fostered and supervised by Pope, to whose coterie Brooke's return was welcome.' Pope's 'supervision' probably refers to both *Universal Beauty* and *Gustavus Vasa*. See H. M. Scurr (1922) 'Henry Brooke' (unpublished doctoral thesis, University of Minnesota), p. 14.
4. H. Brooke and C. H. Wilson (1804) *Brookiana* (London: Richard Phillips), II, pp. 9–10. The letter is undated but prompted a reply from Pope sent from Bath on 'December 1 1739' (see Pope [2000] 'Letter 192' in H. Erskine-Hill [ed.] *Alexander Pope: Selected Letters* [Oxford: Oxford University Press], p. 303).
5. (1993) 'Introduction' in M. Mack (ed.) *Twickenham Edition [...], Vol. III.i*, p.xlvii.
6. (1981) 'Introduction' in J. Sambrook (ed.) *The Seasons* (Oxford: Clarendon Press), pp. xvii–xcv.
7. See, for example, Shaftesbury's *Soliloquy, or Advice to an Author*: 'the horrid discord of jingling rhyme' and *Miscellany V*: 'that monstrous ornament which we call rhyme' in A. A. Cooper, Third Earl of Shaftesbury (1999) *Shaftesbury: Characteristics of Men, Manners, Opinions, Times*, L. E. Klein (ed.) (Cambridge: Cambridge University Press), pp. 98, 450.
8. Scurr, 'Henry Brooke', p. 15.
9. 'Henry Brooke', p. 16.
10. J. Arbuthnot (1734) *Gnothi Seauton. Know Your Self* (London: J. Tonson), pp. 1–2. Further references are by page number to this edition and are placed in parentheses following the quotation.
11. J. Locke (1979) *An Essay Concerning Human Understanding*, P. H. Nidditch (ed.) (Oxford: Clarendon Press), Book 2, chapter 27, 'Of Identity and Diversity'. The chapter was added in the 2nd edition of the *Essay* published in 1694.
12. (1984) *Pope's 'Essay on Man'* (London: George Allen & Unwin), p. 76.
13. (1981) *The Seasons*, J. Sambrook (ed.), lines 849–55. The text of *The Seasons* is that published in 1746. The passage differs only very slightly from the 1728 *Spring*.
14. S. Johnson (1905) 'Akenside' in *Lives of the English Poets*, G. Birkbeck Hill (ed.) (Oxford: Clarendon Press), III, p. 418.
15. *The Seasons*, p. 305.
16. (1728) 'Advertisement' in *The Works of Mr. Henry Needler, Consisting of Original Poems, Translations, Essays, and Letters*, 2nd edn (London: J. Watts).
17. For another example of Brooke's poetics of excess see I.39 in which he portrays a cornucopian world of 'high *Plenty*'.
18. In *An Essay on Criticism* (1711), Pope famously criticizes unnecessary alexandrines, writing: 'A *needless Alexandrine* ends the Song, / That like a wounded Snake, drags its slow length along.' (Pope [1993] *An Essay on Criticism* in E. Audra and A. Williams [eds] *Twickenham Edition [...], Vol. I* [London and New York: Routledge], pp. 237–326, lines 356–7.) I take it that Pope's lines do not apply here! However, in Part III, Brooke's lines 282: 'And wreathing, circulate their am'rous Ring' and 284: 'And clench'd retentive, gripe the topmost Bough' approach Pope's ideal that 'The *Sound* must seem an *Eccho* to the *Sense*' (*An Essay on Criticism*, line 365). The first line does so in its

expression of the entwining movement, and the second where the formulation seems to mimic the effort expended in straining upwards.
19. See *Oxford English Dictionary Online*, online at: www.oed.com; S. Johnson (1755) *A Dictionary of the English Language* (London: J. & P. Knapton). Johnson gives Milton as his source here. The other sense Johnson proposes 'importunately forward' (Shakespeare) would be out of place.
20. (March 1928) 'Brooke's *Universal Beauty* and Modern Thought', *PMLA*, 43:1, 198–209 (p. 209).

3
Argumentative Emphases in Pope's *An Essay on Man*

Tom Jones

The subject of this chapter is the way in which changes of mind in Pope's presentation of *An Essay on Man* impact upon the philosophy it offers us. The history of the poem's composition and revision is rich and complex, with the movement of large parts of text from one position to another, and local interventions into lines that make central assertions. This chapter focuses on local rather than broader organizational changes, but will try to suggest that consideration of the poem as an evolving text shows that slight presentational changes are argumentatively very significant, and that they also contribute to the distinctive scope of Pope's poetico-philosophical argument. Thinking about the poem in this way lends weight to one perennial response to it: its defence of order, fixity and a providential scheme that nevertheless admits the force of chaos, flux and contingency. Earlier in his career, Pope presented himself as having a claim to be a poet only because he possessed 'the power of rejecting his own thoughts', a claim that suggests he is able to isolate that thought which it is his fixed intention to present in his text.[1] Yet *An Essay on Man* itself is the co-presence of different thoughts, and of different paths through the conceptual possibilities of the moment. That is what the poem's textual evolution illustrates of its argumentative tendencies.

The *Essay* is a poem in four verse epistles. Maynard Mack summarizes the publication history of the poem during Pope's lifetime thus:

> The four epistles of the *Essay on Man* were published successively on 20 February, 29 March, 8 May 1733, and 24 January 1734. Of Epistles I–III there were other folio issues, but none of textual interest except Griffith's 'Issue I' of Epistle I, which shows extensive revision and rearrangement. Pope went on correcting the poem till he died; first

in the collected editions, folio and quarto, of 1734; then in editions of the *Works*, vol. II, of 1735, 1736, and 1739; and finally in the Pope-Warburton quarto dated 1743, where several passages were inserted.[2]

There were also collected editions of the four epistles in folio and quarto in 1734. Mack calls the Pope-Warburton text 1743b. To this print history may be added the two MSS of the poem, in likely order of composition: the Morgan Library Manuscript (MLM) and the Houghton Library Manuscript (HLM). One further item of particular interest is a copy of the 1736 *Works* which Pope corrected for the press by hand; most of the corrections to be found in this copy, however, fail to survive in later printed texts of the poem. I will refer to this book by its shelfmark in the British Library: C.122.e.31. In this chapter I will refer to variants found in the two MSS, the collected print edition 1734a, the second volume of *Works* 1736 (together with Pope's hand-written corrections to that text) and to the Pope-Warburton edition 1743b (details for these editions are provided in the endnotes).[3]

Putting aside questions of its intellectual genesis, and the broader poetico-philosophical scheme of which it was to form a part (the *Ethic Epistles*), the *Essay* is an evolution from MSS to the final (more or less) authorial version (1743b) through various different incarnations that, though successive, are also contemporary.[4] Older versions of the text do not disappear once they are superseded by a new edition. Indeed, in the second volume of the 1735 *Works* Pope includes a set of variant readings from earlier editions of the *Essay*, noting where lines had been altered from or, in one case (IV.387–8), 'Omitted by mistake' in an earlier edition.[5] As Mack notes, 'Poetry, in what seems to be Pope's conception of it, is not history, but a form of action within history that has a history: his completed poem presents itself not as a species of Scripture or Revelation, but as a configuration of elements arranged in dramatic and dynamic poise by an entirely human wit that is ever susceptible to second (and even third) thoughts.'[6] Pope does not succeed in rejecting all the thoughts that are present in these different states of the text: they live on in one another, in the hints and suggestions of nervous stress in the language of the poem. These hints and suggestions are heightened or flattened in different forms of textual presentation, but never altogether eliminated. The variations in the text of the poem remind us that we make slight shifts in its arguments in deciding where to weight its lines, even if we have no textual history and no list of variants in front of us.

Other readers of Pope have recently paid close attention to details of textual presentation and the argumentative contribution of Pope's versification. James McLaverty has shown how the smallest details in the presentation of Pope's text can make a significant difference to the way the poem is read; or, perhaps, that the way in which the poem is read can lead to small but significant differences in its mode of presentation. At II.97–100, *TE III.i* gives:

> Passions, tho' selfish, if their means be fair,
> List under Reason, and deserve her care;
> Those, that imparted, court a nobler aim,
> Exalt their kind, and take some Virtue's name.

Passions, when they have reason imparted to them, become nobler, become virtues. To arrive at this sense Mack has imported a comma from the 1751 text of the poem edited by William Warburton. The 1743b text, Mack's copy text, has 'Those that imparted'. McLaverty notes that C.122.e.31 gives 'Those which *imparted*, court a nobler aim'. The sense of the line McLaverty produces is that when passions are imparted, that is, focused on people other than ourselves, they are exalted into virtues. McLaverty points out the large philosophical difference this small detail of presentation makes: 'Warburton [by punctuating as he does] negates irrational power in order to emphasize freedom; Pope attempts to interrelate the two. [...] The alternative and, I believe, correct reading [...] points to the potential of some, but not all passions, to become virtues.'[7] Pope's punctuation says that modes of self-love (passions) can be virtues when they take on a social aspect. This is a real difference: Pope is not one of those Augustinian moralists who believe virtues are often just concealed vices; he is happy to accept that a passion really can be a virtue.[8] Indeed this attitude is perhaps the most distinctive feature of Pope's thought in the *Essay*, going further even than, say, Francis Hutcheson in the rehabilitation of the passions, so often in the history of ideas thought best subjected entirely to reason.[9] The emphasis that shifts sentence meaning has consequences for the moral vision of the poem.

Simon Jarvis has tried to suggest another way in which minute attention to poetry can have philosophical consequences – that is, by considering the cognitive contribution of prosody. He asks students of poetry to 'imagine an account of Pope's prosody which could think of it neither simply as an accumulation of symbolic capital, nor, naively, as an accomplished set of miniature mimeses of the semantic content, but rather as a form of knowledge whose furious pursuit of the rule (and thus of the felicitous transgression of the rule) internalises, yet also exceeds and knows, the polish requisite to domestic luxuries and gentlemanly sociability alike'.[10] Pope's prosodic practice is the way in which Pope's knowledge (cultural, scholarly, linguistic, political and so on) 'lives along the line' (*Essay*, I.218, of the spider's touch). It is not the mastery of a set of rules, nor the knowledge of a set of quantities; it is the habitation and extension of thought in language, achieved by means of emphasis, accent and the direction of energy. This chapter will argue that a specific kind of knowledge is on display in Pope's alterations to his poem: the knowledge that radically different conceptual possibilities are separated, and indeed united, by only slight differences in emphasis.

The coexistence of different thoughts is one reason for many critics feeling that the poem makes incompatible assertions. A. D. Nuttall, for example, sees a tension reaching out from the opposition of pride and humility in Epistle I, identifying:

[a] tension between a view of man which confines him to merely human concerns and the grand metaphysical overview of man in relation to God and the creation, which at one and the same time provides a rationale for the first view and violates it.[11]

Likewise Judith Shklar remarks that the excoriation of injustices wrought by man (she focuses on the injustices man works on animals) in the poem is incompatible with its assertion that 'whatever is, is right'.[12] Such tensions are integral to the poem. I propose that Pope's poem is an exemplary *philosophical* poem because it presents an alternation between the world coming to us as natural contingency, and as divine necessity. That is, Pope's poem captures the aspect shift between these views that are characteristic of a human world, even constitutive of it, if we believe that knowledge of the world, as a set of natural, mechanical systems, can or ought to be reconciled with our feeling that we are free to shape our actions somehow in accordance with those systems or some principle ulterior to them (providence, evolution, social theory, for example).

Pope expresses the desire to steer 'betwixt the extremes of doctrines seemingly opposite', in being '*temperate* yet not *inconsistent*' and believing that the '*force* as well as *grace* of arguments or instructions, depends on their *conciseness*' ('The Design'). I propose that the *Essay* is an exemplary philosophical *poem* because the ambiguity of its moderate, temperate, concise language involves its readers in the sometimes uncomfortable, sometimes exhilarating alternation between aspects.

I propose that the textual history of the poem, in whole as well as part, is an articulation of those concurrently entertained aspects. Controversy in the poem's reception history, then, as to the orthodoxy or heterodoxy of the poem's natural theology, whether it is banally optimistic, or collapses God into the world, is not to be settled one way or another. Rather, it is evidence of the kind of truth that the poem represents: the articulation of a moment of various possible conceptual alternatives, with the poem as a scheme of possibilities that different emphases in different texts make more or less palpable. The knowledge Pope displays in his versification is tacit knowledge of the moment he occupies in the history of thought, his sense of the paths of thinking available and his refusal (inability?) to commit entirely to any one of them.

Two more remarks are required before taking a more sustained view of the poem. The first is to confirm that italicization and capitalization had in the mid-eighteenth century roughly the same import in a printed text that they have for readers now. In 1755 John Smith enumerated the uses of italic thus: 'for varying the different Parts and Fragments, abstracted from the Body of a work – for passages which differ from the language of the Text – for literal citations from Scripture – for words, terms, or expressions which some authors would have regarded as more nervous; and by which they intend to convey to the reader either instructing, satyrizing, admiring, or other hints and remarks'.[13] It is the last of these uses that is most significant for the study of the *Essay*. Smith also notes that some authors 'denote their emphatical expressions, by beginning them with Capitals, whether they be of the substantive kind, or otherwise', and that 'Small Capitals are mostly used to denote, that a more particular stress and emphasis is intended by the Author, on such words and expressions as are distinguished by them'.[14] That is, italics and caps are used for emphasis. The emphasis of caps is unqualified. The emphasis of italic type may have an affective or evaluative quality.

Second, and consequently, the work that emphasis does in print can help the reader to know what the writer is talking about. In terms that are more or less indigenous to the early eighteenth century, emphasis can help to determine what is the subject, and what the attribute that is being asserted of the subject in the complex propositions that for the most part make up a poetic utterance such as the *Essay*. Emphasis can also help to determine not just what perception is being asserted in an utterance, but what judgements about, or reasonings on, perceptions are being proposed.[15] The theory of general or universal grammar makes it clear that the surface structure of propositions may well contain (if not conceal) various other propositions. The Port-Royal Grammar, in talking of the functions of the relative pronoun, gives the example: 'the invisible God has created the visible world'.[16] There is a subtended proposition here that can be revealed by analysing the noun phrase as a relative clause: 'God who is invisible'. Something comparable to this analysis is achieved by emphasis. The effects of emphasis upon propositional content are immediately evident if we say 'the *invisible* God'. For now we are contrasting the invisible with an implied visible God (or making some other contrast, perhaps with an earlier assertion that God is visible in the creation). Typographic emphasis often works in this way in the *Essay*, determining what is subject and what is attribute, and which are the things or qualities in any propositional utterance that are being compared or judged. Emphasis changes the questions to which we take Pope's statements to be answers. Sometimes emphasis saves Pope from the more flagrant illogicalities of the *Essay*. Sometimes emphasis saves Pope from tonal infelicities. Sometimes emphasis does not save him at all. My concern is to demonstrate the scope of possibilities entertained at the level of the verse, not to save Pope.

One tonal consequence of emphasis can be seen in the opening lines of the poem. Epistle I.15–16 describes the attitudes Pope and Bolingbroke will adopt in the dialogue that constitutes the *Essay*. 1743b reads 'Laugh where we must, be candid where we can; / But vindicate the ways of God to Man.' 1736, for example, uses emphasis: 'Laugh where we *must*, be candid where we *can*, / But vindicate the ways of *God* to man.' 1743b says there are times when Pope and Bolingbroke must laugh, no more. The 1736 text suggests that Pope and Bolingbroke resist laughter wherever possible, but laugh perhaps because they cannot resist, or because all other resources have been exhausted in their sustained confrontation with human absurdity. They are candid where they can be, acknowledging that one cannot always be candid, that candour is not a fixed personal quality. These emphases are, in short, more magnanimous than the cleaner 1743b text. They place the participants in philosophical dialogue closer to, even amongst, the absurd humanity at which they laugh. Warburton's note balances mirth against compassion: 'human *follies* are so strangely absurd, that it is not in the power of the most *compassionate*, on some occasions, to restrain their mirth'.[17] The more emphatic text allows compassion and mirth to cohabit more closely.

Pope is working in a context in which one might assert that God made the world according to a scheme partly or mostly comprehensible to humans (Samuel Clarke); a scheme almost entirely incomprehensible to humans (Blaise Pascal); or even that God did not make it, or made it to no scheme at all (Lucretius). How close does Pope allow these various pictures of the world to come to one another? An early and much discussed revision of the text relating to this topic occurs at I.6. The first published text and the earliest MS of the poem give: 'A mighty <u>Maze!</u> of <u>Walks</u> without a Plan' (MLM, *LGA* 207). The later MS (HLM, *LGA* 312) records the revision from the earlier version of the line to the form in which it appears in all other printed texts of the poem: 'A mighty maze! but not without a plan'. The question here is the degree to which Pope can be saying, in his earlier draft, that the creation is a maze, and therefore a work of artifice, and therefore made by an artificer, even though there is no plan. We could allow Pope that opportunity: Mack and Nuttall both do so.[18] We might even suggest that the punctuation of the line allows the lack of a plan to be the attribute of the walks rather than the maze – a plan to our ways through the world, not of its structure. But that would mean that the maze is constituted by the walks, and so has no plan, but is merely the by-product of our contingent tracings through the world. The providential scheme and its availability to humans are brought into question by this earlier text, and its revision is one example of what Richard Wendorf calls Pope's attempt to 'domesticate' the naturalization of religion.[19] Readers were clearly provoked by the alteration. One reader (of the copy BL 11630.e.5.16) wrote the later text in above the text of the first edition. Neither Pope nor his twentieth-century editors or critics can quite undo the radical suggestion of the first draft of these lines. That suggestion may not be enough in itself to justify reference to the 'radical antiprovidentialism' of the *Essay*, but it makes the tension between partial and total views of the universe irresoluble for us as readers, as it may be for us as thinkers.[20]

The degree to which God is present in the creation is also a question between extremes of which Pope seems to be steering rather haphazardly. Both MSS of the poem (*LGA* 257 and 374–5) and the first edition of Epistle III present nature as inanimate: 'See lifeless matter moving to one End'. This line in all later texts becomes 'See plastic Nature working to this end' (III.9). 'Plastic nature' may be distinguished from God: when the *OED* cites Berkeley's *Alciphron* (I.iii.14), 'he is positive as to the Being of God, and that not merely as a plastic Nature or Soul of the World'.[21] This 'plastic nature' is nonetheless more animated and closer to God than 'lifeless matter'. Warburton thinks this reference to 'plastic nature' is an important part of Pope's analogical argument and that the atomic attraction of 'plastic nature' corresponds to divinely ordained human sociability: 'he proves, from the circumstance of *mutual attraction* in matter, that man, while he seeks Society, and thereby promotes the good of his species, co-operates with God's general dispensation'.[22] Pope revises away from a material universe towards terms more appealing to Anglican divines. The story is similar at II.275, where the benevolence of the natural world in providing appropriate desires to various kinds of people, and people in various stages of development, is noted: 'Behold the child, by Nature's kindly law' interested in a rattle. HLM (*LGA* 364–5) has 'Nature's lucky law'. All printed texts but the last of Pope's lifetime, 1743b, omit the passage beginning with these lines. The revised, printed version suggests a less contingent, more benevolent nature, which perhaps shares its nature (kind) with humans. Is it mere chance, or more than mere chance, that different stages of life have different attractions? From Mark Pattison's 1875 edition of Pope's *Essay*, Mack picks up an echo of Francis Hutcheson's sentiments from *An Essay on the Nature and Conduct of the Passions and Affections* (1728):

> We once knew the time when an Hobby-Horse, a Top, a Rattle, was sufficient Pleasure to us. We grow up, we now relish Friendships, Honour, good Offices, Marriage, Offspring, serving a Community or Country. [...] "Our Nature determines us to certain Pursuits in our several Stages; and following her Dictates, is the only way to our Happiness."[23]

Mack also identifies many echoes of his own and one might also point to lines from Rochester:

> A greater fop in business at fourscore,
> Fonder of serious toys, affected more
> Than the gay glittering fool at twenty proves,
> With all his noise, his tawdry clothes and loves.[24]

Textual revision can also affect the allusive scope of the poem, presenting still other possible paths offered by the shifting weights of its argument.

Similarly, textual revisions at IV.113–16 indicate the persistence of potentially limiting accounts of God's providence. 1743b presents the lines thus:

> God sends not ill; if rightly understood,
> Or partial Ill is universal Good,
> Or Change admits, or Nature lets it fall,
> Short, and but rare, 'till Man improv'd it all.

There are numerous views of the nature of evil here: it is necessary to produce a greater good; it is due to the deterioration of the creation over time (change); and the systematic nature of the creation produces evil as a by-product (rather like the first explanation).[25] In any case, it is mostly humans that produce evil, improving it at every opportunity. 1734 is more compact: 'God sends not Ill, 'tis Nature lets it fall / Or Chance escape, and Man improves it all.' The expansion of the lines suggests that Pope did not think the assertion of 'partial Ill' as 'universal Good' was necessary at first, or that he found it a way out of having appeared to allow nature or chance to admit evil into the creation despite God's will. Mack saves Pope from anti-providentialism here by citing Aquinas on the compatibility of chance with providence: chance is the production of effects by a variety of causes interrelating. But it seems hard to remove the sense of a contrast between God and chance (it is not God, but nature or chance ...). Even in the 1743b text, 'partial Ill' as 'universal Good' is only one of three alternative explanations of ill in the syntactic sequence 'or [...] or [...] or'.

These tensions between a providential and a contingent world are in play when we arrive at the closing lines of Epistle I, where the emphasis differs slightly from one text to another. 1743b gives at I.286: 'One truth is clear, "Whatever IS, is RIGHT."' 1736 has 'Whatever *Is*, is RIGHT.' By romanizing 'is', by placing the phrase in inverted commas, 1743b undifferentiates the emphasis of the half-line, and makes it a maxim. The 1736 text commands emphasis on both the first 'is' and 'right', but different forms of emphasis. It seems to me that the 1736 emphasis, doubled (italics as well as caps and small caps) for 'is', lays the stress less on the rightness of the world, and more on the fact that the world's being as it must mean it is the right world – it is the only world.[26] There are of course almost endless nuances that might be drawn out of this phrase once one starts to weigh its words carefully, and some of these will preserve both the providential scheme and the sense in which this world is just making do, and humans merely do their best and worst. Such might be the sense of a possible analogue like this:

> What is evil in the single soul will stand a good thing in the universal system; what in the unit offends nature will serve nature in the total event – and still remains the weak and wrong tone it is, though its sounding takes nothing from the worth of the whole, just as, in another order of image, the executioner's ugly office does not mar the well-governed state: such an officer is a civic necessity, and the corresponding moral type is often serviceable; thus, even as things are, all is well.[27]

A sense of the possible variations of emphasis burns the haze of Panglossian contentment from the line.

The perhaps alarming co-presence of the extremes Pope is supposed to be steering between is sustained in the poem's treatment of human psychology. The key to human happiness, Pope says, is not to aspire beyond the human – hardly an original position, but one that courts contradiction. When Pope describes 'The bliss of man (could pride that blessing find)' (I.189–90), the two MSS both complete the couplet thus: 'Is not to know, or think, beyond Mankind'. Knowing beyond one's position in the creation should just be an impossibility (if you can know it, it is knowledge proper to your station), so it is hard to see how it can be a bliss, let alone a bliss of difficult access. The 1743b text is perhaps an improvement in the consistency of the argumentation. Human bliss 'Is not to act or think beyond mankind.' Here, neither acting nor thinking need imply knowledge beyond the human, nor the achievement of superhuman feats. Acting can be pretending and thinking can be thinking of, not thinking in the manner of – it is bliss not to think of what is more than human, not bliss not to think superhumanly. A more emphatic version of the text saves Pope still more from inconsistency. In 1736, bliss 'Is, not to act, or think, *beyond* mankind.' The marked emphasis indicates that human aspiration might be great, but should not court hubris. Emphasizing the preposition rather than the noun (as may be more intuitive in an unemphatic printing of the line) says that there is a limit beyond which humans will not arrive, but does not preclude the fullest possible extension of human capacities now.

Another central aspect of Pope's account of human psychology is the opacity of our minds to ourselves. Epistle II, line 36 asks if he who could calculate the movement of a comet could 'Describe or fix one movement of his Mind?' Pope's annotated copy, C.122.e.31, here inverts the terms asking if he could 'Fix, or describe' the movements of the mind. David Foxon says 'the transposition to "Fix, or describe, one movement of the mind?" can only be judged subjectively; I feel that it is an improvement, and could rationalize my preference without convincing anyone who felt the converse.'[28] Preferences about the sequence of the verbs will relate to our sense of how to take their inherent ambiguities: is this description following the movement of a line? Or is it providing an adequate verbal account? Is this fixing rendering what is chaotic more predictable? Or is it rendering something transient more permanent and visible (as one fixes a colour)? The order of the verbs in the printed texts (describe or fix) suggests either an inconsequential relationship between them (one or the other, in no particular order or hierarchy), or their equivalence; or it may make 'description' logically or temporally follow fixing and require 'or' to have the sense of 'nay', 'nor even'. (In another correction that fails to find its way from C.122.e.31 into print, Pope changes an 'or' to a 'nay' at IV.264, but there the sequence of terms is governed by social hierarchy rather than logical priority: the person with no equal in arts or business is condemned to drudge 'Without a second, nay without a judge'.) If there is indifference between the two verbs, the fixing or describing likely apply to defined movements. If, however, there is an implied logical sequence to the verbs, then the fixing may be more about giving form to something that previously lacked it: the movement of the mind may not even be a definite thing and the mind may be moving unpredictably, at random. These possibilities (of mental life being rational yet transient, or chaotic and unknowable) coexist in the text. Pope's second thought merely makes their proximity more palpable.

Pope manipulates emphasis to define the politics of the poem also. One of the more famous and controversial couplets of the poem is III. 303–4: 'For Forms of Government let fools contest; / Whate'er is best administer'd is best.' The lines seem to suggest a well-administered tyranny would be better than a badly administered mixed monarchy. Warburton's defence requires one to read a strong continuation of subject across the preceding paragraph break, making the according music of a well-mixed state the subject that is qualified by this statement about the indifference of forms of government, and insisting that Pope is only talking about legitimate governments.[29] In *TE III.i*, Mack transcribes a note in Pope's hand on these lines. The note exists in three forms in BL Egerton MS 1950. ff. 8–10. Mack provides two versions of the note: one in footnotes to the lines and one in an appendix.[30] The one he provides as Appendix B to *TE III.i* (p. 170) from f. 8r removes the two lines of verse that introduce the note in the MS. These lines are of interest because they adjust the poem to bolster Pope's self-defence: 'For Forms of Governm<u>t</u> let Fools contest / <u>That</u> which <u>is</u> best administred, is best.' The underlining attempts to shift emphasis, against any very obvious or successful rhythmic precedent in Pope's versification, from the indifference of 'whate'er' to the actuality of any system of government – what it 'is'. As with 'Whatever IS, IS RIGHT' (I.295), emphasis on 'is' seems half to coerce its audience to an agreement about what is self-evident, and half to put in doubt what 'it' is after all.

Interestingly, a third version of the note not mentioned at all by Mack (he seems to have had only a photograph of the MS provided by George Sherburn) is found on f. 10r:

58 *Tom Jones*

> For Forms of Goverment let fools Contest,
> Whate'er is best administred, is best.
>
> The Author by these lines was far from meaning that no one Form of Goverment is not, in it self, better then another (as that mixed or limited Monarchy, for example, is not preferable to absolute) but that no Form of Goverment, however excellent or preferable in it self, can be Sufficient to make a people happy unless it be administred with Integrity. On the Contrary the Best sort of Goverment when the Form of it is preserv'd, and the Administration corrupt, is most dangerous. ~~In a word, a~~ no   is so bad, but that if   it will be ~~worse~~ ^ Form of Government^ well administerd, is preferable to a   t not being   ~~can never~~
> better, ill administred: ^ ~~Policy and Religion ought to~~
> ~~or in other words it is not~~ the   but the
> ~~be so useful in~~ Theory ~~as in~~ Practise, that must ren
> —der any Government ~~or Religion~~ useful to Society.

(There is a change in handwriting at 'most dangerous', with the hand from that point looking much more like Pope's than the earlier script.) Perhaps Pope's most radical rejected thought here is that religion is only useful to society in practice. It is one thing to suggest that government is of no value in the abstract, another to suggest that the usefulness of religion is dependent upon its human practice. Again one might try to save Pope by saying that he is considering religion only with respect to its social utility, and not with respect to its truth. But this draft note goes further than the following lines of the poem (III.305–8), with their insistence on the primacy of lived faith seem to:

> For Modes of Faith, let graceless zealots fight;
> His can't be wrong whose life is in the right:
> In Faith and Hope the world will disagree,
> But all Mankind's concern is Charity[.]

The draft note is further evidence of the vast scope of commitments Pope might have entertained in the process of composing and revising the poem.

Pope then may not have been as felicitous in the rejection of his own thoughts as he claims in 1717. He may, on the contrary, have been felicitous in the retention of his thoughts. The *Essay* emerges as a poem that does not reject thought, but steers between thoughts, often by such a course that it is not altogether clear to which point the navigator is closer. The poem of multiple and contrasting interpretive possibilities, I suggest, is the poem that we want to keep hold of as readers: it is the poem that has been drafted, revised, commented upon and edited. Pope displays in his visible processes of drafting and revising a type of advanced cultural knowledge, in which the proximity of arguments distinguished only by emphasis is negotiated. The poem moves sometimes this way, sometimes that way along the paths of thought available; it is itself that great undecidedness it describes.

The poem may be truthful in its undecidedness. Jarvis, with reference to a line by Wordsworth in which duty is said to keep the stars in their course, suggests a way of thinking about the kind of assertions poetry, particularly philosophical poetry, makes:

> Its mood is indicative. Yet beneath the indicative syntax sounds an implied optative. [...] The speculative element in Wordsworth's verse can be thought of as a kind of cognitive hypermetricality. It exactly overflows the measure, that is: as a 'spontaneous overflow of powerful feelings' in which poetry blurts out its wish to have back everything which has been taken away by (what is now) sheer common sense. It is an echo of poetry as efficacious as magic, but an echo which knows that there is no such thing as magic. [...] What is blurted out here is a wish believed at the moment of utterance, that poetry may still speak truth: not in the sense of describing or explaining the truth, but in the sense that this utterance be the living event of truth.[31]

In terms of Pope's poem, one might refer to the image of the great chain of being as an example of a similar speculation. As other readers have noticed, this image does not always seem to have a very good grip on the world the poem presents.[32] It may be that the poem presents the image as part of a rhetorical act, whereby indicative descriptions of the world (the world is like this ...) really have the deep grammar of the question 'would it not be better for us if we thought about the world as ...?' Whether the implied optatives behind Pope's indicatives are as burdened with lost desired magic as Wordsworth's is a matter for another chapter. But the attempt to make others think otherwise of their world is in itself a small act of world transformation. What the emphasis of the poem (part of its prosody) shows is the critical importance of its shifts – the different worlds we have if we put the stress here or there. Emphasis is only ever relative, it is heard relationally. Prosodic knowledge is knowledge that the emphasis could fall elsewhere; that it would make a difference if it did; and that the difference is itself a mark of close similarity. If we think of Pope's revisions, and particularly his revisions to emphasis as part of his prosody, the lived event of truth he is blurting out is historical in Mack's sense ('a form of action within history that has a history'); indeed, the truth Pope blurts out might just be that *all* truths will come to us as historical, even providential truths as far as they may be known by humans, in that they will come to us in history and not *beyond* it.

Notes

1. (1936) 'The Preface to *The Works*, 1717' in N. Ault (ed.) *The Prose Works of Alexander Pope, Vol. I* (Oxford: Blackwell), p. 294.
2. (1950) M. Mack (ed.) *The Twickenham Edition of the Poems of Alexander Pope, Vol. III.i* (London: Methuen), p. 3. Hereafter, this edition of the poem will be referred to as *TE III.i.*
3. 1734: *An Essay on Man, Being the First Book of Ethic Epistles. To Henry St. John, L. Bolingbroke* (London: John Wright for Lawton Gilliver), Foxon P852, British Library 1486.d.3.
   1736: *The Works of Alexander Pope, Esq, Vol. II*, 3rd edn (London: Lawton Gilliver), Griffith 430 (see D. Foxon [1991], *Pope and the Early Eighteenth-Century Book Trade [The Lyell Lectures, Oxford 1975–1976]*, J. McLaverty [rev. and ed.] [Oxford: Clarendon Press], p. 222), British Library C.122.e.31.
   1743b: *An Essay on Man. Being the First Book of Ethic Epistles. To H. St. John. L. Bolingbroke. With the Commentary and Notes of Mr. Warburton* (London: J. and P. Knapton), Foxon P865, British Library C.59.e1.
4. For a discussion of these questions, see M. Leranbaum (1977) *Alexander Pope's 'Opus Magnum' 1729–1744* (Oxford: Clarendon Press).
5. (1735) *The Works of Mr. Alexander Pope, Vol. II* (London: J. Wright for Lawton Gilliver), II.199. In this text *An Essay on Man* has its own title page indicating that it is the previous year's collected edition of the four epistles. See also R. Wendorf (2005) *The Scholar-Librarian: Books, Libraries, and the Visual Arts* (New Castle, DE: Oak Knoll Press; Boston, MA: The Boston Athenaeum), particularly the chapter entitled 'Manuscripts, Mazes, and Pope's *Essay on Man*', pp. 61–78 (p. 66).
6. (1984) *The Last and Greatest Art: Some Unpublished Poetical Manuscripts of Alexander Pope*, M. Mack (ed.) (Newark: University of Delaware Press; London and Toronto: Associated University Presses), p. 16. Hereafter, this text will be referred to as *LGA*.
7. (February 2002) 'Warburton's False Comma: Reason and Virtue in Pope's *Essay on Man*', *Modern Philology*, 99:3, 379–92 (pp. 389–90).
8. See, for example, La Rochefoucauld (1976) *Réflexions ou Sentences et Maximes morales Suivi de Réflexions diverses et des Maximes de Madame de Sablé*, J. Lafond (ed.) (Paris: Gallimard), Maximes supprimées 67 (pp. 143–4): 'Nous somme si préoccupés en notre faveur que souvent ce que nous prenons pour

des vertus n'est que des vices qui leur ressemblent, et que l'amour-propre nous déguise.'
9. See (2004) *An Inquiry into the Original of our Ideas of Beauty and Virtue in Two Treatises*, W. Leidhold (ed.) (Indianapolis: Liberty Fund), p. 133, II.iii.15: 'I Know not for what Reason some will not allow that to be Virtue, which flows from Instincts, or Passions; but how do they help themselves? They say, "Virtue arises from Reason." What is Reason but that Sagacity we have in prosecuting any End?' Also, see B. Goldgar (1962) 'Pope's Theory of the Passions: The Background of Epistle II of the *Essay on Man*', *Philological Quarterly*, 41, 730–43.
10. S. Jarvis (December 1998) 'Prosody as Cognition', *Critical Inquiry*, 40:4, 3–15 (p. 12).
11. (1984) *Pope's 'Essay on Man'* (London: Allen & Unwin), p. 54.
12. (1998) 'Poetry and the Political Imagination in Pope's *An Essay on Man*' in S. Hoffmann (ed.) and G. Kateb (foreword) *Political Thought and Political Thinkers* (Chicago: University of Chicago Press), pp. 193–205 (p. 193).
13. (1755) *The Printer's Grammar* (London: W. Owen and M. Cooper), p. 14.
14. *The Printer's Grammar*, pp. 51, 53.
15. A. Arnauld (1753) *A General and Rational Grammar*, T. Nugent (trans.) (London: J. Nourse) [Facsimile Reprint (1967) *English Linguistics 1500–1800*, 73, R. C. Alston (ed.) (Menston, Yorkshire: Scholar Press), p. 23]. For a related discussion in slightly different terms (concerning referring and predicating functions that can differ even in exactly the same sentence), see M. I. Gibson (2004) *From Naming to Saying: The Unity of the Proposition* (Oxford: Blackwell), pp. 139–80.
16. Arnauld, *A General and Rational Grammar*, p. 64.
17. (1756) 'Notes to *An Essay on Man*' in W. Warburton (ed.) *The Works of Alexander Pope*, 9 vols (London: A. Millar et al.), III, p. 4.
18. See *TE III.i*, I.6n, where Mack suggests that 'plan' is a chart or guide to the walks, rather than a scheme or design for them. Also, see Nuttall, *Pope's 'Essay on Man'*, p. 55: 'the earlier version need only imply that we do not possess the plan of the maze'. Mack's citation of Addison's *Cato* reinforces his suggestion that providence and the puzzling maze are compatible:

> The ways of Heaven are dark and intricate,
> Puzzled in mazes, and perplexed with errors,
> Our understanding traces them in vain,
> Lost and bewildered in the fruitless search;
> Nor sees with how much art the windings run,
> Nor where the regular confusion ends.

([1928, repr. 1964] *John Gay's 'The Beggar's Opera' and Other Eighteenth-Century Plays*, J. Hampden [ed.] [London: Dent], p. 8.)
19. 'Manuscripts, Mazes, and Pope's *Essay on Man*', pp. 73–4.
20. S. Ellenzweig (2008) *The Fringes of Belief: English Literature, Ancient Heresy, and the Politics of Freethinking, 1660–1760* (Stanford: Stanford University Press), p. 150.
21. See 'plastic, adj, sense 2', *Oxford English Dictionary*, www.oed.com.

22. 'Notes', III, p. 84.
23. F. Hutcheson (1972) *An Essay on the Nature and Conduct of the Passions and Affections with Illustrations on the Moral Sense* (Menston, Yorkshire: Scolar Press), I.v, p. 131.
24. J. Wilmot (1999) 'Satyr Against Reason and Mankind' in H. Love (ed.) *The Works of John Wilmot Earl of Rochester* (Oxford: Oxford University Press), pp. 57–63, lines 39–42, of a doting bishop.
25. It is interesting to note that at I.147 an interjecting voice, not absurd, but abrupt, enters the poem and makes reference to change in the creation. James McLaverty suggests this is a case in which Pope uses inverted commas 'to bracket certain statements from the main discourse, giving them an equivocal status' ([2001] *Pope, Print, and Meaning* [Oxford: Oxford University Press], p. 122). Pope does, however, at IV.113–6 seem to entertain the possibility of chance alterations in the created world. Samuel Clarke (1956) attempts to resolve the possibility by reference to the contrasting human and divine perspectives: 'The present frame of the solar system (for instance), according to the present laws of motion, will in time fall into confusion; and perhaps, after that, will be amended or put into a new form. But this amendment is only relative, with regard to our conceptions' (see *The Leibniz-Clarke Correspondence, Together with Extracts from Newton's 'Principia' and 'Opticks'*, H. G. Alexander [ed.] [Manchester: Manchester University Press], pp. 22–3).
26. H. M. Solomon (1993) *The Rape of the Text: Reading and Misreading Pope's 'Essay on Man'* (Tuscaloosa and London: The University of Alabama Press), pp. 66–73. These pages do a lot to save Pope on this point.
27. Plotinus (1991) *The Enneads*, S. MacKenna (trans.) and J. Dillon (ed.) (Harmondsworth: Penguin), III.ii, Point 17, p. 155.
28. *Pope and the Early Eighteenth-Century Book Trade*, p. 223.
29. 'Notes', III, pp. 117–18.
30. In the note as cited in the appendix, Pope refers to William Temple's 'Essay on Government pag 83. 8°': W. Temple (1680) 'An Essay on the Origin and Nature of Government' in *Miscellanea* (London: A. M. and R. R. for Edward Gellibrand). Mack's footnote cites passages from (1720) *The Works of Sir William Temple*, 2 vols (London: A. Churchill et al.), I, pp. 105, 259. However, he omits part of the passage on p. 83 of the 1680 text to which it must be inferred Pope was explicitly referring, if we take the verbal echo into account, and which emphasizes 'custom and use' as much as the 'best men' governing:

> it may perhaps be the most reasonably concluded, That those Forms are best, which have been longest receiv'd and most authorized in a Nation by custom and use; and into which the Humours and Manners of the People run with the most general and strongest current.
> Or else, that those are the best Governments, where the best Men govern; and that the difference is not so great in the Forms of Magistracy, as in the Persons of Magistrates'.

Mack's selective citation makes the passage more aristocratic than conservative.

31. (2007) *Wordsworth's Philosophic Song* (Cambridge: Cambridge University Press), p. 21.
32. Shklar, 'Poetry and the Political Imagination', pp. 200–1, notes how unelevated man, as described by the *Essay*, is: 'The [great] chain is revealed less as an explanation of our condition than as an aesthetic object and as such possibly healing.'

4
'Stricken Deer and Digressive Diplomacy':
The Influence of Matthew Prior upon William Cowper

Conrad Brunström

William Cowper's admiration for the poetry of Matthew Prior proved a lifelong source of inspiration. Although Prior remained a very popular poet until the middle decades of the century, Cowper was perhaps unique in retaining a sense of Prior's centrality as far as the end of his life (which coincided with the end of the century). The nineteenth century, by contrast, tended to find Prior somewhat trivial if not smutty and the twentieth century failed to rehabilitate Prior as any kind of literary heavyweight deserving of anything other than the most peripheral and elective pedagogic treatments.

The impact of Matthew Prior upon (among others) William Cowper concerns forms of generic continuity and historical alienation, alongside forms of historical continuity and generic alienation. I have written elsewhere that the important influences on William Cowper could be conveniently abbreviated to just two: John Milton and Matthew Prior.[1] A straightforward reading would neatly assume that Milton was responsible for the more ponderous religious meditations and Prior for the lighter conversational epistles. However, the detailed reality of Prior's influence is rather more complex: it is also a decisive one on Cowper's most serious verse. It would be elegant to suggest that Milton correspondingly influenced Cowper's lighter verse, but this influence is less direct, evidenced by the spoof Miltonic tradition represented by John Phillips' *Splendid Shilling* (1701), which had a very formative influence on Cowper's lighter moments. Indeed, Cowper's very earliest recorded poem is a blank verse meditation on a broken shoe (1748).[2] (Mock-Miltonic blank verse is so prevalent in *The Task* that establishing when the Miltonic thread is being pastiched and when it is to be taken seriously is a very subtle if ultimately very rewarding task.)

Prior's influence on Cowper's light verse is both fully acknowledged (by Cowper) and easily demonstrated. A bantering form of address and a fondness for ballads and for beast fables connect both poets. One of the more interesting pervasive features of Prior's influence on Cowper, meanwhile, is his sheer versatility. Prior employs more verse forms than any other poet of his generation, offering odes, ballads, heroic couplets, Hudibrasts and epigrams. There is, in short, no default setting format to a Prior poem. Likewise, Cowper puts himself to the task of mastering a wide range of verse forms since the very difficulty of versification had its own therapeutic value for him.

The only major verse form that Cowper employs and Prior does not is blank verse, and the only major verse form that Prior employs and Cowper does not is the Pindaric ode. The Pindaric was uncongenial from Cowper's point of view because the Nonsense Club (Churchill, Lloyd, Bonnell Thornton and Colman) that had defined his poetic taste as a young man was famous for its attacks on Thomas Gray, and Lloyd and Colman had earned the approbation of Samuel Johnson when they spoofed Gray's so-called 'Great Odes'.[3] The young Cowper had even written a spoof 'Dissertation on the Modern Ode' and had it published in *St. James Magazine* in 1763. For the whiggish (borderline and actual Wilkesite) wits of the 1760s, Gray and Mason were reactionary quietists, and the ode was therefore a contaminated form. For Churchill, Lloyd and Colman, political quietism was itself a political endorsement of the status quo at a time when the opposition to the Bute and Grenville administrations made civic engagement a positive duty.

Prior's inability and/or refusal to employ blank verse, most particularly for *Solomon* where it might have been of service, can be understood in terms of straightforward prematurity. Cowper's own blank verse stood on the shoulders of Thomson, Young and Akenside, providing the vantage point of a substantial body of work that demonstrated that it was possible to write extended blank verse poems that employed Miltonic techniques without merely parodying them. Prior did not enjoy such a legacy to interpret and adapt. Milton, of course, was a polemicist, content to sound like a voice crying in the wilderness while Prior was a diplomat, professionally and temperamentally out of sympathy with Milton's dominant register. Milton's post-Restoration verse does not seek to flatter or befriend anybody, whereas Prior was professionally devoted to precisely that end.

Prior, therefore, was someone who was unconvinced that heroic couplets could accommodate every poetic topic, but equally unconvinced that any other single measure stood a chance of achieving any comparable versatile pre-eminence. It is in couplets that Prior plotted *Solomon*, his most ambitious and serious poem, and one which Cowper greatly admired. It is Solomon's restless mental anguish that moves and impresses him:

> These cruel Doubts contending in my Breast,
> My Reason stagg'ring, and my Hopes oppress'd,
> Once more I said: once more I will enquire,
> What is this little, agile, pervious Fire,
> This flutt'ring Motion which We call the Mind?
> How does She act? and where is She confin'd?
> Have We the Pow'r to give Her as We please?
> Whence then those Evils, that obstruct our Ease?
> We Happiness pursue: We fly from Pain;
> Yet the Pursuit and yet the Flight is vain;
> And, while poor Nature labors to be blest,
> By Day with Pleasure, and by Night with Rest,
> Some stronger Pow'r eludes our sickly Will,
> Dashes our rising Hope with certain Ill,
> And makes Us, with reflective Trouble see
> That all is destin'd which We fancy free.[4]

For Solomon, all pleasures are ruined by satiety and all intellectual satisfactions come with their concomitant irritations and disappointments. The poet of 'ease' describes someone beset with 'evils' that obstruct that very quality. The sublunary sphere offers nowhere for selfhood to settle. This passage from *Solomon* also reactivates Prior's long-standing fascination with the limits of human agency and the struggle between predestination and free will. The extent to which human beings enjoy subjective autonomy and the comedic, as well as theological implications of the strengths and weaknesses of any such subjectivity, are of recurring fascination for Prior and the topic of predestination provides the title of his final unfinished poem.

Needless to say, William Cowper dwelt on the topic of predestination for just as long, if not longer, than Prior. More idiosyncratic (or mentally unbalanced) than Prior, Cowper decided in 1773 that Divinity had decided to exercise His Sovereignty over his own Calvinist machinery by making Cowper his unique victim, saving him and then damning him again on a fairly arbitrary basis and in defiance of Calvinist theology itself. Among the sources for Cowper's agonized relationship with his maker, few have ever discussed Prior, although Cowper read Prior far more often than he read Calvinist theology. Prior's religious poems have a restless, almost metaphysical quality, which may explain why Johnson was so resistant to them. This reader is inclined, however, to read into their theology something of the flavour of practical diplomacy. When Prior meditates on the Holy Trinity, he offers a sense that the architect of the Treaty of Utrecht is dragging the three parts of Godhead back to the negotiating table to hammer out a workable power-sharing agreement. Long experience of trying to reconcile incompatible objectives gave Prior a natural flair for cadenced theology, for creating metrical balance in the face of logical impossibility.

This theological affinity between Prior and Cowper was superimposed upon more clubbish critical loyalties. Prior was admired in the 1760s by the very people who tended to admire Laurence Sterne and for the same reasons. These people included Cowper – an inconspicuous if attentive member of the Nonsense Club. Even after his evangelical conversion, Cowper remained an admirer of Sterne, as a sermonist and moralist as much as a wit. The line that runs through Prior to Sterne to Charles Churchill to Cowper is a rather jagged, digressive sort of a line, as might well be imagined, a line devoted to digression as a principle of individual identity.

There are other influential authors to be considered. One of Cowper's very earliest poems, 'An Epistle to Robert Lloyd', attempts to pay a Westminster school friend the supreme tribute of being Matthew Prior's principle heir (Cowper's legal training at the Inner Temple never wholly deserted him and legal terminology often surfaces in his epistolary verse):

> 'Tis not that I design to rob
> Thee of thy birth-right, gentle Bob,
> For thou art born sole heir, and single,
> Of dear Mat Prior's easy jingle[.][5]

Robert Lloyd was the most octosyllabic member of the Nonsense Club. Though far more obscure today than even Churchill, in his own (short) lifetime, he was a far more established and prolific published author than Cowper. Cowper is being diplomatic and self-effacing in the presence of a schoolmate who has achieved celebrity and does so by equating his school friend with the diplomatic self-effacement of Prior:

> Thus, the preliminaries settled,
> I fairly find myself *pitch-kettled*;

> And cannot see, tho' few see better,
> How I shall hammer out a letter.
>
> > First, for a thought – since all agree –
> > A thought – I have it – let me see –
> > 'Tis gone again – plague on't! I thought
> > I had it – but I have it not.⁶

The attempt to reproduce a present tense feeling of intellectual frustration enables Cowper to write a poem to the poet while advertising a state of spurious if polite incapacity. The conclusion of the poem reinforces the habitual association of Prior with 'ease' while making the bold suggestion that Lloyd surpasses his mentor in this quality:

> That Matthew's numbers run with ease
> Each man of common sense agrees;
> All men of common sense allow,
> That Robert's lines are easy too;
> Where then the preference shall we place?
> Or how do justice in this case?
> Matthew (says Fame) with endless pains
> Smooth'd and refin'd, the meanest strains,
> Nor suffer'd one ill-chosen rhyme
> T'escape him at the idlest time;
> And thus o'er all a lustre cast,
> That while the language lives, shall last.
> An't please your Ladyship (quoth I,
> For 'tis my business to reply);
> Sure so much labour, so much toil,
> Bespeak at least a stubborn soil:
> Theirs be the laurel-wreath decreed,
> Who both write well, and write full speed;
> Who throw their Helicon about
> As freely, as a conduit spout!
> Friend Robert, thus like *chien scavant*,
> Lets fall a poem *en passant*,
> Nor needs his genuine ore refine;
> 'Tis ready polished from the mine.⁷

Cowper's excessive praise of Lloyd would not long survive Lloyd's death and it is Prior rather than Lloyd whom the mature (and published)

Cowper would continue to cite and imitate. Even this youthful assertion of Lloyd's superiority over Prior treats Prior's distinctive qualities as the qualities against which Lloyd is to be judged. 'Fame' rather than Cowper has already decided for Prior. Martin Priestman notes that this early Cowper poem is fascinated by the 'effort' of ease, the 'labour' of appearing relaxed and spontaneous.[8] This youthful concern with the paradox of effortless work would mature decades later into Cowper's more extended concern with the profound and serious vocational demands of retirement.

The fullest development of Prior's notion of digression as central to sane subjectivity is *Alma*, composed while under house arrest following the whig Hanoverian takeover period of 1714–16. *Alma*, like much of Prior's work, is systematically anti-systematic. As Monroe Spears notes: 'Descartes's conception of the body as "machine de terre," moving according to strict mechanical laws, and related thus narrowly and indirectly to the mind, was evidently repugnant to Prior.'[9] This anti-Cartesianism informs just about everything that Prior ever wrote. His earthiest verses (Chaucerian love-triangular fables) suggest that the body acts on the mind at all times and in all places while his most intellectually curious works suppose that every physical impulse is charged with divine purpose. As *Alma* advertises:

>   My simple *System* shall suppose,
>   That ALMA enters at the Toes;
>   That then She mounts by just Degrees
>   Up to the Ancles, Legs and Knees:
>   Next, as the sap of Life does rise,
>   She lends her vigour to the Thighs:
>   And, all these under-Regions past,
>   She nestles somewhere near the Waste:
>   Gives Pain or Pleasure, Grief or Laughter;
>   As We shall show at large hereafter.
>   Mature, if not improv'd by Time
>   Up to the Heart She loves to climb:
>   From thence, compell'd by Craft and Age,
>   She makes the Head her latest Stage.[10]

From the tippy toes of prenatal kicking to the flaky scalp of decrepitude, consciousness slowly bubbles up the human body. Any human's sense of themselves is always fluid and never stable, and this sense of relentless motion creates a feeling of helplessness, which in turn evokes an idea of destiny, perhaps of predestiny since the mind cannot, it seems, function independently of the body and agency cannot be isolated from biology. The implications of this are as funny as they are serious.

Prior's anti-Cartesian concept of nomadic consciousness may, incidentally, have helped inspire Sterne's description of Uncle Toby reminiscing about a Walloon officer who had his pineal gland shot away during the Nine Years' War and who continued to function subsequently, or at least sufficiently, to offer his brother Walter a practical refutation of Descartes.[11] For Prior and Sterne, the body and soul act upon each other but in complex and inconsistent ways:

> Poor ALMA, like a lonely Deer,
> O'er Hills and Dales doth doubtful err:
> With panting Haste, and quick Surprise,
> From ev'ry Leaf that stirs, She flies,
> 'Till, mingl'd with the neighbouring Herd,
> She slights what erst she singly fear'd:
> And now, exempt from Doubt and Dread,
> She dares pursue; if They dare lead:
> As Their Example still prevails,
> She tempts the Stream, or leaps the Pales.[12]

Majoritarian custom rather than personal deliberation is what dominates individual choice on a day-to-day basis. Cowper, meanwhile, has his own problems with 'herds' and I have written elsewhere that this passage from *Alma* is a probable source for Cowper's celebrated self-image as a 'stricken deer' from Book III of *The Task*.[13] Cowper's errant deer wanders about as follows:

> I was a stricken deer that left the herd
> Long since; with many an arrow deep infixt
> My panting side was charged when I withdrew,
> To seek a tranquil death in distant shades.
> There was I found by one who had himself
> Been hurt by th'archers. In his side he bore,
> And in his hands and feet, the cruel scars.
> With gentle force soliciting the darts
> He drew them forth, and heal'd, and bade me live.
> Since then, with few associates, in remote
> And silent woods I wander, far from those
> My former partners of the peopled scene,
> With few associates, not wishing more.[14]

There are important differences as well as similarities between these passages and their animals. *Alma's* deer is an animal which joined the herd rather than left it. Prior's deer achieves healing by learning to run with the herd, while Cowper has been limping some way behind the herd, has been healed and thereby learns to stop trying to run with the pack, and to defy rather than acknowledge the force of custom. Couplets join Prior's deer to a larger structure whereas Cowper's blank verse wanders, while the word 'wander' is like the deer frozen for an instant at the caesura of the antepenultimate line of this passage. Vincent Newey describes this passage in terms of 'an escape from a general insanity' towards an idiosyncratic sanity.[15] Prior at no point suggests that such individual confidence is ever justified. It is, meanwhile, notable that Cowper's other great literary mentor, Milton, uses the word 'herd' on several pivotal occasions and always in a hostile context.[16]

Before imagining the famous stricken deer from *The Task*, Cowper had already invoked a deer to represent England in the course of his 1782 moral epistle, 'Table Talk':

> Poor England! thou art a devoted deer,
> Beset with ev'ry ill but that of fear.
> The nations hunt; all mark thee for a prey,
> They swarm around thee, and thou stands't at bay.
> Undaunted still, though wearied and perplex'd,
> Once Chatham sav'd thee, but who saves thee next?[17]

'Table Talk' is a conversation poem, featuring the imaginatively christened dialogists 'A' and 'B'. Cowper reflects on the conclusion of the American revolutionary wars, which he (and others) preferred to interpret as a global clash of empires in which Britain (by 1780) stood alone, outnumbered and outgunned by France, Spain, the Netherlands and (to a less important extent) the American colonists. The animal in the passage is a stag at bay, dependent on a divinely appointed 'Judge', like the recently deceased Chatham, to direct her course. Wounded by the loss of the colonies, England the 'devoted' deer resembles a limping creature in peril of annihilation at the hands of opportunistic predators. Appropriately, in the context of the closure of the couplet verse, 'England' the deer is standing still rather than wandering.

Cowper's first volume of poems, *Poems by William Cowper of the Inner Temple* (1782), which opens with this poem, offers a sequence of substantial couplet moral satires which attempt to demonstrate their persuasive authority by illustrating a degree of conversational ease.

'Conversation' (the longest of these poems) attempts to outline errors in sociable discourse and show the extent to which the ends of rational and persuasive communication are too often thwarted:

> Some fretful tempers wince at ev'ry touch,
> You always do too little or too much:
> You speak with life, in hopes to entertain,
> Your elevated voice goes through the brain;
> You fall at once into a lower key,
> That's worse – the drone-pipe of an humble bee.
> The southern sash admits too strong a light,
> You rise and drop the curtain – now its night.
> He shakes with cold – you stir the fire and strive
> To make a blaze – that's roasting him alive.
> Serve him with ven'son and he chuses fish,
> With soal – that's just the sort he would not wish,
> He takes what he at first profess'd to loath,
> And in due time feeds heartily on both;
> Yet still, o'erclouded with a constant frown,
> He does not swallow but he gulps it down
> Your hope to please him, vain on ev'ry plan,
> Himself should work that wonder, if he can –
> Alas! his efforts double his distress,
> He likes yours little, and his own still less,
> Thus always teasing others, always teas'd,
> His only pleasure is – to be displeas'd.[18]

This peevish dinner guest is determined to thwart any kind of creative sociability by failing to resolve antitheses, aptly dramatized by heavily non-predictive caesural verse which deliberately fails to offer either the fluidity of a continuous line or the balance of an equitably pausing line. This is perhaps the most inconsequential passage in 'Conversation' and also perhaps the most enjoyable in terms of its formal dexterity. From a structural point of view, 'Conversation' pivots on a thumbnail sketch of the meeting of two disciples with the disguised resurrected Christ on the road to Emmaus. This pious recollection represents something of a weakness in the context of the logic of the poem as a whole since it presents as the ideal, aspirational conversation a miraculous encounter with the Son of God; this is a somewhat difficult circumstance to replicate in the course of a modern dinner party, and therefore rather obtrusive in the course of the poem as a whole. Cowper excels instead in passages such as these that express while transcending the difficulties of conversational ease. The nightmare conversation, rather than the heavenly conversation, is the more easily digested by the reader.

Like Prior, Cowper regards himself as a diplomat with a predetermined agenda, committed to the successful direction of conversations. He regards it as his task to reconcile well-meaning but secular readers to evangelical Christianity, to preach a particular cause in as polite and sensitive way as possible. The concluding, and perhaps most successful, of these 1782 poems is 'Retirement', which anticipates much that is central to *The Task* (1785). The most effective thumbnail sketch in this final poem involves a retired politician who finds rural life more frustrating and strangely demanding than metropolitan intrigue and who flees back to the corridors of power:

> He chides the tardiness of every post,
> Pants to be told of battles won or lost,
> Blames his own indolence, observes, though late,
> 'Tis criminal to leave a sinking state,
> Flies to the levee, and receiv'd with grace,
> Kneels, kisses hands, and shines again in place.[19]

This resumption of business as usual does not represent a satire on 'retirement' as such. Indeed, as Newey has observed: 'The fickleness of the statesman, like that of Aphius, supplies a measure by which its true value and use – and the knowledgeable sincerity of the author, the poet behind the lines – can be more fully understood.'[20] Rather, it rescues the demanding concept of retirement from the lazily escapist fantasies of a jaded politician. Whereas Prior spent most of his adult life engaged in high-profile political business, seeking comfortable retirement (too) late in life, Cowper's only brush with employment resulted in a cry for help suicide attempt and a decision to devote the rest of his life to 'retirement', increasingly conceived as an important job.

It is only in retirement that Cowper discovers a sense of vocation and professional identity, as suggested by the following verse address, in which Cowper makes a very bold claim for his own status as a poet:

> A POETICAL EPISTLE TO LADY AUSTEN
> DEC. 17, 1781
>
> Dear Anna – between friend and friend,
> Prose answers every common end;

> Serves, in a plain and homely way,
> T'express th'occurrence of the day;
> Our health, the weather, and the news;
> What walks we take, what books we chuse;
> And all the floating thoughts, we find
> Upon the surface of the mind.
>
> But when a Poet takes the pen,
> Far more alive than other men,
> He feels a gentle tingling come
> Down to his finger and his thumb,
> Deriv'd from nature's noblest part,
> The centre of a glowing heart![21]

I have elsewhere glossed this intriguing passage in terms of its impact on the uncertain field of Cowperian sexuality studies, but it is also an example of Cowper's most effective Prioresque register.[22] The poem mocks while celebrating the poet's own status *qua* poet and uses Hudibrasts so subtly that it only takes on a rocking-horse quality in order to note some tedious or predictable circumstance. The poem as a whole also connects to some extent with Prior's unorthodox romantic life. Eschewing marriage, Prior preferred a sequence of long-term partners from somewhat plebeian backgrounds. Cowper (to follow an inverted Sedgwickian logic) seems to have been too heterosociable to be heteronormative and spent decades living an apparently chaste existence with Mary Unwin, a girlfriend of impeccable respectability.[23] Mrs Austen, the addressee of this letter, appears to have regarded Cowper's gallantries as the prelude to a declaration of marriage instead of as an invitation to join a bizarre flirtatious and unconsummated *ménage à trois*, and she fled the scene upon learning the truth. While Cowper himself concludes his poem with the suggestion from 'Solomon' that 'a threefold cord is not soon broken', the overwhelming weight of human experience suggests that such threesomes (celibate or otherwise) are inherently unstable.[24] The poem is, therefore, an effort of triangular diplomacy, all the more rhetorically impressive in light of the implausibility of the cause it serves.

Prior's own domestic arrangements, though far less bizarre than Cowper's, were somewhat unorthodox, and Prior's refusal to commit completely and legally to any one relationship suggests a strange affinity between the two poets. Cowper and Prior are fascinated by a peculiar version of celebrity in which 'the poet' is known and not known at one and the same time, illustrating an enjoyment of the difference between a speaking voice and a character referred to as 'the poet'. The poet who is and is not known forms the subject of Prior's 'The Conversation' (a far more pithy and less abstract poem than Cowper's unarticled moral satire with nearly the same name), and describes the joke of one 'Damon' who discourses at length and with assumed authority upon the political and poetical strengths and weaknesses of Matthew Prior with none other than the poet himself:

> Of all the Gifts the Gods afford,
> (If we may take old TULLY's Word)
> The greatest is a Friend; whose Love
> Knows how to praise, and when reprove:
> From such a Treasure never part,
> But hang the Jewel on your Heart:
> And pray, Sir (it delights Me) tell;
> You know this Author mighty well –
> Know Him! d'ye question it? Ods fish!
> Sir, does a Beggar know his Dish?
> I lov'd him, as I told You, I
> Advis'd Him – here a Stander-by
> Twitch'd Damon gently by the Cloak,
> And thus unwilling silence broke:
> DAMON, 'tis Time we shou'd retire,
> The man you talk with is MAT. PRIOR.[25]

Prior was Cowper's chief influence upon his practice of rambling conversational discourse in verse. Prior's verse conversations, like Cowper's, are far from being stately philosophical dialogues or formal statements of well-structured positions. Prior and Cowper achieve the uncanny knack of reproducing the idea of thought in process, of present tense improvised chit-chat. These practices are all the more demanding and impressive in the context of a four-beat line. Octosyllabic verse is an almost inherently satirical mode of discourse, even more patently so within a culture habituated by pentameters. The pentameter-wired intelligence registers the loss of each and every iambic foot and a sense of artificial compression informs the meaning of every line. The more pronounced bounce of an octosyllabic end-rhyme deliberately foregrounds the suspicion that the reader may be taken for a ride. Prior's Hudibrastic verse therefore makes a virtue of suspicion. The speaker who foolishly claims a friendship with Matthew Prior is himself being 'carried away' by Prior's distinctive rhythms.

Prior was prone to self-deprecation and too many of his too few biographers have taken this self-deprecation too seriously. Prior's high profile and influential identity as a career diplomat has been taken as evidence that he was a part-timer, whose verses are the product of downtime. This version of Prior has prevailed despite the fact that he belongs to a very tiny minority of writers to have ever made serious money out of a volume of original poetry. Prior was not merely a poet and a diplomat – he was a poetic diplomat and a diplomatic poet, and self-deprecation is a necessary, sometimes urgent, diplomatic qualification. The *ars celare artem* are as central to diplomacy as they are to a certain kind of poetry. And something of this self-deprecatory quality was bequeathed to Cowper, with equally significant implications for Cowper's long-term posthumous reputation.

Cowper christened Prior's most characteristic tone as easy writing, while making it immediately clear that it is not in the least bit easy. Vigorously disputing Johnson's description of Prior's 'stiffness', Cowper theorizes as follows:

> To make verse speak the language of prose, without being prosaic, to marshall the words of it in such an order, as they might naturally take in falling from the lips of an extemporary speaker, yet without meanness; harmoniously, elegantly, and without seeming to displace a syllable for the sake of the rhyme, is one of the most arduous tasks a poet can undertake. He that could accomplish this task was Prior; many have imitated his excellence in this particular, but the best copies have fallen far short of the original.[26]

This credo on behalf of a certain kind of poetry is methodologically if not philosophically cognate with Wordsworth's Preface to the *Lyrical Ballads* (1800), a point noted and pondered by Donald Davie back in 1953:

> The Wordsworthian reference is inevitable, for it is another feature of Cowper's comments on Prior that he here comes as near as ever he does to the Wordsworthian principle that 'There neither is, nor can be […] any essential difference between the language of prose and of metrical composition'. Cowper admires Prior for having shown, among other things, how 'To make verse speak the language of prose, without being prosaic'. This is an aspect of the neo-classical attitude to literature which is hardly ever understood, indeed seldom noticed. Johnson, no less than Cowper – in fact, the Augustans in general – insisted, as Wordsworth insisted, that the poet had a duty to the spoken language.[27]

This observation informs Davie's larger project of rescuing late Augustan aesthetics from the disappointed hindsight of Romantic orthodoxy. Having raised the prospect of a Prior–Cowper–Wordsworth collaborative assault on poetic diction, it suits Davie to reaffirm Cowper's essential conservatism:

> In any case there can be no question where Cowper stands. He stands for taste and judgement. In his own eyes, at any rate, he was nobody's precursor, but a poet coming late in an old tradition rich in achievement and based on principles tested in the practice of two centuries.[28]

The admirable rigour of Davie's resistance to the false teleologies of so-called 'proto-Romanticism' notwithstanding, there remains a paper to be written about the indirect influence of the Peace of Utrecht upon Wordsworthian diction. Where Cowper and Prior differ from Wordsworth is that this optimal poetic diction that speaks 'the language of prose' is the result not of any necessarily heightened sensibility, but is rather the culmination of arduous practice, a practice of negotiation (or diplomacy). Although Cowper declared to Lady Austen that a poet was 'far more alive than other men', the octosyllabic bounce of the line diffuses any proleptic Wordsworthian pretensions to vatic singularity. The 'ease' that links Prior and Cowper is an effect and never a cause.

Cowper's attempt to emulate a conversational poet helps to posit a theory of 'influence' that is all but free of 'anxiety', a form of influence that amounts to a conversation, a dialogue with the dead. The key influence of Prior on Cowper has much larger consequences for our sense of how the eighteenth century as a whole imagined the idea of poetic ambition and poetic vocation. Digression, self-deprecation, formal experimentation and a kind of anti-Cartesian fascination with the question of when and where the body begins and the mind ceases are issues which define not merely Prior and Cowper, but the whole combined gravitational pull of both poets, creating lines of influence and allegiance with quite paradoxical consequences. The larger history of egocentricity in verse is bound up with the long shadow of the son of a Dorsetshire joiner turned European peacebroker.

Notes

1. C. Brunström (2004) *William Cowper: Religion, Satire, Society* (Lewisburg: Bucknell). Note especially the chapter on 'The Anti-Visionaries of the Nonsense Club', pp. 43–68.

2. (1980) 'Written at Bath. On Finding the Heel of a Shoe' in J. D. Baird and C. Ryskamp (eds) *The Poems of William Cowper, 1748–1782*, 3 vols (Oxford: Clarendon Press), I, pp. 3–4.
3. For a detailed literary treatment of the Nonsense Club, see L. Bertelsen (1999) *The Nonsense Club: Literature and Popular Culture, 1749–1764* (Oxford: Clarendon Press).
4. (1971) in H. Bunker Wright and M. K. Spears (eds) *The Literary Works of Matthew Prior*, 2nd edn, 2 vols (Oxford: Clarendon Press), I, pp. 306–85, III.619–34.
5. In *The Poems of William Cowper, 1748–1782*, I, pp. 54–7, lines 1–4.
6. lines 31–8.
7. lines 67–90.
8. (1983) *Cowper's Task: Structure and Influence* (Cambridge: Cambridge University Press), pp. 20–2.
9. (December 1946) 'The Meaning of Matthew Prior's *Alma*', *ELH*, 13:4, 266–90 (p. 274).
10. In *The Literary Works of Matthew Prior*, I, pp. 470–516, I.251–65.
11. (1967) *The Life and Opinions of Tristram Shandy*, G. Petrie (ed.) (Harmondsworth: Penguin), p. 162.
12. III.113–22.
13. C. Brunström, *William Cowper: Religion, Satire, Society*, pp. 79–81.
14. (1995) in J. D. Baird and C. Ryskamp (eds) *The Poems of William Cowper*, 3 vols (Oxford: Clarendon Press), II, pp. 107–263, III.108–20.
15. (1982) *Cowper's Poetry: A Critical Study and Reassessment* (Liverpool: Liverpool University Press), p. 95.
16. Note, for example, the elitist anti-populism of Milton's Christ in *Paradise Regained* which excoriates the 'herd instinct' that prevents the general population from embracing the cause of pious (and republican?) virtue:

> For what is glory but the blaze of fame,
> The people's praise, if always praise unmixed?
> And what the people but a herd confused,
> A miscellaneous rabble, who extol
> Things vulgar, and well weighed, scarce worth the praise,
> They praise and they admire they know not what;
> And know not whom, but as one leads the other;
> And what delight to be by such extolled.
> To live upon their tongues and be their talk,
> Of whom to be dispraised were no small praise?

J. Milton (1968) *Paradise Regained* in J. Carey and A. Fowler (eds) *The Poems of John Milton* (Harlow: Longmans), pp. 1061–1167, III.47–56.
17. In *The Poems of William Cowper*, I, pp. 241–61, lines 362–7.
18. In *The Poems of William Cowper*, I, pp. 354–77, lines 325–46.
19. In *The Poems of William Cowper*, I, pp. 378–98, lines 475–80.
20. *Cowper's Poetry*, p. 83.
21. In *The Poems of William Cowper*, I, pp. 453–6, lines 1–14.
22. C. Brunström (2006) 'Leaving the Herd: How Queer was Cowper?', *Journal for Eighteenth-Century Studies*, 29, 157–67.

23. Note, Eve Sedgwick's theorization of homo-sociability of heteronormativity, as developed particularly in (1985) *Between Men: English Literature and Male Homosocial Desire* (New York: Columbia University Press).
24. 'A Poetical Epistle to Lady Austen', line 106.
25. In *The Literary Works of Matthew Prior*, I, pp. 523–5, lines 71–86.
26. (1981) 'Letter to the Rev. William Unwin of 17 January 1782' in J. King and C. Ryskamp (eds) *The Letters and Prose Writings of William Cowper*, 5 vols (Oxford: Clarendon Press), II, p. 10.
27. (1992) 'The Critical Principles of William Cowper' in *Older Masters: Essays and Reflections on English and American Literature* (Manchester: Carcanet), pp. 214–21 (p. 220).
28. 'The Critical Principles', p. 221.

Part II
Science and Nature

5
'When Universal Nature I Survey'
Philosophical Poetry Before 1750

Megan Kitching

A philosophical poem treats the human condition, including our place in the world, the nature of our mind and what it knows and how we develop wisdom. From the mid-seventeenth century onwards, the spread of new scientific knowledge across Europe was profoundly altering the way poets thought and wrote about these questions. This chapter examines the poetry of natural philosophy in Britain in the first half of the eighteenth century. In this Newtonian period, a new confidence in the rational interpretation of the cosmos according to universal laws brought about equally confident verses aiming to depict God's creation in all its harmonious beauty. Following the publication in 1709 of *Death's Vision*, the 'first consciously scientific long poem' of the century, came a cluster of productions from, among others, Richard Blackmore, Henry Baker, Moses Browne and Henry Brooke.[1] With the possible exception of Blackmore's *Creation*, few of these poems have received much sustained critical attention. Philosophical poetry in its more didactic guise seems to lack the imaginative dimensions or emotional appeal of, say, the blank verse meditations of Mark Akenside, Edward Young or William Wordsworth. Yet these less canonical poets were also grappling with how to (re)conceive the world as the object of both empirical and aesthetic enquiry. Setting themselves the ambitious goal of surveying the known universe, they attempted to embody in their verses the order that the sciences revealed in the world and, by placing humanity within this order, to turn questions raised by natural philosophy towards their moral and theological implications. Serious in intent and encyclopaedic in scope, these works help us understand how poetry participates in cultural shifts in understanding and how it creates new knowledge at the boundaries of ignorance.

During the first decades of the eighteenth century, a growing body of literature addressed the burgeoning public interest in the sciences. Philosophical poems join the periodicals, treatises, catalogues, pedagogical literature and diverse other forms in which eighteenth-century readers in London and the provinces consumed natural philosophy. New knowledge circulating through these networks fed poets' appetite for nature and novelty. As one example, we can trace the theory of a plurality of inhabited worlds from William Whiston's *New Theory of the Earth* (1696) to his lectures in Button's coffee house, which Joseph Addison helped arrange, from Addison and Steele's *Spectator*, to Blackmore's *Creation* and to Alexander Pope's *An Essay on Man*, whose author had possibly been in Whiston's audience in Button's.[2] Clear and conversational, the rhyming couplets of these latter works capture the controversies surrounding this socialized science as well as its sublime aspects. Poetry had other advantages for entertaining and instructing its audience. It retained a certain cachet among polite readers and patrons and could reach those 'whose Years, Sex, or Inclinations' deterred them from Latin treatises or mechanical demonstrations.[3]

Though many philosophic poems profess didactic aims, these are not sufficient in themselves to explain their intentions. Doubts were periodically raised, even at the time, about how suitable verses were for conveying scientific knowledge. 'If this writer has any important ideas to communicate to the Public on philosophical subjects', one reviewer wrote of a later work, 'they would probably appear to more advantage in plain prose'.[4] One way to account for why this anonymous author embarked on their six-book opus in verse is to consider the poetic possibilities opened to them by the heterogenous tradition of natural-philosophical poetry that by this time, the 1780s, had established certain shared formal features apart from its subject matter. The resources of the annotated poem in particular gave poets an answer to the opinions of those who wanted their facts in prose. In creating hybrids of verse and notes, they could set up productive dynamics between discourses. Marjorie Hope Nicholson's foundational work demonstrates how much can be gained by considering consciously literary responses to natural philosophy during this period. As she shows at length, Pope, Thomson, Akenside, Hughes and a host of others explored the sublime shifts in perception opened by Isaac Newton's astronomy and optics, or the insights into Scriptural history offered by the earth sciences.[5] The full spectrum of eighteenth-century 'scientific' verse emerges from William Powell Jones's *The Rhetoric of Science*. Prior to 1750, he shows, such poetry was chiefly concerned with astronomy and its theological ramifications, and organized around the imaginative possibilities offered by the microscope and the telescope.

Replacing a transmission model with one of transformation, we can appreciate how successfully poets used what Jones terms 'scientific ideas and imagery' for their own ends.[6] So far this approach has tended to favour poetry that conforms to canonical measures of value – for Jones, sublime nature description is its ideal – and to assume a relatively unquestioned category of the scientific. There is the sense that poetry and science form two extremities of a range, and that poems should naturally fall towards the literary end of the scale. A comment by Helen Margaret Scurr, author of a 1922 dissertation on Henry Brooke, nicely illustrates the problem of how to account for those often quite substantial works that fall in between. 'In the first half of the eighteenth century', she observes, 'a populous school of poetasters were writing pseudo-philosophic, didactic verse. Whether the philosophy was real philosophy, or the poetry genuine poetry, is debatable.'[7] Scurr becomes almost tongue-tied in the alliterative tangle Brooke has made by trying to do two things at once, and doing neither well. Since these studies appeared, historians of science and literature alike (not to mention scholars of religion) have broadened and redefined their objects of study to the point where we might now claim to have transcended this debate. Whether or not we agree with Scurr about their aesthetic shortcomings, these pre-disciplinary texts invite revisiting in our interdisciplinary era in which attention has turned to the social and cultural production of knowledge in all forms.

The first philosophical poem to attract the notice of critics in Britain was Richard Blackmore's *Creation*. Published in February 1712, it had gone into the second of many editions by May that same year.[8] Although its physician author was already known for two patriotic Virgilian epics, *Creation* was a distinct and timely offering. As Blackmore's contemporary John Reynolds remarked, this was a 'Philosophical Age' in which 'such Problems have been Resolv'd, and Discoveries made, as no Ages are known to have been blest with before'.[9] Reynolds was an Oxford-educated Presbyterian minister who had published his own 'philosophical sacred poem' in 1709. These poets were quite different figures, but united by their desire to celebrate Britain's new comprehension of the earth and heavens in verse. They shared too a distaste for the bad manners and impiety of satire. When Thomas Sprat in his 1665 *History of the Royal Society* called for poets to support the new experimental philosophy, he was at the same time appealing to wits not to undermine the fledgling institution.[10] His appeal fell on deaf ears: the decades around the turn of the century are rich in caricatures of scientific virtuosi and their Laputian pursuits.[11] Author of the ironically-titled *Satire on Wit*, Blackmore had engaged in print skirmishes with Dryden and Pope in his quest to purge poetry of triviality and impiety. Reynolds approved of satire's reforming aims, but felt too that poets should amplify the grandeur of natural philosophy. His *Death's Vision* is an irregular ode, the same form Cowley had chosen for his 'To the Royal Society' which introduces Sprat's history. In his own preface, Reynolds admits that while natural philosophy could be 'heavy and dull' (p. 2), when well treated it could 'Advance and Reform our Poetry' (p. 4). Here he echoes the title of John Dennis's 1701 work which argues for religion to play this role as it had done for the ancients.[12]

Framing natural philosophy as a bridge to higher things rescued it from the satirists while preserving its poetic importance. Since the 1680s, a raft of writers had been preaching the remarkably successful synthesis encapsulated in the title of William Derham's 1713 treatise, *Physico-theology: or, a demonstration of the being and attributes of God from His works of creation* (*Astro-theology* followed two years later).[13] Stephen Gaukroger suggests that physico-theology is best understood as a 'tri-angulation', with the assets of both fields 'converging on fundamental truths'.[14] Gaukroger's formulation emphasizes how, for a time, the two bases of the triangle were brought into equivalence. Reynolds offers an interesting take on this triangular relationship by arguing that philosophy and religion should support and advance poetry. His *Death's Vision* uses the conceit of disembodied flight later employed by John Hughes, Mark Akenside and elegists of Newton to convey the other-worldly excitement of new knowledge.[15] On the moral side, it is the desire to escape his degraded mortality that helps propel the speaker's soul into space. Exploring the sublime heights of Newtonian astronomy, he is granted insights into the workings of the cosmos that parallel religious revelation. Blackmore's *Creation* sets at the apex of the triangle the proposition, 'there is a God'. Natural philosophy gives him the rational arguments to prove this statement true. Aligning the study of nature with praise or proof of its maker was such a successful strategy that it would remain a theme of most scientific verses published in Britain up to the 1780s and even beyond.

Physico-theological poetry answered the desire of natural philosophers to see their convictions in verse. As early as 1697, William Molyneux, founder of what became the Dublin Philosophical Society, had suggested to Blackmore that he write 'a philosophick poem'; though Molyneux wrote asking his friend John Locke to repeat the request, it was another 15 years before *Creation* appeared.[16] When Reynolds read this letter shortly before *Death's Vision* went to press, he hastened to assure his readers that he was not presuming to supply 'one of the *Desiderata* in the learned world' (p. 9). This did not prevent his opportunistic publishers adding to the 1713 second edition of his poem the unlikely claim: 'Writ at the request of the famous *Mr. John Lock*'. The learned world appeared to have given the stamp of approval to this new project. What Blackmore eventually wrote was quite different from what Molyneux (who did not live to see his *desideratum* in print) had envisaged. Rather than simply describing those 'great and admirable phenomena of the universe' that inspire 'sublime thoughts', *Creation, a philosophic poem in seven books* is an extended argument against atheism.[17] Blackmore confronts the threat of materialism contained within the physical and mathematical sciences themselves, and associated with one particular source.

Before poets could agree with Dennis that the ancients excelled the moderns when they wrote with religious fervour, they needed to address the prominent exception to this rule. Titus Lucretius Carus (c. 99–c.49 BC) wrote his six-book Latin poem *De Rerum Natura* to expound the atomistic theories of Epicurus. Rediscovered in the fifteenth century, *On the Nature of Things* reached Restoration England in several translations and exerted a profound influence on scientific and literary culture well into the eighteenth century.[18] As Reynolds wrote, in words closely echoed by Blackmore, the Epicurean philosophy 'had ne're lived so long as it did, had not the Poet so adorn'd and dress'd it' (p. 7).[19] They had reason to regret this longevity. *De Rerum Natura* contains a cosmogony where the universe is created from the chance cohesion of atoms, where the material soul returns to the world after death and where gods are superstitious delusions. Its particle-theory of matter helped establish mechanism as the fundamental physical theory of the early modern period. To his poetic successors, Lucretius bequeathed an entire theory of the universe, complete with ethical guidelines and psychological consolations for mortality. *Creation*'s seven books of verse are an explicit rebuttal of Lucretius's six. Blackmore's poem shares certain formal features of the translation most eighteenth-century readers would have known: Thomas Creech's 1682 edition, which renders the poem into heroic couplets and appends a lengthy anti-atheist preface and notes. In this way it signals like many long philosophical poems that it has inherited the classical didactic tradition. Its supporters even hinted that the poem was worthy of the mantle of English epic. Both Molyneux and Joseph Addison praised *Creation* in the same breath as *Paradise*

Lost.[20] Samuel Johnson expressed the spirit of the work more closely as 'reason[ing] in verse'.[21] Dennis, meanwhile, declared that the poem 'has equal'd that of Lucretius, in the Beauty of its Versification, and infinitely surpass'd it, in the Solidity and Strength of its Reasoning'.[22] It is a well-structured poem for a well-structured world.

Blackmore's *Creation* is organized around two axes: cataloguing instances of divine design in the natural world, and refuting the hypotheses of pagan or unorthodox philosophers. Discerning the nature of things was no longer a matter of determining their Aristotelian essences but of observing their relative place in a vast plan. So philosophical poets aimed to build a picture of the universe itself that depicted its organization and utility as well as its beauty. Even when showing the elements in a dynamic balance, Blackmore emphasizes how each has its place:

> The glorious Orbs, which Heavn's bright Host compose,
> Th'imprison'd Sea, that restless ebbs and flows,
> The fluctuating Fields of liquid Air,
> With all the curious Meteors hovering there,
> And the wide Regions of the Land. (I.42–6)

All movement here remains in vertically stratified layers; even the meteors hover rather than fall. The key to this arrangement is in Blackmore's title: this is a cosmos deliberately created to serve the purposes of a deity, primarily the maintenance of human life. Consider this passage where Blackmore rebuts Aristotle's belief that nature fulfils its own innate purposes:

> On this be laid the Stress of this Debate;
> What wisely acts, can never act by Fate.
> The Means and Ends must first be understood,
> The Means, as proper, and the Ends, as good.
> The Act must be exerted with intent
> By using Means to gain the wish'd Event. (V.397–402)

Pared down to their bare bones of repetition, parallelism and antithesis, these couplets exemplify Blackmore's functional approach in what he terms the 'Philosophical and Argumentative Parts' of his poem. A lengthy debate runs throughout these passages in which the heroes Locke and Newton demolish the hoary Aristotle and Copernicus and the irreligious Hobbes and Leibniz. Blackmore's intent is to render philosophies (primarily Epicureanism) based upon chance and non-hierarchical relationships inferior to those asserting higher control, whether in the religious or social sense.

The idea of chance as a creative factor was anathema to the Boyle lecturers and physico-theologists determined to prove that the principles underlying the universe were 'Order, Fitness, Harmony, / Use and Convenience' (III.637–8). The resulting paeans can seem complacent, but Blackmore's emphatic, sometimes hectoring rhetoric would not be necessary if everything were that simple. Reynolds's *Death's Vision*, though it celebrates the earthly knowledge of natural philosophy, is concerned primarily with how to interpret scripture, live a moral life and prepare for death and the revelations that will follow. *Creation* argues that God has given mortals the capacity and, therefore, the duty to understand the world. He exclaims:

> But oh! how dark is human Reason found,
> [...]
>   when he [Man] essays
> To trace dark Nature, and detect her Ways[.] (I.271, 273–4)

The limitations of reason suggest that not all knowledge is available through the study of nature alone. Thus the tone for most philosophical poetry to come remained one of uneasy confidence.

In the decade following Newton's death in 1727 the poetics of cosmic order became established, even conventional. When Moses Browne presented readers with *An Essay on the Universe* in 1739 he rather disingenuously remarked that he knew of no one apart from Blackmore who had 'publish'd any thing of this kind'. 'Several little pieces have appeared', he admitted, 'which by their titles have seem'd to promise a Resemblance; but upon Enquiry I could not find any one of them had fallen upon my Design'.[23] Recently published had been *The Beauties of the Universe* (1732), *The Universe: A Poem* (1734), *Universal Beauty* (1735), *An Essay on the Universe* (1733) and Browne's poem of the same name. The overshadowing presence here is clearly *An Essay on Man* (1733–4). Bernard Fabian argues that the 'subtle and complex' allusive connections between the *Essay* and *De Rerum Natura* would have marked the former work for contemporary readers as anti-Lucretian in the same vein as *Creation*, while Harry Solomon has gone to some lengths to posit Blackmore's poem as a source for Pope.[24] Yet *An Essay on Man*, as we have it, fills only the first part of a proposed four-book work on man, knowledge, government and morality; of the *Essay* itself, the natural-philosophical material is mostly confined to the first two epistles. Pope's powerful expression of the reach and limits of science is also an examination of the role of the social self in the theatre of the cosmos. As such, it undoubtedly helped shape these less canonical presentations of our 'middle state'. The *Essay* also gave contemporaries a generic tag appropriate for the conditional confidence of their endeavour.

Rather than the ode form of Cowley or Reynolds, or the long, combative argument of Blackmore, it was the 'poetical essay' that carried philosophical poetry forwards. The prose genre, as developed by Michel de Montaigne, was subjective and tentative with a 'skeptical despair of achieving any unified cosmological view'.[25] What made the essay ideal for Robert Boyle when recording his experiments also made it incompatible with the kind of physico-theological poem which sought precisely this view. More appropriate was its association with treatises, and with Pope's literary fame. While appropriating his title, these verses expanded into those corners of speculation where his lens, more focused upon human nature, did not care to reach. The author of the 1733 *An Essay on the Universe* had praised Pope's portrait of short-sighted humanity. Since we can know nothing completely, 'How then, explore the Ways of Providence / Profound – or gather information hence?' (27–8). The poet leaps on:

> Yet, since this boundless All each View invites,
> [...]
> Then only let us, as We can, aspire,
> To trace it, that We may the more admire! (29, 34–5)

These couplets bring to mind Pope's 'Ask for what end the heav'nly bodies shine', and the ironic reply, '"Tis for mine'.[26] To believe that the stars were made to inspire our awe and humility is still to assume that they exist for our sake.

These poems describing the universe seek to evoke both grandeur and homogeneity. Inducing a sense of sublime insignificance by confronting readers with mind-boggling scenes is part of their aim; showing how this system remains comprehensible is another. Thus it was possible for one poet to begin: 'When Universal Nature I survey [...]'.[27] The word 'universe' entered written English around the same time as the geocentric system exploded, providing a useful singular noun for what had become an infinity of suns with countless orbiting worlds.[28] For the pioneer of experimental method Robert Boyle, universal or general nature had simply meant all matter as acted upon by the laws of motion – the famous clockwork cosmos.[29] Post-*Principia Mathematica*, poets could seize upon phenomena that were literally universal, since gravitation and the laws of refraction operated across space and time. 'God is uniform in all his Ways', Henry Baker wrote in *The Universe*, 'And rules by Laws eternally the same'.[30] While both Boyle and Newton sought to partition their physical enquiries from unwanted metaphysical implications – Boyle warned, for example, against speaking of nature's 'works' as if some principle apart from the deity was doing the working – poets had greater license to explore the analogies physicotheology encouraged.[31] Thus, in *An Essay upon the Laws of Nature* (1716), Blackmore argues that laws imposed upon us by divine authority need not be solely physical, and that they even include ethical precepts and, contra Locke, innate tendencies towards virtue.[32] John Reynolds, meanwhile, compared the Newtonian law of gravitational attraction to both magnetism and to sexual love. In this stable system, metaphors from social, political and natural realms interlocked with ease.

'Like some grand Building is the Universe', Henry Baker wrote, 'Where evr'y part is useful in its Place' (p. 33). The same might be said of the works of this versatile author, whose poetry and prose complement each other to convey the scientific views of his day. Baker (1698–1774) had a lifelong interest in communication, beginning as a bookseller's apprentice before establishing himself as a speech therapist and deaf educator. *The Universe: A poem intended to restrain the pride of man* (1734) is sometimes dated 1727, but its clear debt to *An Essay on Man* suggests the later date.[33] This short, moralizing, philosophical poem on a single theme bears an obvious relationship to Baker's essays for his periodical *The Universal Spectator and Weekly Journal*, founded in 1728 with his future father-in-law Daniel Defoe as contributor.[34] Fascinated by the microscope, Baker later wrote two popular guides to this instrument as well as scientific papers treating crystals and the freshwater polyp. His certificate of election to the Royal Society may be unique in commending him as the 'Author of a very beautiful Poem called the Universe, with many Curious Notes regarding Natural History'.[35] To celebrate his new status as FRS, he retitled the second 1746 edition of this work 'a *philosophical* poem'. He also cited his couplets in his *Philosophical Transactions* papers.[36] That Baker's poetry is lucid and presents accepted knowledge no doubt assisted these moves between generalist and specialist domains.

The Universe takes full advantage of the compressive power of verse. In less than 300 couplets Baker aims 'to sketch out a Plan of the Universe; that, by considering the Grandeur of the Whole, MAN might be made sensible of his own Littleness and Insignificance, except in the very Place he stands' (p. 6). This is a conveniently large exception, and Baker nowhere denies that humans are superior on earth by virtue of possessing reason. However, he, like Pope, uses the chain of being in which we are merely one link to humble our position. Extending across the material–immaterial divide, the chain joined physical to metaphysical and the lowliest worm to God. Microscopists like Baker could use similar logic to defend their study of 'animalcules' and fleas, a favourite target of satirists' mockery. Quite a lot of work was needed to reveal such creatures as 'exquisite contrivances', as Catherine Wilson puts it nicely, and not vermin.[37] Baker in his poetry dignifies insects by marvelling at the full if brief lives they must lead. By drawing analogies between the discoveries of the microscope and the telescope, he and his contemporaries work to endow micro-science with the dignity of astronomy. The whiteness of the Milky Way, Moses Browne remarks in a note, results from a 'vast number of small Telescopic Stars' just as the pale bloom of plums comes from myriads of tiny insects.[38] The universal nature of these verses invests the apparently chaotic earthly environment with the serenity of the heavens while transferring the marks of design from the terrestrial to the skies.

Since the search for such marks had traditionally relied upon the observation of living things, poets used the idea of a plenitude of beings to invest the planets with life. The theory of a plurality of worlds, like the image of the chain, was nothing new. However, the *kosmoi* of Greek thought and the pre-Copernican spheres were relatively self-enclosed systems, isolated from human speculation.[39] By the 1730s it was possible to speak of numberless systems of worlds and even multiple hypothetical universes.[40] Baker considered that the hypothesis that each fixed star was a sun around which planets orbited was 'generally agreed to by the learned World' (p. 10). Before 1750, the idea that these planets were inhabited found more support among imaginative writers than scientists. For physico-theologists, the vaster and more numerous God's creations, the more glorious and humbling. Returning to the Great Chain, Baker asks reasonably where else might we find 'those numberless Orders of more glorious Beings which are betwixt Us and our Creator' (p. 7), if not on other planets? Moses Browne too denies that such a vast expanse as the field of fixed stars can be barren:

> O! Rather think, since form'd with equal Pow'rs,
> Heav'n meant their systems as compleat as ours.
> O'erwhelming image! what a boundless scene
> Breaks on the mind! (III.127–30)

The oxymoronic image of a 'boundless scene' captures beautifully what the universe meant to these poets. It is the dizzying descent into the opposite end of the scale that brings Baker's *Universe* to a halt. Confronted by the progression of insects towards the minuscule, the poet breaks off, reins in his 'unbounded Fancy' (p. 39) and dreams of the day when his disembodied soul will transcend his senses and reveal all.

The cosmic nature of these 1730s poems bridges a transition whereby modern disciplinary terms, astronomy and physics, gave way to botany, zoology and geology as the scientific fields with most aesthetic appeal and explanatory power in the public imagination. Thus 'nature' began to replace 'universe' in the titles of philosophical poems. This was in part due, as Jones notes, to the influence of *The Seasons* and the subsequent explosion in natural history publishing. Their importance to physico-theology had always ensured the non-mathematical sciences a place in philosophical poetry, even if in generalized terms. Baker's *The Universe* devotes a long passage to the representative species of the chain of being: the lion for wild mammals, the horse for domesticated ones, the eagle for birds and the whale for fish. In *An Essay on the Application of Natural History to Poetry* (1777), John Aikin would later dismiss as derivative the fiery stallions and proud peacocks that populate Baker's verse. Aikin's twentieth-century successor John Arthos observes that this is an early case of measuring literature against the assumed truth-standards of science. With a focus upon didactic verse, Arthos shows that the 'stock diction' used by these authors reflected their belief in a stable orderly environment as well as the need for standardized epithets among the growing scientific community (of which Baker was a member).[41] The emblematic animals of the chain represented the full plenitude of life while also reminding readers of their subjection to higher orders. Once physico-theology had given natural philosophy the standing it needed, the natural sciences remained important to poets for other reasons. The physics of matter and void seemed increasingly incapable of providing one fundamental theory of phenomena. Mechanism, it became plain, had trouble accounting for processes such as the reproduction of plants and animals. This period when Newtonianism became most widespread therefore preceded new developments in the life sciences that turned attention towards living beings.

An early expression of this transfer of interest from matter to life is *Universal Beauty*, by the Irish writer and playwright Henry Brooke. Brooke's debut philosophical poem was published in six parts in 1735. Although still built upon physico-theological foundations, *Universal Beauty* begins to transfer an interest in God's intentions for his creation to a fascination with creation as nature for its own sake. Like that of Thomson in *The Seasons*, especially *Spring*, Brooke's verse has a Shaftesburyian flavour and depicts nature as a theatre of change and sociability. This emerges vividly from his descriptions of plants. On one level these passages defamiliarize seeds, roots and tendrils by portraying their processes as if with the slow-motion lens of a nature documentary. Brooke is unafraid to strew both verse and notes with botanical terms and to observe the anatomical analogies between plants and animals. He then uses these analogies to extend a series of biological and social metaphors. Creepers, he writes in one section, 'spring with mutual Aid; / Officious, brace their amicable Band [in] reciprocal Communion'.[42] Intertwining the language of poetry and love, of science and of civil and political relations, this passage culminates by reproaching humanity for our lack of social cohesion. Only in our better moments can we aspire to the 'wedded Plexures' of the lovers' grotto or the muse's shady bower (297). Humanity is a 'blot' on nature (88). Brooke even gives us an ecological version of Pope's 'whatever is, is right', stating 'all is right – tho' Man be wrong' (91).

As marvelling at nature from a distance gave way to studying nature on the ground, the tendency to uphold the environment as exemplar did not change. Reynolds had called for natural-philosophical poetry that reformed and was reforming, while Blackmore had made moral indignation the sustaining mood of his public verses. Browne's *An Essay on the Universe* shows that in the late 1730s this stance could still justify philosophical poetry as a tonic for 'degenerate taste' and impiety.[43] The *Essay* is dedicated to Frances Seymour, Countess of Hertford and later Duchess of Somerset, patron of numerous poets including James Thomson. Like Thomson, Browne rhetorically addresses those whose taste and intellect are informed by the active investigation of nature, using Seymour to cast his poem towards the growing number of female enthusiasts and practitioners of natural philosophy. The sciences are explicitly presented here as 'Works purely intended for the Improvement of Sobriety, Reason, and Virtue'.[44]

Within the frame of his dedication, Browne also uses the association of poetry with high-mindedness to distinguish his verses from a growing body of popular science writing in prose. Here he singles out two successful astronomy texts, Bernard Le Bouvier de Fontenelle's *Entretiens sur la pluralité des mondes* (1686), and John Harris's *Astronomical Dialogues between a Gentleman and a Lady* (1719). Harris's volume recasts the French academician's witty account of a flirtation under Cartesian stars as a far chaster tale for Anglophone Newtonians. Yet Browne accuses even Harris of removing the 'Grandeur and Solemnity' of his subject by writing in a familiar style.[45] His own model of instructive conversation was not a work of astronomy, but of fishing: Izaak Walton's *The Compleat Angler* (1653). The first book and concluding hymn of *An Essay on the Universe* aim to reinvigorate pastoral by replacing the swain with the sportsman and cultivator, and the shepherdess with the amateur botanizer or star-gazer. Proponents of the sciences, such as Browne, wished to encourage wealthy landowners to study natural philosophy (and to patronize its poetry) to improve both themselves and their lands. Denouncing the person who believes all nature is made for their benefit, Browne and Baker echo wider contemporary debates around individualism, greed and luxury.

The transition from the meadow to the universe in Browne's philosophical poem involves several false starts as he writes himself into new conventions. The 'Rural Notes' of his *'lowly* Theme' will hardly reach to the stars, nor will lingering in 'Groves where *Hermit Inspiration* dwells' (I.1-4) allow the speaker's soul to roam freely around and beyond the earth. Before he commences his tour of the solar system, Browne settles his speaker in a bucolic cottage. Here understanding the world philosophically restores its Edenic freshness. Wherever we look we see a 'Field of Contemplation' endlessly 'pleasing, innocent and new'; we should 'Fear not thro' all her harmless Maze to stray' (I.733-6). Natural philosophy is a choice synonymous with virtue and directly opposed to vice:

> Behold! Philosophy thy Choice invites
> How safe a Guide, how harmless her Delights!
> [...]
> When Vice to low and base Delights Persuades,
> Retire, and lose her in these purer Shades. (I.729-30, 739-40)

Here Browne abandons the metaphor of 'leading' from one discourse to the other and simply situates natural philosophy, religious virtue and poetry in the same shady grove.

From this paradigmatic retreat of muses, *An Essay on the Universe* then ranges far into space, drawing on the connections between astronomy and navigation to celebrate British discoveries of 'New Worlds, New heavens' (III.184). With these comparisons come familiar anxieties. Some stars are clearly vastly more ancient than our sun, others have disappeared and still others were being born: 'Whence are these changes in the mighty Void? / Are Worlds created there, and Worlds Destroy'd?' (III.219-20). The poem descends into a series of rhetorical questions, behind which lie implications for Earth, particularly the relative insignificance, geographical and historical, of the nation and its achievements. Browne breaks off here to invoke the spectre of hubris in the foil to his brave explorer: a rash traveller who aims for the moon, but perishes in the cold, dark vacuum of space. In a startling image, his body remains orbiting above as a warning to others: 'Eternal Ages fix'd, thou must appear / Of suff'ring fools a Monument severe' (III.369–70). This modern Icarus underlines his point that the only thing unchanging is human pride. The poem comes full circle by concluding with a hymn to the virtuous life.

As the century moved on, the synoptic grand view of things became less available to philosophical poets. Natural philosophy abandoned the search for a unified theory that had made physico-theology such an urgent endeavour and separated its interests further from those of religion. Between 1747 and 1751, Church of England clergyman James Fortescue published a quartet of poems. One paean to order and one to providence are both entitled *Nature*, while two poems entitled *Science* treat first the 'philosophical life', then 'a Religious view' of the same.[46] The latter now enjoy their own *ESTC* subject heading of 'Science Fiction Poetry–to 1800', but predict the future only in this segregation of earthly knowledge from Christianity. Tastes in longer-form verse changed, with the turn towards melancholy subjectivity balancing the celebration of British liberty, as universal nature became absorbed into the national landscapes of loco-description and georgic. As the disciplines under natural philosophy formalized and institutionalized their methods, practices and equipment, it became harder too for the clergyman- or physician-poet to contribute to knowledge. In some fields, such as botany, the opportunities for women and amateurs widened, but the poets of natural philosophy later in the century include remarkable polymaths like Erasmus Darwin, Humphrey Davy and Samuel Taylor Coleridge. In his early career Coleridge imagined a decade-long project to steep himself in 'universal science' before attempting an epic poem never realized.[47] Darwin's *The Botanic Garden* (1789, 1791) and *The Temple of Nature* (1803) were simultaneously some of the most successful philosophical verses of the period and among the last, as Darwin's evolutionary views and Epicurean praise of pleasure became radicalized by the heated political climate of his times.[48]

This remains in many ways the story of an unattainable ideal, the vain hope of the human mind to understand everything including its own doubts. At one point in *Creation*, Blackmore issues a challenge to Lucretius:

Let Atomes once the Form of Letters take,
By Chance, and let those huddled Letters make
A finish'd Poem by a lucky Hit,
Such as the *Grecian*, or the *Mantuan* writ;
Then we'll embrace the Doctrines you advance,
And yield the World's fair Poem made by Chance. (IV.782–7)

Behind Blackmore's assertion that only God was such a poet lies the impossibility of epic and the inchoate form of the work that might express not only the world but the universe. 'It is indeed a Wonder', Browne commented, 'no sublime Genius has been excited to give us some finished Poem upon this great and delightful Theme'.[49] It is perhaps a greater surprise that so many philosophical poems were produced and finished. That the separation of scientific disciplines, and of the sciences in general from literature, is often cited as a reason for their decline is also testament to their ambition and scope. Even with the current interest in Romantic science, the works of Blackmore, Baker or Brooke are too often dismissed as isolated curiosities, with little connection to each other or to works since. This chapter has sought to show that philosophical poetry was a persistent presence throughout the first half of the eighteenth century. While concerned to convey the facts of natural-philosophy, these poems are invested in analysing the intellectual and emotional qualities of reason, observation and devotion that allow these discoveries to be interpreted and enjoyed.

Notes

1. W. Powell Jones (1966) *The Rhetoric of Science: A Study of Scientific Ideas and Imagery in Eighteenth-Century English Poetry* (London: Routledge and Kegan Paul), p. 79.
2. M. J. Crowe (1986) *The Extraterrestrial Life Debate, 1750–1900: The Idea of a Plurality of Worlds from Kant to Lowell* (Cambridge: Cambridge University Press), pp. 30–3.
3. M. Browne (1752) 'Preface' in *The Works and Rest of the Creation* (London: A. Millar), pp. i–viii (p. iii).
4. (1786) 'Review of *Nature: A poem in six books*' in *The Monthly Review, Volume 74* (London: R. Griffiths), p. 564.
5. M. Hope Nicholson (1946) *Newton Demands the Muse: Newton's 'Opticks' and the Eighteenth Century Poets* (Princeton, NJ: Princeton University Press); (1959) *Mountain Gloom and Mountain Glory: The Development of the Aesthetics of the Infinite* (Ithaca: Cornell University Press; Oxford: Oxford University Press); (1968) *"This Long Disease, My Life": Alexander Pope and the Sciences* (Princeton: Princeton University Press).

6. *The Rhetoric of Science*, p. vii.
7. H. M. Scurr (1922) 'Henry Brooke' (unpublished doctoral thesis, University of Minnesota), p. 25.
8. See the Bibliography appended to A. Rosenberg (1950) 'The Life and Works of Sir Richard Blackmore' (unpublished doctoral thesis, Queen Mary, University of London).
9. (1709) *Death's Vision, a Philosophical Sacred Poem* (London: Thomas Varnum and John Osborn), p. 3. Further references are by page number to this edition and are placed in parentheses following the quotation.
10. (1667) 'Experiments will be beneficial to our Wits and Writers' in *The History of the Royal Society of London, for the Improving of Natural Knowledge* (London: J. Martyn), pp. 413–18.
11. See Powell Jones, *Rhetoric of Science*, chapter entitled 'Satire on Science, 1660–1760', pp. 65–78; G. Lynall (2012) *Swift and Science: The Satire, Politics, and Theology of Natural Knowledge, 1680–1730* (New York: Palgrave Macmillan).
12. (1701) *The Advancement and Reformation of Modern Poetry* (London: Richard Parker).
13. (1713) *Physico-theology[...]* (London: W. Innys). This was the published version of Derham's 1711–12 Boyle lectures. The lecture series, endowed by Robert Boyle to counter atheism and deism, commenced with Richard Bentley in 1692.
14. (2010) *The Collapse of Mechanism and the Rise of Sensibility: Science and the Shaping of Modernity, 1680–1760* (Oxford: Oxford University Press), p. 2.
15. J. Hughes (1720) *The Ecstasy: An Ode* (London: J. Roberts); M. Akenside (1744) *The Pleasures of Imagination* (London: Robert Dodsley), I.183–211; J. Thomson (1963) 'To the Memory of Sir Isaac Newton' in J. L. Robertson (ed.) *The Complete Poetical Works of James Thomson* (Oxford: Oxford University Press), p. 436, lines 1–2.
16. (1708) 'Mr. Molyneux to Mr. Locke, Dublin, 27 May 1697' and 'Mr. Locke to Mr. Molyneux, Oates, 15 June 1697' in *Some Familiar Letters between Mr. Locke, and Several of His Friends* (London: A. and J. Churchill), pp. 219, 223.
17. 'Mr. Molyneux to Mr. Locke, Dublin, May 27, 1697' in *Some Familiar Letters*, p. 219.
18. On the influence of Epicurus, see R. Markley (1993) *Fallen Languages: Crises of Representation in Newtonian England, 1660–1740* (Ithaca: Cornell University Press) and C. Wilson (2008) *Epicureanism at the Origins of Modernity* (Oxford: Clarendon Press).
19. Blackmore wrote: 'I persuade myself the Epicurean philosophy had not liv'd so long, nor been so much esteem'd, had it not been kept alive and propagated by the famous Poem of Lucretius.' R. Blackmore (1712) *Creation* (London: S. Buckley and J. Tonson), p. xxxiii. Further references are by book and line number to this edition and are placed in parentheses following the quotation.
20. 'Mr. Molyneux to Mr. Locke, Dublin, May 27, 1697' in *Some Familiar Letters*, p. 218; J. Addison and R. Steele (1965) '(29 March 1712) *Spectator* 339' in D. F. Bond (ed.) *The Spectator: 1711–1714*, Vol. 3 (Oxford: Clarendon Press), pp. 254–61 (p. 261).
21. S. Johnson (2010) *The Lives of the Poets* in J. H. Middendorf (ed.) *The Yale Edition of the Works of Samuel Johnson*, Vol. 22 (New Haven and London: Yale University Press), p. 775.

22. (1717) *Remarks Upon Mr. Pope's Translation of Homer* (London: E. Curll), pp. 4–5.
23. (1739) 'The Preface' to *Essay on the Universe* in *Poems on Various Subjects. Many Never Printed Before* (London: Edward Cave) [no page].
24. B. Fabian (1974) 'Pope and Lucretius: Observations on "An Essay on Man"', *The Modern Language Review*, 74, 524–37 (p. 528); H. M. Solomon (1993) *The Rape of the Text: Reading and Misreading Pope's 'Essay on Man'* (Tuscaloosa: University of Alabama Press).
25. J. Paradis (1987) 'Montaigne, Boyle, and the Essay of Experience' in G. Levine and A. Rauch (eds) *One Culture: Essays in Science and Literature* (Madison: University of Wisconsin Press), pp. 59–91 (p. 60).
26. [B. Morrice] (1733) 'To the Author of the Essay on Man' in *An Essay on the Universe* (London: John Oswold), pp. 5–8; A. Pope (1950) *An Essay on Man* in M. Mack (ed.) *The Twickenham Edition of the Poems of Alexander Pope, Vol. III.i* (London: Methuen), I.131.
27. A Gentleman of the Navy (1732) *The Beauties of the Universe* (London: J. Roberts), p. 1.
28. 'universe, n.', *Oxford English Dictionary Online*, online at: www.oed.com [accessed 14 September 2014].
29. (1996) *Robert Boyle: A Free Enquiry into the Vulgarly Received Notion of Nature*, E. B. Davis and M. Hunter (eds) (Cambridge: Cambridge University Press), pp. 36–7.
30. ([n.d.] [1734]) *The Universe. A Poem. Intended to Restrain the Pride of Man* (London: T. Worrall), pp. 11–12. Further references are by page number to this edition and are placed in parentheses following the quotation.
31. *A Free Enquiry*, pp. 27–8.
32. (1716) *An Essay upon the Laws of Nature* (London: George Grierson), pp. 5–7.
33. On the dating of this poem see G. R. Potter (1932) 'Henry Baker, F. R. S. (1698-1774)', *Modern Philology*, 29, 301–21.
34. Baker produced the *Universal Spectator* psedonymously until 1733. Defoe contributed to the first number. See E. W. R. Pitcher (2004) *The Universal Spectator (London 1728–1746): An Annotated Record of the Literary Contents* (Lewiston, NY: Edwin Mellen Press).
35. Cited in G. L. E. Turner (1974) 'Henry Baker, F.R.S.: Founder of the Bakerian Lecture', *Notes and Records of the Royal Society of London*, 29:1, 53–79 (p. 57).
36. H. Baker (1739) 'The Discovery of a Perfect Plant in Semine', *Philosophical Transactions of the Royal Society*, 41, 448–54 (p. 454).
37. (1995) *The Invisible World: Early Modern Philosophy and the Invention of the Microscope* (Princeton, NJ: Princeton University Press), p. 86.
38. (1739) *Essay on the Universe* in *Poems on Various Subjects. Many Never Printed Before* (London: Edward Cave), pp. 291–390, note to II.99. Further references are by book and line number to this edition and are placed in parentheses following the quotation.
39. Crowe, *Extraterrestrial Life Debate*, pp. 4–5.
40. The *Oxford English Dictionary* gives the first use of sense 1.b. of 'universe, n.', as a 'hyptothetical or imagined cosmos', an 'alternate reality', or 'independent system', as of 1738. 'Universe, n', www.oed.com.
41. 'Stock diction' is a phrase Arthos takes from Thomas Quayle, and covers 'compound epithets; Latinisms; personifications of abstract ideas; archaisms; and technical terms' which are somehow stereotyped or conventional either

in their meaning or their formation. J. Arthos (1949) *The Language of Natural Description in Eighteenth-Century Poetry* (Ann Arbor: University of Michigan Press), pp. 2–3.
42. H. Brooke (1735) *Universal Beauty. A Poem. Part III* (London: J. Wilcox), lines 292–4. Further references are by line number to this edition and are placed in parentheses following the quotation.
43. 'To the Reader', *Essay on the Universe* in *Poems on Various Subjects* [no page].
44. 'To the Reader', *Essay on the Universe* [no page].
45. 'Dedication', *Essay on the Universe* in *Poems on Various Subjects* [no page].
46. J. Fortescue (1747) *Nature, a Poem. Tending to Shew, That Every Part in the Moral World Is, in a Beautiful Variety, Regularly Ordered and Adjusted [...]* (London: M. Cooper); Fortescue (1748) *Nature a Poem; Being an Attempt Towards a Vindication of Providence[...]* (London: M. Cooper); Fortescue (1750) *Science: An Epistle on It's Decline and Revival [...]* (Oxford: J. Fletcher); Fortescue (1751) *Science; a Poem, (in a Religious View) on It's Decline and Revival* (Oxford: J. Fletcher).
47. (1956) '[Early April 1797] Letter to Joseph Cottle' in E. L. Griggs (ed.) *Collected Letters of Samuel Taylor Coleridge, Vol.1* (Oxford: Clarendon Press), p. 320.
48. N. Jackson (2009) 'Rhyme and Reason: Erasmus Darwin's Romanticism', *Modern Language Quarterly*, 70:2, 171–94.
49. 'Preface', *Essay on the Universe* [no page].

6
Metering Mineral Resources
Verse Jewels on Earth's Treasures

Kevin L. Cope

Shortly after the calendrical but well within the long eighteenth century, John Scafe, a poet of unknown qualifications who sought the favour of the Geological Society of London, unveiled his *King Coal's Levee, Or Geological Etiquette* (1819). It is an unprecedented and apparently inimitable attempt to combine Miltonizing mock-heroic ribaldry with deep mineralogical knowledge in a sometimes comical, always ploddingly didactic portrayal of the treasures within the earth. Simple in conception but long in execution, Scafe's attempt to update *The Splendid Shilling* (1701) into *The Splendid Schist* juxtaposes 1200 lines of mineralogical banter against a 20,000 word critical apparatus – an apparatus in which the scientific basis of Scafe's every quip, turn or witticism is colloquially explained. The economically attuned Scafe pens a compendium of a drama in which King Coal, the personification of the most energetic and profitable of underground materials, summons his courtiers, earth's assorted courtier gems, stones, substances and rocks, to his castle:

> King COAL, the mighty hero of the mine,
> – Sprung from a dingy, but a far-fam'd line,
> Who, fathoms deep, in peace our earth possest,
> Curb'd but in sway by ocean's billowy breast, –
> Would hold a Levee.[1]

Following a roll-call of attendant sylphs, naiads and sprites, the poem surveys a large ensemble of rocky suitors who, in a previously untried poetic strategy, appear in order of stratification:

> Duke GRANITE first; – a hoary-headed sire,
> Yet blest with symptoms of primæval fire,

> That beam'd across the traces of decay,
> As vivid tints illumine departing day.
> Of *solid* parts, of judgment ne'er asleep,
> And through life been reckon'd *very deep*.
> [...]
> Next, Marquis Slate that aged pair reliev'd,
> And was indeed most graciously receiv'd.[2]

For the remainder of the poem, Scafe struggles to balance his encyclopaedist's drive to catalogue all the minerals with his post-Popean taste for quick turns, concise wit and whimsically compact dramatization. He hovers, and hovers for a very long time, over the faintly drawn boundaries between teaching and delighting – between offering a dramatic verse comedy in which stones are the stars and delivering an informative appraisal of the mineral world and the science appertaining thereto.

The untalented Scafe may stumble over the stones that he turns, but few can rival him for the novelty as well as the totality of his commitment to versified geology. Admittedly, the idea of making a 'light science' accessible to partially educated readers who seek edifying entertainment was far from new in the later, longer eighteenth century. Even specialist disciplines such as entomology gave rise to pop science handbooks.[3] Nevertheless, Scafe's project remains, if not innovative, at least close to unique. For most of the sciences that underwent popularization, the glamour of the topic distracts readers from the oddity of verse bowdlerization. The brilliance of the stars *ipso facto* justifies artful versification of astronomical lore; the social behaviour of animals encourages the composition of allegories; and the majesty of the main eases the transition from oceanography to rhapsody. In the dirtier case of geology, inspiration arises by fits and starts. Any poetaster can laud diamonds or describe mountains, but few scribblers hear the muse when gawking at aluminium ore. Fewer still enthuse over marl. The long eighteenth century was a period that experienced an unusually high number of earthquakes and volcanic eruptions; developed travel and expedition technology allowing for journeys to underground venues such as prominent mines or 'show caves'; found cachet in those premium clay pits that sustained fine plate foundries, geology, mineralogy; and saw plain old rock-hounding enjoy an extraordinarily high prestige – a prestige that could even attract ambitious rhymesters.

This chapter seeks to open a shaft leading to the mother lode of subterranean verse that transects the long eighteenth century. It aims to use the space available within a preliminary study to define a few categories that will help to explain, organize and revive this large but dispersed literature – a literature that often appears within other prose compositions and that, therefore, eludes modern search techniques. Admittedly, it is easy to encourage the appreciation of a verse decidedly lacking in subtlety. Falling rocks, swinging sledgehammers, merciless pickaxes, explosions, gushers, blasts of steam, noxious gases and excavations are hardly the material of the refined poetry of insinuation, irony and telling detail that has flourished since the Romantic period. Poets of the eighteenth century also still contended with expectations pertinent to decorum. Possession of a store of mineral or mining lore sufficient to fill out a poem of even middling length could suggest that the poet's pedigree fell short of nobility. Worse, precedents among 'the ancients' for the introduction of mundane minerals into exalted verse were few in number. Even mechanically-minded painters, such as Joseph Wright of Derby, tended to focus on process more than on substance – to depict the use of an astrolabe or the research activity of an alchemist rather than to portray the harvesting of the metals that comprise laboratory equipment.

As the excerpt from John Scafe's mineralogical mini-epic suggests, advancement of the economy is a key idea for cutters of gem verse. Heavy-handed in its celebration of utility and relentless in its pushing of themes no matter what the cost for technique, underground verse reminds readers that poets in and after the Augustan age expected sound and sense not only to echo one another, but to coincide. Read in retrospect, eighteenth-century neoclassical poets and critics, with their rules, unities, decorum, precepts and opinions, seem nascent formalists, yet the emergence of a utility-obsessed verse that emulates neoclassical practices reaffirms the dominance of substance over style. Scafe, after all, offers an inventory – a roll-call – of the minerals, which is a gesture that harkens back to Homer's and Virgil's catalogues of ships, weapons and personnel. In its assertive presentation of hard mineral objects, though, it redirects attention to the content that epic conventions organize. Eruptions of heroic formality often occur amidst avalanches of plodding practicality. Mining expert Thomas Heton, for example, probably never expected to hear opera house ovations following the reading of his highly technical, detailed, but artless handbook, *Some Account of the Mines, and the Advantages of them to this Kingdom* (1707). Heavy-handed Heton offers adamantine advice on everything from prospecting, to shaft construction, to dealing with miners' superstitions. His relentless celebration of mineral wealth will never qualify him for membership in the social sensitivity association. Yet, at the conclusion of his preface, which hammers away at all the benefits of mining without the slightest genuflection toward belles-lettres, a place is allocated for a panegyric by 'Mr. Yalden' (Thomas Yalden [1670–1736]), who sounds as if he would compose a petrified version of Alexander Pope's *Windsor Forest* (1713):

> How are thy Realms, *Triumphant Britain*, blest!
> Inrich't with more than all the distant *West.*
> Thrice happy Land! from whose Indulgent Womb,
> Such unexhausted store of Riches come!
> Whose *Native Mines* a noble Fund maintain,
> To humble *France*, and check the Pride of *Spain.*
> Thy Sons no more betrayed with hopes of Gain,
> Shall tempt the dangers of a Faithless *Main*;
> Trafficke no more abroad for *Foreign* Spoil,
> Supply'd with Riches from their *Native* Soil.[4]

Yalden's effusion is notable for its unremitting acceptance of the Augustan way of doing poetic business. Unambiguously end-stopped lines vie with eye-exhausting clarity, unchallenging prosopopœia and obvious personification to highlight the denotative, intensely semantic communication in a way that would make a quasar look like candlelight. It is as if the shimmer of valuable minerals shook off all alloy, closing any distance between meaning and ornament while sending out shock waves against Britain's bamboozled competitors. Yalden's is a verse in which form and content converge and co-operate in a way that eludes superior but audience-concerned poets such as the effect-chasing Pope and Dryden. Those two greater authors set up long progresses to culminating crescendos, but Yalden and his ilk work in the ever-exciting present, living perpetually in the climactic moment.

What Yalden and Heton epitomize is a characteristic seldom associated with the complex critical postures of our day: simple and simplifying confidence. Everyday poets, such as those who applaud the mining industry, take it for granted that heroic diction ennobles any topic and that colloquial enterprises, such as the harvesting of earth's bounty, merit an epic treatment. Free of mock-heroic puckishness, geological poets assume that everyone recognizes the Homeric potential of bauxite, copper and coal. The unparalleled virtuoso of these uninhibited poets is surely Edward Manlove, who presents in *The Liberties and Customs of the Lead-Mines* (1653) the full range of mining lore: from the discovery of plentiful veins to the eventual inheritance of mines, in a rock-solid, appropriately thumping heroic verse. Manlove, whose verse renderings of mining lore address such workaday and even legal topics as the staking of claims, the sale of assets and the maintenance of mining equipment, never backs away nor modulates his relentlessly grandiose tone when confronted with the dark side of the mineral industry. In one passage, for example, he proves himself something of a local Homer not, as the ancient bard might, by presenting Olympic-quality funerary games, but, rather, by recounting the procedures for dealing with the remains of mine accident victims:

> If by mischance a Miner damped be,
> Or on the Mine be slain by Chance-medley,
> The Barghmaster or else his Deputie
> Must view the Corps before it buried be,
> And take inquest by Jury, who shall try
> By what mischance the Miner there did die;
> No Coroner or Eschetor aught may do
> Nor of dead bodies may not take their view.[5]

It would be easy enough to dismiss Manlove as a quirky versifier – as someone who aims to amuse his audience deploying mainstream techniques to portray offbeat subject matter. He, however, lived during the development rather than the maturation of the mock-heroic tradition. The remainder of his poem certifies him as free of wit and irony as organic fruit is free of pesticide. Manlove displays a respectful relish for language, composing long passages comprised of vocabulary-building lists of mining terminology. Few poets in the history of rhyme could accomplish more in the art of compiling dialect-originated nouns:

> Bunnings, Polings, Stemples, Forks, and Slyder,
> Stoprice, Yokings, Soletrees, Roach, and Ryder,
> Water holes, Wind holes, Veyns, Coe-shafts and Woughs,
> Main Rakes, Cross Rakes, Brown-henns, Budles and Soughs,
> Break-offs, and Buckers, Randum of the Rake,
> Freeing, and Chasing of the Stole to th' Stake,
> Startling of oar, Smiltings, and driving drifts,
> Primgaps, Root-works, Flat-works, Pipe-works, Shifts,
> Cauke, Sparr, Lid-stones, Twitches, Daulings, and Pees,
> Fell, Bous, and Knock-barke, Forstid-oar, and Tees,
> Bing-place, Barmont Court, Barghmaster, and Stowes,
> Crosses, Holes, Hange-benches, Turntree, and Coes,
> Founder-meers, Taker-meers, Lot, Cope, and Sumps,

Stickings, and Stringes of oar, Wash-oar and Pumps,
Corses, Clivies, Deads, Meers, Groves, Rake-soil, the Gange,
Binge-oar, a Spindle, a Lampturn, a Fange,
Fleaks, Knockings, Doestid, Trunks and Sparks of oar,
Sole of the Rake, Sytham, and many more.[6]

These lists celebrate the arcana of the mineral trade in the same way that Homer honours the inventory of warships or the roster of weapons. This capacity for utter straightforwardness – for the uncritical affirmation of not only the heroic status of industry but also of the wonderful orderliness with which its calamities are addressed – is more than a talent that we may well regard as justifiably discarded. Manlove dares readers to treat his work as a serious anthropological and philological effort. Having noted the roughness and modesty of miners' jargon, he challenges readers to sample the wild side of linguistic life: 'Both strange and uncouth, if you some would see, / Read these rough verses here Compos'd by me.'[7] Manlove thus opens a window to a re-evaluation of the full range of good and bad Augustan poetry: verse that tempts modern critics to look for dark sub-texts or for allegories of exploitation but that also teaches readers to measure good against bad, to compare competence against blundering and to revel in the positive balance resulting from such assessments. Poetry such as Manlove's measures the distance between what contemporary interpreters want the eighteenth century to be and what neoclassical writers affirmed that it was.

Long eighteenth-century telluric poets wielded considerable expertise in the art of not only superimposing form upon, but of actively and empirically seeing artful form in, natural, mineralized experience. The eighteenth century was the first great period of show caves (caves that tourists would pay to inspect) and of cave-like installations that, for the price of admission, would stir the imagination. Both species of show cave attracted poets. One master of the art of excited seeing, William Seward, stylizes, in 1801, the great Yordes Cave into a Sinai-style tablet of divine instruction, the content of which remains vague but the effect of which is sublime. The entrance to the cave – what might be called Seward's ticket window – takes an outright textual form:

With stedfast eyes I now did look around,
The Alphabet in letters all I found:
The figures all of every sort and size,
Are here expos'd to view of human eyes.
But now to let the cunning artist know,

> His tools their forms did never undergo.
> In size exact they at small distance stand,
> Indeed they're form'd by the Almighty's hand.[8]

Inspection then shows this rocky text to include the names of 'all since Adam', or at least all those who played a role in the soteriological history of the world. As Seward takes his reader through the cave, the naturally – or, rather, supernaturally – occurring mineral formations become increasingly complex. Deep within the cave, he, unveiling stalagmites and stalactites, encounters a veritable primer on the history of columns: 'the Orders all contain / The Tuscan, Doric, and Corinthian'.[9] Seward finds himself lost in a mixture of purposes: in the simultaneous suggestion that Yordes Cave is an orderly history of architecture and that Yordes Cave should stimulate visitors who enjoy wild profusion, chaotic variety and unaccountable sublimity. He seeks two diverging goals: he wants to control or at least guide perception of the cave, but he also would pitch up the cave into the supernal realm where reason is overawed and passions are aroused. The result is a strange, as well as inadvertent, awkwardness or even comedy as Seward's imaginary visitors stumble through a bizarre miscellany of mineral forms and mineral messages.

Seward's poem moves through a cycle that is common enough in Augustan, neoclassical and heroic verse. The poet shapes what is seen, sees it and then interprets what is seen in order to confirm his and others' expectations. A poet such as William Seward follows this course while touring a putatively natural cave, but other show cave enthusiasts work in manufactured underground habitats. Jane Brereton pens an offbeat poem in 1735 set in Queen Caroline's grotto, a cave-like environment in which the aforementioned royal personage installed busts of prominent virtuosi. The slightly incoherent storyboard for this poem features the sorcerer Merlin. He brags about his achievements but, while viewing the busts of the Royal Society members, admits that their feats exceed his own. Although the busts in Queen Caroline's grotto accrue from human artifice, they nevertheless seem to emanate naturally intelligible ideas in the same way as do Seward's divinely wrought stalactites. In the visages of the worthies of science, Merlin discovers indications of their accomplishments:

> Here, by the Sculptor's Art, are well design'd,
> The Busts of Those, who dignify'd their Kind.
> Locke, Boyle, and Newton, Woolaston, and Clarke,
> Brighten those Paths which Ignorance made dark;

> Reason, and Arts, Truth moral, and Divine;
> In their immortal Works, unclouded shine.
> Resemblance, the well-judging Eye delights,
> And th' active Soul, to semblant Thought excites:
> Intent, Sh' exerts her Faculties, and Powers,
> Rises in Thought, in Contemplation towers.
> Reason, that Emanation of the Mind,
> Breaks forth in Locke; diffusive, and refin'd.
> The moral Duties *Woolaston* displays,
> And Nature's Laws, the firm Foundation lays.
> In *Clarke*, the Christian Purity appears,
> Reveal'd Religion, he divinely clears.[10]

The initial task – shaping what should be seen – is outsourced to an anonymous sculptor and to Queen Caroline. The detection of that pre-installed meaning remains the work of the poet. Placement of the sublimities in an underground facility, in the cool shadows, facilitates this process by occluding the first steps in the production of this cave, thereby emphasizing the appearance of discovery.

For Brereton and Seward, caves offer the poetic equivalent of a *tabula rasa*: a slate that is all but blank. In virtue of its darkness, deepness, unfamiliarity and seemingly unlimited capacities, the cave provides an enormous but well-primed canvas on which to project any of a thousand ideas. It captures the hope of amateurish as well as accomplished eighteenth-century poets that almost anything could be versified and that verse could accomplish almost any assignment involving teaching or entertaining. Poetry pertaining to the world's underground thus exhibits an astounding range. Heroic verse is not the only available genre. In *The Hill of Caves* (1818), for example, William Read portrays a ferocious, pitted landscape in the Spenserian stanza, all with an aim to create a folkloric atmosphere:

> Aspiring mountain! Could thy Genius speak,
> What tales of other times would charm the ear!
> For there are monuments on every peak
> Which prove the hand of man once mighty here –
> Altars on high, and caverns deep and drear,
> Whereon old scars of mining steel remain: –
> The mystic Druid, lonely and severe,
> Thought human temples, as their builders, vain;
> And worthier of a God this cliff-piled mountain fane.[11]

Read invokes a remarkable combination of industrial history, imaginary antiquity and religious kitsch by way of highlighting the dark otherness of this cavern-pitted mound. Literary explorer John Hutton, in contrast, takes the piecemeal approach, punctuating his 1781 tour of the caves around Ingleborough with a smattering of literary quotations and allusions. He takes a line from here or there, whether from Milton or from folk rhymes, as the need, mood and particular cave environment requires. Always sourcing new ingredients for his pastiche, Hutton specializes in quick turns and juxtapositions of mood. In visiting a spring that emerges from the earth in Giggleswickscar, Hutton conjures the Romantic ambience of this venue but then immediately turns to a doggerel poem by a certain 'drunken *Barnaby*' that comically describes the ebbing and flowing of this water source.[12] Alternation between sources – vacillation between the hieratic Milton and the babbling Barnaby – underwrites a kind of meta-poem in which the interplay of quotations demonstrates the immense and diverse literary possibility embedded in the English underground.

The remarkable tonal flexibility of the eighteenth-century underground idiom – this post-Shakespearian ability to oscillate between low comedy and epic tragedy, between Will Kempe and David Garrick – suggests that subterranean poetry not only contains but is fundamentally *about* variety. The tendency to accept neoclassical theory at face value, and thereby to assume that eighteenth-century verse aspires to thematic coherence, leads to the neglect of disruptive variety as a theme, substance or even core of Augustan rhymes. In long eighteenth-century science, the paradoxical practice of unified, even teleological research about miscellaneousness is easily resolved by neo-Baconian virtuosi such as John Ray, Joseph Glanvill or John Woodward. These men were data, artefact and anecdote collectors who perused, reviewed and otherwise recorded the infinite variety of nature in the expectation that overarching physical laws would emerge from the interplay of diverse evidence. As is demonstrated by various productions, such as Alexander Pope's anecdote-filled verse essays and James Thomson's globally descriptive verse, the proposing of a definitive topic or theme for a composition often only preceded or justified the roving perusal of scattered topics or reports. *The Vanity of Human Wishes* (1749) may address the single issue of ego-supported futility, yet its lines are filled with assorted accounts of celebrity mishaps that occurred in the many scattered venues that our extensive planet provides.

Since the time of Aristotle, poetry has abided adjacent to the parapoetic discipline of drama. Eighteenth-century playwrights, especially those who produced comical entertainments or theatrical spectacles, regarded earth's mineral abundance as a suitable background for easygoing and entertaining, but nevertheless purposive, encounters with a high level of variety that occupied their more sober counterparts in the natural sciences. Entertainer John O'Keeffe revels in the rough diversity of mining culture. One long comical scene in his *Wicklow Mountains* (1797) centres on a caricature of a prospector named 'Dross', who is at once rustic Irishman, a social climber, a virtuoso and an enthusiast with visions of great prosperity from his stake in the mines:

DROSS: Productive! The stream shall equal the Portugal Tagus, the Italian Padus, the Thracian Hebrus, the oriental Ganges, and the Asiatic Pactolus.

DON[NYBROOK]: Oh he has some wise stupid plans for improving his acres. An odd young fellow. (*aside*.) Why Sir, the hills are stony, but by the help of a little gunpowder and undermining, as you remark, they might produce grain.

DROSS: And dust, just so, golden grain, and lovely dust! so pure, we want no refiner, my lucky boy. (*Claps him on the back*.)[13]

In other scenes, O'Keeffe offers dazzling performances composed of variations on the theme of colourful mining jargon:

DROSS: I tell you it black Jack, mere zink, is it soluble to aqua regulis? never mind my lad, I'll bring it to liquefaction, tho' you've got a little cash by it, you mus'nt set up for a gentleman, white and delicate as my hands seem, I have blacken'd them with charcoal. I despise the fear of vapours
[...]

SULL[IVAN]: Oh no, Sir, I'm sure you understand, transmutation, distillation, sublimation, calcination, evaporation, volatilization, exhalation, dephlequation, concentration, rectification, saturation, crystallization, precipitation, conflagration, and botheration.

FRANK[LIN]: What could Sir Richard mean by chusing such a guardian as this for me—certainly touched! (aside)

SUL: As to the edict of dioclesian or Pope John, that we mustn' mind either in our pursuit in the mountains, or over the mountains, after metallurgy, antimony, mercury, ductility, alchemy, and ballinamonyoro, you may

FRANK: perceive Sir, that I have had a solid fixity over the furnace of Homogenous fluids, as taught us by Boyle, and Bacon—
Boil'd bacon! a curst vulgar fellow this! No, he shall have no concern in my addresses to his daughter.[14]

Clearly no technician, O'Keeffe conducts a symphonic pop-style performance of mineral music, enjoying the harsh creativity of ore's orators while accessing a tradition of entertainment through artful deployment of jargon. This tradition began with Dryden's *Annus Mirabilis* (1667) and Butler's *Hudibras* (1661–77). O'Keeffe combines delighting with teaching, per Aristotle, granting his chortling audience a modest introduction to the terminology current among geologists.

The strange convergence of, if not delight, then extreme emotion and hyperbolic excitement with Aristotelian didacticism comes to a grotesquely perfect climax in John Sargent's popular but puzzling 1785 would-be masterpiece, *The Mine: A Dramatic Poem*. It is a versified closet drama that retells the story of Paul Hiffernan's *The Heroine of the Cave* (1775) – another overwrought work that was itself derived from the already hypertrophic *The Cave of Idra* by Henry Jones.[15] The lineaments of this melodramatic tale are simple and predictable: following a duel, a nobleman is sentenced to death, but, owing to his lineage, receives a commuted sentence of lifelong labour in the mines of Istria, which is a sentence tantamount to gradual capital punishment. The nobleman's adoring wife follows him into the punitive pits, where they undergo excruciating torments while experiencing the outer limits of mutual devotion. In the end, the loser in the aforementioned duel recovers and nobly sues his prince for a pardon for his old antagonist, whereupon fortunes are restored and everyone lives happily ever after above ground, in the full and happy light of day. In the hands of the poetical Sargent, this simple story becomes a rack on which to hang a variety of striking scenes and special effects. It is an indication that, even in 1785, the drive towards organic form and aesthetic coherence that was about to emerge in Wordsworth and Coleridge had not yet picked up all those seeking passage aboard the trolley of English poetry. *The Mine* attempts the impossible task of combining miscellaneousness of mood – it ranges from the offhand songs of whimsical sylphs to tormented, desperate soliloquies spoken in the deepest abysms of the earth – with the encyclopaedic review of minerals and their properties and a heavy admixture of moral exemplification and sentimental effusion. Accompanied by a preface that credits the idea for the inclusion of gnomes and other 'subterraneous spirits' to mock-heroic expert

Alexander Pope, and encumbered with an extensive critical apparatus that includes annotations on a vast array of geological phenomena, *The Mine* veers in every possible direction from modern to postmodern taste.[16] It explores a bewildering array of reactions to and explanations for what its stock, stereotyped characters experience underground. On the one hand, Sargent, in the songs that he assigns to the company of gnomes, celebrates the wonder and above all the foreignness of the underground world:

> Ye Gnomes, ye puissant Spirits, who delight
> To range th' unfathomable depths of night;
> Who these stupendous realms undaunted sway,
> To whom this cold is heat, this darkness day;
> Speed thro' the earthy layers your fluid course,
> Loose the soft sand, the marle obstructive force;
> Of latent rills the bubbling fount unlock,
> And gem with crystal every glistening rock.[17]

Into these enthusiasms, however, Sargent infuses long passages ballasted by heavy annotation elucidating the properties of earth's resources:

> 'Midst flinty crags, on bed of glittering spars,
> Spread the red Mineral of indignant Mars:
> Tho' fierce, he rushes to the Magnet's side,
> And as an ardent bridegroom clasps his bride[.][18]

Listeners to, or readers of, Sargent's sprawling passages may well sustain a bit of emotional vertigo as this most vacillating of poets wavers between the whimsies of the theatrical intermezzo, the flights of emotion experienced by his characters and what look for all the world like versified encyclopaedia entries. This extraordinary variation in tone coincides with a similar variation in metre. According to the mood, the rank of the speaker, the situation and the level of emotional pressure, Sargent intersperses his main measure, blank verse, with incantations in heroic couplets; ballads; odes; and, of course, his frequent (and often distracting, albeit informative) footnotes. Indeed, Sargent is probably one of the few poets who somewhat successfully annotates an impassioned song. It would be easy enough to suggest that he is tone-deaf with regard to the myriad variations within his work and that he utterly lacks any sense for dramatic staging, as is evidenced by the bathetic effect of his lead character's baleful address to a wall of rocks:

> [...] Ye rocks,
> Witness her tender spirit, her mild zeal,
> That blunts affliction's edge![19]

At stake, however, is something far more, if not profound, then at least pertinent to the history of verse, especially that subset of verse caught in the interstices between what are too easily designated as the 'classical' or 'Romantic' periods and modes. In his excess of enthusiasm of all kinds, whether for unending devotion or for the extraction of ore, Sargent attempts to create poetry that is not only evocative and compelling in the Coleridgean sense, but evocative and compelling with respect to *every* aspect of experience, or at least to that huge range of experience that pertains to earthen treasures. Sargent tries to accord, if not sublimity, at least decorously grand status to an astounding range of phenomena. He finds an appropriately epic articulation for everything from fossils – 'The barren Petra, giant queen' (an ejaculation that elicits a footnote on competing theories about fossilization) – to the bad smells attending mine exhalations:

> [...] What odours now
> Breathe thro' the winding cavern, and o'erpow'r
> My drowsy sense?[20]

He then goes on to whirlpools, volcanoes and, in sum, nearly every extreme or offbeat phenomenon that nature can deploy. Unlike neoclassical poets, such as Dryden or Thomson who set out to accomplish primarily one purpose (whether the condemnation of satiric butts or the description of landscapes), and unlike more exalted yet also more monaural poets, such as Shelley or Keats (who, in each verse, intone a single mood), Sargent is a multi-purpose poet: a poet for whom the variety of the mineral kingdom enables the simultaneous use of every tool in the poetic workshop.

Unusual juxtapositions or even contrasts of tone and purpose also abound in such theatrical spectacles as Ralph Wewitzer's musical pantomime, *The Magic Cavern* (1785), where fancy and frivolity arise from more-or-less correct use of mineral lore in the on-stage evocation of fantasy underground environments.[21] In Reverend Mr Horton's *Account of the Earthquakes which Happened at Leghorn in Italy, Between the 5th and 16th of January, 1742*, readers experience a neo-Elizabethan take on seismic activity as the author pens a sonnet on the might of the earth and the moral message of mass destruction.[22] Even more extravagantly,

Stephen Duck, the poet as well as the manager of Merlin's cave, a 'Necromantick' tourist attraction themed to sorcery, takes a sublime, pseudo-Pindaric approach to the underground as a venue from which mysteriously entertaining as well as clumsily satiric prophecies may issue. In *The Year of Wonders* (1737), for Duck, it is the clash of various forms of incompetence that gives rise to sublimity. An impromptu excavation reveals a discarded urn bearing an inscription in the degenerate Latin of the Roman church – language which, the story goes, Duck, his neighbours and a superannuated priest translated from 'Monkish Rhimes' into 'a sort of a Prose Translation' and thence into passable Augustan verse.[23] From the collision of languages, verse idioms and avocations emerges a poem that can lend form to a highly heterogenous event.

Stephen Duck may be something of a human masterpiece in our own counter-culturally focused eyes. Every idiom, including that of subterranean poetry, also includes, in its canon, a genuine masterpiece. Qualifying for this role is *Wonders of the Peak* (1681) by Charles Cotton, which presents a sprawling tour in couplets of the Derbyshire Peak District. Analysis and annotation of Cotton's detailed rhyming review of early outdoor ecotourism would require, if not a book, at least an extended study. The space of this introductory chapter allows only for an acknowledgment of Cotton's extraordinary range, which extends from comic reportage of odd local customs to elaborate settings in which baroque lighting and offbeat perspectives create scenes worthy of Eidophusikon impresario Philippe de Loutherbourg. Cotton's polyvalent poem not only covers the full index of geological attractions in the Derby area, but it also spans the full spectrum of tonal and genre possibilities: from theological questions about the wisdom of God in inflicting so pitted a landscape on so humble a people, to critical remarks on accommodations, to summaries of tourist attractions and to sidebar comments on special attractions. One cave, Eldon's Hole, elicits Cotton's nimble bathos, as this man for all moods and poet for all possibilities draws together elements from geology, theology, sublimity and hair loss therapy:

> A formidable fissure gapes so wide,
> Deep, black, and full of horror, that who dare
> Look down into the chasm, and keeps his hair
> From lifting off his hat, either has none,
> Or for more modest curls cashiers his own.
> It were injurious, I must confess,

> By mine to measure braver courages:
> But when I peep into 't, I must declare
> My heart still beats, and eyes with horror stare.
> And he, that standing on the brink of Hell,
> Can carry it so unconcern'd, and well
> As to betray no fear, is, certainly,
> A better christian, or a worse than I.[24]

Strange, bumpy and offbeat as well as off the beat, startling, sublime and appropriately awkward, Cotton's guileless and not altogether mocking heroic verse captures an Augustan sense for promising yet inscrutable multiplicity – a taste that we have lost. Cotton finds it exciting to gawk not into a Miltonic vast abyss but into yet another partially explored sinkhole. He speculates on how much might be learned while also testing various possible reactions and taking time to comment on his own shortcomings and on the incommodious character of travel.

For this Columbus, the ocean may be no larger than an underground pool, yet the combination of moods and opinions that Cotton brings to his three-hour visit well exceeds anything found in the monaural logbooks of the aforementioned and determinedly optimistic Genoan explorer. By metering earth's mineral resources – by affirming that the standard heroic measure can provide a baseline from which to measure the tonal, ideological and semantic deviations of assorted and miscellaneous phenomena – Cotton shows that the metre will run for a long time and that far more research will be required to measure both the value and the extent of long-eighteenth-century subterranean poetry. Perhaps in that time we will also recognize the role that offbeat rhymesters such as Cotton played in creating our own modern conception of deep, cosmological time: in using humble metre and rhythmic verse to discover the deep antiquity and deeper future of our planet and of the universe through which it rolls.[25]

Notes

1. J. Scafe (1819) *King Coal's Levee, Or Geological Etiquette, with Explanatory Notes. To which is added the Council of the Metals*, 2nd edn (Alnwick: J. Graham), lines 8–12.
2. Scafe, *King Coal's Levee*, lines 84–9 and 108–9.
3. For a discussion of the interaction between entomology, popular science and theology see K. L. Cope (forthcoming b) 'Tea at a Hexagonal Table? Gregarious Insects and the Outer Limits of Eighteenth-Century Sociability' in N. Col and A. Cossic (eds) *Transversales: Sociability in the Enlightenment*

(Paris: Le Manuscrit); and also K. L. Cope (forthcoming a) 'Notes from Many Hands: Pierre Lyonnet's Redesign of Friedrich Christian Lesser's Insecto-Theology', *Religion and the Age of Enlightenment*.
4. T. Heton (1707) *Some Account of the Mines, and the Advantages of them to this Kingdom* (London: W.B. for John Wyat), 'The Preface'.
5. E. Manlove (1653) *The Liberties and Customes of the Lead-Mines Within the Wapentake of Wirkswarth in the County of Derby* (London: [n. pub.]), p. 7.
6. Manlove, *The Liberties and Customes*, p. 8.
7. Manlove, *The Liberties and Customes*, p. 8.
8. W. Seward (1801) *A Tour to Yordes Cave* (Kirkby Lonsdale: A. Foster), p. 12.
9. Seward, *A Tour to Yordes Cave*, pp. 22–3.
10. J. Brereton (1735) *Merlin, A Poem* (London: Edward Cave), pp. 14–16.
11. See W. Read (1818) *The Hill of Caves* (London: Henry Colburn), p. 15, Canto I, stanza xiii.
12. See J. Hutton (1781) *A Tour to the Caves, in the Environs of Ingleborough and Settle, in the West-Riding of Yorkshire*, 2nd edn (London: [n. pub.]), pp. 47–8.
13. J. O'Keeffe (1798) *The Wicklow Mountains: Or, The Lad of the Hills, a Comic Opera* in *The Dramatic Works of John O'Keeffe*, 4 vols (London: T. Woodfall), II, pp. 111–92, III.i. (p. 175).
14. O'Keeffe, *The Wicklow Mountains*, III.i, pp. 176, 181.
15. J. Sargent (1796) *The Mine: A Dramatic Poem*, 3rd edn (London: T. Cadell, Jun. and W. Davies). For an account of the composite history of *The Heroine of the Cave*, see (March 1797) *The European Magazine and London Review*, Vol. 31 (London: Philological Society of London), p. 358. *The Caves of Idra* by Henry Jones remained unfinished at the end of his life. It must, therefore, have been written (in part) before 1770. It has no true publication date because it never made its way into print and remained in manuscript form.
16. Sargent, *The Mine*, p. 7.
17. Sargent, *The Mine*, p. 7.
18. Sargent, *The Mine*, p. 8.
19. Sargent, *The Mine*, p. 33.
20. Sargent, *The Mine*, pp. 28, 27.
21. See R. Wewitzer (1785) *Songs, Choruses, and Recitative in the Pantomime of the Magic Cavern; Of, Virtue's Triumph* (London: J. Almon).
22. Rev. Mr Horton (1750) *Account of the Earthquakes which Happened at Leghorn in Italy, Between the 5th and 16th of January, 1742* (London: E. Withers).
23. See S. Duck (1737) *The Year of Wonders, Being a Literal and Poetical Translation of an Old Latin Prophecy Found Near Merlin's Cave* (London: J. Johnson).
24. C. Cotton (1744) *The Wonders of the Peak*, 2nd edn (Nottingham: [n. pub.]), p. 23.
25. An excellent evaluation of the emergence, during the early modern to modern period, of an idea of deep time can be found in S. J. Gould (1987) *Time's Arrow, Time's Cycle: Myth and Metaphor in the Discovery of Geological Time* (Cambridge: Harvard University Press).

7
Deserted Village and Animated Nature
An Ecocritical Approach to Oliver Goldsmith
Brycchan Carey

The eighteenth century has not until now been fertile ground for ecocritics, unless one includes a host of articles concerning the relationship of the early Romantic poets with nature. The attitudes of pre-Romantic eighteenth-century poets towards the natural environment has for the most part been examined through the dichotomy of town and country, through the lens of the sublime and picturesque or as part of a neoclassical tradition of pastoral verse. Taken together, this body of critical literature offers considerable insights into the ways in which eighteenth-century poets engaged with landscape in particular, but the methodology is often dated, frequently emerging from Marxist approaches rooted in the political conditions of the mid-twentieth century. Since the 1990s, by contrast, critics studying many periods of literary history have offered newly theorized readings of literature's engagement with the environment under the banner of 'ecocriticism'. This critical approach has been defined as 'the study of the relationship between literature and the physical environment' or, even more broadly, as 'the study of the relationship between the human and the non-human, throughout human cultural history'.[1] The approach encompasses a broad range of methodologies, but most ecocritics emphasize the political utility of ecocriticism in the face of 'the most pressing contemporary issue of all, namely, the global environmental crisis', as well as it being 'unique amongst contemporary literary and cultural theories because of its close relationship with the science of ecology'.[2]

Ecology and environmental crisis may seem remote to the eighteenth century, anachronistic even, but this overlooks the fact that the century saw the beginnings of both agrarian and industrial revolution, the adoption of fossil fuel as a major energy source, the start of exponential population growth, as well as the development of scientific methodologies and technologies that would enable precise understanding of environment, evolution and ecology in the following century. At the same time, a great many eighteenth-century writers were closely involved with nature, whether as farmers, naturalists, explorers or simply lovers of the pastoral and the picturesque. Despite its reputation for an urban, sophisticated, satirical or sentimental worldview characterized by artificial poetic diction, from Alexander Pope's views on landscape gardening, through Erasmus Darwin's poetic musings on evolutionary theory, to William Blake's invocation of the Satanic steam-powered Albion Mill, eighteenth-century poets were deeply immersed in the natural world, and increasingly aware of the threats it faced. Critics so minded may discern in eighteenth-century literary discussions of nature both the origins of the science of ecology and the origins of the current global environmental crisis.

This chapter offers an ecocritical reading of a well-known eighteenth-century poem that dramatizes a local social and environmental catastrophe: the abandonment of a rural community and its reversion to nature. Oliver Goldsmith's *The Deserted Village* is by any measure an environmental poem. It represents an environmental crisis, takes a moral position regarding it, and is throughout informed by the poet's own interest in natural history and the rural economy. Although Goldsmith's political views are somewhat fuzzy and not entirely consistent with contemporary debates, the poem's attempt to take a position in regard to environmental change makes it an ideal candidate for an ecocritical study. Such an approach, however, whether in relation to Goldsmith's poem or to any other work of eighteenth-century literature, must go beyond vague generalizations about landscape or currents in eighteenth-century natural history. Instead, we should respond to the countryside historian Oliver Rackham's lament that 'many historians confine themselves to the written word or, worse still, to the literary word; they are reluctant to put on their boots and to see what the land itself, and the things that grow on it, have to say.'[3] In the case of *The Deserted Village*, booting up and visiting the site is not literally possible. Nevertheless, a practical understanding of botany, zoology and hydrology can and should be brought to bear on the poem's depiction of the village after its abandonment, and may help us to understand one of the most enduring debates in literary history: the location of the community at the heart of the poem. At the same time, reading the poem alongside Goldsmith's own writings in natural history may aid our understanding of the text's ecological significance as much as its social and cultural importance.

Neither Oliver Goldsmith (1730–74) nor *The Deserted Village* (1770) require much introduction. Goldsmith, the Anglo-Irish poet, playwright, historian and novelist, was at the height of his literary career when the poem was composed.[4] In approximately 400 lines, it contrasts the happy, bucolic, sentimental past of a village called Auburn with its desolate and abandoned present. It is a famous example of pastoral elegy, a poetic form that laments the passing of old rural ways, and thus its form arguably dictates its subject just as much as the fact that it was written at the height of the enclosure movement in the English Midlands (often taken as the central feature of the eighteenth-century agrarian revolution). The poem was extremely popular, and to a certain extent remains so. It has thus been subjected to a much wider range of critical analyses than can be reviewed here. No unambiguously ecocritical reading of the poem has yet been attempted; although, in the two and half centuries since its composition, critics have read it in the context both of the enclosure movement in England and of land management and mismanagement in Ireland. A key question that resurfaces, therefore, is the location of Auburn, with some critics seeing it as Irish, some as a generalized English village and others as the specific location of Nuneham Courtenay in Oxfordshire. Choosing between these radically alters the political message of the poem, as several critics have argued. In a survey of the debate, Alfred Lutz has shown that early readings of the poem emphasized its allegedly radical critique of enclosure, but that nineteenth-century critics increasingly depoliticized the poem, a tendency that 'was reinforced by biographical readings'.[5] Such approaches highlighted the poem's supposed explorations of nostalgia and childhood memory, which could divorce the poem from the politics of the English countryside and, although Lutz does not mention it, could encourage readers to relocate Auburn to the Ireland of Goldsmith's youth.

In more recent years, there has been a return to interpretations of the poem that locate it within contemporary English debates about enclosure and land use more generally. In particular, Mavis Batey has located the poem not merely in a generalized English landscape at the time of enclosure, but has more specifically argued that Auburn is Nuneham Courtenay in Oxfordshire, a village which, in 1760–1, Simon Harcourt, 1st Earl Harcourt, had demolished and moved a mile away to make space for the park for his newly built Nuneham House, which overlooks the Thames about five miles south of Oxford. There seems little doubt that Goldsmith witnessed this event (which Batey notes in fact did not cause 'any actual hardship or depopulation') and wrote about it in

June 1762 in an essay for *Lloyd's Evening Post* called 'The Revolution in Low Life'.[6] The essay clearly gives voice to some of the nostalgic sentiments that are later also expressed in *The Deserted Village*, but whether Auburn was directly modelled on Nuneham Courtenay remains to be seen. Indeed, as Nigel Wood has put it, 'The urgency with which critics have attempted to locate Auburn is perhaps inescapable [...] but the most striking detail is how elusive the village proves to be.'[7] This is no doubt because there is no literal Auburn waiting to be revealed. Instead, the poem almost certainly offers us an amalgam of places, both real and imagined, set forth as much to meet the demands of the pastoral elegy form as to comment on genuine events in the English or Irish countryside. This does not mean, however, that all attempts to read Auburn in the landscape must fail. The imagined village reflects genuine experiences and genuine environments, even though those times and places are various and sometimes contradictory. This chapter accordingly interrogates the poem in its ecological context and in relation to *An History of the Earth and Animated Nature*, Goldsmith's eight-volume popular natural history which was published in 1774, a few years after the publication of *The Deserted Village*, but which Goldsmith had been working on since 1769.[8] Its central argument is twofold. It shows that Goldsmith's understanding of both British and American natural history has been underestimated by critics, but it also argues that the ecological evidence in the poem does not support the thesis that the poem is a direct response to the destruction of Nuneham Courtenay.

Although Auburn may be a literary construct, *The Deserted Village* was nonetheless an avowedly environmental poem in its own time, considering the effect on human beings of four distinct environments – London, America, a flourishing British village and a deserted British village – as well as entering into an emerging debate about population growth. All of these aspects of the poem are amenable to ecocritical readings. Goldsmith himself begins with a dedication to Joshua Reynolds in which he addresses the question of rural population. Since the publication of Paul Ehrlich's *The Population Bomb* in 1968, the spectre of global overpopulation has become one of the most contested issues in modern environmentalism, and literary representations of population growth and decline are accordingly of great interest to ecocritics.[9] Ehrlich's thesis, that growing population would outstrip the global food supply, was of course merely a restatement of the central concerns of Thomas Malthus's *Essay on the Principle of Population*, which had been published in 1798 and warned that 'The power of population is so superior to the power of the earth to produce subsistence for man, that premature death must in some shape or other visit the human race.'[10] Malthus's views were striking because they were new. For most eighteenth-century observers, the strength of a country was derived from its population. The principle fear was depopulation, with its attendant shortage of labourers to farm the land and troops and sailors to defend the nation. This is the context within which Goldsmith is writing, and in his dedication to Reynolds he explicitly invokes the fear of a declining population, while simultaneously raising doubts about the accuracy of his observation:

> How far you may be pleased with the versification and mere mechanical parts of this attempt, I do not pretend to inquire; but I know you will object (and, indeed, several of our best and wisest friends concur in the opinion) that the depopulation it deplores is nowhere to be seen, and the disorders it laments are only to be found in the poet's own imagination. To this I can scarcely make any other answer than that I sincerely believe what I have written: that I have taken all possible pains, in my country excursions, for these four or five years past, to be certain of what I allege; and that all my views and inquiries have led me to believe those miseries real which I here attempt to display.[11]

Goldsmith was wrong about the size of England's population and, despite his protestations to the contrary, it seems clear that he knew he was wrong. We now know that England moved into an exponential phase of population growth in about the 1750s, but although the figures could not be known until national censuses began in 1801, it was widely understood at the time that the population was increasing.[12] Although Goldsmith recognizes that many of the poem's readers would have found that 'the depopulation it deplores is nowhere to be seen', his defence that he has himself witnessed these 'disorders' should not be dismissed out of hand. Large-scale social and economic change is often locally disruptive even when it is nationally benign or beneficial. Microeconomic conditions, such as the death of a local landowner, the building of a new road that bypasses the village or the failure of a local harvest, might tip a village into poverty and spur outward migration. If Goldsmith indeed enquired about depopulation while making his 'country excursions', local examples would no doubt have been pointed out to him. His unscientific research may have led him into a form of confirmation bias in which he would have sought out and believed evidence that supported his poetic hypothesis, causing him genuinely 'to be certain of what I allege'. In any case, if Goldsmith's country excursions were indeed scientific or quasi-scientific, his pastoral elegy did not require scientific legitimacy and there is no reason to believe that Goldsmith thought that it should. Depopulated Auburn is at once hyperbole, amalgam and synecdoche. Bringing together and exaggerating many dispersed instances of rural depopulation in a single poetic creation that could represent national, social and environment change was a stroke of poetic genius, but did little to represent the true state of the nation. The primary purpose of the poem was more clearly moral than representational; the intention, as Goldsmith assures Reynolds in the final paragraph of his dedication, was to 'inveigh against the increase of our luxuries' (p. vi). This homely aim accords well with the traditions of pastoral verse and was a consistent theme in Goldsmith's work more broadly, while the depopulation is necessary to render the poem elegiac. Goldsmith's entry into the population debate is a facet of his rhetorical ethos or poetic persona rather than a reliable statement of researched fact.

Much the same could be said of Goldsmith's attempts to represent locations available to those emigrating from the village. These are represented by the extreme environments of London and the British American colonies rather than simply nearby market towns, or neighbouring villages. Again, London and America are hyperbolic and synecdochic, representing the totality of possible locations for migrants and making the moral case that the destruction of the individual must inevitably follow the decline of the village. Ecocritics are, however, more interested in physical than moral spaces. Goldsmith's London, where 'the black gibbet glooms beside the way' (p. 20) and 'Tumultuous grandeur crowds the blazing square' (p. 20), is not short on physical detail. It is a place of confused sensations, of synaesthesia, of beauty and excitement, but also of sickness and premature death. Ultimately, though, it is a social space more than a geographic location. Goldsmith's America, by contrast, is couched almost entirely in environmental rather than social terms and provides a wealth of detail for ecocritical analysis. He invokes:

> The various terrors of that horrid shore;
> Those blazing suns that dart a downward ray,
> And fiercely shed intolerable day;
> Those matted woods where birds forget to sing,
> But silent bats in drowsy clusters cling;
> Those poisonous fields with rank luxuriance crown'd,

Where the dark scorpion gathers death around;
Where at each step the stranger fears to wake
The rattling terrors of the vengeful snake;
Where crouching tigers wait their hapless prey,
And savage men more murderous still than they;
While oft in whirls the mad tornado flies,
Mingling the ravag'd lanscape with the skies. (p. 21)

The putative location is 'wild Altama', Goldsmith's rendering of the Altamaha River: the major waterway in the then colony and now state of Georgia. On a first reading, the passage seems wildly inaccurate to anyone familiar with the region. Georgia does suffer tornadoes, but it is an exaggeration to say that it is 'ravaged' by them. Tigers are of course absent from North America. Fields are not generally poisonous. Birds do in fact sing in Georgia. These details have provided amusement for generations of American students, but closer attention to the underlying ecology suggests that Goldsmith was nearer to the truth than is often supposed. As long ago as 1945, Edward D. Seeber notes in a reading of the poem that in the eighteenth century the word 'tiger' might be applied to any large cat.[13] Goldsmith himself, in his *History of the Earth and Animated Nature*, speaks of 'an animal of America, which is usually called the Red Tiger, but Mr. Buffon calls it the Cougar, which, no doubt, is very different from the tiger of the east'.[14] To clarify the point, Goldsmith went to the menagerie at the Tower of London, where he was able to compare a tiger (*Panthera tigris*) and a cougar (*Puma concolor*) and to conclude that they were different species.[15] Other details become similarly less dubious as one explores them, and as one realises that Goldsmith's understanding of natural history was both current and comprehensive. For example, he discusses rattlesnakes at some length in his *History*, recounting anecdotes about their venomous nature from Pennsylvanian and Virginian settlers.[16] His general discussion of snakes demonstrates that his ecological understanding of this suborder of reptiles closely correlates with his moral perception of American colonization as a response to agrarian change at home. 'Nature', he argues, seems to have placed snakes 'as centinels to deter mankind from spreading too widely, and from seeking new abodes till they have thoroughly cultivated those at home'.[17] He likewise assigns a moral and a national character to scorpions, which are certainly common in Georgia, 'whose shape is hideous, whose size among the insect tribe is enormous, and whose sting is generally fatal. Happy for England, the scorpion is entirely a stranger among us!'[18] Bats too are discussed at length in his

History, and while Goldsmith does not specifically mention them, the Brazilian free-tailed bat (*Tadarida brasiliensis*) is a very familiar species which closely fits his description in that it roosts in large numbers, albeit more often in caves than in trees, remaining silent through much of the day, if becoming noisy at night.[19] Those poisonous fields are also not entirely imaginary. Poison ivy (*Toxicodendron radicans*) and poison sumac (*T. vernix*) abound in Georgia, the latter particularly in the fertile wetlands of the Altamaha river floodplain, which today are managed as important nature reserves. In such eutrophic conditions, competitive plants do indeed grow with 'rank luxuriance' (in biological terms, the word 'rank' means vigorous due to excessive fertility). The more one looks, the more convincing Goldsmith's account seems. Even the curious aside about tropical and subtropical birds forgetting to sing appears to have been a contemporary poetic trope. The Scottish poet James Grainger, for example, describes this phenomenon at length in his georgic poem *The Sugar Cane* (1764), set in the tropical Caribbean island of St Kitts:

> What tho' no bird of song, here charms the sense
> With her wild minstrelsy; far, far beyond,
> The unnatural quavers of Hesperian throats!
> Tho' the chaste poet of the vernal woods,
> That shuns rude folly's din, delight not here
> The listening eve; and tho' no herald-lark
> Here leave his couch, high-towering to descry
> The approach of dawn, and hail her with his song.[20]

Grainger read this poem out loud to 'assembled wits' at Joshua Reynolds's house in 1763, a year before Reynolds, Goldsmith and Samuel Johnson, among others, founded the famous Literary Club. Goldsmith may not have been at the party, but he would surely have known Grainger's poem.[21] Considered in both its scientific and literary contexts, and when allowance is made for poetic diction, Goldsmith's depiction of 'wild Altama' begins to seem less spurious and more mainstream; it is a selective but otherwise reasonably accurate reflection of what an educated general British reader might know about Georgia in 1770.

Indeed, one begins to form the impression that Goldsmith's environmental politics, more generally, is shrewder and better informed than the dedication's apologetics would suggest. He was certainly wrong about British population growth, and apparently knew it, but the local picture is more nuanced. Like Georgia, Auburn too has a wealth of both physical and ecological detail, and understanding this may both enhance our appreciation of the poem and lead us to some insights into Goldsmith's political purpose, as well as the putative location of Auburn itself. As with Georgia, contrasting the description of Auburn with Goldsmith's nature writing in the *History of the Earth and Animated Nature* gives us valuable insights into the significance he may have attached to various geographical and biological features. Although initially inspired by the elder Pliny's *Naturalis Historia*, much of the *History* was based on the Comte de Buffon's then incomplete *Histoire naturelle*, a borrowing Goldsmith freely admits to in his preface. He does, however, note that 'though many of the materials are taken from him, yet I have added, retrenched, and altered, as I thought proper'.[22] These alterations are largely taken from the writing of other naturalists, not always clearly referenced, but at least some must have come from observation. Goldsmith, of course, had first-hand knowledge of the flora and fauna of the British countryside and, unlike his representation of Georgia, his depiction of Auburn must in part have been based on personal knowledge. From 1768, Goldsmith spent his weekends at his cottage at The Hyde, now a rather grim North London industrial estate close to the British Library's newspaper library at Colindale, but at that time a pleasant rural hamlet. He signed the contract for the *History of the Earth and Animated Nature* in 1769 and must therefore have at least been bearing natural history in mind during the final stages of composition of *The Deserted Village*.[23] We should thus note carefully that in his dedication to Reynolds, Goldsmith claims to have 'taken all possible pains, in my country excursions, for these four or five years past, to be certain of what I allege'. As both a reader of natural histories, and an observer of the rural landscape, Goldsmith's observations could hardly have been accidental. An important passage from early in the poem is a case in point:

> Sweet smiling village, loveliest of the lawn,
> Thy sports are fled, and all thy charms withdrawn;
> Amidst thy bowers the tyrant's hand is seen,
> And desolation saddens all thy green:
> One only master grasps the whole domain,
> And half a tillage stints thy smiling plain;
> No more thy glassy brook reflects the day,
> But, chok'd with sedges, works its weedy way;
> Along thy glades, a solitary guest,
> The hollow-sounding bittern guards its nest;

> Amidst thy desert walks the lapwing flies,
> And tires their echoes with unvaried cries.
> Sunk are thy bowers in shapeless ruin all,
> And the long grass o'ertops the mouldering wall;
> And, trembling, shrinking from the spoiler's hand,
> Far, far away thy children leave the land. (pp. 8–9)

The opening lines of this passage can be interpreted in various and contradictory ways. In one reading, the phrases 'the tyrant's hand is seen' and 'One only master grasps the whole domain' support the contention that Auburn is a representation of Nuneham Courtenay, and the single tyrant is the landowner Simon Harcourt who moved his Oxfordshire village. Goldsmith's village is explicitly 'deserted', however, not demolished and relocated like Nuneham Courtenay. An alternative reading might interpret the 'the whole domain' synecdochically, reading Auburn as a fictional example of the more general national enthusiasm among landowners for enclosing and consolidating land that had previously been managed as strips and smallholdings. In this reading, Auburn might easily represent the type of village in the English Midlands where enclosure was having its most noticeable effect. By the same token, it might be a community in Ireland dispossessed of its hereditary lands, now controlled by 'one only master', an English absentee landlord perhaps, rack-renting the land and siphoning off its profits to enlarge his English estate. All these readings are possible. The last part of this chapter attempts to steer a course between them not by trying to understand the 'whole domain', but instead by more narrowly considering the hydrological, botanical and zoological references in the passage.

Goldsmith dedicates two chapters of the *History* to terrestrial hydrology, and a further three to oceanography, in which he demonstrates a solid understanding of what is now known as the hydrological cycle: the process of evaporation, transpiration, rainfall and runoff by which water moves between land and ocean. He describes in detail the relationship between river flow speed and discharge, the effect this has on erosion and riverbed formation and the impact of canalization on watercourses.[24] Although detailed study for the *History* most likely took place after composition of *The Deserted Village*, it is nevertheless unlikely that his description of the transformation of Auburn's brook is entirely naïve. In the first place, although Auburn has a brook, we should note that Nuneham Courtenay lies on the Thames, then and now one of the principle waterways in England and certainly no brook. Before the village's desertion he describes the brook as 'glassy', but afterwards it is 'chok'd with sedges' and 'works its weedy way'. Neither description fits the eighteenth-century Thames. A glassy surface is consistent only with a relatively low-turbulence flow, which means a clear and relatively deep channel such as a mill stream. These minor watercourses were important resources in rural communities and were carefully managed and frequently cleared of vegetation. What Goldsmith means by sedges is not entirely clear, as the word may have referred to many species in the eighteenth century, and not merely the genus *Carex* which we now think of as the true sedges. Goldsmith may be referring to sedges, rushes or reeds, but in every case these are plants associated with shallow water and, in particular, with the succession from a riparian to a wetland habitat. They are not associated with free-flowing rivers such as the Thames, or even minor brooks, except at the very edges of such bodies of water, and not always then if the lake or river was actively managed, steep-sided or embanked. Neither a Harcourt maintaining the banks of the Thames, nor an enclosing landlord seeking to maximize profits from the land, would encourage the development of wetland. What Goldsmith describes is consistent only with the total abandonment of a village along with any attempt to manage even its minor watercourses.

The birds that Goldsmith mentions support this thesis. Water and wetland habitats give rise to a great diversity of bird species, while at the same time birds, which are highly visible and easy to identify, are very useful indicators of the underlying habitat type. Birds also occasion a complex web of literary and folkloric symbol, metaphor and allusion and, unsurprisingly, are the subject of two volumes of Goldsmith's *History*. The Thames supports many species, particularly ducks such as mallard (*Anas platyrhynchos*), pochard (*Aythya ferina*) and tufted duck (*Aythya fuligula*), as well as other open water fowl such as great crested grebe (*Podiceps cristatus*) and mute swan (*Cygnus olor*). English rivers are also home to such colourful birds as the grey wagtail (*Motacilla cinerea*) and common kingfisher (*Alcedo atthis*). Goldsmith mentions none of these. Instead, 'The hollow-sounding bittern guards its nest; / Amidst thy desert walks the lapwing flies'. The bittern (*Botaurus stellaris*), though relatively common in the eighteenth century, is now a very rare heron in the British Isles, but its habitat is reed beds, marshes and fens, not open water. Goldsmith is alluding to its ominous 'hollow-sounding' booming call, but that call would not normally be heard in carefully-managed riversides and certainly not in park or arable land. The lapwing (*Vanellus vanellus*), a type of plover, is a relatively common bird which today can be found in a variety of habitats including estuaries and flood plains. A favoured habitat, however, is pasture and meadow – flat, often poorly drained fields and open places which are sometimes submerged but rarely entirely saturated. Some enclosed hay meadows and pasturelands would fit this bill, as would the Thames flood plain at certain times of year, but much enclosed arable land is too intensively managed and carefully drained to attract lapwing in great numbers. The ideal place for lapwing is neither parkland nor carefully drained enclosed land but instead more traditionally farmed arable land or rough, poorly drained grassland – the kind of habitat that might be created by abandoning a mill stream and letting its waters find their own level.[25]

Goldsmith's choice of bittern and lapwing was almost certainly carefully considered, both for their resonance in folklore and popular culture as well as for their scientific accuracy. Like all British citizens at the time, Goldsmith was deeply immersed in the symbolism of the 1611 Authorized Version of the Bible, which had freely translated the names of various middle-eastern animals into species familiar in England. Herons and lapwings are explicitly mentioned as 'abominations' in Leviticus and as 'unclean birds' in Deuteronomy: both texts forbid eating 'the stork, and the heron after her kind, and the lapwing, and the bat', although in the late-nineteenth-century Revised Version, 'lapwing' is translated as 'hoopoe'.[26] The bittern is mentioned much later in Isaiah (and echoed in Zephaniah). In 'the day of the LORD's vengeance' the land shall be destroyed by 'brimstone' and 'burning pitch'. Of what is left:

> The cormorant and the bittern shall possess it;
> the owl also and the raven shall dwell in it:
> and he shall stretch out upon it the line of confusion,
> and the stones of emptiness.
> They shall call the nobles thereof to the kingdom,
> but none *shall be* there,
> and all her princes shall be nothing.
> And thorns shall come up in her palaces,
> nettles and brambles in the fortresses thereof:
> and it shall be an habitation of dragons, *and* a court for owls.[27]

As with 'lapwing', 'bittern' was a highly speculative translation not widely agreed upon by other biblical translators: the 1560 Geneva Bible renders 'the cormorant and the bittern' as 'the pelican and the hedgehog'; the Victorian Revised Version suggests 'the hawk and the porcupine'; the New International Version offers 'the desert owl and the screech owl' with a footnote remarking that 'the precise identification of these birds is uncertain'; while the popular modern Good News translation cuts the reference entirely.[28] The scientific veracity of the translation is less important, though, than the associations the birds would have conjured up in Goldsmith's mind and the mind of his readers. However translated, the Bible did not locate these species in either rivers or carefully managed agricultural land. Both birds were instead associated with decay and abandonment at best, and God's vengeance at worst. These associations in fact predated the Authorized Version of the Bible, and probably influenced its translators. As Mark Cocker and Richard Mabey have pointed out in their voluminous survey of the cultural history of British birds, Geoffrey Chaucer, John Gower, William Caxton and William Shakespeare all represented the lapwing as false and treacherous after its habit of feigning injury to distract predators away from its nest. Furthermore, 'a bittern's distinctive booming note in spring', they inform us, 'was an omen of disaster'.[29] In both biblical and folkloric tradition, the two birds symbolically represented deceit and disaster, while also being metonymically associated with decay and dereliction – which in the rainy British Isles is often synonymous with the encroachment of wetland.

For evidence of the prophetic reputation of the bittern, Cocker and Mabey turn to Goldsmith's *History*, quoting from his account of his memory of the bird as a child in Ireland: 'I remember in the place where I was a boy with what terror this bird's note affected the whole village', Goldsmith recalls, and how 'they considered it as the presage of some sad event; and generally found or made one to succeed it'.[30] But as well as a memory of the bird's role in Irish popular culture, Goldsmith also had a scientific understanding of the bird and its habitat. Of the bittern, he writes: 'Those who have walked in an evening by the sedgy sides of unfrequented rivers, must remember a variety of notes from different water-fowl: the loud scream of the wild goose, the croaking of the mallard, the whining of the lapwing, and the tremulous neighing of the jack-snipe. But of all those sounds, there is none so dismally hollow as the booming of the bittern'.[31] From a literary perspective, Goldsmith's emphasis on the bittern's 'dismally hollow' call is noteworthy since his representation of the bird's melancholy sound is consistent in both his poetic and his scientific discourse. From an ecological perspective, however, the key words are 'sedgy' and 'unfrequented'. Even in the eighteenth century the bittern was not associated with busy rivers and maintained watercourses such as would be found near enclosed farmland, and Goldsmith understands that well. He reiterates the point a page later, noting that the bittern is 'a retired timorous animal, concealing itself in the midst of reeds and marshy places, and living upon frogs, insects, and vegetables. [...] [It] lays its nest in a sedgy margin, or amidst a tuft of rushes'.[32] Goldsmith likewise characterizes the lapwing as a bird of uninhabited wetlands. 'In summer', he reports, 'they frequent such marshes as are not dried up in any part of the year; the Essex hundreds and the fens of Lincolnshire. There, in solitudes formed by the surrounding marshes, they breed and bring up their young'.[33] He recognizes, however, that lapwing is also at times a bird of meadow and pasture, particularly 'In winter', he notes, when 'they come down from their retreats, rendered uninhabitable by the flooding of the waters; and seek their food about our ditches and marshy meadow-grounds.'[34] None of this suggests that Goldsmith associated lapwing with prosperous, well-maintained and well-frequented aristocratic parkland, even if in reality lapwing probably were found at Nuneham Courtenay in winter. Instead, Goldsmith again reiterates that 'The place these birds chiefly chuse to breed in, is some island surrounded with sedgy moors, where men seldom resort.'[35]

Whatever historical sources may suggest, the ecological evidence in the poem does not well support the thesis that Auburn was directly inspired by Goldsmith's experience at Nuneham Courtenay. He clearly knew his birds and understood the habitats in which they were found and so the mention of the bittern and lapwing in the poem must have been deliberate and informed rather than accidental or naïve. This means that we can ascribe strong meaning to them, both literary and scientific. It is also hard to understand why Goldsmith would use the bathetic term 'brook' to describe the Thames if his poem was a direct critique of the destruction of Nuneham Courtenay. Taken together, the ecological observations support a reading in which Goldsmith is offering us a village that for whatever reason has been deserted and which has reverted to wetland, as in fact the title of the poem suggests, and not one that has been moved at the whim of a local aristocrat. The ecological evidence may not finally settle the debate over the putative location of Auburn, of course, and in any case we should be under no illusions that Auburn is anything other than an imaginary village, reflecting multiple and perhaps contradictory viewpoints of a changing landscape and to some extent constructed to meet the demands of the pastoral elegy form. Nevertheless, it does suggest that Goldsmith's political protest, if that is not too strong a term for a poem that is more elegy than satire, was predominantly a response to his perception of the general state of the rural economy rather than a critique of the depredations, real or imagined, of tyrannical landowners. Finally, and more broadly, this assessment of the poem may also be seen as a response to Oliver Rackham's call to cultural historians 'to put on their boots and to see what the land itself, and the things that grow on it, have to say'. In this case, binoculars may have been more beneficial than boots, but the point remains. Combining ecological reading with textual analysis offers us a method to re-evaluate familiar texts, and it is hoped that this approach will be useful both to literary critics and to environmental historians in the future.

Notes

1. C. Glotfelty (1996) 'Introduction: Literary Studies in an Age of Environmental Crisis' in C. Glotfelty and H. Fromm (eds) *The Ecocriticism Reader: Landmarks in Literary Ecology* (Athens: University of Georgia Press), pp. xv–xxxvii (p. xviii); G. Garrard (2012) *Ecocriticism*, 2nd edn (Abingdon: Routledge), p. 5.
2. Glotfelty, 'Introduction', p. xv; Garrard, *Ecocriticism*, p. 5.
3. O. Rackham (1986) *The History of the Countryside* (London: J. M. Dent), p. 6.
4. No satisfactory biography of Goldsmith exists. The best recent brief biography is J. A. Dussinger (2009) 'Goldsmith, Oliver (1728?–1774)', *Oxford Dictionary of National Biography*, online at: http://www.oxforddnb.com/view/article/10924 [accessed 15 August 2014].
5. (1998) 'The Politics of Reception: The Case of Goldsmith's *"The Deserted Village"'*, *Studies in Philology*, 95:2, 174–96 (p. 188).
6. (1968) 'Nuneham Courtenay; an Oxfordshire 18th-century Deserted Village', *Oxoniensia*, 33, 108–24 (p. 124). See also M. Batey (1974) 'Oliver Goldsmith: An Indictment of Landscape Gardening' in P. Willis (ed.) *Furor Hortensis* (Edinburgh: Elysium Press), pp. 57–71. For 'The Revolution in Low Life', see A. Friedman (ed.) (1966) *Collected Works of Oliver Goldsmith*, 5 vols (Oxford: Clarendon Press), III, pp. 195–8 (originally published in *Lloyd's Evening Post*, June 14–16, 1762).
7. (Spring 2011) 'Goldsmith's English Malady', *Studies in the Literary Imagination*, 44:1, 63–83 (pp. 73–4).
8. For discussion of the *History of the Earth*, see R. M. Wardle (1957) *Oliver Goldsmith* (Lawrence: University of Kansas Press), pp. 283–7.
9. (1968) (New York: Ballantine Books). For discussion of population and apocalypticism in environmental literature, see Garrard, *Ecocriticism*, pp. 104–9.
10. (1798) *An Essay on the Principle of Population, as it affects the future improvement of society with remarks on the speculations of Mr. Godwin, M. Condorcet, and other writers* (London: J. Johnson), p. 139.
11. (1770) *The Deserted Village, A Poem* (London: W. Griffin). The dedication is at pp. v–vi. Further references are by page number to this edition and placed in parentheses following the quotation.
12. A. Rusnock (2002) *Vital Accounts: Quantifying Health and Population in Eighteenth-Century England and France* (Cambridge: Cambridge University Press); D. V. Glass (1973) *Numbering the People: The Eighteenth-Century Population Controversy and the Development of Census and Vital Statistics in*

Britain (Farnborough: D. C. Heath); E. A. Wrigley and R. S. Schofield (1989) *The Population History of England 1541–1871: A Reconstruction* (Cambridge: Cambridge University Press).
13. (1945) 'Goldsmith's American Tigers', *Modern Language Quarterly*, 6:4, 417–19.
14. (1774), 8 vols (London: J. Nourse), III, p. 226.
15. *History*, III, pp. 244–5.
16. *History*, VII, pp. 208–14.
17. *History*, VII, pp. 160–1.
18. *History*, VII, p. 291.
19. *History*, IV, p. 134–46.
20. In (2000) J. Gilmore (ed.) *The Poetics of Empire: A Study of James Grainger's The Sugar Cane* (London: Athlone Press), pp. 87–163, lines 553–60.
21. J. Boswell (1964) '21 March 1776' in G. B. Hill (ed.) and L. F. Powell (rev.) *Life of Johnson*, 6 vols (Oxford: Clarendon Press), II, pp. 453–4 and p. 533.
22. Goldsmith, *History*, I, p. xi.
23. Dussinger, 'Goldsmith, Oliver', O*DNB Online*.
24. See especially Chapter XIV 'Of the Origin of Rivers', *History*, I, pp. 193–227.
25. If left completely unmanaged, farmland in the UK and Ireland would normally revert first to rough grassland, then scrub and then to woodland. Unmanaged, it might remain good lapwing habitat for a decade or so. The standard work on European birds and their habitats is S. Cramp et al (1977–96) *The Birds of the Western Palearctic*, 9 vols (Oxford: Oxford University Press). For the bittern, see I, pp. 47–52. For the lapwing, see III, pp. 250–66.
26. Leviticus XI.19; Deuteronomy XIV.18.
27. Isaiah XXIV.8–13. See also Zephaniah II.14.
28. From almost 200 different biblical translations available at *BibleGateway* (Nashville, TN: Harper Collins Christian Publishing), online at https://www.biblegateway.com [accessed 17 August 2014].
29. M. Cocker and R. Mabey (2005) *Birds Britannica* (London: Chatto and Windus), pp. 202–7, 44.
30. *History*, VI, p. 4.
31. *History*, VI, pp. 1–2.
32. *History*, VI, pp. 3–4.
33. *History*, VI, p. 29.
34. *History*, VI, p. 29.
35. *History*, VI, p. 32.

8
Footnotes to a Nation
Richard Llwyd's *Beaumaris Bay* (1800)

Elizabeth Edwards

In March 1800, the Anglesey labouring-class poet Richard Llwyd (1752–1835) published *Beaumaris Bay, A Poem; with Notes, Descriptive and Explanatory*, the book-length work he had probably been working on for much of the 1790s. A loco-descriptive poem written in heroic couplets, *Beaumaris Bay* was his first major publication. Yet although its opening page looks conventional enough (Figure 8.1), it quickly becomes clear that this is no ordinary place poem. Only a short way into this work, the main text becomes increasingly pushed for space on the page by an abundance of lengthy footnotes, which offer geographically and culturally particularized glosses on the area around Anglesey and Snowdonia. At 434 lines, *Beaumaris Bay* is, at most, a short long poem, comparable with around a single book of Robert Bloomfield's four-part *The Farmer's Boy* (1800), its direct contemporary (the two poems appeared in the same month). The poem as a whole, however, stretches to 48 pages, with a further six-page appendix, because of the notes, which make up around 80 per cent of its total word count (see Figure 8.2).

This three-part chapter looks at the meanings of the notes, in relation to the poem on which they comment, and in the context of Welsh Romantic literature and culture more generally. The first section describes *Beaumaris Bay* and examines the nuances and implications of its (generally very positive) critical reception. The second section considers the content of the notes in more detail, before contemplating the poem apart from its notes. Both of these sections work through questions of Romantic-period perceptions of national literature/s, and of class, but the notes also, this chapter argues, represent an act of literary resistance. Though Llwyd at no point in his published work explicitly rejects union with England, or Britain, the space he creates in the margins of *Beaumaris Bay* for presenting the specificities, and especially the

BEAUMARIS BAY, &c.

BRIGHT foars the morn, in Summer's* fplendor dreft,
And throws o'er eaftern fkies her ruddy veft;
Whofe darting beams, with varied radiance gay,
Gild the tall cliff, and on the ocean play.

O thou, whofe fmiles upon the teeming earth,
Can lead her latent bleffings into birth,
Raife from the parent foil the infant grain,
And fpread the verdant velvet o'er the plain—
Refill the rifing herb with healing powers,
And Nature's varied furface deck with flowers.
Great fource of light! renew thy race benign—
Refulgent on the vaft creation fhine!
Roll through the blue expanfe thy radiant way,
And give the favor'd Mufe a cloudlefs day.

And thou! dear inmate! of the Grecian grove,
(The tuneful offspring of paternal Jove)
Recording Clio, leave the claffic climes,
Where war and havoc fwell the roll of crimes;
Where Mecca triumphs in a barb'rous reign,
And Learning fhuns the defolated plain—

    * " Ag awyr erwyr araf,
     " A'r byd yn hyfryd yr hâf."
              D. ap. G. Cowydd i'r hâf.

In Summer, earth is lavifh of delight,
And Heaven's expanded arch ferene and bright.

A

Figure 8.1 R. Llwyd (1800) *Beaumaris Bay, A Poem; with Notes, Descriptive and Explanatory* (Chester: J. Fletcher), p. 1

23

Thy towers Carnarvon*—triple fummits,† Llŷn,
That diftant clofe the vaft and varied fcene.

* This neat and compact town, is the *Arfonian* capital, the offspring of the Roman *Segontium*, and the *birth-place of the unfortunate Edward II.

" The fhrieks of death through Berkley's roofs that ring—
" Shrieks of an agonizing King!"   *Gray.*

Its caftle is the moft elegant and entire of the three great fortreffes built by Edward I. on the fubjugation of the country, and from whatever point it is approached, has a ftriking and magnincent effect.

" Ple mae Edwart, plwm ydych!
" Gwr a wnai y Gaer yn wych:
" Mae ei ddelw, pe meddylien.
" Wych yn y porth, uwch y pen;
" Ynteu yn fud hwnt yn ei fedd;
" Dan garreg dew yn gorwedd."   *Sir D. Trefor.*

Where! ye now aftonifh'd cry—
Where does mighty Edward lie?
He that gave thefe ramparts birth,
When proftrate Cambria lean'd on earth;
Here ftill his image, rais'd on high,
Attracts the thoughtful, curious eye;
But he, long humbled from a throne,
Far diftant lies beneath a ftone.

As a proof of the progrefs of rational refinement, and the habits of different ages, it may not be amifs to mention here, that an order was iffued, in the reign of Edward I. as hiftory informs us, that the chamber of that Monarch fhould be furnifhed with *clean ftraw every week!*

† Three beautiful and (from hence) uniform conic fummits, of the *Reifl* ridge, in the promontory of *Llŷn*. The *Rivals*, a name by which they are frequently called, feems to be the mere echo of the Britifh 'r eifl, but of very different fignification.

The diftrict extending from thefe hills to the confines of Carnarvon, formed, in the ninth century, the territories of *Cilmyn droed du* (or of the black leg) nephew to *Merfyn Frych* (who defeated the Saxons at *Llanfaes*) and Founder of one of the Fifteen Tribes. *Glynllifon* (his feat) continued to be that of his defcendants till of late years, when Frances, daughter and heirefs of John Glynn, Efq. beftowed it, with her perfon, on Thomas Wynn, of *Boduan*, Efq. grandfather to Lord Newborough. From *Cilmyn* is defcended, Sir Stephen Glynn, of Hawarden, Bart. the Glynns of London and *Nanlle*, the Lloyds of *Maes y porth*, and the Hugheses of *Bodrwyn*; from him alfo were the Glynns of *Lleiar*, *Pláfnewydd*, and *Elernion*, now extinct.

Cilmyn bore quarterly 1 *and* 4, *argent, an eagle difplayed with two heads fable*; 2 *and* 3, *argent, three fiery rugged flakes gules*; *and on an efcutcheon furtout argent, a man's leg couped fable*; perhaps an allufion to his name.

* The cradle of this Prince is faid to be ftill preferved in the family of a clergyman in Gloucefterfhire, defcended from one of his attendants.

perceived injustices, of Welsh history produces a voice tuned to resistance nonetheless. The final section of this chapter, then, reads his practice of annotation through ideas of Wales's colonial history, offering a postcolonial interpretation of the aesthetics of the hybrid, fragmenting work that made his name.

Richard Llwyd was born in Beaumaris in 1752, the son of a naval man turned coastal trader. There is no reason to think that his family was poor in the early part of his life, but the death of his father, quickly followed by those of his two siblings, forced Llwyd and his mother into much-reduced circumstances (and, in the case of his mother, what appears to be a serious episode of depression).[1] According to a note in one of his poems, he attended the Beaumaris Free School for around nine months, before beginning a career as a domestic servant at the age of 11.[2] There is little evidence to explain just how Llwyd became one of the most learned Welsh antiquaries of his day, but it is likely that his employment in gentry houses, and consequently his access to books, was an important part of his self-education. The sequence of events through which he became a published poet is only slightly less obscure, but in the 1780s he began submitting his work to the radical-sympathizing newspaper, the *Chester Chronicle*. By the 1790s, he had become something of a favourite, if occasional, contributor to this paper. More than that, the *Chronicle*'s support for his work played a decisive role in his unfolding writing career because the newspaper's owner-printer, John Fletcher, was also responsible for printing *Beaumaris Bay*. Llwyd evidently sustained his relationship with his associates at the newspaper over a long period of time, and at least sometimes in person: when, for example, he was directing correspondents to send to him 'at Mr. Fletchers Printer, Chester' in 1800, it is likely that he was at the *Chronicle*'s offices to oversee the production of his typographically difficult poem.[3]

I 'Where Britain westward spreads her rocky shore': *Beaumaris Bay* (1800)

Beaumaris Bay describes the events of a single summer's day, a conceit almost certainly borrowed from James Thomson's *Summer* (1727), a work that Llwyd knew.[4] It takes the form of a topographical tour, beginning at dawn on Ynys Seiriol (or Puffin Island), a rocky island just south-east of Anglesey, before turning to a series of views of Anglesey, Snowdonia, the Llŷn Peninsula and the Menai Straits, which runs like a central spine through the poem. It concludes with a flourish, returning to Ynys Seriol, moving along the Straits by boat as evening closes in:

'The DAY is clos'd – the fluttering sails are furl'd – / And Night, in shade and stillness, folds the world!'[5] The poem's opening is similarly assured, creating a colourful, kinetic seascape that locates the poem within the scene suggested by its title:

> Bright soars the morn, in Summer's splendour drest,
> And throws o'er eastern skies her ruddy vest;
> Whose darting beams, with varied radiance gay,
> Gild the tall cliff, and on the ocean play. (1–4)

Although this is a confident beginning, Llwyd's sunrise scene is also a study in marginality, set as it is at the notoriously liminal shoreline, on an island (Ynys Seiriol), off an island (Anglesey), off an island (Britain). Being at the nation's edge establishes a political mood for the poem: there are intimations of the progress poem in the opening pages of *Beaumaris Bay*, but one in which the voice of the poem calls the muse not just westwards from classical Greece or Rome to modern Britain in general, but to a kind of devolutionary challenge:

> Recording Clio, leave the classic climes,
> Where war and havoc swell the roll of crimes;
> [...]
> Come, where the Arts illume th' alluring way,
> And smiling Science feels a fostering sway;
> Where Thames triumphant wafts a richer Fleece,
> And either world salutes the modern Greece.
> Thy pinions Muse, expand – the space explore,
> Where Britain westward spreads her rocky shore,
> Looks back on worthies she delights to trace,
> And still preserves a remnant of her race;
> Her hoary cliffs in wild confusion crowds,
> And wraps their tow'ring summits in the clouds. (17–30)

For readers not familiar with its territory, Llwyd seems to acknowledge, *Beaumaris Bay* reveals the new and unfamiliar scenes of north-west Wales's relatively unexplored 'rocky shore'. It is possible to read this moment in the context of the 'home tour' movement that was reaching a height of popularity around 1800, and drawing Romantic tourists along increasingly well-travelled Welsh pathways.[6] But it is also an act of cultural remapping, an attempt to draw the literary gaze to the borders of the British nation – perhaps necessarily a stress point – and, in portraying Anglesey as the place of 'a remnant of' the aboriginal British, to its racialized Celtic past.

The poem as a whole is also substantially an attempt to highlight the existence of a Welsh-language literary past, a project begun in the reference on the first page to the fourteenth-century lyric poet Dafydd ap Gwilym. This note, to Dafydd ap Gwilym's poem 'Yr Haf' ('To Summer'), is the first piece in the detailed intertextual patchwork of literary and antiquarian references that becomes a vital feature of *Beaumaris Bay*. And the poem is pluralistic in other ways. From its solitary, reflective opening, the voice of the poem shifts into one of sociable tourism, sweeping the reader through panoramic prospect views, vignettes of island life and close-ups of particular local detail. In this sense, it can easily be seen as a kind of guidebook to the area, but its digressive structure, constantly changing scenes and aggressive annotation complicate matters from a readerly perspective. I discuss the often fruitful, often strained relations between the text and notes in the poem in more detail later in the chapter, but characterizing the interrelation of text and note in terms of space and form will prepare the ground for that discussion.

The footnotes are highly condensed, multivalent spaces. The brief reference to Dafydd ap Gwilym on the first page, for example, contains a particular textual history that would have been familiar to many (but not all) of Llwyd's first readers, since it refers to a body of medieval manuscripts that had been collected and published in 1789.[7] In this way Llwyd brings together different kinds of space, physical and literary, through *Beaumaris Bay*'s form. A west-lying landscape already characterized in the poem as relatively unknown becomes associated with new spaces carved out in Welsh literary history; topographical or touristic space is described, contextualized and attenuated by the typographical space of the poem, particularly the footnotes. Llwyd's description of Priestholm (yet another name for Ynys Seiriol) on page two leads, for example, to a note explaining the background to the island's various names:

> Hibernia's eastern sea† here Cambria laves,
> And pours on either shore its restless waves,
> While Menai's‡ currents with its waters play –
> Now roll to meet, or refluent fill the Bay;§
> And, circling PRIESTHOLM, ‖ shews its oval steep,
> Emerging boldly from the briny deep. (30–6)

‖ A small island, divided by the narrow channel called the Sound, from the eastern extremity of Anglesey; its British name, *Ynys Seiriol*, is derived from the residence of *St. Seiriol* upon it, in the sixth century; the compound name of *Priest-holm,* originated in its being the occasional retreat of the religious of the neighbouring Priory of *Penmon. Holm,* the Norse word for island, was probably added here as in South Wales, *Gresholm, Stockholm,* &c. by our northern invaders in the ninth century. – It is also frequently called *Puffin island,* from its being annually resorted to by these birds for the purpose of breeding. (35n)

This explanation drifts, via a lesson in local history, into a light-hearted stanza on the Welsh saints Seiriol and Curig by the fifteenth-century court poet Lewis Glyn Cothi (fl. 1447–89), quoted in the original with an English translation:

> "Gurig lwyd dan gwr ei go'l,
> Gwâs arall, a ddug Seiriol."

> Beneath his cloak, the begging Friar bore
> The guardian charm, grey *Curig,* to the door;
> Another *Seiriol's* healing image sold,
> And found the useful Saints like modern gold.

Llwyd repeats this pattern of juxtaposition and suggestion throughout the poem. 20 pages later, for example, his depiction of the Menai Straits snaking across a panoramic view of Anglesey, Snowdonia and the Llŷn Peninsular brings to the footnotes a quotation from the little-known sixteenth-century bard Lewis Menai:

> The Landscape's various charms the Muse explores,
> The Druid† haunts, and Mona's hallow'd shores,
> High Arfon soaring o'er the humbler isle,
> The winding Menai* – Daniel's† mitred pile;
> Thy towers Carnarvon* – triple summits,† Llŷn,
> That distant close the vast and varied scene. (209–14)

> * "Ymmyl Môn, am ael Menai
> O hyd, gwyn i fyd, y fai."*Lewis Menai.*

> On shady Mona's sacred side,
> Where Menai rolls her saline tide,
> How blest my lot, could I through life abide. (212n)

There is, however, plenty of opportunity for disorder in the process of switching between subjects, forms and literary registers, and Llwyd's vision of Snowdonia's clouded 'wild confusion' in the progress poem passage may hint at the difficulties that lie ahead. As a writer, he is, in general terms, a conciliatory figure, loyal to the British union. But as the poem unfolds, it becomes clear that it is impossible to write about Wales and its history without more troubled perspectives emerging.

Although Llwyd is all but forgotten today, *Beaumaris Bay* received a range of good reviews from the London press; he was subsequently styled 'the Bard of Snowdon' by contemporary readers (a title he also claimed for himself).[8] However, the London reviewers sealed their positive responses with certain reservations, and the following section examines the nuances of their comments on the poem. The *Monthly Review* picked out, on the evidence of *Beaumaris Bay*, Llwyd's 'amiable temper, the liberal views, and the many excellent qualities which he displays'.[9] The *Antijacobin Review* praised the poem for its 'strong, nervous, and correct verse', while the *British Critic* judged it 'very spirited and good [...] [the] versification is extremely pleasing', though regretting that no illustrations accompanied it: 'We would rather have seen this Poem in a quarto form, with a sketch of Beaumaris Bay attached, which we think would have reinforced its durability.'[10] The same reviewer observed that the footnotes 'indicate an intimate acquaintance with local history'. Though the writer for the *Critical Review* admired Llwyd's 'smooth couplets', and quoted the closing section as a 'fair specimen', s/he went further, reflecting that the poem 'seems to have been written as a vehicle for the learning in the notes. These are full of miscellaneous information which will chiefly be interesting to the author's countrymen.'[11] The reviewer for the *Monthly* commented on the (easily discerned) fact that the poem 'contains more annotation than text', and when the *British Critic* approvingly quoted from *Beaumaris Bay* as part of its review, it chose a passage with almost no annotation, as though implicitly identifying the real poem as one without the notes.[12]

In the short preface he wrote for *Beaumaris Bay*, Llwyd himself brought up the issue of the footnotes, describing the poem as

> a vehicle for the introduction (by way of note) of a variety of historical and other matter, now scattered in obsolete or expensive books, to be found only in the collections of the curious; yet necessary to throw light on past times, and the events of a district peculiarly inviting in the variety of its combinations, and the sublimity of its features.

In characterizing the notes as the main purpose of the poem, and as addressing a local audience, these reviewers may, then, have been repeating Llwyd's own words, but the point sounds quite different coming from a London periodical. And if the *Critical* was playing back Llwyd's statement, then its conclusion that *Beaumaris Bay* would mainly interest the Welsh is entirely its own. Although these are comparatively good reviews – hugely warmer, for example, than the devastating responses Llwyd's 1804 *Poems* would face – there is a sense in which these reviewers confine the poem to the local and regional on the grounds of its geographical and cultural specificity. But it is one thing to claim a local purchase and relevance, another to be consigned to it from without.

Beaumaris Bay also had a longer and more diffuse reception history, part of which exists in contemporary and later references to the poem by tourists to north-west Wales who read the poem as they travelled.[13] Despite the support of the *Chester Chronicle*, however, there was in 1800 little possibility of reviews that did not come from a centrally English perspective. No regional reviewing culture existed that might have offered alternative impressions of Llwyd's work, and in this he was at a distinct disadvantage compared with, for example, the Scottish writers who were by this point benefitting from the alternative national print culture and public discourse circulating from an Edinburgh centre. As a publishing hub, and as the cradle of Enlightenment thought, Edinburgh was a nodal point for the emergence of a distinct Scottish cultural voice.[14] But little comparable space existed for the development of a cultural voice for Wales, aside from the displaced public sphere that existed among the expatriate Welsh in London in this period.[15] Starting from this point, the following two sections further explore the national contexts and aesthetic and formal aspects of what Llwyd was attempting in the poem, focusing on the Enlightenment project of the notes, and particularly the ways in which this project fragments as if from within.

II '[H]istorical and other matter': the footnotes

Llwyd was by no means alone in this period in his extensive use of notes. Footnotes are everywhere in Romantic-period texts, filling the margins of political writings, narrative ballads, oriental fictions and national tales, dictionaries and grammars, parliamentary registers, scientific tracts and antiquarian writings, to list just some of the genres in which they appear. Though the notes to *Beaumaris Bay* are mainly literary and historical, they also allow for a significant degree of generic mixing, switching between science, visual culture, topography, industrial development, charity and moral economy. The broad overall sweep of the notes also levels or blurs some of the distinctions of time, class and place. Contemporary real-life figures appear in them as well as historical ones, while people who could only have been known in local contexts share the page with nationally eminent figures. The text as a whole becomes a cumulative compendium of quotations and commentary; the resulting interplay between the different textual zones on the page is its most surprising and problematic, but also most distinctive, aspect.

It is possible to see almost endless nuances in the intersecting map of references in the margins, and in this sense Llwyd's dead-pan claim for the poem as an introduction to 'historical and other matter' seems too simple and understated. The central metaphor of his preface may reveal more. The notes are, he says, 'necessary to throw light on past times' – or the vital element of an Enlightenment project. References drawn from Welsh-language literature tip the balance of the notes. Quotations from now canonical writers, such as the fifteenth-century poets Guto'r Glyn (fl. c.1435–c.93) and Lewis Glyn Cothi, are set alongside those from lesser-known ones. But Llwyd is just as likely to refer to literature in English, quoting Shakespeare, Milton and Gray in the notes in a manner unusual for a labouring-class poet of this period.[16] At the same time, major historiographical works in Welsh and English pull the poem into complex scholarly networks, from *Bonedd y Saint* (literally 'The Lineage of the Saints'), a manuscript genealogical tract documenting Welsh and British saints, probably dating from the thirteenth century, to Edward Hall's (or Halle's) *Chronicle* (1548), William Camden's *Britannia* (1586) and John Speed's *Historie of Greate Britaine* (1611), respectively a vernacular history of England, and topographical and cartographical surveys of Britain and Ireland.

Viewing these references in the aggregate may suggest that Llwyd's footnotes explore a unionist history of Britain, not just artistic and intellectual contexts for Wales at the turn of the nineteenth century. While it may be impossible to separate the two in this text, Llwyd's use of Welsh histories does suggest resistance to British incorporation. For example, there are several references in *Beaumaris Bay* to the first printed history of Wales, David Powel's *The Historie of Cambria* (1584), a work described by John Kerrigan as belonging within a group of sixteenth-century histories that reveal 'the development of collective consciousness among [the] newly empowered gentry' in the emergent British state, such as Hall's *Chronicle* and George Buchanan's *Rerum Scoticarum Historia* (1582).[17] A more recent perspective on this text suggests, however, that

Powel's *Historie* is part of a larger 'historical narrative that refuses to relinquish a separate Welsh identity in the aftermath of England's union with Wales', thereby resisting contemporary attempts to represent Wales in ways that 'validate Tudor control of the Principality and its people'.[18] It is telling that the footnotes endlessly supply *Beaumaris Bay* with microhistories and counterhistories – a priest murdered near Penmon Priory by English soldiers under the Marcher Lords; details of first-millennium battles on Anglesey; mineral extraction on the island; or its history of charity and philanthropy – giving accounts of individuals and events prompted by the turns of the landscape as we travel through it, and not necessarily or obviously related to narratives of the state. Instead, the notes allow for histories told at multiple levels, and for competing voices, ensuring that the reader remains at once within and outside the real time of the poem as it clocks its way through the day. As a result, the scene of *Beaumaris Bay* is not just constantly remade by the framing devices of the tour, or the passage of time, but by the kaleidoscopic way in which the pieces of the poem slot into new configurations by the action of the notes. No single or stable viewpoint emerges, a detail which, read through the recent turn to coastal history, may also be linked with the poem's island condition. As Isaac Land has observed, '[a]n island [...] does not even face in a single direction', and as a result it 'invites the historian to tell stories from multiple perspectives'.[19]

Place and antiquarianism had already been established as a model for writing about Wales by Thomas Pennant in the 1780s – a writer sometimes quoted without acknowledgement in *Beaumaris Bay* – so Llwyd's use of scholarly detail does have precedents in the period. But in braiding local and antiquarian detail onto an otherwise fairly conventional topographical poem, Llwyd was breaking new ground in Welsh writing. As much as *Beaumaris Bay* is not that well-known today, its place in the Anglophone tradition of Wales has long been recognized. Extracts of the poem were included, for instance, in a landmark anthology published in 1984, Raymond Garlick and Roland Mathias's *Anglo-Welsh Poetry 1480–1980*. This is an important moment for the reception history of *Beaumaris Bay*, at a point when labouring-class poets and peripheral voices were far more marginal in literary studies than they are now, but there are problems with this version of the poem: sections are left out (without ellipses to indicate where), and the footnotes are missing (nor is there any indication that there are any footnotes).

It is, of course, possible to read the poem without the footnotes, even in its originally published form. There are advantages to reading it without them: it becomes more legible as a Romantic place poem, the shape of the narrative becomes easier to follow and the influence of earlier eighteenth-century topographical poetry, such as Thomson's, becomes more visible. Footnotes have sometimes been seen as an interruption or obstacle and a distracting and potentially irrelevant 'outgrowth' of the main text, and it is possible that this view of the margins lies behind Garlick and Mathias's decision to remove Llwyd's notes.[20] As Alex Watson has argued in his recent study of Romantic annotation, footnotes challenge a sense of the organic unity of the Romantic text that has traditionally been much valued: 'practices such as citation and quotation' expose the 'incompleteness and imperfection' of the Romantic poem.[21]

Perhaps few poems of this period look as fragmentary or incomplete as *Beaumaris Bay* in its most heavily annotated passages, in which a single line of the poem hovers uncertainly above an entire page of notes. The result is that even a quick glance at *Beaumaris Bay* makes it difficult to see annotation as in any way secondary or marginal in this text, as its earliest reviewers sensed. Instead, the tensions between the notes and the main text (or centred text, to avoid hierarchical terms) dramatize power relations, creating 'a zone of confrontational transactions between different forms of textual and political authority'.[22] There are several ways of explaining why Llwyd used footnotes in the way that he did, not least a scholarly anxiety about his learning, and perhaps a need to prove the extent of his self-taught knowledge with endless evidence. As the notes spread across the surface of the text, gathering momentum from the bottom of the page, they may seem to reflect or record Llwyd's boundless or uncontainable excitement about antiquarian discovery. But it is surely not a coincidence that a writer who could be seen as marginal in a number of ways – Welsh, labouring-class, dealing in a nearly-lost manuscript native literature – should write so much of his career-defining poem in the margins. To conclude, the final section of this chapter explores the idea that the annotated Romantic text reflects, reveals and contests the shifting nature of 'geopolitical identities' in this period, as the nation-state was consolidated, and as British imperialism expanded, offering an account of why the balance of power seems to lie – albeit uneasily – with the footnotes.[23]

III '[T]he victories or the woes of Cambria' – postcolonial annotation

In December 1801, Llwyd's emergence on the literary scene was marked by a biographical sketch in the *Monthly Mirror*, 'Anecdotes of the Author of Beaumaris Bay', signed from Beaumaris by one William Toone. Despite his long life, much of Llwyd's biography remains frustratingly obscure – none of his literary manuscripts and few of his letters survive – so Toone's piece offers tantalizing, if unreliable, glimpses of him. His comments on Llwyd's poor background ('uncultured genius emerging from obscurity, and bursting through the almost insuperable barriers of poverty and contempt'), and career as a 'gentleman's menial servant' are spot on, while the claim that he 'read with avidity the works of the ancient Welsh bards, and cultivated his taste for poetry' is easily illustrated by the range of Llwyd's literary references.[24] Shakier, because there is no other evidence for it, is the suggestion that at some point in his writing life Llwyd became an itinerant minstrel:

> Disgusted [...] at a situation so unfavourable to his genius and literary pursuits [...] he commenced minstrel, and, being a tolerable performer on the Welsh triple-pipe, he traversed the whole of North Wales, and part of Scotland, like his ancestors, the bards, celebrating the victories or the woes of Cambria; by this means earning a scanty and but precarious subsistence.[25]

In a letter of February 1802 to the London-based editor and lexicographer William Owen Pughe, Llwyd commented that the *Monthly Mirror* piece contained 'inaccuracies', though he did not elaborate on these.[26] But whatever the errors in Toone's sketch, his sense of Llwyd as a patriotic, historically engaged, modern-day bard, taking the national past as his guiding theme, is surely beyond dispute.

Labouring-class writers have long been seen as the custodians of oral tradition, but in Llwyd's case this position is complicated by the historical role of the bard in Wales, a figure charged with a particular public duty to memorialize the past. As both the archivist and voice of national memory, Llwyd was clearly playing a bardic part in *Beaumaris Bay*, though the poem allows for a definite shift from an oral culture to a written one in the compendium or album-like quality of the notes. His reinvention of the bardic role in this way is continuous with the eighteenth-century antiquarian movement, but it also needs to be seen in the context of Romantic-period shifts towards new models of print culture and public discourse. Again, the example of Scotland may bring the situation in Wales into some relief. Sharon Alker and Holly Faith Nelson have recently argued that James Hogg played the new Scottish public sphere to his advantage in this period, 'amass[ing] cultural capital by presenting himself as an intermediary between the oral traditions of the Scottish Borders and the print culture of the urban Edinburgh literati'.[27] By comparison with Hogg, it is striking that Llwyd was positioning himself as an authoritative collector of manuscript and printed sources, recovering, above all, a wide-ranging written Welsh poetic tradition. Despite the structural and institutional challenges that his project faced, it seems very much as though *Beaumaris Bay* should be read as an attempt at excavating and amassing cultural capital and as an intermediary between nineteenth-century Wales and its disappearing national past.

Alker and Nelson persuasively show that even Scottish writers laboured under changing, and at times ambivalent, perceptions of patriotism and national centres in this period. John Gibson Lockhart, writing from Edinburgh in the early nineteenth century, characterized Thomson and Smollett as 'emigrants' who had had 'no relation to their country in particular, or its modes of feeling', and who exported their work to the imperial centre of London rather than publishing within Scotland.[28] In *Peter's Letters to his Kinsfolk* (1819), Lockhart's fictional narrator Morris (who is Welsh) concludes that earlier eighteenth-century Scottish writers relied on an English literary system, and urges nineteenth-century writers instead to 'emulate' Walter Scott by responding to Scotland's 'own national character as a mine of intellectual wealth, which remains in great measure unexplored'.[29] In this context, the impulse of Hogg's writing, mediating between oral and literary cultures, looks like Romantic Enlightenment. So, too, does Llwyd's, even though there was no corresponding Welsh centre or apparatus of a public discourse to write to, within or against.

The difficulties of attempting to sustain such a project in these circumstances brings *Beaumaris Bay* to the verge of collapse as a literary work. This reading of the poem enables us, however, to consider the footnotes as an effect or expression of Wales's postcolonial condition, written into the structure of *Beaumaris Bay*; something it performs rather than simply describes. Llwyd was, as we have seen, writing out of a moment particularly marked by touristic interest in north Wales, especially Snowdonia. But, like his friend the artist Edward Pugh (who makes a cameo appearance in the footnotes when Llwyd claims him as the successor to Richard Wilson in Welsh painting), Llwyd's depictions of Anglesey and mainland north Wales also define these places as places, not just scenes to be viewed.[30] As John Barrell has recently shown, in Pugh's paintings, inside knowledge of a place's history and current politics can result in a deep defamiliarization of spaces viewers and readers may have thought they knew well.[31] Discussing Pugh's 1794 portrayal of a war widow near Ruthin, for instance, Barrell sums up the painting as one that brings the Revolutionary war home to north-east Wales in an understated but deeply unsettling fashion:

> the image approaches us with the power of what Freud called the *unheimlich* [...] the appearance of the unfamiliar, ghostly presence in what would have been to Pugh's north Welsh customers a familiar street in a fully recognizable landscape.[32]

The dense local particularity of *Beaumaris Bay* releases structurally similar possibilities, presenting Anglesey scenes with a level of insider knowledge that transforms them from Romantic spectacle to sites of historical trauma, via the theme of bardic lament that runs through the poem, or, in its simultaneously Whiggish political outlook, sites of industrial innovation and commercial progress.

The effect registers spatially on the page in *Beaumaris Bay*. Critics of labouring-class poets have recently stressed the need to pay more attention to the artistry and aesthetic achievements of their work: 'to the ways in which labouring-class writers subvert, adapt and reconfigure the styles and modes available to them'.[33] Elsewhere in his poetry, Llwyd can be seen reconfiguring contemporary forms in just this way, remaking narrative ballads in Welsh contexts, or adapting Welsh medieval poetry as contemporary Gothicized dramatic monologue.[34] In *Beaumaris Bay*, a work faintly outlined as a Welsh progress poem, he refashions verse topography as native history lesson. Furthermore, his literary authoritativeness in relation to the scenes he writes about also renders those scenes as labouring-class space, in the sense that Anne Milne has recently observed, that '[a] more pointed attentiveness to "place" in literary studies' reveals

> a sense of belonging-in-place that belies common class-based exclusionary practices enacted upon labouring-class poets and, indeed, deeply legitimises and authorises them to speak of, in, and about place and their specific and special relationship to it.[35]

Finally, the notes to *Beaumaris Bay* allow Llwyd to reconceive locodescriptive poetry as postcolonial space. From the reader's perspective, the poem's footnotes can feel overwhelming – difficult to navigate relative to, or assimilate to the centred text (see Figure 8.2). From a postcolonial perspective, however, the revisionary nature of the notes means that this is exactly as they should be. It has long been recognized that 'the rereading and the rewriting of the European historical and fictional record is a vital and inescapable task at the heart of the postcolonial enterprise.'[36] But Llwyd's attempt to create such a wide-ranging portrait of a nation in a single long-short work means that the attempt was almost certain to run into trouble. In one sense, the attempt goes very wrong: the halting, fractured experience of reading the poem is the opposite of the highly controlled, forward-moving panegyric of earlier eighteenth-century poems of nation such as Thomson's.[37] But viewed through the lens of postcolonial Wales, Llwyd's ability to disorientate his reader – to make his work dangerously discontinuous, almost unreadable in the conventional way – is an act of resistance that makes Romantic Wales inaccessible to its readers in the act of guiding them on a tour of the area.

The history-in-fragments that characterizes *Beaumaris Bay*'s relentless footnotes, puncturing and slowing the progress of the poem, produces a form of the Gothic that has been seen as applying particularly to Wales. Kirsti Bohata has argued that '[t]he manifestation of the past in the present and a sense of the inescapability of the past', a key feature of Gothic writing generally,

> is an apt representation of the postcolonial experience of history and a pervasive feature of Welsh writing. Wales is characterised by internal fractures and uncanny doublings which emanate not least from the uneasy history of the two languages of Wales.[38]

Llwyd's mastery of the margins, of the spaces of the poem whether they are loco-descriptive or antiquarian, Welsh-language or English-language, produces imagined and aesthetic spaces unlike anything else in the Anglophone Welsh poetry of this period. William J. Christmas has recently made the case that '[a] critical focus on poetic genre means taking a fresh look at poems still largely ignored, even in our new literary histories, and recalibrating our analytical focus with regard to form and content, or more precisely form's relationship to content and the ways meaning is construed.'[39] In the case of *Beaumaris Bay*, the political message of Llwyd's poem, its levelling, revisionist accounts of place and history, emerges in full only by reading the strained relations between form and content. It is only by applying pressure to the typographical presentation of the poem, reading from the margins and between the lines, that the more ambitious and disruptive aspects of his topography of a national past and modern condition come into view. Llwyd's technical ability in the main body of *Beaumaris Bay* and elsewhere in

Richard Llwyd's Beaumaris Bay *(1800)* 149

his poetry suggests that he could easily have written a much more conventional looking topographical work. That he decided instead to spend page after page after page allowing his chosen genre to unravel speaks directly to Christmas's challenge.

Notes

1. This account of Llwyd's life is based on the memoir of him written by a Chester printer, Edward Parry, which prefaced Parry's posthumous edition of Llwyd's works. See (1837) 'Preface' in *The Poetical Works of Richard Llwyd, the Bard of Snowdon* (London: Whittaker and Co.), pp. xxvii–cxv.
2. Parry, 'Preface', p. xxxv.
3. See 'John Henry Burges to Richard Llwyd, 11 March 1800', National Library of Wales (NLW) MS 1562 C.
4. Llwyd refers to *The Seasons* by name in 'The Vision of Taliesin' in (1804) *Poems, Tales, Odes, Sonnets, Translations from the British* (Chester: J. Fletcher), pp. 136–44 (p. 143).
5. R. Llwyd (forthcoming) *Beaumaris Bay* in E. Edwards (ed.) *Richard Llwyd: Beaumaris Bay and Other Poems* (Nottingham: Trent Editions), lines 433–4. Further references are by line number to this edition and are placed in parentheses following the quotation.
6. For an overview of domestic tourism in this period, see B. Colbert (ed.) (2012) *Tourism and Travel Writing in Britain and Ireland* (Basingstoke: Palgrave Macmillan).
7. See (1789) *Barddoniaeth Dafydd ab Gwilym* (Llundain [London]: H. Baldwin).
8. See Llwyd's poem on the invasion threat of 1803 in (2013) 'The Address of the Bard of Snowdon, to his Countrymen' in E. Edwards (ed.) *English-Language Poetry from Wales 1789–1806* (Cardiff: University of Wales Press), pp. 195–202.
9. (1800) *The Monthly Review [...] From May to August, inclusive, M,DCCC,* Vol. 32 (London: R. Griffiths), p. 318.
10. (1800) *The Antijacobin Review and Magazine [...] From April to August (Inclusive),* Vol. 6 (London: T. Crowder), p. 82; (1800) *The British Critic, for January, February, March, April, May, and June,* Vol. 15 (London: F. and C. Rivington), p. 672.
11. (1800) *The Critical Review; or, Annals of Literature,* Vol. 29 (London: S. Hamilton), pp. 235–6.
12. *The British Critic*, p. 672.
13. Travel writers who quote Llwyd include the novelist James Norris Brewer, whose tour of north Wales appeared in the *Universal Magazine* in 1805; E. Butcher (1805) *An Excursion from Sidmouth to Chester in the Summer of 1803, Part I* (London: C. Whittingham); and W. Fordyce Mavor (1806) *A Tour in Wales, and through several Counties of England* (London: R. Phillips).
14. M. Pittock (2008) *Scottish and Irish Romanticism* (Oxford: Oxford University Press), pp. 7–8.
15. For recent surveys of Wales and Enlightenment, see R. J. W. Davies (2004) 'Was There a Welsh Enlightenment?' in G. H. Jenkins and K. O. Morgan (eds) *From Medieval to Modern Wales: Historical Essays in Honour of Kenneth*

O. Morgan and Ralph A. Griffiths (Cardiff: University of Wales Press), pp. 142–59 and C. Kidd (2010) 'Wales, the Enlightenment and the New British History', *Welsh History Review*, 25:2, 209–30.

16. For example, line 160n quotes Gray's 'The Bard' (lines 35–8); line 185n quotes from *Paradise Lost* (IV.139–41); and line 416n quotes from *King Lear* (IV.iv.11–15). Tim Burke and John Goodridge note that Shakespeare, Milton and Thomson – all reference points for *Beaumaris Bay* – were not easily available as literary models for labouring-class poets of this period. See (2010) 'Retrieval and Beyond: Labouring-Class Writing', *Key Words: A Journal of Cultural Materialism*, 8, 8–14 (p. 12).
17. (2008) *Archipelagic English: Literature, History and Politics 1603–1707* (Oxford: Oxford University Press), p. 42.
18. G. Jones (2013) 'Early Modern Welsh Nationalism and the British History' in S. Mottram and S. Prescott (eds) *Writing Wales, from the Renaissance to Romanticism* (Aldershot: Ashgate), pp. 21–38 (p. 22).
19. (Spring 2007) 'Tidal Waves: The New Coastal History', *Journal of Social History*, 40:3, 731–43 (p. 732).
20. For a discussion of footnotes as an 'outgrowth' of the centred text, see A. Watson (2012) *Romantic Marginality: Nation and Empire on the Borders of the Page* (London: Pickering and Chatto), p. 5.
21. Watson, *Romantic Marginality*, p. 5.
22. Watson, *Romantic Marginality*, p. 3.
23. Watson, *Romantic Marginality*, p. 5.
24. W. Toone (December 1801) 'Anecdotes of the Author of *Beaumaris Bay*', *The Monthly Mirror*, 12, 371–2 (p. 371).
25. Toone, 'Anecdotes of the Author of *Beaumaris Bay*', p. 371.
26. 'Richard Llwyd to William Owen Pughe, 1 February 1802', NLW 13222C, f. 739.
27. (2008) 'Introduction' in S. Alker and H. F. Nelson (eds) *James Hogg and the Literary Marketplace* (Farnham: Ashgate), p. 15.
28. Quoted in Alter and Nelson, 'Introduction', p. 8.
29. Alter and Nelson, 'Introduction', p. 8.
30. Llwyd writes, '*Snowdon, Cader Idris*, and other impressive features on the Cambrian countenance, have been rendered familiar even to untravelled eyes, by the admired pencil of a Wilson: others will probably be so, by that of a native artist, Mr. Pugh'. See *Beaumaris Bay*, line 378n.
31. (2013) *Edward Pugh of Ruthin, 1763–1813[:] 'A Native Artist'* (Cardiff: University of Wales Press), pp. 62–81.
32. Barrell, *Edward Pugh of Ruthin*, p. 77.
33. Burke and Goodridge, 'Retrieval and Beyond', pp. 11–12.
34. See Edwards, *English-Language Poetry from Wales*, pp. 255–347, for examples of these and other forms.
35. (2010) 'Ecocriticm', *Key Words*, 8, 46–8 (p. 46).
36. B. Ashcroft, G. Griffiths and H. Tiffin (1989) *The Empire Writes Back: Theory and Practice in Post-Colonial Literatures* (London: Routledge), p. 196.
37. For this view of Thomson, see S. Kaul (2000) *Poems of Nation, Anthems of Empire: English Verse in the Long Eighteenth Century* (Charlottesville: University Press of Virginia).

38. (2009) '"Unhomely Moments": Reading and Writing Nation in Welsh Female Gothic' in A. Smith and D. Wallace (eds) *The Female Gothic* (Basingstoke: Palgrave Macmillan), pp. 180–95 (p. 182).
39. (2010) 'Genre Matters: Attending to Form and Convention in Eighteenth-Century Labouring-Class Poetry', *Key Words*, 8, 38–45 (p. 39).

Part III
Women's Verse and Genres

9
'I wish the child, I call my own'
[Pro]Creative Experience in the Poetry of Jane Cave Winscom

Ashleigh Blackwood

> I wish the child, I call my own,
> A soul that would adorn a throne!
> With keen sensations, soft, refin'd,
> A noble, but an humble mind.[1]

Jane Cave Winscom's 'To My Dear Child' imagines a child, as yet unborn, with descriptions that are as pregnant as the poem's speaker, and represents one of the author's 'birth poems'. These poems, of which I define there to be six ('Written a few Hours before the Birth of a Child', 'The Author's Address to her first Child previous to its Birth ['My Dear Child']', 'To My Child, If A Son', 'To My Child, If A Daughter [Including a Letter]', 'Written a Month after the Birth of the Author's Son' and 'On the Death of Mrs Blake, who died in Child-Bed [of her sixth Child]'), cover issues including maternal health and mortality, infant care and childhood guidance.[2] As a collective these poems capture a strong sense of the importance of reproduction as a cultural concept in the late eighteenth century and require further exploration in order to offer a full depiction of how the creative identity of a female writer may have been affected by any procreative experiences. This chapter aims to offer specific insight into the work of Jane Cave Winscom, a female poet whose work has often been overlooked in examinations of eighteenth-century women's verse. I will first examine a gap in historiography and criticism relevant to Winscom and her work, before moving on to an analysis of the range of poems based on the subject of maternal experience that were included in a series of editions of her published collection, *Poems on Various Subjects, Entertaining, Elegiac and Religious*, across a period of almost 20 years. Furthermore, this chapter will consider the place of her 'birth poems' in wider traditions of maternal instruction literature and advice poetry.

Reproduction, in both its medical and cultural contexts, influenced women's literary creativity throughout the long eighteenth century. A growth in professional medical interests towards reproductive medicine and surgery, as well as the admission of the male practitioner into the lying-in chamber from the late seventeenth century in England, brought the events of childbirth further into public culture than social norms had previously allowed. Alongside a rapid increase in the amount of medical literature that had been made available in relation to maternity and neonatal care, women's own interpretations of procreation also emerged within literature ensuring that maternal voices and narratives were plentiful in poetic form. Roger Lonsdale's anthology, *Eighteenth-Century Women Poets*, contains no less than nine poems which address birth as a central subject and Paula Backscheider and Catherine Ingrassia have dedicated an entire section of their anthology *British Women Poets of the Long Eighteenth Century* to the subject of motherhood.[3] Like 'To My Dear Child', poems from female authors, including Isabella Kelly, Anna Laetita Barbauld and Joanna Baillie, attempt to depict the experience of motherhood whether during pregnancy, or through descriptions of infant care and parenting. Some of these authors were mothers themselves, while others were not. Joanna Baillie, for example, while never giving birth herself, was the niece of famed obstetric practitioners William and John Hunter and sister of physician Matthew Baillie.[4] Regardless of their own reproductive history, women could rarely avoid the events of birth altogether, as attendance on other women was still a traditional and regular duty within female social culture during the late eighteenth and early nineteenth centuries. The Duke of Sutherland highlighted the expectations placed on women in families when writing of the events surrounding the unexpected timing of the birth of a grandchild, by his daughter Constance, Lady Grosvenor. In an account of household events, he recollected that 'the ladies were all in attendance on Constance who has been moved from her temporary place of rest into Elizabeth's room.'[5] Even if not giving birth themselves, women often bore witness to the birth of infants that were the children of relatives or close friends.

Although *Poems on Various Subjects, Entertaining, Elegiac and Religious* was published in at least four editions during Winscom's lifetime (along with one additional reprint of the final edition a year later), very little critical coverage of her works has emerged.[6] From over

100 poems produced and published by Winscom, A. Elizabeth McKim has produced one of the only studies devoted entirely to her output, focusing on three particular works: 'The Head-Ach, Or An Ode to Health', 'Written the first Morning of the Author's Bathing at Teignmouth' and 'An Invocation to Death'. McKim collects these three under the label of the 'Headache poems' due to their 'valuable historical record of the treatments [...] in England in the 1790s', and their 'account of the physical and psychological effects of [Winscom's own] experience of headache'.[7] McKim's article was published in 2005, but only recently has another article appeared that focuses exclusively on Winscom and her literary output. Norbert Schürer's 'Jane Cave Winscom: Provincial Poetry and the Metropolitan Connection' offers the most detailed biographical research to date on Winscom's life before also examining the implications of the Winscom family locating themselves in provincial towns rather than a metropolitan centre of commerce and publishing, such as London, on the wider recognition of her poetry within contemporary scholarship.[8] His review of places where Winscom's name appears, as well as places where it is omitted, reveals that the scarce few references to her that do exist, such as those offered by Sarah Prescott, Roland Mathias and Catherine Brennan, have been inclined to focus predominantly on her nationality as a Welsh writer.[9] Although Winscom held strong familial connections to Wales, as well as having lived there for some time, she was, in fact, born of equal Welsh and English descent and spent much of her life in England meaning that her work might be included in both English and Welsh Anglophone categories of eighteenth-century poetry.

While Schürer's analysis in particular considers a range of themes from Winscom's poetry, such as politics, religion and local communities, he misses out significant themes of others, including birth – by no means one of the author's most obscure topics of choice. Similarly, of the six Winscom poems selected by Lonsdale for inclusion in his anthology, only one of these is about maternity: 'Written a Few Hours Before the Birth of a Child'.[10] Though a short verse, her poem, offered in poetic prayer, reveals much about the fears and anxieties of a woman submitting herself to the pains of labour in the hope of producing a healthy, living child. The poem itself gives no indication as to whether author and speaker are in fact one and the same; yet, what is evident throughout Winscom's body of work is that there was much of the poet in her poetry. Across her wide range of subject matter and themes, many involved people, events or experiences that surrounded Winscom or her family at the time of her writing.[11] As Schürer and McKim have both claimed in relation to the 'Headache Poems', Winscom herself was the sufferer of debilitating headaches thought to have been migraines. The connection between Winscom and her subject matter in the headache poems has been proved further by Schürer's having found that 'The Head-Ach, or an Ode to Health' appeared in *Bonner and Middleton's Bristol Journal* in May 1793, prior to its publication in Winscom's volume of 1794.[12] In this version she included a correspondence address for readers to contribute their own treatments and remedies for head pain. When read together, these three 'Headache Poems' indicate that one of Winscom's interests as a poet lay in creating a patient narrative of her own life and bodily experiences.

When considering Winscom's own reproductive experiences and her position as the author of birth poetry, it is important to acknowledge that the first edition of her poetry, printed and sold in 1783, gave her name as 'Miss Jane Cave', thus indicating that she was not married at the time of its publication. As might be expected from these dates, while 'On the Death of Mrs Blake, who died in Child-Bed (of her sixth Child)' was featured, the first volume did not include any of her other birth poems. Jane Cave had married Thomas Winscom on 17 May 1783, most likely a relatively short time after the publication of the first edition of *Poems on Various Subjects, Entertaining, Elegiac and Religious*.[13] It was then only in the second edition of the collection, in 1786, that 'Written a few Hours before the Birth of a Child' was printed alongside 'The Author's Address to her first Child previous to its Birth ('My Dear Child')', 'To My Child, If A Son' and 'To My Child, If A Daughter', each of which discusses a woman's imaginings of her unborn child.[14]

Genealogical records make clear that these poems were not based on her pregnancy with her first surviving child on record, Thomas, who was not born until October of the following year, making it impossible for the timings suggested in the text to refer to this pregnancy and birth.[15] Given that the Winscoms had been married approximately three years by the time the second edition of Jane's poetry was published, however, it may well be the case that they were based on her own personal experience of giving birth to her daughter Harriot, for whom a date of birth remains unknown, or another child who did not survive to adulthood.[16] In another of the birth poems, 'To My Child. If A Daughter', Harriot is named, suggesting that she was the expected child during the year that these poems were possibly written, and certainly published.[17] Like the identification of her daughter Harriot in her earlier poems, the last of her birth poems to appear in print, 'Written About a Month after the Birth of the Author's Son', published in her 1789 collection when

Thomas, whose name is given in the first line, was approximately two years old, clearly demonstrates that the speaker is Winscom herself.[18]

Although these indications do indeed point towards the authenticity of Winscom's birth poems being based on her own maternal experiences, we may at least question the legitimacy of the claim made by the title of 'Written a few Hours before the Birth of a Child'. As the timing of the writing in relation to the event of the birth itself is given in retrospective terms as 'a few Hours before', it would be reasonable to assume it was at least titled after the event itself, or may not be accurate to any particular number of hours. Her key interest in this poem is to document both the psychological and emotional preparations that a woman might make before giving birth, rather than any physiological sensation or pain which she was likely to have felt prior to delivery. The poet's choice of language surrounding the physical aspects of childbirth, anticipating birth with the phrase 'prepare me for that hour', suggests that the time period which she points towards is that which either narrowly precedes or follows the onset of early labour.[19]

The poem's form meets many of the contemporary expectations of how an eighteenth-century hymn would be composed. Winscom uses common metre, a popular choice of the period, and her prefacing words to subscribers of her volume, which appeared as early as the first edition, include a list of authors, 'Seward, Steele [and] More' whose works she may have tried to emulate, or may have referred to during the production of her hymns and other poetry.[20] While literary influences were undoubtedly significant to Winscom, this poem, along with a number of other hymns in her collection, including 'An Hymn for Consecration, sung at the Opening of the Countess of *Huntingdon's* Chapels in *Brecon, Worcester, &c.*' and 'An Hymn for a Child who has lost its Father or Mother', suggests that the hymnal form was equally important, if not more so, as a signifier of the poet's own faith.[21] The specific details of Winscom's personal religious beliefs have been debated by literary critics for some time. This issue of biography is particularly important to Winscom's birth poetry given that this small collection is predominantly made up of spiritual meditations on both motherhood and raising children. Even though many of her poems and aspects of her biography give a clear indication that she was Methodist, the details of whether her own Methodism was that which subscribed to Calvinist or Wesleyan teachings appears to be an issue that has not yet been fully resolved. Roland Mathias interprets Winscom's having written in English as a clear sign that she was a follower of 'Wesley's Methodism rather than that of Daniel

Rowland and the Calvinist followers of Whit[e]field'.[22] Alternatively, Sarah Prescott argues against this, asserting the belief that Winscom's poetry 'clearly aligns her with the Calvinist Methodism which flourished in, and was associated with, Wales'.[23] Prescott's view is derived from close analysis of a variety of Winscom's poetry, including three of her elegiac verses: 'On the Death of Mr. Whitefield', 'On the Death of the Rev. Mr. Howell Harris' and 'On the Death of the Rev. Mr. Watkins'. Though Schürer does not establish a firm position on either assessment, but does admit that Winscom's elegy for Harris is 'more personal in tone, figuring him in terms of friendship and family', his own findings include reference to evidence of correspondence between Jasper Winscom, Jane's father-in-law, and John Wesley and even between Wesley and Jane herself.[24] These exchanges of letters between the family and Wesley draw attention to the distinct possibility that Jasper Winscom, if not Thomas, her husband, also, raised his family as followers of Wesleyan Methodism.

While Prescott looks to the first edition of Winscom's poetry to evidence her Calvinist beliefs, the only version published prior to her marriage, Schürer refers to the later 1794 edition which may account, at least in part, for some of the differences in interpretation.[25] As each edition was edited, the poems published within each were subject to revision and variation – some poems were removed and newer material was added. Where the 1783 edition includes the three examples of elegiac verse that Prescott believes indicate Winscom's Calvinist beliefs, only 'On the Death of the Rev. Mr. Watkins' remains included in the 1794 printed text. Schürer takes this as a sign that 'Winscom was trying to make her volume less Welsh', yet also admits that, if this was the case, the question remains why was 'On the Death of Mrs. Maybery, of Brecon' not also removed.[26] This type of editing might also indicate a shift in her religious beliefs, away from the earlier Calvinist teachings which she had received towards a Wesleyan model, in the passage of time since her marriage. Poems such as those elegies, written as tribute to Calvinist minsters, were replaced with others which, as Prescott comments, 'deal specifically with her experience of marriage, childbirth and motherhood'.[27] By the time Winscom wrote her 'birth poems' she had been married to Thomas for some time and may well have integrated his family's Wesleyan beliefs into her own faith and religious practices.

Among those poems printed in subsequent editions of Winscom's collection, there was an increasing number that focused on matters of health, discussing headaches as well as childbirth, indicating that she may have taken some interest in Wesley's views specifically in relation to links between physical and spiritual health. Wesley is documented as having treated medical care with an almost equal respect to that he awards religious faith in his published guidance to his followers. In his treatise *Primitive Physick*, Wesley claims "[t]is probable, Physick as well as Religion, was in the First Ages chiefly traditional'.[28] His narrative indicates that he pursued an active interest in research and publications by practitioners, including Thomas Sydenham among others, yet also maintained a strong belief in the power of prayer as a means of communicating bodily needs for purposes of encouraging divine intervention and supernatural cures for physical ailments. Furthermore, Wesley also recognized the possibility for a public shift away from viewing religious worship as a means of improving health and curing illness in favour of professionalized, empirical medical discourses. In addition to his discussion of 'Regimen, or Manner of Living', made up of medical advice 'chiefly transcribed from Dr. *Cheyne*', Wesley also advises '[a]bove all, add to the rest, (for it is not labour lost) that Old, Unfashionable Medicine, Prayer. And have faith in GOD, who "killeth and maketh alive, who bringeth down to the Grave and bringeth up."'[29] This belief of his is not dissimilar to that Winscom draws attention to in 'Written a few Hours before the Birth of a Child' in which she contemplates the possibility of death in childbirth and prays to God as an acknowledgment that only God's will shall control the events of birthing. Similarly Winscom, like Wesley, shows a degree of familiarity with commonplace domestic medical literature that would have been accessible during her lifetime in a later volume, *Prose and Poetry, on Religious, Moral and Entertaining Subjects*. Although this volume is an anonymous collection of work, Schürer convincingly identifies the author as Winscom.[30] In this work she makes direct reference to Hugh Smythson's *The Compleat Family Physician*, yet her sentiments, as expressed in 'Written a few Hours before the Birth of a Child', equally parallel Wesley's faith in the power of prayer and in God over life and death rather than seeking to introduce forms of practical medical care to this already complex equation.[31] As the poem describes the feelings of a woman who readies herself for 'pain, or agony, or death' (p. 116), all reasonable apprehensions in the context of eighteenth-century birthing, the verse also points towards religious devotion as both a means of self-medicating and as an emotional coping mechanism in response to fears relating to the painful and physically exhausting work of giving birth.

Winscom's poetic prayer demonstrates her deference and willingness for God to determine the outcome of the delivery, claiming '[w]ith joy shall I give up my breath' (p. 116) should any complications result in her death. As these personal hopes and fears unfold, she asks for strength as well as 'patience to submit, / To what shall best thy goodness please' (pp. 115–16). Her final request is still more revealing about her personal apprehensions of childbirth as she asks that

> If death thy pleasure be;
> O may the harmless babe I bear
> Haply expire with me. (p. 116)

This request, initially startling to the modern reader, is underpinned by a fear of leaving her child without a mother's care should she die in childbirth. Winscom was by no means alone in these fears nor was she the only woman to express these feelings through poetry. Elizabeth Hands, a writer whom, much like Winscom, was 'born in obscurity, and never emerg[ed] beyond the lower stations in life', also drew on her own maternal experiences and fears of birth for her poem 'On the Author's Lying-In, August, 1785'.[32] Hands' poem shares a number of features with Winscom's birth poems, most closely with 'Written a few Hours before the Birth of a Child'. Also written like a prayer (although, the hymnal stanza is not used), the poem takes the possibility of death in childbirth as its central focus. In contrast to the perspective of Winscom's poem, in which the speaker reflects upon her fears of death in childbirth prior to actually giving birth, however, Hands' speaker gives thanks to God for preserving her life. She exclaims:

> I live! my God be prais'd, I live,
> And do most thankfully receive,
> The bounty of my life[.][33]

These joyful expressions are suggestive of the range of fears which the speaker experienced both prior to and during the delivery of her infant daughter and the relief she now feels having been safely guided through the ordeal so that she may 'live, still longer'.[34] The realities of childbirth during the eighteenth century included the risks of both infant and maternal mortality, or potentially both. Statistics provided by Robert Woods suggest that, at the time of Winscom's writing, 90 in every 10,000 deliveries in England resulted in maternal death.[35] Winscom herself experienced pregnancy on at least two occasions during a period which mostly saw declines, with only intermittent or small increases in infant and maternal mortality as well as stillbirths. Yet the remaining loss of life and the memories of generations of women who had faced higher risks, often with lesser medical care, were still present within public consciousness.

Arrangements made specifically for Winscom's confinements are among biographical details which remain unknown. It is likely that she gave birth at home given that, as Schürer indicates, her life was spent in provincial rather than metropolitan areas, such as London or Manchester, where public lying-in facilities were more likely to have been readily available to a middle-class family such as the Winscoms.[36] Even in rural and provincial towns maternity care was subject to much improvement by the late eighteenth century and the number of medical manuals offering instruction and advice to attending practitioners had increased steadily since the mid-sixteenth century. As Helen King notes, the female reproductive body became subject to 'intense interest', particularly from male medical professionals whose academic training had not prepared them for the seemingly social and non-professional duties of managing childbirth.[37] While these developments contributed to decreasing rates of mortality for women and children, medical literature continued to make no secret of the pains of labour and delivery. Manuals offered by female midwives, including Jane Sharp and Elizabeth Nihell, and male practitioners, such as Henry Bracken, Thomas Denman and Giles Watts, openly acknowledged the hard and painful process of 'travail' or labour before delivery.[38] In spite of this though, there was considerably less content directed specifically at women's particular fears and apprehensions surrounding birth. Martha Mears' midwifery guidance text *The Pupil of Nature*, published in 1797, was one of the earliest manuals to address such personal issues as anxiety during pregnancy through an in-depth discussion. 'Essay III', of the 11 that make up her text, examines the psychological journey that women undertake throughout pregnancy and childbirth, highlighting a number of key issues which were liable to affect women's mental wellbeing, as well as the development of her unborn infant, and methods for managing a healthy progression of gestation. With regards to fears, similar to those expressed by Winscom, Mears warns that '[o]ne of the first and most prevailing passions in the breasts of pregnant women is fear. The happiness of becoming mothers is sourly checked by preposterous ideas of danger.'[39] 'Hope', she continues, is 'so justly, so emphatically called the *balm* and *life-blood* of the soul', a message not dissimilar to the hope and comfort which Winscom's speaker finds in her own prayer and reflection.[40] In both literary and medical texts of the late eighteenth century, such as those written by Winscom and Mears, an increased level of public discussion around women's experiences of childbearing, especially those that were personal, is apparent.[41]

In addition to beliefs surrounding supernatural intervention and healing, those who subscribed to the Methodist faith during the eighteenth century, as Robert Webster comments, 'saw themselves fitting into an *ars moriendi* tradition that attempted to value the experience of a good death. In various narratives that depicted final hours of suffering a glimpse was offered into the state of the departing soul [...] often the desire for healing was eschewed by the faithful in favour of transportation into another realm of existence where peace and harmony were actualized.'[42] 'Written a Few Hours Before the Birth of a Child' can be read as a final hours prayer in which, in the face of uncertainty, Winscom attempts to reassure herself of a 'good death'. In addition to descriptions which, not only obey, but readily acquiesce to the will of God, Winscom also seeks to convey honesty, integrity and a candid approach to being guided by divine will through the poem's form and language. Her plain vocabulary and her use of a ballad quatrain make the poem accessible to the broadest possible readership.

These written reflections indicate that Winscom had spent time seriously contemplating the possibilities of delivery and was not unrealistic in her assumptions about the risks and potential complications associated with giving birth. Like the final lines of 'Written a Few Hours Before the Birth of a Child', anxieties surrounding maternal death and subsequently leaving an infant without a mother's care are echoed in other poems written by Winscom, including 'To My Dear Child', an address to her as-yet-unborn child.[43] Her verse describes these fears in detail:

> What unknown cares obstruct my rest,
> What new emotions fill my breast!
> I count the days so oft re-told
> E'er I my infant can behold.
> Thought after thought intrudes a dart,
> And strange forebodings fill my heart. (p. 118)

These 'new' feelings which pervade the mind of an expectant mother, disturbing her happiness and contentment at the prospect of the birth of her child, bear striking similarities to those which Mears later described in her medical manual. Although dark in their very nature, Winscom's thoughts are only those that contemporary readers, a female audience in particular, would be likely to empathize with, and would be understood as part of her preparations for birth and a potential transition from life into death. The poem contains two particular wishes. The first, like 'Written a few Hours before the Birth of a Child', desires that, in the event of her fear of maternal death being realized, the infant might 'breathless with thy mother lie' (p. 119). In the second, the speaker more optimistically hopes 'Perhaps I yet may live to see / My child grow up and comfort me' (p. 119).

Though chiefly foreboding and fearful, these thoughts are quickly expanded upon by an intrinsically practical approach to the possibility of the unborn infant being left without a mother's care. The stanzas of the poem that follow are dedicated to providing a written record of hopes and advice which the child, should they survive, would be able refer to in later life, again in the event that

> Perhaps the time which gives you life,
> Deprives Eusebius of his wife;
> And you for circling years may spare,
> Who ne'er will know a mother's care. (p. 118)

The figure of Eusebius is one which not only occurs in 'To My Dear Child', but also in another of Winscom's 'birth poems', 'On the Death of Mrs Blake'. Here Eusebius represents a husband left widower and is, again, used as an indication of maternal mortality as the name is a substitution for the presumably real Mr Blake. 'The fond Eusebius view[ing] his lovely wife' initially appears to have seen his wife recovering from the birth of her sixth child, but then sees her die within a week of delivery.[44] At first glance, the choice of the name Eusebius specifically to depict a loving husband and father appears puzzling, and one wonders whether Winscom had in fact read a history of the life of the Roman historian Eusebius that is now lost to modern readers. On deeper examination, however, a more likely source for these references to him is William Darrell's *The Gentleman Instructed, in the Conduct of a Virtuous and Happy Life*. Darrell's manual was first published in 1704 and was reprinted on many occasions, meaning that although the text predates Winscom's own birth, it is nevertheless likely to have been an accessible and appealing read. Darrell offers guidance on the instruction of young gentlemen through a dialogue between an instructor and his pupil; Eusebius advises Neander on a series of topics including the 'Duties of a Christian'.[45] It is not difficult to see why the manual may well have attracted the eye of Winscom whose interests in parenting and the instruction of children are evidenced in her birth poetry as well as others within her collection including 'To a Youth, inclinable to Gaiety', 'A Poem for Children, on Cruelty to the Irrational Creation' and 'To a Young Gentleman much addicted to Detraction'.[46] In the preface to his text Eusebius, Darrell explains, represents *'a* Scholar, Soldier *and* Courtier, *and in all these States a* Saint', thus providing Winscom with a model figure on which to base her advice to her unborn child.[47] In addition to these desirable traits, Darrell's Eusebius is also noted to have *'had the good Fortune to be born of a Mother, whose Wisdom vied with her Piety, and both indeed were extraordinary: She trained him up from the Cradle in the Duties of a Christian'*, attributes which Winscom herself would have been likely to aspire to in raising her children.[48]

'To My Dear Child' goes on to offer guidance, in the form of maternal instruction, and undertakes to express a variety of directions for intellectual, social and emotional wellbeing. The two poems that immediately follow this poem in Winscom's volumes, 'To My Child, If A Son' and 'To My Child, If A Daughter', also present practical instruction to an unborn infant intended for later life. So much are these two prepared in the same spirit as the previous poem that, without additional titles and entries into the contents pages of the volume, they might be mistaken for one and the same verse. Although, unlike 'To My Dear Child', both of these poems are specific to the gender of the child that they address and the advice contained within each is focused on issues of courtship. In 'To My Child, If A Son', Winscom's speaker is keen to encourage her son to exercise caution over his affections and treat the object of his desires with care and respect. First, her primary interest lies in protecting her son against entering into a marriage which he may later regret:

> If you, my son, should e'er incline
> In Hymen's careful bands to join
> Observe the maid who suits your heart.

Progressing to more serious warnings, she advises: 'With ardour seek — her love obtain — / Then to desert and give her pain'.[49] She cautions, with more than a hint of apprehension, that her unborn son might, without guidance, fall into a pattern of insalubrious behaviour with regard to his treatment of women.[50] In her guidance to her daughter, Winscom warns, 'External beauty has no charms, / If disengaged from Virtue's arms' (p. 126), stressing that her unborn child Harriot should pay close attention to the cultivation of her mind and manners, regardless of how comely she may be in her appearance. Like 'To My Child, If A Son', the poem then turns to courtship as its chief matter of concern. While Winscom is not necessarily troubled by her daughter's duty and behaviour towards male suitors in the way she is of her son, her speaker stresses the need for young women to be watchful of 'Whom to accept and whom to refuse' (p. 127). Her maternal anxieties for her daughter's future focus on the possibility that 'the deep deceits of men' (p. 127) might go undetected during courtship, later entrapping Harriot in a loveless marriage. Moreover, she is painfully aware of the fact that her poem 'own[s] a task beyond [her] pen' (p. 127), and that her advice may yet prove ineffective in her daughter's future relationships. A letter, also addressed to an unborn child, is printed alongside 'To My Child, If A Daughter' as a further explanation of the poem itself.[51] The letter, while being noted as being attached to one poem only, makes no specific reference to gender and might apply as well to Winscom's poem addressed to a son, as to that addressed to a daughter. The poet makes clear that, as is the case with all of Winscom's birth poems with the exception of 'On the Death of Mrs Blake (which still deals directly with maternal death), the 'To My Child' poems are intended as guidance in the event of maternal death before she herself could administer the advice.

The series of considerations made by a mother in preparing her child for later life is a theme which remains consistent in the majority of poems examined here and provides another valid justification for viewing Winscom's birth poetry as a collective beyond the generic subject of the poems themselves. If displayed in isolation, any one of these verses would be incomplete at least without the other two advice poems, if not the whole body of Winscom's work, which is centred on pregnancy, birth and the experience of motherhood. In each instance the speaker's imagination is projected so as to be experiencing motherhood purely through her own imagination, yet the advice presented might be real enough. These three poems locate Winscom within two different yet connected literary traditions: maternal instruction manuals for children and advice poetry. Like Winscom, earlier women writers, including Dorothy Leigh, Elizabeth Joscelin, Susannah Bell and Elizabeth Grymeston, had also written and published records of advice to their unborn offspring in the event that they might die during childbirth.[52] While the unfortunate truth behind these documents is that many of these women anticipated their own fate and did in fact die due to complications related to giving birth, Winscom was not among them. Happily the date of her death, in 1812, indicates that, perhaps as a result of improved delivery methods, she was able to offer her advice to her children in person.[53]

Winscom claimed within her collection that most of her 'birth poems' were 'not intended for publication, nor would they have been inserted here, but in compliance with the request of several friends', but, given that her work suggests her to have been an avid reader, she was most likely to have been aware of contemporary trends of viewing poetry as material through which one might reflect on matters of lifestyle, including parenting.[54] As Patricia Meyer Spacks explains, alongside the popular genre of conduct literature, which had continued to be a source of guidance, eighteenth-century readers also 'turned to poetry for investigation of such matters as how one should live, not primarily because of the absence of other resources, but rather because they believed poetry a particular authoritative literary mode'.[55] Although it may have been the case when Winscom initially set down her thoughts about maternity on paper that these poems were written as personal reflections, the fact that they had been seen by others at all suggests that they were not completely private documents, or that the statement was inserted as a purely cautionary measure. She may well have perceived that her reflections on maternity were not the stuff of canonical poetry, or even remotely similar in content to the works of those authors, such as Steele and More, that she so admired. Yet, as Schürer alludes to on more than one occasion, Winscom appears not to have made any attempt to establish herself within higher profile, London-based literary circles, and never published there.[56] Perhaps it was the very fact that she remained within small-town surroundings that gave her the freedom to publish poetry of a different kind. Spacks draws attention to the work of well-known poets who offered advice in their writing, such as Alexander Pope and the Countess of Winchilsea; yet, even poetry of the most personal nature could provide advice to a wider audience than might first be perceived.[57] Ann Yearsley, writing in 1795, offered a range of views on child-rearing from the earliest days of motherhood expressed through a dialogue of friendship, one mother to another, in her poem 'To Mira, On the Care of her Infant'.[58] Winscom's own approach assumes a position of authority as a mother, extending her advice beyond her own children to readers through publication, about the early days of parenthood while also acting as an advocate for self-medication against the pains of labour through the medium of prayer.

Notes

1. J. Cave Winscom (1794) 'To My Dear Child' in *Poems on Various Subjects: Entertaining, Elegiac, and Religious* (Bristol: N. Biggs), pp. 117–124 (p. 117). Further references are by page number to this edition and are placed in parentheses following the quotation. The poem is alternatively titled 'The Author's Address to her first Child previous to its Birth' in the contents page of the volume. For purposes of consistency across Jane Cave Winscom's work I will refer to the 1794 edition of her collection throughout the chapter, the first volume in which all of her birth poems feature, unless otherwise stated.
2. There are more than six poems in Winscom's complete collection that make reference to birth or children, those which I have selected as 'birth poems' are those that make direct reference to pregnancy, birth or an unborn infant.
3. R. Lonsdale (1990) *Eighteenth-Century Women Poets: An Oxford Anthology* (Oxford: Oxford University Press) and P. R. Backscheider and C. E Ingrassia (2009) *British Women Poets of the Long Eighteenth Century: An Anthology* (Baltimore: Johns Hopkins Press).
4. D. McMillan (1998) 'Dr Baillie' in R. Cronin (ed.) *1798: The Year of the Lyrical Ballads* (Basingstoke: Macmillan), pp. 68–92 (pp. 70–1).
5. J. Schneid Lewis (1986) *In the Family Way: Childbearing in the British Aristocracy, 1760–1860* (New Brunswick: Rutgers University Press), p. 162.
6. Critical scholarship remains largely undecided over whether to refer to Jane Cave Winscom as 'Cave' or 'Winscom' due to the fact that in each edition of her collection after the first she is referred to as 'Miss Jane Cave. Now Mrs. Winscom'. As she is listed as married on all but one edition, I will refer to her as Cave Winscom or Winscom.
7. (2005) 'Making Poetry of Pain: The Headache Poems of Jane Cave Winscom', *Literature and Medicine*, 24:1, 93–108 (p. 93).
8. (2013) 'Jane Cave Winscom: Provincial Poetry and the Metropolitan Connection', *Journal for Eighteenth-Century Studies*, 36:3, 415–31 (pp. 416–17).
9. S. Prescott (2010) 'Anglophone Welsh Women's Poetry 1750–84' in J. Labbe (ed.) *The History of British Women's Writing, 1750–1830* (Basingstoke: Palgrave Macmillan), pp. 102–24; R. Mathias (1980/81) 'Poets of Breconshire', *Brycheiniog*, 19, 27–49; C. Brennan (2003) *Angers, Fantasies and Ghostly Fears: Nineteenth-Century Women from Wales and English Language Poetry* (Cardiff: University of Wales Press), p. 37.
10. *Eighteenth-Century Women Poets: An Oxford Anthology*, pp. 376–7.
11. Winscom is known to have lived in Brecon or Talgarth, Bath, Winchester, Chagford, Bristol and Monmouthshire. See Schürer, 'Jane Cave Winscom: Provincial Poetry', p. 421.
12. Schürer, 'Jane Cave Winscom: Provincial Poetry', p. 420. Winscom herself made reference to the fact that the poem was inserted 'in the Bristol Newspaper' but does not give the name of which local newspaper: see Winscom, 'The HEAD-ACH, or An ODE to HEALTH', pp. 152–5 (p. 152).
13. Schürer, 'Jane Cave Winscom: Provincial Poetry', p. 418.
14. The only poem which had appeared in the first edition was 'On the Death of Mrs Blake, who died in Child-Bed (of her sixth Child)'. It was originally included in a larger section entitled 'Elegies'.

15. Schürer, 'Jane Cave Winscom: Provincial Poetry', p. 420.
16. Schürer, 'Jane Cave Winscom: Provincial Poetry', p. 420.
17. Winscom, 'To My Child, If A Daughter', pp. 126-9. Further references are by page number to this edition and are placed in parentheses following the quotation.
    Although no records have been found to prove Harriot Winscom's date of birth, 'To My Child, If A Daughter' would suggest that she was in fact older than her brother Thomas and would have been born between 1783 and 1786. Alternatively, there remains the possibility that the expected child referred to in these poems was neither Harriot nor Thomas, or in fact another infant named Harriot who did not survive into adulthood. Another poem in Winscom's collection does address childhood mortality but there is no suggestion that the child's mother is Winscom herself. Unlike the birth poems, 'Written By Desire of a Mother who had lost only Child' includes no first-person reference to the poem's speaker and as it appeared in the 1783 edition would have been likely to have been written before or around the time of Wincom's marriage, whereas the 'Mother' in the poem is referred to as a 'Widow' in the 1794 edition. See Winscom, 'Written By Desire of a Widow on the Death of her only Child', pp. 49-50.
18. J. Cave Winscom (1789) 'Written About a Month after the Birth of the Author's Son' in *Poems on Various Subjects: Entertaining, Elegiac, and Religious* (Shrewsbury: T. Wood), pp. 182-7.
19. 'Written a Few Hours Before the Birth of a Child', pp. 115-16 (p. 115). Further references are by page number to this edition and are placed in parentheses following the quotation.
20. J. Cave (1783) *Poems on Various Subjects, Entertaining, Elegiac and Religious* (Winchester: J. Sadler), unpaginated address 'To the SUBSCRIBERS'.
21. Winscom, 'An Hymn for Consecration, sung at the Opening of the Countess of *Huntingdon's* Chapels in *Brecon, Worcester, &c.*' and 'An Hymn for a Child who has lost its Father or Mother', pp. 83-5, 103-4.
22. Mathias, 'Poets of Breconshire', p. 35.
23. Prescott, 'Anglophone Welsh Women's Poetry 1750-84', p. 105.
24. Schürer, 'Jane Cave Winscom: Provincial Poetry', p. 419.
25. Mathias does not refer to any specific edition of Winscom's poems.
26. Schürer, 'Jane Cave Winscom: Provincial Poetry', p. 422.
27. Prescott, 'Anglophone Welsh Women's Poetry 1750-84', p. 106.
28. J. Wesley (1747) *Primitive Physick: or, an easy and natural method of curing most diseases* (London: Thomas Trye), p. vi.
29. Wesley, *Primitive Physick*, pp. xviii-xix.
30. Schürer, 'Jane Cave Winscom: Provincial Poetry', p. 423.
31. J. Cave Winscom [n.d.] *Prose and Poetry, on Religious, Moral and Entertaining Subjects* (Bristol: George Routh), p. 3. See also H. Smythson (1781) *The Compleat Family Physician: Or, Universal Medical Repository* (London: Harrison and Co.). As well as its original 1781 print, Smythson's domestic medical manual was also reprinted in 1785. It is unknown which copy Winscom was familiar with; however, for the page in the original 1781 edition which she refers to see Smythson, *The Compleat Family Physician*, p. 396.
32. E. Hands (1789) *The Death of Amnon. A Poem. With an Appendix: Containing Pastorals, and other Poetical Pieces* (Coventry: N. Rollason), unpaginated dedication 'To Bertie Greatheed, Esq.'

[Pro]Creative Experience in the Poetry of Jane Cave Winscom   171

33. Hands, 'On the Author's Lying-In, August, 1785' in *The Death of Amnon*, pp. 123–4 (p. 123).
34. Hands, 'On the Author's Lying-In, August, 1785', p. 123.
35. (2009) *Death before Birth: Fetal Health and Mortality in Historical Perspective* (Oxford: Oxford University Press), p. 95.
36. Schürer, 'Jane Cave Winscom: Provincial Poetry', p. 420.
37. (2007) *Midwifery, Obstetrics and the Rise of Gynaecology: The Uses of a Sixteenth-Century Compendium* (Aldershot: Ashgate Publishing), p. 9.
38. See J. Sharp (1999) *The Midwives Book: Or the Whole Art of Midwifry Discovered*, E. Hobby (ed.) (Oxford: Oxford University Press), p. 131; E. Nihell (1760) *A Treatise on the Art of Midwifery* (London: A. Morley), p. 153; H. Bracken (1737) *The Midwife's Companion; or, a Treatise of Midwifery: Wherein the Whole Art is Explained* (London: J. Clarke and J. Shuckburgh), p. 117; T. Denman (1786) *An Essay on Natural Labours* (London: J. Johnson), p. 3; G. Watts (1755) *Reflections on Slow and Painful Labours, and Other Subjects in Midwifery* (London: G. Keith), p. 3.
39. (1797) *The Pupil of Nature* (London: Faulder, Murray and Highly), p. 27.
40. Mears, *The Pupil of Nature*, p. 28.
41. G. J. Barker-Benfield (1996) *The Culture of Sensibility: Sex and Society in Eighteenth-Century Britain* (Chicago: University of Chicago Press), p. 160.
42. (2012) '"Health of Soul and Health of Body": The Supernatural Dimensions of Healing in John Wesley' in D. Madden (ed.) *'Inward & Outward Health': John Wesley's Holistic Concept of Medical Science, the Environment and Holy Living* (Eugene: Wipf & Stock), pp. 213–32 (p. 215).
43. As well as 'To My Dear Child', Winscom also produced another poem on a similar theme entitled 'A Hymn for a Child who has Lost its Father or Mother'. These poems, alongside 'On the Death of Mrs Blake', suggest that Winscom was familiar with families who had children in her local community and had suffered the loss of at least one parent. See Winscom, 'A Hymn for a Child who has Lost its Father or Mother', pp. 103–4.
44. Winscom, 'On the Death of Mrs Blake', pp. 54–6 (p. 55).
45. (1704) *A Gentleman Instructed in the Conduct of a Virtuous and Happy Life*, 2nd edn (London: E. Evets) pp. 45–76.
46. Winscom, 'To a Youth, inclinable to Gaiety', 'A Poem for Children, on Cruelty to the Irrational Creation' and 'To a Young Gentleman much addicted to Detraction', pp. 37–40, 51–3, 148–9.
47. Darrell, *A Gentleman Instructed*, unpaginated section, 'The Preface'.
48. Darrell, *A Gentleman Instructed*, unpaginated section, 'The Preface'.
49. Winscom, 'To My Child, If A Son', pp. 124–6 (p. 124).
50. 'To My Child, If A Son', p. 125.
51. Winscom, 'Letter', pp. 129–30.
52. See D. Leigh (1616) *The Mothers Blessing* (London: John Budge); E. Joscelin (1624) *The Mother's Legacie to her Unborne Childe* (London: John Haviland); S. Bell (1673) *The Legacy of a Dying Mother to her Mourning Children* (London: John Hancock Senior and Junior); E. Grymeston (1604) *Miscelanea. Meditations. Memoratiues* (London: Melch Bradwood).
53. Schürer, 'Jane Cave Winscom: Provincial Poetry', p. 421.
54. Author's note accompanying 'To My Dear Child', p. 117.
55. P. M. Spacks (2009) *Reading Eighteenth-Century Poetry* (Chicester: Wiley-Blackwell), p. 7.

56. For references to Winscom's life in provincial settings and her lack of connections to the London literary market, see Schürer, 'Jane Cave Winscom: Provincial Poetry', pp. 415–16, 420, 423, 428.
57. For examples, including work from Alexander Pope and Anne Finch, Countess of Winchilsea, see Spacks, *Reading Eighteenth-Century Poetry*, p. 38.
58. (1796) 'To Mira, On the Care of Her Infant' in *The Rural Lyre; A Volume of Poems Dedicated to the Right Honourable the Earl of Bristol, Lord Bishop of Derry* (London: G. G. and J. Robinson), pp. 115–16.

10
Figs and Fame
Envisioning the Future in Women's Poetry
Mascha Hansen

In *The Bell Jar* (1963), Sylvia Plath describes her protagonist's metaphoric struggle with the future: 'I saw my life branching out before me like the green fig tree in the story. From the tip of every branch, like a fat purple fig, a wonderful future beckoned and winked.'[1] Esther's vision implies agency, the possibility of doing something as well as the necessity to (re-)act and a future that must be shaped. Plath's fig tree, however, is a twentieth-century conception of futurity, not an eighteenth-century one. The future seemed more contingent in the early modern period and less accommodating to the visions of the individual.[2] In this chapter, I would like to trace eighteenth-century women's conceptions of the future in poetry, as their poems reveal aspects of agency, here taken to mean specifically the possibility to shape and influence their future. 'Agency', Paula Backscheider asserts, 'may be assessed in proportion to perceived ambition'.[3] Ambition is an aspect of futurity implying the hope of some future rewards. It is also an important indicator of the more general impressions conveyed by women's poetry of what it was possible to think and to express in the eighteenth century. Anyone writing poetry with even the slightest thought of publication in mind – and I dare say most of the women who found their way into print did have that thought in mind, no matter how much they protested the contrary – had dreams or visions of a future, however unusual. Many women poets expressed their desire for future fame, and their uneasiness at the boldness of such desires, as did Elizabeth Singer Rowe in 1737:

> [...] in spight
> Of your ill-natur'd Prophecy I'll write
> And for the future paint my *thoughts* at large.[4]

Even if fame was denied them in their own day, they voiced the ambition that their writings should survive and be read by future generations, since, after all, 'sacred Verse will ne'er decay', in the words of Jane Brereton.[5] This line in Brereton's verse letter, 'To Mr Thomas Griffith' (wr. 1720; pub. 1744), makes it quite clear that she does not mean religious verse but all great poetry, since, to her, 'an Addison conveys / Immortal verse to future days' (she does not seem to have envisioned a future in which poetry would be the least popular genre).[6] The limitations of genre are of course crucially important here, but, in this chapter, my focus is on the figurative language women used to explore their visions of the future – the figs of my title – and the way in which they made use of poetic traditions to make sense of, in Charles Taylor's words, 'the inescapable temporal structure of being in the world'.[7]

The 'figs' of my title, however, are not merely to be understood as an abbreviation of figurative language. While Plath's inability to make up her mind in the face of too many options is very much a twentieth-century problem, her use of figs (instead of, say, apples) and their symbolic value – here promising sweetness, fame and fertility, but also threatening decay if not plucked in time – makes them an appropriate vehicle for visions of the future which can be found already in early modern women's poetry. Figs, despite such belittling expressions as 'not worth a fig', were considered worth having in the eighteenth century, cultivated in greenhouses and valued as sweetmeats among the better-off: in Susanna Blamire's 'The Bower of Elegance' (wr. 1780; pub. 1842), for instance, the girls gain 'a prize of sweet, sweet figs' for being good needlewomen, and the boys of her 'Stoklewath; or The Cumbrian Village' (wr. c.1780; pub. 1842) are rewarded with 'a raisin or a fig' for doing something perceived to be good by their teacher.[8] The fig was used to symbolize possibility and promise; its emblematic value spread with the popularity of oriental tales and, of course, the plant's frequent appearance in the Bible. While figs may stand for fertility in connection with literary works, their spiritual dimension should not be underestimated either. Most women poets would have been familiar with the biblical symbolism of fig trees and leaves. The use of fig leaves in Genesis would have been the most familiar one, signifying awareness and knowledge on a higher level, and thus, as in the Song of Songs II.13 or Luke VI.13, spiritual maturation.[9] In Elizabeth Tollet's 'Hypatia' (1724), which begins with an appeal to 'a future Age', the cultivated mind is particularly distinguished from one in which 'an hateful Crop succeeds / Of tangling Brambles, and pernicious Weeds'.[10] By contrast, Charlotte Smith's vindication of the melancholy mood of her poems, echoing Matthew VII.16, 'Are grapes gathered from thorns, or figs from thistles?', was not meant to reflect specifically on the future, but it does have implications for the poems she expected to write.[11] Her grapes and figs, contrasted with thorns and thistles, emphasize her unhappiness and seem to imply that she would write better if her means – presumably material rather than spiritual – were more adequate. While she cannot be accused of literary barrenness – these 'thistles' proved quite fruitful, after all – her figs may well stand for the (financially) rewarding aspects of writing poetry. Luke VI.44 ('For of thorns men do not gather figs, nor of a bramble bush gather they grapes') echoes Matthew's more famous line, but while Matthew writes 'Ask, and it shall be given you' (VII.7), Luke transforms to 'Give, and it shall be given unto you' (VI.38). It is the latter line, with its insistence on faith, which explains Anne Finch's demand, in her 'Petition for an Absolute Retreat' (1713), 'Give me, O indulgent Fate! / Give me yet before I die', reiterating the unusually direct plea (almost a command) 'Give me' twice in the first two lines and a further three times in the course of poem.[12] Finch elaborates on her retreat, as she envisions:

> Grapes with juice so crowded up
> As breaking through the native cup;
> Figs yet growing candied o'er
> By the sun's attracting power.[13]

Here, the fig drying in the sun may stand not only for spiritual maturation, but also quite literally for the process of ageing, somewhat euphemized as being 'candied o'er'. Finch, moreover, specifically asks to be given 'Contemplations of the mind' as a compensation for the 'pleasures left behind' – those of youth.[14] The fig also has some connection with age and ageing in the Bible. In Luke XIII.6–9, Jesus tells the parable of the barren fig tree, which is not to be cut down before the gardener has once more tried his best to make it bear fruit. Immediately after, however, Jesus heals a woman who has 'had a spirit of infirmity' for 18 years. Unable to 'lift up herself', she, too, is like the fig tree: barren but not beyond salvation, even in this world. The fig is thus a symbol of hope; indeed, it is unusually rich in symbolism, and, perhaps to an eighteenth-century woman writer, less dangerously sexualized than the apple, even if both male and female sexual organs are symbolically associated with the fig, one of the attributes of Venus. The fig leaf, moreover, covered more than one sin: in Richardson's *Clarissa* (1747–8), Lovelace declares a husband to be a 'fig-leafed apron for a wife', while

Lady Mary Wortley Montagu rejected Richardson's indecent revelation of the character's thoughts in *Clarissa* with the same metaphor: 'Fig-leaves are as necessary for our Minds as for our Bodies'.[15] The fig is thus a fitting emblem for sinful literary ambition in a discussion of early modern women's writings. The many ambiguities implied in its symbolic values reveal rather than hide women's difficulties with the notions of futurity: with contemplating marriage and sexuality, maturation, ageing and finally immortality, in heaven or in print.

Literary fame and immortality

When Mme d'Arblay in 1823 remembered her mentor Samuel Crisp's words of advice to her as a young letter-writer, she recalls that he told her he 'would not give one fig' for her letters if she thought about what she wrote or what her words might possibly reveal about her.[16] When he urged her to accept an offer of marriage, however, he used a different metaphor to express his fears for her future: 'the Tide is lost & You are left in the shallows, fast aground, & struggling in Vain for the remainder of your life to get on'.[17] To Burney, any fig seems to have been more palatable than poor Thomas Barlow, her soon-to-be rejected suitor. We do not know whether at that time she actually hoped to be able to live as an independent author, but she must have been aware of the fact that her chances on the marriage market were slim. Burney's rejection of both her suitor and her beloved mentor's advice proves that she allowed herself to think and act for herself, more so, perhaps, than even her own fictional heroines. Her refusal to comply with their wishes implies a different vision of the future, whether it was more of a shudder at the thought of living with a man like Barlow or a glorying vision of herself as an independent author.

It is quite conceivable, however, that Crisp's warning to Burney could only be delivered towards the end of the eighteenth century: first, of course, because before then most women were not allowed to decide on such important matters, and, second, because Shakespeare's tide is an image belonging to a perception of time as cyclical: the tide may not return within the same man's life, but it is a cyclically returning moment belonging to men's lives. Social historians point out that in the late eighteenth century the impression was voiced that time itself was accelerating. This impression, or perception, was accompanied by the notion that one *could* decide on a future career path, because the future was no longer either far off and 'otherworldly' or cyclical, routinely offering more of the same, but somehow within one's reach.[18] Reinhart

Koselleck, a German historian, claims that eschatology had limited people's expectations until the mid-seventeenth century: that experience and expectation were thus tied together and could not diverge beyond a certain limit.[19] The past explained the present, and the future was a matter of prophecy because it could be explained by recurrence to past events.[20] This is a principle, for instance, still upheld in Elizabeth Tollet's *Hypatia*, first published in 1724, where man is enabled 'With Rays reflected on the Past to shine, / And thence the distant Future to divine'.[21] By contrast, the late eighteenth century saw the advent of 'new time'. It was experienced as new because events such as the French Revolution could not be explained by searching for parallels in the past any more. While the Christian belief in salvation still mingled with the new philosophy of progress and prognostication, the future, in Koselleck's view, changed from 'prophesied' to 'prognosticable'.[22] Crisp has, I think, translated Shakespeare's metaphor to a different perception of time, and a woman's time at that: young only once and quickly doomed to poverty and obscurity unless she catches that one moment now, or rather catches *at* that one offer. To Crisp, the danger a woman without a portion ran was not a matter of prophecy; for him, Fanny's future was so certain, so 'prognosticable' that the one road had to be foreclosed and the other secured at any cost to the present.

Women's time had changed in more than one respect. However, while eighteenth-century women poets were quite open about their wishes for a life without the restricting hand of husbands (see, for instance, Mary Chandler's 'A True Tale' [1744]), much of their poetry seems to reflect past conventions rather than branching out into something new when it comes to creating their own visions of their personal futures.[23] Even the many poems on children invariably seem to contain a line or two deploring the miseries the child is certain to face in the future. For instance, Henrietta O'Neill in 'Written on Seeing her Two Sons at Play' (c. 1797) declares:

> Even now, a mother's fond prophetic fear
> Sees the dark train of human ills appear
> Views various fortune for each lovely child,
> Storms for the bold, anguish for the mild.[24]

Most poets were less fearful but similarly conventional when contemplating their personal future. This is neatly expressed in two poems collected by Joyce Fullard, the anonymously published 'The Female Wish' (1733) and 'My Wish' by Mary Chandler, published at around the same time (1736).²⁵ Both, like Finch, envision a future retreat to spend their time in, preferably together with a (female) friend, preferring a quiet, uneventful life that will end just as 'gently' as it has passed. This wish is expressed in various other poems throughout the century, but rarely with such serenity. In these two poems, even if such a retreat may be unattainable to the speaker, they do not ask for anything else; in fact, they seem to portray the kind of life that most women actually led. In Finch's 'Petition', the vision is much more enticing, and more urgent. Her poem is ultimately translatable into the demand of something to hope *for*: even if it is an unworldly, Edenic retreat rather than, say, fame. The conventional wish is turned into something less self-restricting, more hopeful in Finch's version, whereas the last stanza of 'The Female Wish', preceding Gray's more famous complaint in the elegy that 'Full many a flower is born to blush unseen, / And waste its sweetness on the desert air', accepts that very fate without a murmur:

> Just so some tender blossom that has stood
> In the recesses of some secret wood,
> Unruffled by the winds, feels slow decay,
> Hangs down its head, and gently dies away.²⁶

As the poem has still not been attributed to a particular poet, the speaker seems to have had at least part of her wish granted: obscurity.

In later poems expressing a similar desire for rural tranquillity, the wish for fame is openly scorned as it threatens the simplicity of life the poets cherish. Mary Jones's humorous reflection on her own (dis-)interest in fame (wr. c.1736; pub. 1750) is also concerned with future options. Chiding a friend, Lady Bowyer, for her desire that she should write, she makes fun even of her own ambition:

> What's fame to me, who pray, and pay my rent?
> [...]
> Well, but the joy to see my works in print!
> Myself too pictured in a mezzo-tint!²⁷

The poem goes on to describe the life of an impecunious poet trying to gain the attention of some wealthy patron only to reject such a life: 'Fortune her favours much too dear may hold'.²⁸ One of the biblical fig trees similarly refuses to emerge from the well-known retreat to give up its comforts, claiming that it is not because it wishes to avoid the burden of responsibility but because it fears to be put above the rest. In Judges

IX.8–15, the trees seek for a king, asking the olive tree, the fig tree and the vine in turn. The fig tree replies: 'Should I forsake my sweetness, and my good fruit, and go to be promoted over the trees?' This, again, seems to be a fig(-tree) women could identify with. And yet, it was not so much the life of attendance women feared, as Jones avers, but the envy levelled at one who was perceived to set herself above others, described by Anne Killigrew. She openly voiced her preference for poetic laurels over a 'crown of gold', but warned against the allure of fame in her complaint 'Upon the Saying that my Verses were made by Another' (1686):

> How strong, how sweet, Fame, was thy influence!
> [...]
> But, ah, the sad effects that from it came!
> What ought t'have brought me honour, brought me shame![29]

It is remarkable, however, with what assurance Killigrew assumes that her verses ought to bring her honour, and the poem ends on a similarly defiant note: 'So deathless numbers from my tuneful lyre / Do ever flow [...] I willingly accept Cassandra's fate'.[30] She rages against, but is also quite flattered by, the implication that her verses were thought to be those of a famous male poet, an implication which her poem certainly flaunts. At the same time Killigrew also avers that Katherine Phillips' being a woman had made her famous. It set her above the rest indeed, but so far above as to be beyond earthly envy: 'Nor did her sex at all obstruct her fame / But higher 'mong the stars it fixt her name'.[31]

Life's progress

At the beginning of the eighteenth century, in 'Addressed to –' (wr. 1736; pub. 1749), Lady Mary Wortley Montagu characteristically doubted that death would bring immediate happiness though she did not seem to doubt that there would be an afterlife:

> With toilsome steps I pass through life's dull road,
> No Packhorse half so weary of his load;
> And when this dirty journey will conclude,
> To what new realms is then my way pursued?[32]

She maintains that life's progress is 'dull' and that the road offers neither amusement nor opportunities for either self-improvement or spiritual maturation. There is, to her, no happiness in ageing and no compensation for the loss of youth. Unconventional both in comparing herself to a packhorse and in contemplating suicide in this poem, she nevertheless cannot anticipate any future that would differ from the present, except perhaps after death. Similarly, Anne Finch's 'Life's Progress' (1709) as yet uses the term 'progress' to mean a movement towards decay rather than maturation, even if, to gay youth, the future beckons as an enticing place.[33] Everybody, moreover, passes through the same (and in that sense recurring or cyclical) periods of time: life, to her, is not a highly individual experience. She uses the image of undesirable thorns, not figs, and the 'we' of the poem (presumably men as well as women) are just too glad to sink into an eternal rest.[34] There is no hope even of salvation in this poem, only the 'crowds following' indicate that there is a future, perhaps implying future readers.[35] The working-class poet Mary Collier, too, found life's progress weary, and feared a future yet worse than the present. Although she hoped to make some money with her poems (only to be disappointed), there is no hope at all for the washerwomen in her poem, *The Woman's Labour*. Time is cyclical still in 1739, especially in the countryside, and it passes all too quickly as 'the Time runs on too fast', forcing the women to work night and day.[36] Worse, there is no consoling vision of salvation. To underline the hopelessness of the situation, Collier proclaims: 'For all our pains no prospect can we see / Attend us, but old age and poverty'.[37]

While it was still common to express the notion that hope was confined to youth (evident in Anne Hunter's 'Song' [1802] and Charlotte Smith's 'Sonnet X: To Mrs. G' [1786]), there are some notable exceptions to this tradition of depicting life's progress in the works of some later poets.[38] They explored the notion that, even if advancing age inevitably brings about the loss of youth and beauty, there is also a gain in the form of experience. This is already partly expressed in Finch's poetry. In the poem on 'Clarinda's Indifference at Parting with her Beauty' (wr. 1689, pub. 1713), Finch characteristically describes fading beauty as a loss for its owner for which there is recompense, except perhaps in the speaker's growing indifference:

> I see, indeed, thy certain ruin near,
> But can't afford one parting sigh or tear,
> Nor rail at time, nor quarrel with my glass,
> But unconcerned, can let thy glories pass.[39]

The speaker cannot 'afford' rage or grief, as she is in no position to do so (with 'afford' being used in terms of sense III, definition 5 in the *OED*).

Unconcern is not much of a choice; it is the only option left. Long before Frances Greville (c.1757), Finch seems to have favoured indifference. She considered both prophecy and prognostication an error, at least in her fables. In 'The Hog, the Sheep and Goat, Carrying to a Fair' (1713), the hog demands to know what will happen; a demand considered to be stupid in the moral, since the animals will of course be killed. The farmer admonishes that, as thinking will not avert fate, 'he, who though th'unhappy future pries' is unwise as it will only prolong his sufferings.[40] In another fable, appropriately called 'There's no tomorrow' (1713), Finch denies the future altogether, again expressing the notion that it is stupid to put one's hopes into future events.[41] A young man, having promised to marry his pregnant nymph 'tomorrow', denies that he ever has to fulfil his promise since tomorrow will never arrive:

> For when it comes in place to be employed,
> 'Tis then to-day: to-morrow's ne'er enjoyed!
> The tale's a jest, the moral is a truth:
> To-morrow and to-morrow cheat our youth.
> In riper age, to-morrow still we cry,
> Not thinking that the present day we die.[42]

This is still in keeping with a perception of life's 'progress' as a movement towards death and decay, a cyclical movement only because there will be a resurrection. To Finch, the present was just as dangerous as the future ('the present day we die'); while time was still circular, the present day was not far removed from the next. On earth, the future was merely the winter season, offering, if not more of the same, then just a little less.

This perception changes towards the end of the century. Charlotte Smith's generally melancholic poetic persona, who could look at graves with envy ('Sonnet Written in the Church Yard at Middleton in Sussex' [1789]) and complain that, for all time's cyclical movements, happiness had no second spring ('Sonnet Written at the Close of Spring' [1782]), was nevertheless quite able to gather, if not figs, then some small grapes.[43] The first three stanzas of 'Thirty-Eight' (1791) seem to follow the poetic tradition of seeing youth as the only time of enchantment:

> In early youth's unclouded scene,
> The brilliant morning of eighteen,

> With health and sprightly joy elate,
> We gazed on youth's enchanting spring,
> Nor thought how quickly time would bring
> The mournful period – *thirty-eight*!⁴⁴

And yet, the very title suggests that she is making fun of clichés, and so do her crisply paced tetrameter lines, underlining her self-irony. The next seven stanzas reveal that there is a compensation for the loss of juvenile happiness, and the pleasures of eternity are by no means all that remain to look forward to once youth is gone:

> The transient roses fade away,
> But Reason comes at – *thirty-eight*!
>
> Her voice the anguish contradicts
> That dying vanity inflicts;
> Her hand new pleasures can create,
> For us she opens to the view
> Prospect less bright – but far more true[.][45]

Reason is the voice of agency, enabling the writer to *create* pleasures. Smith here echoes the last lines of Johnson's *The Vanity of Human Wishes* (1749), where, however, it is 'celestial wisdom' who 'makes the happiness she does not find'.[46] Similarly alluding to Johnson, even if only in the title, Mary Whateley's 'The Vanity of External Accomplishments' (1764) describes the loss of beauty that society's belles will inevitably sustain, and then goes on to ask: 'But who would waste their bloom, and not engage / One friend to soothe the wintry storms of age?'[47] The speaker actively seeks for a remedy, in this case a friend as well as personal improvement. Inspired by reason's applause for her indifference to the signs of age, the speaker can hope for 'health, and poetry, and peace', and envisage her life as 'vanish[ing] in a tuneful sigh' – a far more positive image than the drooping flower offered by earlier writers.[48] Hester Mulso, in 'To Stella' (wr. c.1751; pub. 1775), similarly saw pleasures at least in friendship to compensate for lost youth and love.[49] Elizabeth Carter finally celebrated in 1758 a complete lack of concern about ageing that, in 1713, Finch's Clarinda had not quite managed to convey:

> The vain coquet, whose empty pride
> A fading face supplies,

> May justly dread the winter gloom,
> When all its glory dies.
>
> Leave such a ruin to deplore
> To fading forms confin'd:
> Nor age, nor wrinkles discompose
> One feature of the mind.[50]

Carter looks forward to eternity in this poem, certain that it is within her reach.[51] A similar trust is expressed by her friend Catherine Talbot in a poem presumably written in 1770, 'Writ on New-Year's Eve, While the Bells Were Ringing Out the Old Year':

> Farewell ye seasons! roll away,
> I wish not to prolong your stay,
> Tho [sic] age brings up the rear.
>
> Cheerful I trust, for future good,
> The hand which all the past bestow'd[.][52]

Towards the very end of the century, however, with the French Revolution upsetting all conventions, there was a backlash and the future again became a fearful prospect. In 'Ode to My Beloved Daughter, On her Birth-Day, October 18, 1794', Mary Robinson again worries about the future:

> We are but busy ants;
> We toil thro' Summer's vivid glow
> To hoard for Winter's wants;
> Our brightest prospects fraught with woe[.][53]

The only remedy Robinson can envisage is, like Finch's sheep, to focus on the present hour, and not to try and explore 'the mysteries of fate'.[54] The speaker here hopes quite conventionally that 'revolving years' will bring more virtue – there is no hint in the poem that the future might be shaped in any way.[55] In a poem written roughly a decade later (1802), Anne Hunter romanticizes the past in the light of an uncertain future, rhetorically asking: 'Yet will it be, as when the past / Twin'd ev'ry joy and care and thought?'[56] Time, indeed, had not accelerated for all. In 1799, Lady Catherine Rebecca Manners wrote 'A Review of Poetry, Addressed to a Son', in which she still recommends reading history (and poetry) to be able to understand the future: 'Pale experience, all aghast / Reads the future in the past'.[57] Just a little earlier (wr. 1782, pub. 1796), Eliza Dorothea Tuite had defiantly maintained the old ideals in a celebration of friendship which piles up terms associated with cyclical time, such as 'each returning year', 'perpetual', 'forever', 'season', 'each revolving year' and ends with a line declaring that her love is indeed 'by Time unmov'd'.[58] Despite such comforts, her time is measured by (returning?) cares:

> We measure life by time, and time by care;
> And I with Prior think that "Fame's a breath,
> And Life an ill, whose only cure is death."[59]

Fame is not timeless, but only too short-lived: for Tuite, life still led but to the tomb. In this kind of melancholia, sociologist Hartmut Rosa sees a state of being marked by a temporal emptiness, of feeling unconnected to either past or future. To him, this was a reaction to the sense of acceleration which was only enhanced by the 'nervousness' of the age of sensibility.[60] And yet, the female poets discussed here, while often steeped in melancholic brooding over a past clearly romanticized, expressed feeling not empty, but resigned, much as early modern women had always done. In a poem merely called 'Elegy' (1796), Tuite accuses the 'giddy crowd' of not wanting to see their own 'sad prospects', declaring that her Muse will 'calmly wait [...] the various will of Fate'.[61] In spite of her intention to be resigned, however, a little defiance creeps in, and she bids her Muse 'to cease':

> Mourn for the present, not the future ill,
> The past thou may'st with deep concern review,
> But to the future prospects hope is due
> [...]
> Still be this maxim on thy thoughts imprest,
> Since God is just, "Whatever is, is best."[62]

With the last line, Tuite not only echoes but exceeds Pope: now suddenly the present is best.[63] It is as if these turn-of-the-century women poets had taken up the age-old admonition to make the most of their time, not indeed to favour lovers but to enjoy the time at hand. Amelia Opie, in 1802, thus bids 'Pleasure, come!' since 'Future suns may set in sorrow, / Or in sorrow dimly rise', and Susannah Blamire asks: 'O why should mortals suffer care / To rob them of their present Joy?' (wr. before 1794, pub. 1842).[64] She, however, refuses to follow 'chariot's wheel', tomorrow had better not be contemplated today.[65] This does not, however, contradict Rosa and others who see time accelerating in that period, even if none of them, as far as I could make out, discuss women's reactions to that impression. Rosa maintains that the very injunction to make the most of one's time is in keeping with that notion, because time becomes ever more precious and has to be used as if it were, in Benjamin Franklin's words, money.[66] Even if young women seemed to have so much time on their hands, like Rosamond in *Middlemarch* or the girls admonished by the Fordyces of the period, clearly women like the fictional Clarissa Harlowe did not 'waste' their time but carefully measured every minute.

Koselleck claims that, to the eighteenth century, perfection, no longer restricted to the hereafter, finally seemed attainable on earth.[67] The possibility of self-perfection, neatly tied in with Protestant notions of self-scrutiny, was a notion clearly appealing to early modern women. In *The Ladies Defence*, published in 1701, Mary, Lady Chudleigh, could imagine a better future for her own sex only if they strictly committed themselves to the ardent task of self-perfection:

> O that my Sex would all such Toys despise,
> And only Study to be Good, and Wise:
> Inspect themselves, and every Blemish find,
> Search all the close Recesses of the Mind
> [...]
> Thro' all the Labyrinths of Learning go,
> And grow more humble, as they more do know.[68]

There is not yet a vision of what the world could be like for women, all is conditional. However, she continues in another key: 'By doing this, they will respect procure, / Silence the men, and lasting fame secure'.[69] Though she does not, cannot, see all women 'doing this', she can envision a time in which women have gained respect and fame. Only the doubt creeping into the first lines ('O that my sex would') does make that time seem rather far off.

This is different in 1774, when Mary Scott published *The Female Advocate*, predicting 'future female intellectual triumphs'.[70] Her Muse contemplates the future with rapture, watching women pursue the various sciences:

> With matchless Newton now one soars on high,
> Lost in the boundless wonders of the sky;

> Another now, of curious mind, reveals
> What treasures in her bowels Earth conceals;
> Nature's minuter works attract her eyes;
> Their laws, their powers, her deep research descries,
> From sense abstracted, some, with arduous flight,
> Explore the realms of intellectual light[.][71]

She, too, envisages men paying respect to female intellectual achievements. Her future, however, is not conditional on women's reformation (though they study with unremittent ardour in the poem in line 23); it is not even far off: in fact, it has already begun. Women were pursuing these studies already at the time. In 1786, Caroline Herschel would discover the first 'lady's comet': women's time was accelerating.

'In the literary culture of early modern England it was commonplace to regard posthumous remembrance as the ultimate fulfilment of human life', Keith Thomas writes, but even he finds only Margaret Cavendish in the seventeenth century openly desiring fame as a woman.[72] Along with the assurance that women do have reason and poetry, however, came a time that allowed women to voice their desire for fame. No longer like Finch's muse, cautioned not to try for admiration, the early nineteenth-century poet Letitia Elizabeth Landon can openly express her overwhelming desire for the immortality of fame in 'Lines of Life' (1827):

> Why write I this? Because my heart
> Towards the future springs
> The future where it loves to soar
> [...]
> My first, my last, my only wish,
> Say, will my charmed chords
> Wake to the morning light of fame
> And breathe again my words?[73]

Landon hopes for, but ultimately doubts, salvation ('Alas! My dream is done').[74] And yet, the lines I just quoted do not, in their almost childlike insistence, differ much from Anne Finch's demand in 'The Petition for an Absolute Retreat' to 'Give me yet before I die'. Surprisingly, though, the earlier poet hopes for a future on earth, and the later one looks for rewards after death. Like Finch, however, Landon ultimately seems to ask less for immortality than for fulfilment: the fulfilment of knowing that her verse will survive.

Notes

1. S. Plath (2005) *The Bell Jar* (London: Faber and Faber), p. 73. Esther's figs 'wrinkle and go black' while she looks at them, however, denying her even the possibility of agency.
2. See, for instance, R. Koselleck (2013) *Vergangene Zeiten: Zur Semantik geschichtlicher Zeiten* (Frankfurt am Main: Suhrkamp), p. 173.
3. (2008) *Eighteenth-Century Women Poets and Their Poetry: Inventing Agency, Inventing Genre* (Baltimore: Johns Hopkins University Press), p. 26.
4. See J. Fullard (1990) 'Introduction' in J. Fullard (ed.) *British Women Poets, 1660–1800: An Anthology* (New York: Whitston Publishing Company), pp. 1–13 (pp. 5–7); E. Singer Rowe (1737) 'To a Friend who Persuades me to Leave the Muse' in *Philomela: Or, Poems by Mrs. Elizabeth Singer, [Now Rowe,] Of Frome in Somersetshire*, 2nd edn (London: E. Curll), pp. 128–31 (p. 128) (quoted in Backscheider, *Eighteenth-Century Women Poets and Their Poetry*, pp. 118–19).
5. (1744) 'To Mr Thomas Griffith, at the University of Glasgow. Written in London, 1720' in *Poems on Several Occasions: by Mrs Jane Brereton. With Letters to her Friends And An Account of Her Life* (London: Edward Cave), pp. 53–62 (p. 60). (An excerpt of this poem, including these lines, is available in R. Lonsdale [ed.] [1990] *Eighteenth-Century Women Poets: An Oxford Anthology* [Oxford: Oxford University Press], p. 80.) In this poem, written in 1720, the speaker does not dare present herself as being among the number of immortal poets, though she had already published two books of poetry (Lonsdale, *Eighteenth-Century Women Poets*, pp. 78–9).
6. p. 60.
7. (1989) *Sources of the Self: The Making of the Modern Identity* (Cambridge, MA: Harvard University Press), p. 47.
8. (1842) 'The Bower of Elegance' and 'Stoklewath: Or, The Cumbrian Village' in *The Poetical Works of Miss Susanna Blamire, with a Preface, Memoir, and Notes by Patrick Maxwell*, H. Lonsdale (ed.) (Edinburgh: John Menzies), pp. 61–9 (p. 67) and pp. 1–40 (p. 8). (Excerpts of these poems, including these lines, are available in *British Women Poets*, pp. 169–71 and pp. 210–15).
9. See (1975) *The Erdmans Bible Dictionary*, A. C. Myers (ed.) (Kampen: J. H. Kok), 'fig tree', pp. 381–2.
10. (1724) 'Hypatia' in *Poems on Several Occasions: With Anne Boleyn to King Henry VIII. An Epistle* (London: John Clarke), pp. 61–6 (pp. 61, 62). (An excerpt of this poem, including these lines, is available in *Eighteenth-Century Women Poets*, pp. 99–100.)
11. Charlotte Smith is quoted in K. Juhas (2008) *"I'le to My Self, and to My Muse Be True": Strategies of Self-Authorization in Eighteenth-Century Women Poetry* (Frankfurt am Main and Oxford: Peter Lang), p. 236.
12. (1987) 'The Petition for an Absolute Retreat' in D. Thompson (ed.) *Anne Finch: Selected Poems* (Manchester: Fyfield), pp. 53–61, lines 1–2.
13. lines 38–41.
14. lines 281–2.
15. (1985) *Clarissa, or, The History of a Young Lady*, A. Ross (ed.) (Harmondsworth: Penguin), p. 1040. Lady Mary Wortley Montagu is quoted in T. Keymer and P. Sabor (2005) *'Pamela' in the Marketplace: Literary Controversy and Print*

188 Mascha Hansen

      Culture in Eighteenth-Century Britain and Ireland (Cambridge: Cambridge University Press), p. 109.
16. (1846) *The Diary and Letters of Mme d'Arblay*, C. Barrett (ed.), 7 vols (London: Colburn), VII, p. 373.
17. Samuel Crisp is quoted in (1990) *The Early Journals and Letters of Fanny Burney, 1774–1777*, L. Troide (ed.), 5 vols (Oxford: Oxford University Press), II, p. 123.
18. See Koselleck, *Vergangene Zeiten*, pp. 266–7.
19. *Vergangene Zeiten*, p. 361.
20. *Vergangene Zeiten*, pp. 30–3.
21. Tollet, 'Hypatia', p. 64. See also Backscheider, *Eighteenth-Century Women Poets and Their Poetry*, p. 71. Backscheider asserts that late eighteenth-century poets not only wrote more on history but also assumed a 'prophetic stance' (p. 14), and that 'Poets such as Pope and Johnson had insisted on the high calling as a judge and prophet, and the women poets at the end of the century took up this calling' (p. 374).
22. *Vergangene Zeiten*, pp. 33, 336. Prognostication, he says, implies – or even presupposes – expectation (p. 359).
23. In *Eighteenth-Century Women Poets*, pp. 153–5.
24. In *Eighteenth-Century Women Poets*, p. 459, lines 13–16.
25. In *British Women Poets*, pp. 238, 239. See Backscheider, *Eighteenth-Century Women Poets and Their Poetry*, chapter 6, for a longer discussion of the genre she calls retirement poetry.
26. T. Gray (1969) 'Elegy Written in a Country Church Yard' in R. Lonsdale (ed.) *The Poems of Thomas Gray, William Collins, and Oliver Goldsmith* (London: Longmans), pp. 117–40, lines 55–6; Anon, 'The Female Wish' in *British Women Poets*, lines 11–14.
27. 'An Epistle to Lady Bower' in *British Women Poets*, pp. 45–8, lines 27 and 29–30.
28. Jones, 'An Epistle', line 126.
29. In *British Women Poets*, pp. 21–2, lines 33–4.
30. lines 60–1.
31. lines 53–4.
32. In *Eighteenth-Century Women Poets*, pp. 68–9, lines 1–4.
33. In *Eighteenth-Century Women Poets*, pp. 8–9, lines 8–10.
34. lines 41–5.
35. line 45.
36. In *British Women Poets*, pp. 306–12, line 167.
37. lines 200–1.
38. In *British Women Poets*, pp. 275, 263.
39. In *Anne Finch: Selected Poems*, p. 22, lines 32–5.
40. In *Eighteenth-Century Women Poets*, p. 18, line 29.
41. This tradition is, of course, much older: see, for instance, Dryden's translation of Horace's Ode:

> Happy the man, and happy he alone,
> He, who can call today his own:
> He, who secure within, can say
> Tomorrow do thy worst, for I have liv'd today.

(2007) *Dryden: Selected Poems*, P. Hammond and D. Hopkins (eds) (Harlow: Pearson Education), pp. 343–9, lines 65–8.
42. In *Anne Finch: Selected Poems*, p. 66, lines 14–17.
43. In *Eighteenth-Century Women Poets*, pp. 367, 367–8.
44. In *Eighteenth-Century Women Poets*, pp. 368–9, lines 1–6.
45. lines 23–9.
46. (2000) in *Samuel Johnson: The Major Works*, D. Green (ed.) (Oxford: Oxford University Press) pp. 12–21, lines 367–8.
47. In *Eighteenth-Century Women Poets*, pp. 260–1, lines 52–3. Whateley's poem is a rather conventional satire on women for the first part, and then offers a much more hopeful vision of ageing than Johnson's.
48. lines 67 and 71.
49. In *Eighteenth-Century Women Poets*, pp. 238–40.
50. 'To Miss Hall' in *British Women Poets*, pp. 255–6, lines 25–32.
51. Backscheider points out that Carter, too, enjoyed writing graveyard poems in which she celebrates the tomb as her 'future peaceful Bed'. Yet even here, Carter seems to 'flirt with sentimentality' rather than indulge in melancholia (see *Eighteenth-Century Women Poets and Their Poetry*, p. 249).
52. In *British Women Poets*, p. 257, lines 10–14.
53. In *British Women Poets*, pp. 173–5, lines 50–3.
54. line 62.
55. line 71.
56. 'To my daughter, on being separated from her on her marriage' in *British Women Poets*, p. 178, lines 7–8.
57. R. Manners (1799) *A Review of Poetry* (London: J. Booth), p. 3. (An excerpt of this poem, including these lines, is available in *British Women Poets*, pp. 57–9.)
58. 'To a Friend. Written, 1782' in *British Women Poets*, pp. 84–5, lines 2, 26, 29, 36, 42.
59. 'To a Friend', lines 26–8.
60. (2012) *Beschleunigung: die Veränderung der Zeitstrukturen in der Moderne* (Frankfurt am Main: Suhrkamp), p. 87. He sees a return of that reaction at the end of the nineteenth century with its fashionable wave of 'ennui'.
61. In *British Women Poets*, pp. 87–9, lines 1, and 71–2.
62. lines 85–7 and 91–2.
63. 'Whatever is, is right' is the final line of Epistle I of A. Pope (1950) *An Essay on Man* in *The Twickenham Edition of the Poems of Alexander Pope, Vol. III.i*, M. Mack (ed.) (London: Methuen).
64. 'Song' in *British Women Poets*, pp. 457–8, lines 13 and 9–10; 'O Why Should Mortals Suffer Care' in *British Women Poets*, pp. 453–4, lines 1–2.
65. Blamire, 'O Why', line 17.
66. *Beschleunigung*, p. 93.
67. *Vergangene Zeiten*, p. 362.
68. (1993) *The Ladies Defence* in M. J. M Ezell (ed.) *The Poems and Prose of Mary, Lady Chudleigh* (New York and Oxford: Oxford University Press), pp. 15–40, lines 549–52 and 559–60.
69. lines 561–2.
70. Lonsdale, 'Introduction' in *Eighteenth-Century Women Poets*, pp. xxi–xlvii (p. xxxiv).

71. In *British Women Poets*, pp. 319–32, lines 444 (Muse's contemplation) and 450–7.
72. (2009) *The Ends of Life: Roads to Fulfilment in Early Modern England* (Oxford: Oxford University Press), p. 236.
73. (1830) 'Lines of Life' in *The Poetical Works of L.E.L.* (London: Longman), pp. 265–74, lines 73–5 and 93–6. See also Juhas, *Strategies of Self-Authorization*, p. 258.
74. Landon, 'Lines of Life', line 68.

11
Women Poets and the Mock-Heroic Elegy

Joanna Fowler

Discussion of mock-heroic verse has focused predominantly on the works of Augustan male poets, with Anna Laetitia Barbauld's 'Washing Day' (1797), arguably, being the most widely analysed female-authored example of this mode.[1] Attention on this poem, and its supplication to the 'domestic Muse', can be attributed to the recent critical interest in the 'poeticising [of] the domestic' and, as Adeline Johns-Putra considers, 'the way in which so much of [...] [the] work [of late eighteenth-century women poets] foregrounds, even celebrates, the homely, the private and, as such, the resolutely un-poetic'.[2] From the early 1700s, though, Jane Spencer notes that women were coming up against 'a new ideology of femininity' which meant that 'women were more highly valued [than in the sixteenth and seventeenth centuries], but also more confined to a special feminine sphere, as guardians of the home and of moral and emotional values'.[3] Despite this sense of restriction, Paula Backscheider stresses that 'women were writing all of the kinds of poetry that men were' and, throughout the century, female poets, such as Lady Mary Wortley Montagu, Elizabeth Thomas, Mary Jones, Sarah Dixon and Anna Seward, were employing the mock-heroic to explore a variety of themes, including illness and the loss of beauty it can cause (Montagu in 'Saturday: The Small-Pox' [wr. 1716; pub. 1747]), false lovers (Dixon in 'Cloe to Aminta. On the Loss of her Lover' [1740]) and the recipe for pot-pourri (Seward in 'Receipt for a Sweet Jar' [pub. 1810])![4] The mock-heroic mode would have represented a provocative option for women writers: although the elevated diction and style of this kind of verse, as well as the link to erudition, traditionally, would have been viewed as the jurisdiction of male writers, the trifling subject matter and the potential overlap with occasional verse would be seen as within the scope of women's writing. Also it would have proved intriguing because, as Richard Terry asserts, the 'mock-heroic provided a formula for thinking through a range of personal or social issues, ones involving ideas of triviality, disproportion, condescension or degradation' – issues close to the hearts of women facing this 'new ideology of femininity'.[5] Terry goes on to say that

> Women's forced withdrawal from active life, their presumed susceptibility to the ruses of consumer culture, and the age's construction of femininity in terms of a sickly delicacy of both body and mind, all rendered women both peripheral and trivial. Women's triviality, in fact, became a crucial issue within masculine discourse during the eighteenth century.[6]

It was also a 'crucial issue' for women, though, as they sought to address their treatment in society and literature, both in fictional poems and prose, and non-fictional periodicals.

As well as mock-epics and mock-heroic verse, the mock-elegy was widely experimented with during the period and the subject of the poem could be either human or animal. In her essay on pet elegies and epitaphs, Ingrid H. Tague writes that

> It was during the eighteenth century that pet keeping first developed as a widespread phenomenon, and this period also saw the rapid growth of literary works dealing with pets. More than a hundred epitaphs or elegies for pets were published in the British Isles during the century, including at least six for monkeys, twelve for canaries, seventeen for cats, and fifty-three for dogs.[7]

While Tague does refer to several examples of female-authored pet mock-elegies, she also makes the point that 'these poems were largely produced by men', perhaps because 'The objects of these poems – both the animals themselves and their owners – were often female, and there is, of course, a long tradition of using animals to satirize women.'[8] Numerous pet mock-elegies by men tap into a 'social discourse infused by mock-heroic' that, according to Terry, 'is the rhetoric of gallantry addressed towards women which the eighteenth century termed "fair-sexing"'.[9] For instance, in the widely anthologized Thomas Gray's 'Ode on the Death of a Favourite Cat, Drowned in a Tub of Goldfishes' (wr. 1747; pub. 1748), the downfall of Selima the tabby, the female overreacher whose death is a result of her love of treasure – fish, leads to the gendered moral in the final stanza:

> From hence, ye beauties, undeceived,
> Know, one false step is ne'er retrieved,
> And be with caution bold.
> Not all that tempts your wandering eyes
> And heedless hearts, is lawful prize;
> Nor all that glitters, gold.[10]

Selima may have been promoted to the role of doomed heroine, worthy of a Horatian ode in her honour, but she is portrayed, overall, as a greedy woman lacking in sense, highlighting Terry's point that 'Fair-sexing was a way of elevating women, but in terms that were consistent with a general subjugation'.[11] Both Tague and Margaret Doody note how, in both literature and art, a woman's relationship with an animal is often the site of male critique and fantasy, with the latter suggesting that female passion is seen as 'momentarily wasted and misdirected' towards an animal rather than towards a human, particularly a male friend or relation. Women writers, Doody suggests, are fully aware of this male frustration and play on it, stating: 'Women, it seems to me, consistently though not inevitably disturb the order of the affections when they introduce animals – even though officially they are not going out of the bounds of playfulness or of realism.'[12] This idea can be upheld when looking at pet mock-elegies by women poets because, as Backscheider asserts, they sometimes 'played with the form [of the elegy] for the amusement of their friends and themselves'.[13] This chapter will focus on examples of this type of verse by Elizabeth Thomas, Mary Jones and Mary Masters. As Roger Lonsdale indicates, many poems that mourn pets, such as 'laments for dead birds and small animals', demonstrate 'the insipidity of the fashionable poetry of this period', but, at the same time, Tague notes that 'The wide variety of literary approaches and quality [of mock-heroic animal elegies] reflect the variety of purpose that these works served, and it is one reason they are useful sources for students of eighteenth-century culture.'[14] She alludes to Masters in her essay, albeit only very briefly and, instead, she focuses on more sentimental examples of female-authored pet mock-elegies by later writers, such as Ann Francis and Anna Laetitia Barbauld. These poems are certainly interesting regarding the representation of the human–animal bond, but it is the, often comic, mock-heroic poems that, in some way, address and manipulate widely held views about female behaviour. What makes them particularly striking as poetic expressions of the human–animal relationship is that they adopt a mode often used to disparage women, and, with origins that can be traced back to Ovid and Catullus, to make a point about women as poets.

Mary Jones was not a poet who had ambitions to publish but was eventually persuaded to do so by her friends and was modest about her talents.[15] However, in her allusive 'Elegy on a Favourite Dog, suppos'd to be poison'd' (1750), added to the recently published third edition of Fairer and Gerrard's *Eighteenth-Century Poetry: An Annotated Anthology*, she does implicitly address the topic of female authorship by re-appropriating lines of verse by eminent male authors. As Backscheider asserts, 'Women like Mary Jones learned strategies that allowed them to acknowledge and covertly counter the increasing gendering pressures.'[16] Her poem may exhibit similarities to the archetypal male-authored pet mock-elegy with a dog – evocatively called Sparky, linking him to the 'foppish' kind of man often attacked by men of wit – and doting female owner, but she tweaks the presentation of these motifs to defy expectations.[17] Jones is commonly linked with Alexander Pope in criticism as there are several instances of her alluding to his work in her own and, as Fairer and Gerrard highlight, *The Rape of the Lock* (1714) is echoed on four occasions in this elegy.[18] In the opening heroic couplets (another link to Pope), dogs from all walks of life, including 'Shocks', are called upon to 'join the dismal howl' and mourn Sparky the dog.[19] Like Shock, Belinda's dog in *The Rape of the Lock*, Sparky is a lady's companion and some of his actions towards her are described bawdily. For instance, the poem employs what Laura Brown calls 'the familiar inter-species bed fellow scene [...] [that] becomes the locus classicus of the figure of the lady and the lapdog in the poetry of this period'.[20] In a couplet that even utilizes the same rhyme as Pope's corresponding couplet, we are told how the dog woke the lady in the morning and that '[...] when the balmy slumber I prolong, / [You] Ascend the stairs, and wake me with thy tongue' (38–9).[21] As a beloved dog, Sparky's fate was set because, according to the elegy and with a nod to Pope, 'all ye favourites fall! / Dogs, parrots, squirrels, monkeys, beaus and all' (26–7).[22] However, Sparky's mistress is no Belinda as this elegy is keen to point out: while the 50 sylphs failed to protect Pope's heroine, with the loss of her hair being prefigured by the assertion that a lady's petticoat or 'sev'nfold Fence' as a means of protection can 'Oft [...] fail', Sparky was always there to protect his mistress' honour as, regarding her suitors: 'Well he distinguish'd 'twixt brocade and sense, / And growl'd contempt beneath the sev'n-fold fence' (58–9).[23]

As well as Pope's mock-epic, as Fairer and Gerrard note, Jones also alludes to Shakespeare's *Hamlet* in a witty section of the poem in which the cat of the house is personified and depicted as one who is perfectly content with her fellow pet's demise (as she now is the recipient of Sparky's luxuriant treats of 'cream' and 'bread and butter soak'd in tea' [62]), with lines 64–5 of the poem declaring, the 'proud vixen [...] often seems to say, / "Peace to his shade! – each dog must have his day."'[24] Here, Jones takes the now famous proverbial phrase and uses it ironically: the usual sentiment of the phrase – that an underdog will eventually have his moment of glory – is replaced by the cat's snide remark that each favourite's time has to come to an end. It is this reminder of the transitory nature of life that is used to counteract the grief caused by Sparky's demise. However, it is not the idea that you should make the most out of life that offers consolation – instead it is thoughts of revenge. Earlier in the poem, the hope is expressed that Sparky's murderer will live a miserable life:

> O that kind fate would poison all thy life
> With some smart vixen, very much a Wife!
> And when the end of thy chastisement's near,
> May'st thou want ratsbane then – to poison Her. (12–15)

The idea of retribution is revisited to conclude the poem, with the wish that a lady's smile could bring Sparky back to life so that she could 'aid his vengeance at the pois'ner's heel' (77) or, in other words, so that he could come back and bite his attacker's heel! Jones's mock-elegy, then, ends with consolation, but twists the notion of gaining solace from thoughts of life-after-death by considering the idea that a woman's love and imagination can allow someone special to live again (and find retribution).

As is traditional with mock-heroic verse, Sparky is not portrayed as a humble pet but as a special companion and, even at times, like an epic hero. He may not have descended from gods, but he is illustrious because of his breeding. Lines 30–4 of the poem read:

> Thy high descent, thy ancient royal race!
> Thy length of ears proclaim'd the gen'rous seed,
> Hereditary heir of Charles's breed;
> And had not William chang'd the face of things,
> Might'st still have barked beneath the throne of kings.

However, despite the claim that Sparky, as a King Charles spaniel, still would have been the choice of kings if it was not for William III and the growing prominence of the pug, he is less celebrated for his beauty and more for his battle with his mistress' unwanted suitors.[25] Sparky knew to leave the room when a welcome 'Beau' was present, but 'when the ruddy 'Squire grew loud and vain' (52) and

> [...] practis'd all the noises of the plain;
> With sneaking step, at distance he'd retire,
> Then mount his tail, and ev'n out-bark the well-mouthed
>   'Squire. (53–5)

The spaniel becomes a tactical solider who uses his best weapon – his bark. Obviously, Jones's intention here is to be comic, but at the same time she is taking the relationship of the lady and the lapdog, often used to comment on a woman's sexuality, and instead employs it to present a dog, although a little jealous, concerned for his owner's welfare and honour.

While Mary Jones provides a different angle on the female pet owner, Mary Masters extends on the story of a female pet's death and eulogizes her. In her 1755 *Familiar Letters and Poems on Several Occasions*, her second published collection, Masters reprinted Thomas Gray's 'Ode on the Death of a Favourite Cat' (albeit under the more protracted title 'On a female Cat nam'd Selima, who fell into a China Cistern with Gold Fishes in it, and was drown'd; by Mr De Grey') and followed it up with two companion pieces of her own about Selima the cat. However, whilst it is well known that Gray wrote his poem about Horace Walpole's cat, Masters's first response, as declared in the title, is aimed at 'Selima's Mistress, to comfort her for the Loss of her Favourite'.[26] By changing focus to a female owner, Masters is immediately highlighting her intention to create a piece that will reposition Selima, as heroine, away from being the subject of Gray's cautionary tale. Gray's account of the cat's death offers no sense of consolation and, instead, uses it as a means to critique female behaviour. As Lonsdale highlights, 'Gray blends [...] some elements of the animal fable, which always concludes with a lightly moralistic application of the story to humanity, [...] [with] a kind of poem which moralizes ironically about women.'[27] Masters, although alluding to events in Gray's poem, playfully fights back and celebrates Selima's beauty, repositioning her from example in a fable to beloved of the Muses and the Gods.

In her biographical entry on the poet, Patricia Demers declares that Masters 'was [...] an adept imitator whose skill verged on parody'.[28] She draws attention to the fact that it was not only Gray's work that she responded to in her verse – in the same 1755 collection, Masters reprinted Dryden's 'Catullus to Lesbia' and then presented 'An Imitation of the foregoing Verses, by way of Reply' in which she 'adroitly turns the tables' on the accusatory male voice by retorting with accusations from Lesbia.[29] This 'turning of the tables' occurs in her second riposte to Gray. The first of the two focuses on Selima's charmed and Utopian life after her death; we are told that 'Tho ev'ry wat'ry God was deaf', 'Phoebus', the God of poetry, was not.[30] It is he that saved Selima as she is 'The only worthy of her Kind, / To breathe poetic Air' (p. 252) and so she now lives on Parnassus, where

> [...] hid from human Eyes she sports,
> On Clio's Lap Divine;
> And with her Purring swells the Notes,
> Of Phoebus and the Nine. (p. 253)

The poem is made up of seven ballad quatrains and the use of end-stopped common measure means that the story of Selima's rescue is presented in a step-by-step manner. Therefore, when the reader reaches the end of the poem, the implication is that the tale of Selima has come to an end, with Masters offering a different and more consolatory, although ridiculous, closure. This expectation is comically deflated by the title of the next poem in Masters's collection, though, which states that 'A Gentleman having read the foregoing Verses, ask'd what Reason could be given for Phoebus interesting himself in the Affair? This Question occasion'd the following Lines'.

In this second poem, Selima is elevated to even headier heights as she keeps company with, and is admired by, Thalia, 'the Muse of comedy and idyllic poetry', and Calliope, 'the Muse of epic poetry'.[31] On this occasion, Masters discards her previous poem's verse form, almost as if the humble ballad stanza is no longer suitable for her even loftier subject matter, and reverts to the stanza form used by Gray which is now known as the 'Song to David' stanza. Most of this poem hyperbolically expands on Selima's newly found status as set out in the initial composition, and it is almost as if Masters uses the first six stanzas to demonstrate her prosodic skill and knowledge of mythology. However, in the seventh stanza, the response to the Gentleman's question posed in the title is presented: why was Selima saved? The answer is that the God of Poetry wanted to impress a woman! We are told that Selima 'Sprung from an ancient honour'd Race / Of Daphne's fav'rite breed' (p. 257) so Phoebus, now humorously reduced from his high stature and referred to colloquially as 'the Don' (p. 257), had to save his lover's favourite cat. It seems as if everything that has come before has led to this – a comic dig at men. No matter his status, a man is always going to be at the whim of a woman, confirmed by the rhetorical question that follows the revelation about Phoebus's rescue which asks:

> Tell me ye mortal Lovers all,
> In such a case, at such a call,
>   Could the bright Beau do less? (p. 257)

This enquiry does not end the poem as Masters takes her tongue-in-cheek rewriting of Selima's fate that bit further by making a witty point about male and female poets. The final stanza reads:

> Phoebus, for Reasons unreveal'd,
> From his own Son her Fate conceal'd,
>   But told a kindred Dame.
> Yet GRAY to gain his Father's Praise,
> Sung all her Charms in pleasing Lays,
>   And won a Poet's Fame. (p. 258)

To humorously explain why Selima's complete story has not been disclosed until now, Masters cheekily suggests that Phoebus withheld information from Thomas Gray but let her in on the secret. By referring to Gray as the 'Son' of the God of Poetry and herself as the 'kindred Dame', rather than a 'Daughter' or even a 'Poet', she can be seen to be making a point about the different levels of recognition afforded to a male bard over a female one. As Demers point out, by reading Masters's two collections of poems, including the prefatory matter in which she refers to her father's distaste for women writing, it is evident that she was interested in 'proto-feminist issues'.[32] By continuing the story of Selima, she is not only responding to another poet's piece of work, but demonstrating her sense of humour, and also calling attention to the literary position held by women.

In her 1722 collection, Elizabeth Thomas also used a follow-up piece to a mock-elegy to address the issue of women writing. 'Jill. A Pindarick Ode' does not exhibit the bawdy comedy of Jones's work or the sustained mythologizing of Masters's piece and actually exhibits sincere emotion at points. However, its status as a mock-elegy is confirmed once the diction, imagery and irregular 'Pindarick' ode verse form are analysed. In her *Miscellany Poems on Several Subjects*, Thomas also uses the irregular ode for philosophical pieces and literary imitations like 'A Pindarick Ode In Imitation of Spencer's Divine Love, inscribed to Mrs Katherine Bridgeman', as well as for straight elegies, such as that 'To the Pious Memory of Mrs. Diana Bridgeman', highlighting the bathetic nature of her using the same form for a poem about a domestic animal.[33] The other pet mock-elegy that she writes is actually in trochaic tetrameter catalectic couplets, which is the only time she chooses this verse form in her collection; her decision on this occasion can be explained, though, by the assertion that 'Canario. To the Same. On the Death of Her beloved Bird' is meant to be 'In Imitation of Anacreon'.[34] While it is clear that the Lady Dowager de la Warr's bird will be extolled as an excellent example of the species in this poem, with his name being a conflation of 'canary' and the suffix often attached to a heroic name, 'Jill' holds different implications with Thomas seemingly playing on its negative connotations as 'A familiar or contemptuous term applied to a woman'.[35] Jill may have a lower status than most subjects of epics and odes, but she is elevated to their rank throughout the poem.

Thomas seems to have been incredibly aware of views on decorum and appropriateness when it came to women's verse, but rejected them through her writing. For instance, in the extremely sarcastic poem, 'A Panegyrick. To an Attorney', Thomas comically attacks men of the law, adopting the esoteric diction of this profession to shine a light on, what she sees as, their greed and inflated egos. Initially the poem appears to be a puff piece with the man being addressed as 'the Fav'rite of Apollo' but then the irony takes hold as she refers to her lower position, asking

> Permit me then, the hindmost of the Rear,
> To render Tribute due,
> Altho' too mean for you.
> Since I can't write heroick Verse,
> Nor durst presume I to rehearse
> A Merit so exact,
> As you each Moment make appear,
> In ev'ry Word and Act.[36]

Here Thomas is acknowledging the belief that epic/heroic verse was not a mode seen as suitable for women to attempt. She then goes on to use Latinate phrases and bombastic diction to disprove this assertion and in her mock-elegy she further challenges her supposed limits by endeavouring to turn Jill into a kind female hero.

The beginning of the poem elevates Jill to a god-like status. Although the traditional 'Invocation' of the epic is rejected as the voice of the poem declares to herself that 'Thy fatal Loss admits of no Relief, / And does all fruitless Aid refuse', Thomas raises Jill by having her evoke jealousy in one of 'the brightest stars of the northern winter sky'.[37] We are told that she has been 'Slain' by 'Syrius' because 'The spiteful Star had envied her' (p. 192) as 'His Lustre by her Eyes [had been] out-shin'd' (p. 193). By having Jill's demise come as a result of Sirius, Thomas is demonstrating her knowledge of beliefs that can be traced back to antiquity. Jay B. Holberg explains that 'several themes [...] continually reappear [...] in Greek and then Roman literature, which reveal popular ideas and beliefs concerning Sirius. [...] [It] is a "death star" used by Homer [in Book 11 of *The Iliad*] to convey the fate of doomed Hector in his battle with Achilles.' He also notes that, in Book 22, Homer alludes to 'the association of Sirius with dogs, and fever and again as a sign of betiding woe'.[38] It is highly likely that Thomas's awareness of the mythology surrounding the star came from literature as Sirius is often alluded to in both poetry and prose. The probability of this suggestion becomes even clearer when we take note of Thomas's description of Jill's actual death, as we learn that 'He [Sirius] shot a baleful Influence, / And snatch'd his beauteous Rival hence' (p. 193). Translations of *The Iliad* see Sirius described as 'baleful' and, in *The Shepheardes Calender for Julye*, Edmund Spenser talks about the 'Dogge of noisome breath' and uses the same adjective to describe the star, stating that his 'balefull barking bringes in hast / Pyne, plagues, and dreery death'.[39] Of course, Thomas is not just being allusive with her choice of death for her canine subject, she is also being humorous and facetious with Jill being killed by the 'dog-star' who is personified as an envious male getting revenge on a beautiful female.

The overtly hyperbolic vein used to address the dog's death continues as Jill's character is explored. Like Sparky and Selima, she is portrayed as exemplary in both appearance and temperament because of her good breeding, with it being declared that 'Two stately Dew-laps dangled o'er her Breast / Th'hereditary Ensigns of her Race' (p. 193) ('dew-laps' refer to the 'loose skin under the throat of dogs') and her body is described as being of 'Unspotted Whiteness' (p. 193), with the implication that she is both physically and morally pure.[40] However, her most treasured quality seems to be that her 'Kindness did improve: / [And] No Change of Fortune could thy Love prevent' (p. 195). This sentiment would have appealed to Thomas considering the personal difficulties that she faced in her own life; biographical sketches on the author make clear that she faced financial difficulties from, at least, 1718 onwards.[41] Tague suggests that, in general, 'elegies and epitaphs for pets throughout the eighteenth century'

> [...] help us understand how people thought about the relationship between humans and animals, and how that thinking changed over the century [...]. As ideas about animals and nature were transformed, satires increasingly gave way to works dominated by sentiment and an emphasis on the close bonds between human and beast.[42]

Thomas's poem blurs the line between the characteristically mock-heroic elegies of the earlier years of the century and the more emotional compositions of later years. This is what sets her poem apart from Jones's and Masters's elegies and indicates that this is a more experimental poem in terms of mock-elegy conventions. While Jones and Masters end their poems with a comic flourish, Thomas concludes with a more traditional search for consolation. The final stanza of the poem threatens to culminate in utter distress with the employment of parallelism to emphasize that Jill will 'No more' (p. 196) be amongst the living; however, the final use of this phrase, which coincides with an unfinished and unrhymed line as the dog's owner pauses for reflection, indicates a change in tone and attitude. Addressing a contemporary topic, Jill's owner finds solace from remembering her dog's actions at her death and declares that

> [...] when her Actions I review,
> I vow! I could almost believe
> The Metempsychosis is true. (70–2)

According to Tague, 'The Pythagorean belief in metempsychosis, the transmigration of souls, was widely known and frequently served as a starting point for thinking about animal souls in elegies and epitaphs.'[43] Therefore, while providing a sense of genuine solace, the close of Thomas's poem, furthermore, indicates her engagement with current meditations.

Although connections can be drawn between 'Jill. A Pindarick' and later mock-elegies in terms of tone and purpose, its closing couplet, designed as an inscription on a tomb, points to Thomas's knowledge of her literary predecessors as Ovid's mock-elegy to Corinna's parrot ends similarly.[44] Further references to the history of the pet mock-elegy are made in the companion piece that is entitled 'Apology for the foregoing

Ode'. In this poem, Thomas imagines the responses that her adaptation of the irregular ode will evoke. Starting with two emphatic triplets (the second being capped with an iambic heptameter), she writes:

> And now, methinks, some Criticks smiling cry,
> How Folly does that Sex betray
>   To superstitious Vanity!
> Could nothing less, than Pindar's lofty Verse,
>   Adorn a paltry Mongril's Hearse?
> Sure she's insufferably dull, or nobler Themes are scarce.[45]

She responds to potential disparagement of her choice of verse form, the beliefs expressed and the celebration of her domestic subject by listing Roman poets, such as Catullus, Scribonius, Goddeus, Ovid, Melancton and Lipsus (p. 197), and the animals that they wrote about in their elegies. Her powerful rebuke aimed at potential critics, opinionated about women poets and what they see as appropriate topics for them to address, ends emphatically with a punchy dig aimed at her attackers that proclaims:

> Cease then this Elegy to scorn,
> The Verse my Subject suits,
> Tho' Jill was but a Bitch in Form,
> Her Sense was more than Brutes. (p. 198)

Thomas is defiant – she knows what charges she will face in writing this poem, but is asserting herself as a knowledgeable and skilled versifier. Even though her other mock-elegy on 'Canario' is also very allusive, it does not have a wider target and purpose like 'Jill. A Pindarick Ode' (perhaps because the Lady Dowager de la Warr, who is the subject or addressee of five of Thomas's poems, requested this poem on her pet).[46] The poem on her canine heroine sits alongside poems like 'The True Effigies on a Certain Squire', 'To Pulcheria, On Her Saying behind my Back, I made my self ridiculous by writing Verses' and 'On Sir J—S— saying in a sarcastic Manner, My Books would make me mad' that are proto-feminist in their approach and address women, writing and education.[47]

By looking through anthologies on eighteenth-century women's verse, such as Roger Lonsdale's, Joyce Fullard's and Paula Backscheider and Catherine Ingrassia's, it is evident that many female poets wrote about the 'experience of writing' and the 'experience of reception' (those two phrases are actually subtitles in Backscheider and Ingrassia's collection).[48] These 'experiences' are addressed both explicitly and implicitly and through the medium of numerous different genres: for example, Jane Brereton and Mary Barber use verse epistles in 'Epistle to Mrs Anne Griffiths' and 'To a Lady, who commanded me to send her an Account in Verse' respectively, while Mary Whateley's 'On the author's Husband Desiring her to Write Some Verses' is an occasional poem and Hannah More's 'Epilogue to the Search after Happiness' is a pastoral dialogue. By using the pet mock-elegy to present varying degrees of comment on women's writing, Mary Jones, Mary Masters and Elizabeth Thomas take a mode of writing, often used to critique and/or patronize their sex, and invert its purpose, raising questions about what is acceptable in terms of poetic genre, verse form and subject matter for a woman writer to employ. Jones and Thomas both create mock-elegies that could also be identified as friendship poems, with Sparky and Jill presented as true and honest companions. However, Backscheider states that 'the friendship poem is the unique poetic kind in which women do not have to appropriate or accommodate to a space already claimed by men.'[49] In writing in the form of the mock-elegy, Jones and Masters, arguably, did have to 'claim a space' for their work and did so by knowingly alluding to and challenging verse by their male contemporaries and predecessors. In writing about a pet, all three women adopted a subject that was 'suitable' in that it came from the domestic sphere; however, they would then have been faced with, as Tague points out, 'a common [and negative] contemporary association between women, fashion, and pet keeping'.[50] While Jones and Masters play up to this association, with the former incorporating, but tweaking, common images of the lady and the lapdog, and the latter making Selima a pampered pet even in the afterlife, Thomas justifies Jill's special treatment by attributing human characteristics to the dog, talking of 'the Beauties of her fairer Mind' (p. 193). Perhaps most striking of all is how the three women take mock-heroic discourse, which as Terry says can be linked to the discourse of gallantry, to draw attention to their literary status: Jones plays with the words of Pope and Shakespeare; Masters usurps Gray's place next to Phoebus; and Thomas questions why she cannot write in a similar mode to a man without being criticized. These women, to use Demers phrase, 'turn the tables' and move from subjects of the mock-heroic to inventive creators of verse in this mode.

Notes

1. I refer to the mock-heroic as a 'mode' rather than a 'genre', drawing on a point made by Richard Terry (himself drawing on Alastair Fowler). He writes: 'Most previous criticism has tended to see mock-heroic as a genre, a distinct category of work, not as a fugitive "effect" flickering to life in a variety of contexts. Yet this is one of the directions in which mock-heroic evolves in the eighteenth century; indeed it is a mark of its full absorption in the literary culture of its day. This phenomenon is one that conforms to the process outlined by Alastair Fowler, by which a high-level "kind" devolves over time into a "mode", figuring, that is, as a building-block or flavouring within a more encompassing form, a destiny that in the eighteenth century can be seen as already having overtaken older forms such as the epigram or character.' See R. Terry (2005) *Mock-Heroic: Butler to Cowper* (Aldershot and Burlington, VT: Ashgate), p. 26.
2. A. L. Barbauld (1990) 'Washing Day' in R. Lonsdale (ed.) *Eighteenth-Century Women Poets: An Oxford Anthology* (Oxford: Oxford University Press), pp. 308–10, line 3; A. Johns-Putra (2010) 'Satire and Domesticity in Late Eighteenth-Century Women's Poetry', *Journal for Eighteenth-Century Studies*, 33:1, 67–87 (pp. 67, 68).
3. (1986) *The Rise of the Woman Novelist: From Aphra Behn to Jane Austen* (Oxford: Blackwell), p. 15. Richard Terry refers to this shift too but his discussion is about women as targets of gallantry and mock-heroic discourse, rather than as authors of such works. See *Mock-Heroic: Butler to Cowper*, p. 114.
4. (2008) *Eighteenth-Century Women Poets and Their Poetry: Inventing Agency, Inventing Genre* (Baltimore, MD: Johns Hopkins University Press), p. 102. Lady M. W. Montagu (1747) 'Saturday. The Small-Pox' in *Six Town Eclogues. With Some Other Poems* (London: M. Cooper), pp. 32–7 (an excerpt of this poem is available in *Eighteenth-Century Women Poets*, pp. 56–8); S. Dixon, 'Cloe to Aminta. On the Loss of Her Lover' in *Eighteenth-Century Women Poets*, p. 177; A. Seward (1810) 'Receipt for a Sweet Jar' in W. Scott (ed.) *The Poetical Works of Anna Seward; with Extracts from Her Literary Correspondence*, 3 vols (Edinburgh: James Ballantyne), I, pp. 110–12 (this poem is discussed at length in A. Johns-Putra, 'Satire and Domesticity', pp. 70–3).
5. *Mock-Heroic: Butler to Cowper*, p. 8.
6. *Mock-Heroic: Butler to Cowper*, p. 117.
7. (2008) 'Dead Pets: Satire and Sentiment in British Elegies and Epitaphs for Animals', *Eighteenth-Century Studies*, 41:3, 289–306 (p. 291).
8. 'Dead Pets', pp. 291, 293.
9. *Mock-Heroic: Butler to Cowper*, p. 9.
10. (1969) in R. Lonsdale (ed.) *The Poems of Thomas Gray, William Collins, and Oliver Goldsmith* (London: Longmans), pp. 78–85, lines 37–42.
11. *Mock-Heroic: Butler to Cowper*, p. 9.
12. (2010) 'Love in All Its Oddness: The Affections in Women's Private Poetry of the Eighteenth Century', *Huntington Library Quarterly*, 63:4, 491–508 (p. 501).
13. *Eighteenth-Century Women Poets and Their Poetry*, p. 276 (Backscheider discusses Jones's mock-elegy on this page).

14. Lonsdale, 'Introduction' in *Eighteenth-Century Women Poets*, pp. xxi–xlvii (p. xxxvi); Tague, 'Dead Pets', p. 291.
15. For biographical pieces on Mary Jones, see Lonsdale, *Eighteenth Century Women Poets*, pp. 155–6; D. Fairer and C. Gerrard (2015) *Eighteenth-Century Poetry: An Annotated Anthology*, 3rd edn (Oxford: Blackwell), p. 361; R. Greene (rev. W. R. Jones) (2009) 'Jones, Mary (1707–1778), poet', *Oxford Dictionary of National Biography*, online at: www.oxforddnb.com [accessed 14 September 2014].
16. *Eighteenth-Century Women Poets and Their Poetry*, p. 108.
17. See 'spark, n2', sense 2a in *Oxford English Dictionary*, online at: www.oed.com [accessed 14 September 2014].
18. In particular, Backscheider talks, in *Eighteenth-Century Women Poets and Their Poetry*, about the connections between Jones's 'Epistle to Lady Bowyer' and Pope's *Epistle to Dr Arbuthnot* (pp. 103–4). See Fairer and Gerrard, 'Notes' in *Eighteenth-Century Poetry: An Annotated Anthology*, pp. 369–70.
19. M. Jones (2015) 'Elegy, On a Favourite Dog, suppos'd to be poison'd' in *Eighteenth-Century Poetry: An Annotated Anthology*, pp. 368–70, lines 3 and 9. Further line references are to this edition and are given in parentheses following the quotation.
20. (2010) *Homeless Dogs and Melancholy Apes: Humans and Other Animals in the Modern Literary Imagination* (Ithaca, NY and London: Cornell University Press), pp. 127–8.
21. A. Pope (1962) *The Rape of the Lock: An Heroi-Comical Poem* in G. Tillotson (ed.) *The Twickenham Edition of the Poems of Alexander Pope, Vol II*, 3rd edn (London: Methuen), pp. 127–206, I. 115–16.
22. *The Rape of the Lock*, IV.120.
23. *The Rape of the Lock*, II.119.
24. According to *The Oxford Dictionary of Proverbs*, the phrase can actually be traced back to 1545; however, it is most famously used in *Hamlet* (see J. Speake [ed.] [2008], 5th edn [Oxford: Oxford University Press], p. 82). The line 'The cat will mew and dog will have his day' appears in V.i.281 of *Hamlet* ([2006] A. Thompson and N. Taylor [eds] [London: Arden Shakespeare]).
25. Fairer and Gerrard suggest that, in these lines,

> Jones draws a playful parallel with the end of the Stuart dynasty ('*Charles's* breed'). At the 'Glorious Revolution' of 1688 the Catholic King James II (Charles's 'hereditary heir') was exiled to be replaced by the Dutch Protestant William III. None of the fruits of Charles's 'gen'rous seed' was legitimate. (p. 369, note)

However, I believe Jones is also referring to the new 'face' of the pug. Katharine Rogers explains that

> Pugs arrived in Europe in the seventeenth century, when Dutch traders brought them from the Far East. One saved the life of William of Orange by waking him when enemy Spanish soldiers were approaching his camp, and he introduced them to England when he became King William III.

See (2010) *First Friend: A History of Dogs and Humans* (Bloomington: iUniverse), p. 94.

26. See C. Frayling (2009) *Horace Walpole's Cat* (London: Thames & Hudson). On p. 27, Frayling notes the different names used for the poem.
27. *The Poems of Thomas Gray, William Collins, Oliver Goldsmith*, p. 80.
28. (2004) 'Masters, Mary (fl. 1733–1755)', *Oxford Dictionary of National Biography*, online at: www.oxforddnb.com [accessed 14 September 2014].
29. 'Masters, Mary (fl. 1733–1755)'; M. Masters (1755) 'An Imitation of the foregoing Verses, by way of Reply' in *Familiar Letters and Poems on Several Occasions* (London: D. Henry and R. Cave), p. 190 (Dryden's poem appears on p. 189).
30. (1755) 'The following upon the same Occasion, was wrote by a Lady, probably to Selima's Mistress, to comfort her for the Loss of her Favourite' in *Familiar Letters and Poems on Several Occasions*, pp. 251–3. (Gray's poem appears on pp. 248–50). Further page references are to this edition and are given in parentheses following the quotation.
31. (1755) 'A Gentleman having read the foregoing Verses, ask'd what Reason could be given for Phoebus interesting himself in the Affair? This Question occasion'd the following Lines' in *Familiar Letters and Poems on Several Occasions*, pp. 253–8 (p. 255). Further page references are to this edition and are given in parentheses following the quotation. See entries on 'Thalia' and 'Calliope' in E. Knowles (2005) *The Oxford Dictionary of Phrase and Fable*, 2nd edn (Oxford: Oxford University Press), pp. 713, 116.
32. 'Masters, Mary (fl. 1733–1755)'.
33. (1722) 'A Pindarick Ode In Imitation of Spencer's Divine Love, inscribed to Mrs Katherine Bridgeman' and 'To the Pious Memory of Mrs. Diana Bridgeman. An Ode' in *Miscellany Poems on Several Subjects* (London: Thomas Combes), pp. 68–76 and pp. 29–38.
34. In *Miscellany Poems on Several Subjects*, pp. 53–6. J. Mason (1749) *An Essay on the Power of Numbers, and the Principles of Harmony in Poetical Compositions*, observation seven of 'Observations on the Trochaic Measure' states: 'Under the Trochaic Measures may be comprehended the Anacreontic Verse. This is usually divided into stanzas, each stanza containing four Lines which Rime alternately to each other; and every Line consists of three Troches and a long Syllable' (London: James Waugh), pp. 65–6. Although Thomas composed her poem before this book was published, and used a varying stanza form, it can be assumed that this view of Anacreontic verse was current during the earlier part of the century too.
35. 'gill/jill n4', sense 1a, *Oxford English Dictionary*, online at: www.oed.com [accessed 14 September 2014].
36. In *Miscellany Poems on Several Subjects*, pp. 122–5 (pp. 122, 123).
37. E. Thomas, 'Jill. A Pindarick Ode' in *Miscellany Poems on Several Subjects*, pp. 192–6 (p. 192). Further page references are to this edition and are given in parentheses following the quotation (an extract of this poem is available in *Eighteenth-Century Women Poets*, p. 42). J. B. Holberg (2007) *Sirius: Brightest Diamond in the Night Sky* (Berlin, New York and Chichester: Springer), p. 15.
38. Holberg, *Sirius*, pp. 17–18, p. 18.
39. E. Spenser (2013) *The Shepheardes Calendar* (Cambridge: Cambridge University Press), Julye, pp. 37–44 (p. 37). Reference found via G. Noonan (1990) *Fixed Stars and Judicial Astrology* (Washington: American Federation of Astrologers), p. 66.

40. 'dewlap, n', sense 1b, *Oxford English Dictionary*, online at: www.oed.com [accessed 14 September 2014].
41. For biographical information on Elizabeth Thomas, see Lonsdale, *Eighteenth-Century Women Poets*, pp. 32–3; R. Mills (2008) 'Thomas, Elizabeth (1675–1731), poet', *Oxford Dictionary of National Biography*, online at: www.oxforddnb.com [accessed 14 September 2014].
42. 'Dead Pets', p. 289.
43. 'Dead Pets', p. 299.
44. (1968) *Amores II.vi* in G. Lee (trans.) *Ovid's Amores* (London: John Murray), pp. 74–9.
45. 'Apology for the foregoing Ode' in *Miscellany Poems on Several Subjects*, pp. 197–8 (p. 197). Further page references are to this edition and are placed in parentheses following the quotation.
46. Similarly, Mary Jones's (1750) 'Consolatory Rhymes to Mrs. East. On the Death of her Canary Bird' (in *Miscellanies in Prose and Verse* [Oxford: Mr Dodsley, Mr Clements, Mr Frederick], pp. 90–3) focuses primarily on providing solace for the bird's owner, with the sentiment that 'When life goes out, the Samian sages say, / We only change our tenement of clay' (p. 91).
47. In *Miscellany Poems on Several Subjects*, pp. 79–85, 85–6, 181–6.
48. See Lonsdale, *Eighteenth-Century Women Poets*; P. R. Backscheider and C. E. Ingrassia (eds) (2009) *British Women Poets of the Long Eighteenth Century: An Anthology* (Baltimore: Johns Hopkins University Press); J. Fullard (ed.) (1990) *British Women Poets, 1660–1780: An Anthology* (New York: Whitston Publishing Company).
49. *Eighteenth-Century Women Poets and Their Poetry*, p. 175.
50. 'Dead Pets', p. 293.

Part IV
Self and Others

12
Getting Personal
Swift's Non-Public Poetry

Allan Ingram

In one sense, all of Swift's poetry was public. He seemed incapable, even in his private correspondence, and even in what eventually became the *Journal to Stella*, of keeping a sense of potential public response out of his writing. In most of his prose works, of course, and in all of his published ones, it is a very public readership he is aiming at, and any sense of self that we see is almost certainly going to be a fabricated one, just as Gulliver, the author of *Tale of a Tub* and the proposer in *A Modest Proposal* are carefully judged constructs. Many of his poems were published during Swift's lifetime, often several years after composition, while many were circulated in manuscript. He was not a poet who wrote primarily for himself, but for public, or at least semi-public, effect. In this respect, his poetry and his prose are different forms of the same enterprise. But in much of his poetry, nevertheless, there is ambiguity, both in the published and, even more, in his unpublished verse. The personal, for all that it is often hidden beneath ironies, voices and forms of expression, is nevertheless a frequently informing presence.

One brief example of the extent of the public/private overlap is in the extempore lines he wrote 'To Mr Harley's Physicians', the inscription he gave it when reporting it to Stella in the *Journal to Stella* on 19 February 1712, almost a year after the knife assault on the Lord Treasurer by the Frenchman Guiscard:

> I dind with my Ld Treasurer to day, & sate with him till 10 [...]. I told him of 4 Lines I writ extempore with my Pencil, on a bitt of Paper in his House while he lay wounded; Some of the Servant[s] I suppose made wastepaper of them; and he never had heard of them. Shall I tell them you [...] [.] Thus On Europe Britain's Safety lyes; Britain is

lost if Harley dyes; Harley depends upon your Skill: Think What You save, or what You kill.[1]

The lines were not published during Swift's lifetime, only appearing in print as part of John Hawkesworth's 1766 edition of the *Journal*, and in their own right when John Nichols brought out his *Select Collection of Poems* in 1782. They would appear, therefore, not to have been intended by Swift for wider circulation beyond Stella, Harley himself and perhaps a few of their circle. Modern editions of Swift's poetry print them from Swift's autograph (not, after all, made into 'wastepaper' by servants), and correct the obvious copying error from the *Journal*:

> To Mr Harlyes Surgeon
> On Britain Europe's safety lyes
> And Britain's lost if Harly dyes
> Harly depends upon your skill,
> Think what you save or what you kill
> J[2]

Irvin Ehrenpreis mentions the lines, rather dismissively, when discussing Harley's surviving the assassination attempt: 'An acclamatory wave of verse and prose celebrated the British patriot who had been struck down by a French papist spy. One of the weaker effusions was an impromptu quatrain by Swift.'[3] But while the quality of the verse as poetry is debatable, its real interest lies in what it brings to the fore of both Swift's public position and his private one, and of their interlocking features.

As a potential public statement, of course, the lines, though never actually made public, represent a very natural response to an event that shocked the nation and, for a while at least, produced genuine uncertainty over the immediate political future. On a more personal note, Swift's feelings, as related to Archbishop King in Dublin in a letter written on the day of the stabbing, while the outcome was still uncertain, come across as composed of genuine anxiety and distress, for many reasons:

> Nothing could happen so unluckily to England at this Juncture, as Mr. Harley's Death, when he has all the Schemes for the greatest Part of the Supplies in his Head, and the Parliament cannot stir a Step without him. Neither can I altogether forget myself, who, in him, should lose a Person I have more Obligations to, than any other in

this Kingdom; who hath always treated me with the Tenderness of a Parent, and never refused me any Favour I asked for a Friend.

He adds, in effect in a postscript: 'I have read over what I writ, and find it very confused and incorrect, which your grace must impute to the violent Pain of Mind I am in, greater than ever I felt in my Life.'[4] Public and private mix inextricably to produce a confused tumult of emotions.

But other factors, drawn from Swift's wider views and prejudices, also exert an influence on the verses, not least his opinion of the medical profession. The *Journal to Stella* contains more private details than the letter to King, or than the quatrain. On the morning of 9 March, he writes:

> Patrick is just come from Mr. Harley's. He slept well till four; the surgeon sat with him: he is asleep again: he felt a pain in his wound when he waked: they apprehend him in no danger. This account the surgeon left with the porter, to tell people that send. Pray God preserve him.[5]

This surgeon was Paul Buissière, a naturalized Frenchman who had achieved considerable distinction in his adopted country. This satisfactory situation, however, from Swift's point of view, changed very much for the worse when the society physician John Radcliffe was called in. As he writes on 26 March, 'All things are at a stop in parliament for want of Mr. Harley; they cannot stir an inch without him in their most material affairs: and we fear by the caprice of Radcliffe, who will admit none but his own surgeon, he has not been well lookt after.'[6] Radcliffe, who prescribed for Swift at times, employed as surgeon a Mr. Green, whom Swift describes on 10 April as 'an ill surgeon', appointed 'by the caprice of that puppy Dr. Radcliffe; which has kept him back so long'.[7] Green, though, was still attending on Harley in July, and Swift reports him dressing the Lord Treasurer's breast, 'that is, put on a plaister, which is still requisite'.[8] By this time, there is also concern over Queen Anne's health: Swift tells Stella that he 'took an opportunity to speak to him of the queen; but he cut me short [...]. I find he is against her taking much physick; and I doubt he cannot persuade her to take Dr. Radcliffe.'[9]

It is, of course, unclear whether Swift is aiming at Buissière or at Green in stipulating 'Think what you save or what you kill.' Either way, the line, sardonic already, takes on an extra resonance when read in the context of Swift's mixed feelings about the profession, but a distinctly personal bias if it is Green and, behind him, the 'puppy' Radcliffe who are being aimed at. But more broadly, 'To Mr Harlyes Surgeon', as a private statement about a very public event, fuelled in its detail by personal animosity, stands as a model of the terrain occupied by so much of Swift's non-public, or semi-public, poetry, whether published by him during his lifetime or not.

Two other unusual lines – indeed, they are unique among his poetic output – reflect, more self-deprecatingly, the fluidity of the private/public borderline in Swift's poetry. These are the curious and enigmatic 'Verses Made in Swift's Sleep': 'I walk before no man, a hawk in his fist; / Nor, am I a brilliant, whenever I list.'[10] These were certainly not published by Swift, and the title is provided by Pat Rogers for his edition of the poems in 1983. They were apparently written during the night of 26–7 December 1733. As Rogers explains:

> Swift's young friend, Rev. John Lyon, transcribed a memorandum containing these lines into a copy of Hawkesworth's *Life of Swift* [1754–5].
> The memorandum runs:
> December 27, 1733.
> I waked at two this morning with the two above lines in my head, which I had made in my sleep, and I wrote them down in the dark, lest I should forget them. But as the original words being writ in the dark, may possibly be mistaken by a careless or unskilful transcriber, I shall give them a fairer copy, that two such precious lines may not be lost to posterity.[11]

The relation between private and public is no less clear for it being spoofed by Swift. The lines themselves, one imagines, would have been meaningless to Swift, and to a wider audience, and therefore of curiosity value to no one but himself – if that. But, characteristically, and aware of his own celebrity by 1733, and very ready to satirize both it and a potentially undiscriminating public taste, he makes a show, in private, of preserving them in a finished copy for 'posterity'.

Swift, though, was very alert to his own presence, not only as a writer who would most likely continue to be read in time to come but also within his own semi-public circle – his friends and social contacts, particularly when permanently resident in Dublin after 1714. This was a circle that included, in various combinations, Stella, Vanessa, Thomas Sheridan, Swift's poetic female friends, like Laetitia Pilkington and Mary Barber, his clerical friends and, after the deaths of Vanessa in 1723 and

Stella in 1728, the Acheson family, Sir Arthur and Lady Anne, of Market Hill in Armagh and particularly Lady Anne. The 'Market Hill' poems, the products of extended visits to the family, represent a distinct rediscovery of Swift's sense of fun in his verse, not least after the despair he felt during the long final illness of Stella. One of the most playful, in fact, is dated 'August 12 1728', and has the title 'An excellent new Panegyrick on Skinnibonia', which was Swift's nickname for the unusually thin Lady Acheson:

> Skinnibonia, brown and bright,
> Consort lean of comely Knight,
> Or, to raise thy Title high'r,
> Sherriffess of Armagh-shire:
> Thou be subject of my quill
> Nut-brown pride of Market-hill:
> Let me, for I know them well,
> All thy various motions tell,
> How thy spirits quick extend
> To each Toe and fingers end;
> Wonder not they travel so,
> Little way they have to go,
> Skin and bone so closely fixt,
> No intruding flesh betwixt.[12]

Given that, as Ehrenpreis says, this was clearly written during Swift's first extended visit at Market Hill (it began in June of 1728 and ended with his return to Dublin in February 1729), the lines are evidence of an extraordinarily high degree of informality, of being at ease in the company of both wife and husband.[13] If the most obvious aspect of 'getting personal' in this poem (and it is 100 lines long) is Swift's freedom to joke about Lady Acheson's physical appearance, the tone and subject matter would also seem to reveal his own contentment in the company of these new friends. The detail of the lines conspicuously portrays the lady's characteristic gestures and restlessness:

> Now each nimble finger skips
> O'r thy Nose, and Chin, and lips,
> O[']r thy Neck with nails respectless
> Scratching round a ruby necklace;
> While the joggings of thy feet
> To thy head in consort meet.[14]

The very fact of Swift's familiarity with them, though, and of his taking the liberty of extracting amusement from them, is evidence of a very attentive interest in Anne's whole personality and mode of being. Indeed, as if to draw attention to an unusual degree of intimacy, Swift actually plays a part within the poem, coming to the rescue when Lady Acheson, out walking, is caught unawares by a gust of wind:

> Leanest, lightest Skinnibony,
> Zephyr's Mistress, Echo's Crony;
> Zephyr, when you chanc'd to stoop
> Strove to get beneath your hoop,
> And to waft you Lord knows where,
> To his Palace high in air:
> But the Dean with counter-charm
> Interpos'd his valiant arm,
> Lent a Pin to make all tight;
> Zephyr fled with grief and spight.[15]

This, certainly, is an unusual representation of 'the Dean': he is 'valiant' like a knight of old (Sir Arthur, the actual 'Knight', by contrast, is only described as 'comely'), and either he is charming in manners, or he is possessed of powers that act as a charm – a 'counter-charm'. His presence in the poem brings benefit, albeit the incident he has chosen to draw attention to might be seen as verging on impertinent, or even as in dubious taste.

As David Woolley says, however,

> As 'family verses of mirth,' this rollicking poem was probably meant to be read aloud, perhaps with appropriate vocal and gestural mimicry, as after-dinner or evening entertainment, like other Market Hill poems that allude humorously to family members, house guests, servants, and neighbours. The new poem also seems designed to manage tensions between Swift and his hosts, including the fact that it was Anne rather than Arthur to whom Swift was particularly drawn.[16]

Stephen Karian points out that this was one of the poems written for a very restricted audience, and probably depending on the manuscript-holder – in this case Lady Acheson – rather than Swift to decide upon the breadth of its circulation. In fact, 'An excellent new Panegyrick', says Karian, appears not to have circulated in manuscript beyond the immediate family during Swift's lifetime.[17] As already noted, it did not appear in print until 2008.

Louise K. Barnett writes of the Market Hill poems that they illustrate

> the complete strategy of self-defense: a speaker portrays Swift as a ridiculous figure, but this portrait is then undercut so that the final result is a triumph over Swift's enemies – that is, friends turned into enemies within the poetic fiction. Under the guise of 'these family verses of mirth,' Swift confronts and exorcises various ridiculous postures in which his friends *might* see him.[18]

'An excellent new Panegyrick' is unusual among these poems in not following the pattern Barnett outlines: Swift, rather, is the amused observer of another's distinctiveness and, in the course of the poem, also the mock saviour of the day. More characteristic, not least in terms of the poet's series of double-takes between private individual, made public by being spoken and written about, but finally rendered private again, within the circle of its recipients, is 'Lady Acheson Weary of the Dean', probably written some time during Swift's visit of 1728–9, and actually published as a broadside in Dublin in 1730, though Karian suggests that this might have been 'unauthorized'.[19] Here is a poem spoken entirely through the voice of Lady Acheson herself, who thus becomes, in Barnett's terms, one of the 'enemies within the poetic fiction'. She is bemoaning Swift's extended visit, and pointing out that this was by no means what they had in mind when making an invitation to him:

> The Dean wou'd visit Market-hill,
>   Our Invitation was but slight
> I said—why—Let him if he will,
>   And so I bid Sir *Arthur* write.
>
> His Manners would not let him wait,
>   Least we should think ourselves neglected,
> And so we saw him at our Gate
>   Three Days before he was expected.
>
> After a Week, a Month, a Quarter,
>   And Day succeeding after Day,
> Says not a Word of his Departure
>   Tho' not a Soul would have him stay.[20]

This, even more explicitly than 'An excellent new Panegyrick', would seem to be 'designed to manage tensions between Swift and his hosts', if only by confronting them directly and challenging the Achesons actually to say in earnest what Swift jests of, or perhaps mock jests of, in the poem: 'But you, my Life', says Lady Acheson to Sir Arthur in the poem,

> may let him know,
>   In civil Language, if he stays
> How deep and foul the Roads may grow,
>   And that he may command the Chaise. (17–20)

Finally, her temper breaks through, and she roundly declares what she would do to Swift that would very soon make him leave, and concludes with an extra burst of resentment at his constant mockery of her:

> Oh! If I could, how I would maul
>   His Tallow Face and Wainscot Paws,
> His Beetle-brows and Eyes of Wall,
>   And make him soon give up the Cause.
>
> Must I be every Moment chid
>   With skinny, boney, snip and lean,
> Oh! that I could but once be rid
>   Of that insulting Tyrant Dean. (37–44)

Unlike 'An excellent new Panegyrick', Swift himself makes no appearance in the poem. There is no need: the poem is entirely devoted to him, the space he occupies in the speaker's mind and resentments as much as within her house, the behaviour that so grates and jars with her and even the physical characteristics, the eyes and beetle brows, that have so engrained themselves that she cannot be rid of them, any more than she can expel their possessor. As Nora Crow Jaffe points out, 'Swift seems unusually conscious of his appearance' in the Market Hill poems.[21] Far from making no appearance, in fact, it is Swift's actual appearance that constitutes the entirety of the speaker's complaint, both the way he looks and the fact that he has appeared at their gate and stayed for month after month.

If this is Lady Acheson's (or 'Lady Acheson's') revenge for the constant mockery of her own appearance and mannerisms, it is, of course, more precisely the expression of an awareness on Swift's part that there is a very public price to pay, potentially, for the personal aspects of one's personality. The private individual, at ease among a circle in which he feels confident enough to write 'An excellent new Panegyrick', also expresses the other side of that freedom by imagining the cost of his presence on the circle itself. What is private for him is public for them, albeit here represented in the process of being spoken in private, between wife and husband. Swift himself is thrust into a very different kind of prominence from the 'valiant' saviour of the day: he is now made public as the social menace who ruins his so-called friends' private existence.

Probably the most extreme of the forms of personal representation, though, in the 'Market Hill' poems and also potentially one of the most revealing, comes in 'Death and Daphne'. This was written in 1730 and first published in the 1735 *Works*. Here it is Swift/'*Death*' himself, rather than Lady Acheson, or '*Daphne*', who is the lead figure. He is ordered by '*Pluto*' to marry in order to help, by producing a brood of 'Young *Deathlings*', to restock the kingdom of the dead after the increased life expectancy on earth following the Peace of Utrecht.[22] A substantial part of the first half of the poem is spent describing how he is furnished out as a beau in order to make his court of a suitable mate upon earth:

> The Owl, the Raven, and the Bat,
> Club'd for a Feather to his Hat;
> His Coat, an Us'rer's Velvet Pall,
> Bequeathed to *Pluto*, Corps and all. (29–32)

'*Daphne*' becomes the joint focus at the halfway point, when '*Death*' enters the room 'where she sat at Cards' and makes an instant impression:

> She, as he came into the Room,
> Thought him *Adonis* in his Bloom.
> And how her Heart with Pleasure jumps,
> She scarce remembers what is Trumps.
> For, such a Shape of skin and Bone
> Was never seen, except her own[.] (57–62)

So enamoured is she that she 'freely made the first Advance' (68), eager, apparently, to be wedded to this most compelling of figures. The poem ends, however, with '*Death*' himself drawing back. This is partly a joke at Lady Acheson's expense, along the lines of 'An excellent new Panegyrick':

> For, when by chance the meagre Shade
> Upon thy Hand his Finger laid;
> Thy Hand as dry and cold as Lead,
> His matrimonial Spirit fled:
> He felt about his Heart a Damp,

> That quite extinguish'd *Cupid*'s Lamp:
> Away the frighted Spectre scuds,
> And leaves my Lady in the Suds. (93–100)

In other words, the skeletonic Lady's body temperature is colder than '*Death*', and she is therefore incapable of arousing '*Death*'s' generative passion. He flees, terrified at having encountered a living being more death-like than himself.

The ending of the poem, though, is not only a joke upon Lady Acheson's extreme thinness: it is also a matter of Swift facing facts, and remorselessly expressing them. At the time of his first visit to Market Hill, in 1728, Swift was 61, fresh from the death of Stella, only five months earlier. Anne Acheson was probably in her early thirties. Like '*Death*' in the poem, he found in her a kindred spirit, one whose lively and appreciative personality brought out a playful inventiveness in his poetry, and no doubt a forgetfulness of his recent personal history. Yet more personal still, in 'Death and Daphne', is the acknowledgement that compatibility in terms of outlook, literary taste and sense of humour should not be mistaken for anything more: 'Cease, haughty Nymph; the Fates decree / *Death* must not be a Spouse for thee' (91–2). Or rather, 'Cease, haughty Dean', perhaps. The moral lesson might be aimed, in the poem, at the Lady, but the personal warning, framed by the poetic voice, is couched as an acknowledgement by '*Death*'.

This is underlined by the realization that the poem reworks earlier Swift territory, that covered in *Cadenus and Vanessa*.[23] This was probably written in 1712–13, and first published in around 1726 – though Stephen Karian points out that unauthorized copies had circulated widely prior to that.[24] It was then included in both the 1727 *Miscellanies. The Last Volume*, which was edited by Pope, and in the *Works* of 1735. By the time of writing, Swift would have been 44 or 45, while Esther Vanhomrigh was in her mid twenties. The age difference is not as great as that between Swift and Lady Acheson, yet the self-representation within the poem if anything exaggerates the gap, not just in terms of years but also personality and outlook. '*Vanessa*', younger in the poem than Esther herself, is described as being 'in her Bloom': she advances 'like *Atalanta*'s Star, But rarely seen, and seen from far'.[25] '*Cadenus*', on the other hand, worn beyond his middle-aged years, is one 'Grown old in Politicks and Wit' (503), one for whom

> [...] Time, and Books, and State Affairs
> Had spoil'd his fashionable Airs;

> He now cou'd praise, esteem, approve,
> But understood not what was Love.
> His Conduct might have made him styl'd
> A Father, and the Nymph his Child.
> That innocent Delight he took
> To see the Virgin mind her Book,
> Was but the Master's secret Joy
> In School to hear the finest Boy. (544–53)

Once '*Cupid*' has successfully wounded Vanessa's heart, however, piercing as he does so a 'feeble Volume' (518) of Cadenus' 'Poetick Works', she sees him as utterly transformed – quite another figure than the exaggerated, prematurely aged pedant as at first represented by Swift:

> *Vanessa*, not in Years a Score,
> Dreams of a Gown of forty-four;
> Imaginary Charms can find,
> In Eyes with Reading almost blind;
> *Cadenus* now no more appears
> Declin'd in Health, advanc'd in Years.
> She fancies Musick in his Tongue,
> Nor further looks, but thinks him young. (524–31)

The impact on Cadenus is powerful, and, Swift makes clear, self-deluding. The formerly staid and remote prelate begins to think of himself as Vanessa clearly thinks:

> *Cadenus*, to his Grief and Shame,
> Cou'd scarce oppose *Vanessa's* Flame;
> But tho' her Arguments were strong,
> At least, cou'd hardly wish them wrong.
> [...]
> His Pride began to interpose,
> Preferr'd before a Crowd of Beaux,
> So bright a Nymph to come unsought,
> Such Wonder by his Merit wrought[.] (744–7; 750–3)

And, retreating for a moment, the poet adds:

> 'Tis an old Maxim in the Schools,
> That Vanity's the Food of Fools.
> [...]

> So when *Cadenus* could not hide,
> He chose to justify his Pride;
> Constru'ing the Passion she had shown,
> Much to her Praise, more to his Own. (758–9; 762–5)

As with 'Death and Daphne', the main thrust of the poem is against the man, the elder, the fool who should have known better than to allow his pride to be flattered by the admiration of a much younger woman.

Such poems are indeed personal, and include various strategies of self-representation, some of them deeply self-critical, or self-condemnatory, albeit beneath a surface of a poetic light touch. Public appearance, though, and an emphasis upon the wider public ethic of moral responsibility filter that which derives from the private and make it fit for a public audience – indeed, in the case of 'Death and Daphne' and *Cadenus and Vanessa,* for inclusion in two collections approved by Swift himself. Apparently, Swift felt that whatever there was of the intensely personal within either poem was sufficiently obscured to allow for wider circulation than simply the person who was subject and recipient. The same holds, too, for most of the poems he wrote to Stella, not least those composed for her birthday, 13th March, most years from 1719 through to 1727. Of these, seven poems in all (there are no poems for 1720 and 1726), all but those for 1722 and 1724 were published by Swift, both in *Miscellanies. The Last Volume* and in the 1735 *Works*. The 1724 birthday poem's absence from publication during Swift's lifetime is explained by the sub-heading: 'Written when I was sick'. There were clearly some aspects of his personal life Swift wished to keep personal. But there is no clear reason why the 1722 poem remained unpublished, particularly as it was one of the three birthday poems copied by Stella into her poembook before Swift ended it in 1722 – indeed, 'To Stella on her Birth-day. Written A.D. 1721-2' was the final poem to be copied in.[26] In the event, it remained unpublished until 1766.[27]

In terms of treatment of the personal, the Stella poems, where one might expect to find them most explicit – after all, this was the woman with whom Swift had the longest and probably most intimate relationship of his life – are generally reticent, more a gentle mocking of both Stella and of himself than any attempt at defining a friendship. If anything, as Irvin Ehrenpreis suggests, they are anti-romances, they dwell 'on what common love songs would hide: her bulk and her age'.[28] So, the very first, 'On Stella's Birth-day. Written AD. 1718–[19]', begins:

> Stella this Day is thirty-four
> (We shan't dispute a Year or more)
> However Stella, be not troubled,
> Although thy size and Years are doubled,
> Since first I saw Thee at Sixteen
> The brightest Virgin on the Green[.][29]

Already the poems are showing themselves untrustworthy in terms of historical accuracy: Stella was in fact 38 in 1719, and Swift had first met her not when she was 16 but eight. Nor is 34 twice 16! But these poems, specific to Esther Johnson when written, fall more into the category of friendship poems, ironically addressed to a less unconditionally admired 'Stella' than Sir Philip Sidney's, once they are published. When they appear in the *Miscellanies* it is quite without gloss: 'Stella' might be anyone, and her birthday poems simply a tongue-in-cheek record of a closeness under the realistic influence of passing time. There is little of the deeply personal, still less of the embarrassingly personal, such as Swift looks to have been engaging with in 'Death and Daphne' and *Cadenus and Vanessa*.

Personal touches there are, though, and personal to Swift, rather than only to Stella. '*Stella*'s Birth-day, 1725', for example, dwells on both of their advancing years:

> At Fifty six, if this be true,
> Am I a Poet fit for you?
> Or at the Age of Forty three,
> Are you a Subject fit for me?[30]

Also, unusually in poems allowed for publication, he elaborates on his own declining physical state – specifically his eyesight:

> 'Tis true, but let it not be known,
> My Eyes are somewhat dimmish grown;
> For Nature, always in the Right,
> To your Decays adapts my Sight,
> And Wrinkles undistinguish'd pass,
> For I'm ashamed to use a Glass;
> And till I see them with these Eyes,
> Whoever says you have them, lyes.[31]

Pat Rogers reminds us that Swift was indeed finding his eyes failing around this time, and was also reluctant 'to use spectacles'.[32] But, interestingly, Swift very much plays down what was in fact a much longer-standing affliction, his deafness:

> No Length of Time can make you quit
> Honour and Virtue, Sense and Wit,
> Thus you may still be young to me,
> While I can better *hear* than *see*;
> Oh, ne'er may Fortune shew her Spight,
> To make me *deaf*, and mend my *Sight*.[33]

Deafness, as Rogers adds, had been acutely problematic during 1724, and something of this recurred in 1725.[34] Swift was clearly willing to acknowledge in print an infirmity that he saw as minor, within the scale of his health problems, but to preserve a deceptive veil over what had been a much more serious anxiety for him, along with, and associated with, his vertigo.[35]

Even in what was probably the most serious and heart-felt of the published birthday poems, '*Stella*'s Birth-day, March 13, 1726/7', the last he wrote and the final birthday of her life, the physical frailty with which he opens is his eyesight, not his deafness or his dizziness:

> This Day, whate'er the Fates decree,
> Shall still be kept with Joy by me:
> This Day then, let us not be told,
> That you are sick, and I grown old,
> Nor think on our approaching Ills,
> And talk of Spectacles and Pills:
> To morrow will be Time enough
> To hear such mortifying Stuff.[36]

And yet, in spite of their factual inaccuracies, their low-key compliments and their jokes about weight and wrinkles, there does emerge – as there does from all the Stella poems, published and unpublished – a very real, very personal sense of value and affection, an affection that is undiminished for all the awareness of passing years. How far this is itself a duplicitous tactic, a concealing of the real nature of the relationship that existed between them, will remain subject to debate. Was it really the case that Swift had to warn himself off the attractions of physical intimacy with Vanessa and Lady Acheson but was able to jog on side by side with Stella over many years without any such alarms? Indeed, if that was the case, was it because the physical intimacy was already present, already taken for granted and of necessity being concealed? In the absence of further evidence this will continue to be inconclusive. Nevertheless, there is, from the Stella poems, a convincing impression of enduring respect and friendship, tempered only by the growing frailties of the participants.

The very real distress that Swift expresses in this poem would also have been influenced by the knowledge that he planned to make a visit to London in the summer and autumn of 1727, raising the possibility that he might not see Stella again once he left. His feelings, and his state of health, are summarized in a letter to his, and Stella's, close friend, the Reverend Thomas Sheridan, from London on 2 September:

> I am still in the same Condition, or rather worse, for I walk like a drunken Man, and am deafer than ever you knew me. If I had any tolerable Health, I would go this Moment to Ireland; yet I think I would not, considering the News I daily expect to hear from you. [...] [T]he last Act of Life is always a Tragedy at best; but it is a bitter Aggravation to have one's best Friend go before one. [...] I long knew that our dear Friend had not the *Stamina Vitae*; but my Friendship could not arm me against this Accident altho' I foresaw it. [...] I know not whether it would be an Addition to my Grief or no, that I am now extreamly ill; for it would have been a Reproach to me to be in perfect Health, when such a Friend is desperate. I do profess, upon my Salvation, that the distressed and desperate Condition of our Friend, makes Life so indifferent to me, who by Course of Nature have so little left, that I do not think it worth the Time to struggle.[37]

As it happened, Swift found himself stuck at Holyhead during the course of his return to Ireland in late September, delayed by bad weather for five days. His 'Holyhead Journal' is a record of the frustrations and deprivations he endured, but also includes several poems which are clearly tempered not only by his enforced immobility but by his awareness of what he regarded as an inevitable outcome of Stella's illness. It is referred to explicitly in 'Holyhead. Sept. 25, 1727':

> I never was in hast before
> To reach that slavish hateful shore:
> Before, I always found the wind
> To me was most malicious kind
> But now, the danger of a friend
> On whom my fears and hopes depend

> Absent from whom all Clymes are curst
> With whom I'm happy in the worst
> With rage impatient makes me wait
> A passage to the land I hate.[38]

It clearly influences, too, the resigned, almost despairing humour of 'Shall I repine':

> If neither brass nor marble can withstand
> The mortal force of Time's dystructive hand
> If mountains sink to vales, if cityes dye
> And lessening rivers mourn their fountains dry
> When my old cassock says a Welch divine
> Is out at elbows why should I repine?[39]

Only the latter poem, with the title 'The Power of Time: Written in the Year 1730', with punctuation suitably inserted, and with a footnote added pointing out the connection to a longer poem by the seventeenth-century French poet Paul Scarron, was published by Swift, in the second volume of his *Works* of 1735. Here, though, mourning is confined to the 'lessening rivers', grieving for the loss of their 'fountains'. In 'Holyhead. Sept. 25, 1727' the grieving is much closer to home, far more directly anticipated and the poem remained unpublished until 1882.

Swift's despair in the letter to Sheridan was down to anxiety over Stella, compounded by his own health problems. His health, though, while a recurrent topic of his letters to friends, appears infrequently in his poetry, perhaps because of a reluctance to see it set down in print. A few published poems address the topic. 'In Sickness', written in 1714, but not published until 1735, in the *Works*, is almost a companion piece to 'Holyhead. Sept. 25, 1727' in that it is to do with Swift's illness in the context of his then recent exile to Ireland, the 'land I hate':

> 'Tis true, — then why should I repine,
> To see my Life so fast decline?
> But, why obscurely here alone?
> Where I am neither lov'd nor known.
> My State of Health none care to learn;
> My Life is here no Soul's Concern.
> And, those with whom I now converse,
> Without a Tear will tend my Herse.[40]

Where the later poem is unpublished and anguished, though, 'In Sickness' reads as tending towards self-pity – confirmed, perhaps, by Swift's choosing not to publish it until over 20 years later, when many of the friends he charges with not caring were dead.

More genuine, finally, not least because Swift was more genuinely sick, and written almost ten years later than *Cadenus and Vanessa*, is the unpublished birthday poem, 'To Stella, March 13, MDCCXXIII-IV [written on the Day of her Birth, but not on the Subject, when I was sick in bed.]':

> Tormented with incessant pains,
> Can I devise poetic strains?
> Time was, when I could yearly pay
> My verse on Stella's native day:
> But now, unable grown to write,
> I grieve she ever saw the light.
> Ungrateful; since to her I owe
> That I these pains can undergo.
> She tends me like an humble slave;
> And, when indecently, I rave,
> When out my brutish passions break,
> With gall in ev'ry word I speak,
> She, with soft speech, my anguish chears,
> Or melts my passions down with tears:
> Although 'tis easy to descry
> She wants assistance more than I;
> Yet seems to feel my pains alone,
> And is a Stoic in her own.[41]

Swift, writing to Charles Ford on 2 April 1724, gives more detail of the illness. He 'fell into a cruell Disroder that kept me in Torture for a week, and confined me 2 more to my Chambr, but I am now rid of it, onely left very weak'. The condition was 'the Hæmorrhoides internæ' and he has been obliged to suffer 'Strangury, loss of Blood, water-gruel and no sleep'.[42] Stella herself, meanwhile, had been developing problems with her stomach and with loss of appetite since at least 1723, problems which were to lead to her death in 1728.[43] The poem is revelatory about Swift's behaviour in his own sick room, the rudeness and impatience with which he treats his closest attendant and the pathetic gratitude he feels to this partner under the relentlessness of passing time and the physical tolls it exacts. It remained unpublished until 1765, when

Deane Swift brought out his edition of Swift's *Works*. It is easy to see why Swift himself would not have published it. It has all the personal vulnerability that his life in writing went to almost excessive lengths to keep hidden. It lacks the subterfuge of poems like *Cadenus and Vanessa* and 'Death and Daphne', the generalizations about ageing of the published birthday poems and the self-mockery of 'Lady Acheson Weary of the Dean'. It is one of those very rare Swift poems: a text that is unashamedly personal. As such, it also stands as a rarity in an age in which even such intensely personal poetic topics as depression, self-doubt and fears of death and the hereafter were conventionally written up as if fabricated, albeit originating in something genuine. Where Pope and Gray, and other more or less contemporaries, were looking to classical and continental models in writing poems on suicide and melancholy, Swift, at least in his less guarded moments, had developed a distinctively direct and personal voice. It suited him.

Notes

1. J. Swift (1948) *Journal to Stella*, H. Williams (ed.), 2 vols (Oxford: Clarendon Press), II, p. 492.
2. (1967) in H. Davis (ed.) *Poetical Works* (London: Oxford University Press), p. 94.
3. (1983) *Swift: The Man, His Works, and The Age*, 3 vols (London: Methuen), II: *Dr Swift*, p. 469.
4. (2001) *The Correspondence of Jonathan Swift, D.D.*, D. Woolley (ed.), 4 vols (Frankfurt: Peter Lang), I, p. 338.
5. *Journal to Stella*, I, p. 212.
6. *Journal to Stella*, I, p. 225.
7. *Journal to Stella*, I, p. 239.
8. *Journal to Stella*, I, p. 315.
9. *Journal to Stella*, I, p. 315.
10. (1983) in P. Rogers (ed.) *Jonathan Swift: The Complete Poems* (New Haven: Yale University Press), p. 537.
11. 'Notes to "Verses Made in Swift's Sleep"' in *The Complete Poems*, p. 879.
12. Quoted from J. Woolley (2008) 'Swift's "Skinnibonia"' in H. J. Real (ed.) *Reading Swift: Papers from the Fifth Münster Symposium on Jonathan Swift* (Münster: Wilhelm Fink), pp. 309–42 (p. 320). The poem, that was unknown until 2003, is part of the 'Acheson manuscript', when the privately-owned collection was examined and verified by James Woolley and Hermann Real. It remained unpublished until Woolley's essay in 2008.
13. *Swift: The Man, His Works, and The Age*, III, pp. 601, 603.
14. Quoted in Woolley, 'Swift's "Skinnibonia"', p. 320.
15. Quoted in Woolley, 'Swift's "Skinnibonia"', p. 322.
16. Quoted in Woolley, 'Swift's "Skinnibonia"', p. 328.
17. S. Karian (2010) *Jonathan Swift in Print and Manuscript* (Cambridge: Cambridge University Press), pp. 74–5.

18. L. K. Barnett (1981) *Swift's Poetic Worlds* (Toronto: Associated University Presses), p. 57.
19. See Rogers, 'Notes to "Lady Acheson Weary of the Dean"' in *The Complete Poems*, p. 787; Karian, *Jonathan Swift in Print and Manuscript*, p. 92.
20. 'Lady Acheson Weary of the Dean' in *Poetical Works*, pp. 370–2, lines 1–12. Further references are by line number to this edition and are placed in parentheses following the quotation.
21. (1981) 'Swift and the "agreeable young Lady, but extremely lean"' in J. Irwin Fischer, D. C. Mell and D. M. Vieth (eds) *Contemporary Studies of Swift's Poetry* (East Brunswick, NJ: Associated University Presses), pp. 149–58 (p. 154).
22. 'Death and Daphne' in *Poetical Works*, pp. 466–8, line 15. Further references are by line number to this edition and are placed in parentheses following the quotation.
23. See the discussion of both these poems in Jaffe, 'Swift and the "agreeable young Lady, but extremely lean"', pp. 155–7: Jaffe adopts a similar line of argument, and makes the same connection between the two texts.
24. See the discussion in 'Notes to *Cadenus and Vanessa*' in *The Complete Poems*, pp. 658–9; Karian, *Jonathan Swift in Print and Manuscript*, p. 91.
25. *Cadenus and Vanessa* in *Poetical Works*, pp. 114–37, lines 305–7. Further references are by line number to this edition and are placed in parentheses following the quotation.
26. On this, see Karian, *Jonathan Swift in Print and Manuscript*, pp. 77–9.
27. See 'Notes on "To Stella on Her Birthday"' in *The Complete Poems*, p. 718.
28. *Swift: The Man, His Works, and The Age*, III, pp. 102–3.
29. In *Poetical Works*, p. 167, lines 1–6.
30. In *Poetical Works*, pp. 292–3, lines 23–6.
31. lines 41–8.
32. 'Notes to "Stella's Birthday"' in *The Complete Poems*, p. 748.
33. lines 49–54.
34. 'Notes to "Stella's Birthday"' in *The Complete Poems*, p. 748.
35. See W. J. Creaser (2004) '"The most mortifying malady": Jonathan Swift's Dizzying World and Dublin's Mentally Ill' in H. J. Real (ed.) *Swift Studies* (Münster: Wilhelm Fink), pp. 27–48.
36. In *Poetical Works*, pp. 318–21, lines 1–8.
37. Swift, *Correspondence*, III, pp. 123–4.
38. In *Poetical Works*, p. 331, lines 19–28.
39. In *Poetical Works*, p. 330.
40. In *Poetical Works*, pp. 153–4, lines 1–8.
41. In *Poetical Works*, p. 260–1, lines 1–18.
42. *Correspondence*, II, p. 493.
43. See Ehrenpreis, *Swift: The Man, His Works, and The Age*, III, pp. 413–15.

13
Blind Woman on the Rampage
Priscilla Pointon's Grand Tour of the Midlands and the Question of the Legitimacy of Sources for Biography

Chris Mounsey[1]

The truth and letters

What counts as a good source for biographical information? This is a question that I want to address as it is, for me, the burning question in both the recovery project of eighteenth-century women writers and the exploration of the experience of disability in the eighteenth century, since we have few objective records of either which would 'count' for traditional biographers. It is also a question to which Bill Overton gave a bold lead that I intend to follow in this chapter.

The problem about evidence for academic biography first came to my attention in the 1990s after Janet Todd's *The Secret Life of Aphra Behn* was attacked by, among others, Michael Dobson for its use of Behn's fictions to make claims about Behn's life.[2] In the *London Review of Books*, Dobson notes that after Behn's

> paradoxically well-documented secret excursion [as a spy to Antwerp], [...] (the letters Behn wrote under cover as agent 160, code-named Astrea, constitute the bulk of her surviving correspondence), the life pretty much disappears, and there remain only the traces of a prolific literary career.[3]

Of course, Dobson, a Shakespeare scholar, was trying desperately to protect the genius of his 'fully fledged author' against a woman writer whom he thought of as no more than a 'scribbler'. However, his paradoxical tactic was to suggest that since Behn's literary creations were so various none of them could be used to find Behn herself:

About the only things [...] [Behn's] works have in common are that they were written in the first instance to please paying audiences rather than to lay bare Behn's soul, adopting a scintillating array of dramatic and rhetorical personae in order to do so, and that most of them suggest considerable scepticism about the very notion of the consistent inner self pursued by modern biography.[4]

At the heart of Todd's riposte to Dobson was her question why a letter, with all its formal literary conventions – that staple source of the traditional biographer pursuing a 'consistent inner self' – should be counted as true to life where other things a writer composed might not. Todd writes:

Our assumptions of the authenticity of private writing [...] mean that we value letters because they have the appearance of genuine, modern subjectivity, and because we often ignore their generic, rhetorical features.[5]

The idea that 'modern subjectivity' in letters is only an appearance should remind us, not only of our oversight about the rhetorical features of letters, but also that if we remain vigilant to the rhetorical features of a piece of writing, fictional or otherwise, we may use it in our recovery of the lives of historical writers, since we are aware of the fictional nature of *all* written sources. Writing, as every literary scholar knows, transforms while it records facts, and letters like any other form of writing are more or less acceptable as the source of biography; this is a truth, as Todd argues at the end of the same paper, 'derived from everyone's perfect knowledge that nothing written was claiming to be exclusively true'.[6] The question that remains is how far can we go into the 'traces' of a writer's 'literary career' before we are accused of basing our literary lives on airy fictions?

In the recovery of women poets of the eighteenth century, and in particular of those who wrote about their disabilities, we have little factual information other than published works. In the case of the blind poet, Priscilla Pointon, we have two collections of poems, one dated 1770 and the other 1794 and almost nothing else.[7] Published works, it is true to say, come surrounded with the machinery of publication: prefaces, dedications, subscriber lists, advertisements and so forth, but, even at the moment of the first recovery, we find that such legitimate sources of information are always supplemented by less objective sources, and even by the most respected of scholars.

Roger Lonsdale's headnote about Priscilla Pointon, in his *Eighteenth-Century Women Poets: An Oxford Anthology*, declares that 'What is known of her derives mostly from the prefaces, by John Jones and Joseph Weston, to her two volumes, *and from her verse itself*.'[8] Thus, we hear of her very long subscription list and the death of her husband after five months' illness. The first of these facts is printed in full at the beginning of the 1770 collection and so is apparently an incontrovertible fact. The death of James Pickering her husband is reported in the 1794 collection of poems in the poem 'Elegy by the Author, on the death of her husband':

> What mighty woes he, patient, did sustain;
> Five dreary months unto his room confin'd,
> With dire disease, that wracked both frame and mind![9]

Should therefore James Pickering's 'Five dreary months' disease also be considered an incontrovertible truth? The question might seem an easy one to answer, but another apparently easy question demonstrates the difficulty with verifying the most basic facts of the poet's marriage. PP (and I shall refer to her as 'PP' from now on as this is the way she referred to herself, and it conflates her father's and husband's surnames in a way I find elegant) published both her collections in Birmingham, while her husband, James Pickering, was a saddler in Chester. There is a piece of incontrovertible fact about his profession in *Adams's Weekly Courant*, which reads:

> Wanted, A Good Hand in the Sadlery and Cap-making Business; he will meet with Encouragement suitable to his Merits, and constant Employ, by applying to James Pickering, Sadler, in Chester.[10]

But was there another saddler in Chester called James Pickering? And there was. In the 1770 subscription list there is an entry for 'James Pickering jun.' so there must have been a 'James Pickering sen.' who might have placed the advertisement, which does not mention whether it was James Pickering 'sen.' or 'jun.'. And which of the James Pickerings married PP?

The marriage license gives the names of both PP and James Pickering, with the epithet that both are 'aged 30 years and upwards'. This means that even with this official document we cannot be sure whether PP was marrying James Pickering 'sen.' or 'jun.', but we can be sure that they married on Thursday 10 August 1780 because, in *Adams's Weekly Courant* of Tuesday 15 August 1780, we read:

Thursday was married, Mr James Pickering, of this City, Saddler, to Miss Priscilla Pointon, late of the City of Litchfield; a Lady possess'd of many amiable Accomplishments, among which her Taste as a Poetess is not the least considerable.[11]

I am being deliberately playful with the interpretation of facts, but underlying my pedantry is a serious biographical question. Why did PP write about 'JP' as being her Valentine three times in her 1770 collection but did not marry him until 1780? There are, I believe, at least nine poems addressed to him in the 1770 collection and five, including the elegy, in the 1794. PP, it might seem, found a true friend in JP as early as 1770, as her most famous poem 'Address to a Bachelor, On a Delicate Occasion' attests.[12] The story describes a party of men at which she is the only woman, when she is plied with drink and needs to relieve herself: 'Tea, wine, and punch, Sir, to be free, / Excellent diuretics be'.[13] She asks for a maid to help her only to be told that it is the maids' night off and that her host, the Bachelor to whom the poem is addressed, will hold a 'bason' for her, the role which the maid would have performed beneath her skirt, and which was out of the question for a man to do. Into the fray steps James Pickering – this time called 'Trueworth' – who leads her to the toilet and comfort. But how can we be sure it is James Pickering who played the role of 'Trueworth', when we could not even be certain from objective facts that it was James Pickering 'sen.' or 'jun.' whom she married? Why should we believe a poem or make the logical deduction that the man to whom she wrote Valentines so often was her rescuer? And if he was, then why did she wait so long to marry him? And why is this important anyway? Perhaps it is because knowing the answers will tell us something about being disabled in the eighteenth century. PP's spikiness when treated in a way she thought was bad comes through a number of times in her poems. Can we perhaps use the evidence from her poems to understand PP as the subject of a biography? Can we read her poems and understand what it was like for her to be blind?

The truth in letters

If letters are, as Janet Todd argues, the easiest forms of writing to evade our literary analysis 'because they have the appearance of genuine, modern subjectivity' then poetry is probably the first we baulk at as a source for facts due to its obvious 'generic, rhetorical features'. However, as Bill Overton's book, *The Eighteenth-Century British Verse Epistle*, suggests, letters that are written in verse 'hover "between manuscript and print'".[14] The idea, which Overton develops from David Fairer, is itself derived from an analysis of epistolarity: the essence of communicating intimate knowledge between the addressor and the addressee of a letter. Overton's analysis of verse epistles needs no rehearsing here, but I do want to develop an idea of his from a later piece 'Journeying in the Eighteenth-Century British Verse Epistle'.[15] This essay contains the first modern analysis of PP's poetry, and in particular of a verse epistle about a journey from Lichfield to Chester made sometime after 1780, which, alongside a number of facts about travel in the eighteenth century, gives a great deal of biographical evidence as well. However, bearing in mind the difficulties of accepting facts from literature discussed in the first section, I would like to begin with Overton's analysis of verse epistles to explore their 'generic rhetorical features'.

The letter is not an ordinary text. An ordinary text throws out its ideas like seed in the hand of the sower in the parable: some to land upon the path, some on stony ground, some among thorns and some on good soil. If St Matthew is not averse to a secular, textual analysis, words that land on the path remain unheard by their intended audience, those that land in stony ground are heard but not understood as they are intended, those that land among thorns are heard by an unreceptive audience and for those that land in good soil meaning becomes communication. On the other hand, what is extraordinary about a letter is, as Overton tells us, 'the extent to which a letter-writer may refer to private knowledge shared with the addressee'.[16] Thus a letter – if I may extend the metaphor of the parable – is like seed sown in prepared compost: the slightest nuance may be a reference to a shared joke and lead to a magnified level of communication. The process may not lead to the complete reconstruction of the intended communication by those other than the addressee, but Overton explains that:

> While, for example, some forms of intimate reference may be unintelligible to external readers, it is possible to present them so as to enable such readers to enjoy the illusion of occupying the addressee's position.[17]

What he might mean by 'it is possible to present' here would seem to be the work of transforming a letter into verse, such that the two forms of communication together, letter and verse, give an even more accessible aspect to the form. With the knowledge of the context of the addressor and addressee, alongside the beguiling language of poetry – the factual and the rhetorical read together – the external reader can believe themselves let into the inside information of the communication between friends.

Illusion it may be but communication by verse epistle can also pass down the centuries. As Overton further notes, the travel verse epistles he analyses 'bring to light a kind of evidence little considered previously about the *experience and representation* of travel in the eighteenth century'.[18] What he argues, in effect, is that the double rhetorical strategies of verse and epistle stabilize the communication so that it can be recovered by those who may be far outside the closed circle of communication that is the addressee and addressor of the original letter. What is ultimately exciting for me in this way of understanding the verse epistle is not just the experience and representation of PP's journey from Lichfield to Chester in the eighteenth century, but also the question of how far we can read this and other verse epistles as evidence for biography. First I shall explore the abundant facts from the subscription list from PP's 1770 collection of verse and discover how the rhetoric of the verse epistles in the collection is necessary to give the bare facts more veracity and relevance. Then I shall explore the verse epistles for evidence of what it was like to be a blind woman in the eighteenth century, which will begin to suggest answers to some of the questions about PP's marriage to James Pickering.

Verse epistles as evidence for a literary life

Probably the most remarkable thing about PP's 1770 collection of verse is the length of the subscription list. She writes of it in a verse epistle 'To a Friend, with whom the Author had been many Years intimate', declaring:

> Fifteen hundred and upwards the list does adorn,
> Lords, Ladies, Knights, Squires, and scores nobly born;
> Divinity, Physic, and Law, it is true,
> Nay the milit'ry Smarts have my int'rest in view,
> And Tradesmen of spirit, the number not few.[19]

In fact the list totals 1577 in all, of which I have traced 914 from contemporary directories, the earliest of which dates from 1784 and that from Leicester 1793. The fact that the people who subscribed were still living up to 20 years after subscribing suggests that many of her subscribers were the same age as her. An analysis of the list, based on the directories, shows – as PP says in her verse epistle:

Gentry   – 196
Clergy   – 107

Lawyers/ Doctors – 94
Soldiers   – 18
Traders   – 441

I have noted 'James Pickering jun.' already and there is a 'Captain John Poynton', who took ten copies and is, therefore, probably demonstrating relative duty.[20] We cannot though be certain that 'Ely Poynton, Hosier, of Exchange, Chester' is a relative, since when PP travelled to that town a verse epistle records that she stayed with 'Mr. A.C.'.[21] Whether the other subscribers with the surname Poynton are relatives is therefore unclear. Another subscriber, 'Sir Harry Parker', was a relative of Sir Hyde Parker, a Rear Admiral who possibly helped two of PP's brothers: the putative brother 'Captain John', who took the ten copies, and the real brother ship's Surgeon, Ned Poynton, to whom she addresses a verse epistle when he took up his post.[22] Other than the trades of the tradespeople, the list itself gives us little further information, except that the distribution of the subscribers covers the Midlands of England.

It is a truth universally acknowledged that subscription lists, while initially exciting, are ultimately disappointing as they add little to our knowledge of the writer of the book. This is the longest list I have ever seen, but there is no Joseph Spence or Samuel Johnson lurking among its number.[23] The closest to literary fame is the name of the Reverend Thomas Seward of Lichfield, Anna's father, to whom PP wrote an elegy in the 1794 collection – so much for facts! However, the verse epistles in the collection bring the list to life, and give us an account of PP as a professional poet, determined to make money out of her skill in poetry, both written and performed. In the 'Preface' to the 1770 collection, John Jones, a schoolmaster poet of Kidderminster, notes that the subscription list was announced in the *Birmingham Gazette* on 12 September 1768, and his introductory poem alludes to lines of verse from her 'Consolatory Ode' on her loss of sight that were published with the advertisement.[24] To bring in 1577 subscriptions, PP did not sit quietly in Lichfield hoping that a single advertisement about a blind poet would go viral and cause an epidemic of sympathetic generosity. But it did. In her local area, a breakdown of the subscription list shows a remarkable uptake:

Lichfield   – 118
Coventry   – 119
Burton upon Trent   – 48

Ashby	–	18
Walsall	–	6

All of these towns and cities are within a day's journey of Lichfield, but PP must have worked hard to bring in such numbers of enthusiasts who were happy to give five shillings in hope of a book that they had not yet read, and which would in the event be made up of poems to and about them. But what did she do – other than being local and blind – to entice people to part with so large a sum?

We get some evidence from the verse epistle PP sent to her brother Ned, 'The following Letter by the Author to her Brother E.P. at *Lichfield*, After her arrival at *Chester*'. The poem tells us that PP took the scenic route:

> Know first of all, to L.D's house I came
> [...]
> My Newport visit next I mean to tell,
> At Mr T. M.'s, all I wish'd did dwell
> [...]
> To Chester, friend, at length, I now am come;
> At Mr A.C's house I make my home.[25]

Reading from the subscription list, 'L.D.' with whom she stayed first is probably Lister Dighton Esq., of Clifford Chambers, a manor house near Stratford upon Avon.[26] The house was a large one, bringing forth speculation about PP's class, but she writes to her brother of her stay thus:

> Know first of all, to L.D.'s house I came,
> And who I ask'd for there, I need not name;
> The hour-glass near twice its course had run,
> Before the nymph, to welcome me, did come;
> And when, at length, she did on me attend,
> All hopes of pleasure disappear'd, my friend; –
> So flat her converse, and so grave her air,
> Instead of nineteen, ninety did appear;
> Wednesday and Thursday, with her stupid past,
> But happy Friday dawn'd, my dear, at last,
> A day not noted much for bliss, I own,
> Tho' Venus rules, yet many fair ones moan.
> With Mrs Friendly home this eve I went,

> And chearful there a week or nine days spent; –
> To make me happy seem'd her chiefest care,
> And I in turn strove to delight this fair.[27]

Why it was dull to stay in Clifford Chambers, and what PP did while with 'Mrs Friendly' that made her happy, we can reconstruct from the subscription list, which shows good uptake numbers from the towns nearby:

Warwick – 66
Stratford – 34
Worcester – 77

It would therefore seem that PP was expecting her 19 year old friend – probably Dighton's god-daughter Lucy Mason – to take her to the local towns where she could solicit subscriptions: something which 'Mrs Friendly' ultimately did.[28] But to this supposition we can add more information from the poems she wrote to the inhabitants of these towns. For the first two, these are called 'Extempore Address to the Inhabitants of Warwick' and 'The following lines were spoken Extempore by the Author, on being requested to compose a complimentary Ode to the Memory of *Shakespeare*, when she was at *Stratford* soliciting a Subscription'.[29] Something like verse epistles, these 'Extempore Addresses' have an addressor, multiple addressees (we know exactly how many and their names and addresses), a roughly datable moment of utterance and a clear context. Their content is formulaic, and in the following for 'Warwick', you might substitute 'Coventry', 'Lichfield', 'Stratford', 'Walsall' or 'Birmingham':

> Cou'd I with skill but tune my artless lyre,
> To sing thy praise, I'd Warwick then aspire:
> But all the Nine, are for the task too faint,
> Shou'd they attempt one half thy worth to paint:
> Such matchless goodness in thy people dwell,
> Their greatest pride's in virtue to excel;
> [...]
> Friends to the poor, benevolent and kind,
> In them good-nature is with prudence join'd:
> Oh! how shall I in humble verse then tell?
> Merit like their's, that sure would volumes swell:
> My artless lays, you'll worthy Friends excuse,
> Nor scorn this tribute of my grateful muse.[30]

I am not sure how self-referential or how ironic the suggestion is that Warwick's merit 'would volumes swell', but PP's practice would appear to be to swell the subscription list of her own volume of poems by performing some of them and ending up with an 'Extempore' effusion about the wonderful town in which she found herself. The business model was obviously a successful one, and we have further evidence of how it worked from verses written in Chester where she remained for a long time and garnered 231 subscriptions. From Chester she published, in addition to two extempore addresses, three poems associated with the theatre. The first two make up a call and response, and are clearly intended as advertisements. J. Wheatley, 'Manager of a Company of Comedians in *Chester*', wrote of PP:

> O Prissy! cou'd my pencil paint
> The portrait of a spotless saint,
> My canvas shou'd with colours glow
> Fairer by far than feather'd snow,
> And more delightful to the eye
> Than is the purest Tyrean dye![31]

To which she replied:

> Sure these encomiums you ne'er meant for me,
> For I'm no saint, if saints on earth there be:
> What arrogance, and ostentation too,
> In me must reign, to think such praise my due.
> Well I remember a wise Author tells,
> *In unjust praise severest satyr dwells*.[32]

The poems are both species of show business hyperbolic banter. From this evidence, it does not seem out of the question to suggest that PP performed her poetry to theatre audiences in the other Midland towns at which she solicited subscriptions. Such an approach would draw the attention of the Traders who appear in the list, but the verse epistle to her brother Ned suggests another business model which would account for a very different social group of subscribers.

Before arriving at Chester PP stayed in Newport with 'T.M.'. Reading the name from the subscription list, it is probably one Thomas Marshall, at whose house:

> Health, peace and Pleasure, daily smiled around,
> And every breast with friendship did abound:

> When here two months, or more, I pass'd away,
> Alas! to me it scarce appear'd a day.[33]

As with the stay with 'Mrs Friendly', time ran swiftly it would appear because PP was gathering subscriptions, but in this area the subscription list is uniquely populated by titled people: Harry Grey of Enville; William Holles Vane of Caverswall Castle; Granville Leveson Gower of Trentham Hall; Thomas Lyttleton of Hagley Hall; Henry William Paget of Beaudesert House; Robert Pigot of Patshull Hall; John Touchet Chetwode of Oakley Hall; William Bagot of Blithfield Hall; William Legge of Sandwell; and Mrs Robert Bosvil of Biana. The last of these, Biana, PP addresses thus:

> Ye bleating Flocks, and feather'd Choir, farewell,
> And dear *Biana*, which does far excel
> Each splendid Court, where Folly's train attends,
> Thy welcome guests must all be Virtue's friends[.][34]

As in the address to the people of Warwick, it appears that people, whatever their quality, become friends of virtue when they have added their names to the subscription, although there are only 48 as a result of two months' work at Biana, while nine days with 'Mrs Friendly' netted 177.

Varieties of a similar business plan, executed in other places, are discernible from relations between other poems and the subscription list, such as the 'Extempore Elegy, on the Death of The Rev. Mr Davenport, Vicar of St. Nicholas, and Master of the Grammar-School in Leicester'.[35] Davenport, whose name appears marked as 'deceased' in the subscription list, might have helped PP in adding 66 names to the list. At the same time, PP may have stayed with him, or with one John Poynton, an ironmonger from the High Street, who might have been another brother. But there are neither a similar poem to a friend, nor convenient relatives, with whom she might have stayed while collecting 52 names from Derby, 74 from Nottingham and 36 from Loughborough. However, there is another poem, 'Wrote upon the Author's Box, By a Friend, Who receiv'd it a few Hours before her Arrival at his House', which is addressed to 'Dear Swain' and that is voiced by the box itself:

> If with one humane sentiment possess'd,
> Within thy cottage let a stranger rest;
> The weakest vassal of the brightest Fair,
> That ever felt – the most afflictive care!
> [...]

> At her command thro' various parts I roam,
> Nor wish without her leave my native home[.][36]

There are two 'Swaines' in the subscription list, one male and one female. The title of the poem indicates that it is addressed to James Swaine of Birmingham, who was the carrier to Barton upon Humber, Beverley, Brigg, Chesterfield, Derby, Edinburgh and so on, and kept the Half Moon and Swan public house. Whether this suggests that PP was not above staying in public houses, or that she merely used carriers to transport her valise between towns while she stayed with friends cannot be certain; however, it is important to consider whether she paid for her accommodation while gathering the 138 names of Birmingham residents, which is the largest number for any town except for Chester. The longer she stayed in a rented room the more she would have to pay out of her receipts.

Another and equally important question is whether she travelled alone. The poem which Overton analyses in the 'Journeying' paper, about a night-time trip by coach from Lichfield to Chester, suggests that she did. No travelling companion is mentioned, and PP is cheated into paying for the wine for the young men on the same coach.[37] However, the verse epistle to her brother, from which I mapped out the earlier and more circuitous journey from Lichfield to Chester via Stratford and Newport, Shropshire, gives us a tantalizing suggestion that she may have been accompanied by an amanuensis. Coming to the close of the long letter, PP says: 'And soon my Writer shall the pen lay down'.[38] But who was 'my Writer'? The evidence I have so far provided suggests that while she travelled PP performed some of her poetry to a group of potential subscribers and then ended up with her 'Extempore Address' to the town in thanks for their generosity. But who wrote all this down? 'My Writer' is annoying in its political correctness: did *he* or *she* put down the pen? It was not her father as we know he was dead since PP addresses Ned, her brother, as 'Father, Brother, Sight and all to me'. Nor was it her mother, to whom the same poem wishes 'health and long to live'.[39] Nor is it likely that if 'my Writer' were her sister or another relation that PP would have failed to send their brother Ned both their good wishes. 'My Writer' may have been 'Mr A.C.' with whom she stayed in Chester, but he may have been an innkeeper, in which case it would be unlikely that he would have had time. 'My Writer' may have even been James Pickering, although she met him for the first time in Chester, so it is unlikely they he would write her first letter home to her brother recording her safe arrival. It is possible that the amanuensis was a servant. Given that PP performed in many of the great houses in the Midlands, she too may have been born into one, which would tend us towards further rumination about her class.

Her sister's address is noted in two poems to her in the 1794 collection: 'An Address to the Author's Sister, Mrs Woollaston, of the Groves, near Enville, On her Recovering from a severe Lameness', and 'On the Death of the Author's Sister, Mrs Woollaston, of the Groves, near Enville'.[40] One 'Mr Woolaston of Apley, Salop' subscribed to the first collection and Apley is one of the greatest houses in Shropshire, but it was the home of the Whitmore family. The National Archives mention one 'Mr Henry Wollaston of the Groves, Enville', and even modern maps show a farm called 'The Groves'. But if this is PP's sister, who was addressed in 'Letter to a Sister Giving an Account of her Wedding Day' and again in 'Extempore Epistle, Occasioned by my Sister neither Writing nor Coming agreeably to promise', then why did PP not stay with her when she was soliciting subscriptions from the great houses of Staffordshire?[41] Her farm was close by Enville Hall, from which PP gained the name of Harry Grey. This is the point at which the facts of the subscription list and the rhetoric of the verse epistle begin to unravel. The present line of argument was intended to answer the question whether PP employed a servant as an amanuensis by discussing the evidence that she might be from a wealthy family, but has led to more questions than answers. While the combination of facts and verse epistles forms a heuristic and convincing picture of PP's business plan, the method can take us so far and no further in the direction of biography.

Verse epistles as evidence of disabled lives

At the same time, however, PP's verse epistles can give us some understanding of the experience of a blind woman who thought that her disability excluded her from the marriage market, and, for which reason we may assume, did actually exclude her from marrying her future husband for ten years. The group of poems to James Pickering in the 1770 collection might be called the 'courting' poems, and those in the second collection, published after his death in 1794, the 'marriage' poems. While only one in the earlier collection is indubitably directed to him, 'An Invitation to J.P., written Extempore', his status as addressee of the others can be convincingly argued from circumstantial evidence.[42] In the 1794 collection there are two verse epistles in the form of Valentines. The first, 'Valentine, On [a] Leap Year', clearly addresses a man whom she wants to call husband:

> Ev'ry grace will I study, my mind for to dress,
> That the hour Hymen join'd us he may ever bless.
> His converse I'll wisely prefer, Sir, to all;
> And scorn all those cheats the world pleasure does call:
> Abroad for amusement I seldom will roam,
> Thrice happy the pair, that are pleas'd best at home.[43]

The second, 'To Mr. J.P. On Drawing him Four Years Successively for a Valentine', gives James Pickering's initials and calls him 'Strephon'.[44] Furthermore, it recalls the poem in the 1770 collection 'A Valentine, Extempore; On Drawing a young Gentleman three times successively'.[45] Thus, it does not seem out of the question to argue that all the poems which use the word 'Valentine' in the title are addressed to James Pickering, as is the 1770 poem which also addresses 'Strephon': 'The following Advice to a gay Bachelor, upon the Marriage State'.[46] Likewise, since the poem in the 1770 collection which addresses 'J.P.' in the title is an invitation, it also seems likely that the male 'friend' in the title of another invitation, 'The following Invitation, Extempore. To a Friend', is also James Pickering.[47] The courtship poems in which the address to James Pickering is less certain are 'Mr. Trueworth' in the 'Address to a Bachelor', and a poem that is much less complimentary, 'To Master Jemmy -----, in his 32nd Year. An Extempore Epistle', which, like the Invitation epistle, describes a man tied to his mother's apron strings, which, if it is Pickering, suggests one reason why he did not marry PP before 1780.[48]

However, there are no grounds to believe that PP ever regarded marriage as a prospect. The first poem to James Pickering declares that although on Valentine's Day it is an ancient courting custom for women to address themselves to men: 'Mine is but Friendship, others may be love'.[49] On one level, PP's attitude derives directly from the strong vein of writing against submitting themselves to men in marriage that marks much of eighteenth-century women's verse:

> But when once wed, we find it, to our cost,
> That in the wife the goddess soon is lost:
> No more you sigh, no more in transport view,
> For strait we're mortals, and mere husbands you.[50]

But at the same time PP recognizes both that she can love although she cannot believe those who claim to love her:

> With me, ye Pow'rs! let friendship ever reign,
> I ask no more, nor let me ask in vain:

> For shou'd I love, and meet with no return,
> How wou'd my bosom, like to *Sappho*, burn!
> Pity on me, perhaps, they might bestow,
> But pity cannot ease the pangs of woe.[51]

I would argue that these lines do not resound with self-pity and weakness of resolve, but rather begin to give us something of the experience of a blind woman who has met more often with the pity of others than with their friendship, let alone their love. Rather like the disabled MP, William Hay, who in his *Deformity: An Essay* gives a rhetorical shrug of his shoulders to all chairmen who call him 'My Lord' because he was a dwarf, so PP's response to people's interest in her is to greet it with the suspicion that it might not be genuine friendship but instead the pitying objectification that is the usual address to disabled people.[52] But she was certainly interested in men.

Of the 42 verse epistles addressed to single people in the first collection, 31 are to men and only 11 to women. Of the poems addressed to women, one is to a celebrated beauty, the deceased Countess of Coventry, one is about not meeting any good looking men during a walk on Chester's roman walls and one is lines requested by a woman-friend to send to her beau.[53] Nor is this to say that PP had no intimate female friends, as is attested in the poem, 'A Lady, with whom the Author had resided some time, requested, on her departure, that she would, as soon as convenient, send her a line, to acquaint her with the situation of her health, and in particular her spirits, which she did in the following manner'. The lines to her girl-friend are some of the most personal about her emotional response to her blindness:

> But how I do, will strait prepare to tell –
> Know then, my friend, sometimes I gay appear,
> Sometimes, as usual, Prissy's low, my dear;
> Each place does spirits much avail,
> I'm under deck, or else top-gallant sail.
> You'll smile at this, and think my humour strange,
> Because alas! thus subject I'm to change:
> Pardon in me this wonderful defect;
> Tho' mutable, I seem in some respect,
> Yet know, dear madam, I will ever be
> Your's to command – and much oblig'd P.P.[54]

In this verse epistle we get as close as possible to the 'genuine, modern subjectivity' which can bring us the 'consistent inner self pursued by modern biography'. The 'letter-writer [...] refer[s] to private knowledge shared with the addressee' in the metaphor of a ship, on which at least one of her brothers served. And although, as Overton says, the 'intimate reference[s] may be unintelligible to external readers, it is possible to present them so as to enable such readers to enjoy the illusion of occupying the addressee's position' – even if you are not blind. For those of us who are the verse rings, perhaps, the more truly.

Notes

1. The author, being partially sighted, cannot read paper copies of books, so references are to pdf copies, which can be read with text-to-voice, most of which do not have page numbers. Thus, in this chapter, unless the page number has been located by a sighted person, the electronic version will be cited. I have chosen this practice as a statement of intent since, as a partially sighted scholar, I cannot easily work with texts that cannot be translated by text-to-voice.
2. J. Todd (1996) *The Secret Life of Aphra Behn* (London: Andre Deutsch).
3. (8 May 1997) 'Shee Spy', *London Review of Books*, 19:9, online at: http://www.lrb.co.uk/v19/n09/michael-dobson/shee-spy [accessed 5 May 2015].
4. Dobson, 'Shee Spy'.
5. (January–April 2000) 'Fatal Fluency: Behn's Fiction and the Restoration Letter', *Eighteenth Century Fiction*, 12:2–3, 417–34 (p. 418).
6. 'Fatal Fluency', p. 434.
7. P. Pointon (1770) *Poems on Several Occasions* (Birmingham: T. Warren); P. Pickering (1794) *Poems by Mrs. Pickering* (Birmingham: E. Piercy).
8. Lonsdale (1990) *Eighteenth-Century Women Poets: An Oxford Anthology* (Oxford: Oxford University Press), p. 275 (italics added).
9. In *Poems by Mrs. Pickering*, pp. 62–3 (p. 62).
10. *Adams's Weekly Courant* (Chester, England), Tuesday, April 10, 1770; Issue 1743.
11. *Adam's Weekly Courant* (Chester, England), Tuesday, August 15, 1780; Issue 2479.
12. A poem reprinted for the first time since 1770 in Lonsdale's *Anthology*, pp. 274–5.
13. 'Address to a Bachelor, On a Delicate Occasion' in *Poems on Several Occasions*, pp. 31–2 (p. 31).
14. (2007) *The Eighteenth-Century Verse Epistle* (Basingstoke: Palgrave Macmillan), p. 63.
15. (2009) 'Journeying in the Eighteenth-Century British Verse Epistle', *Studies in Travel Writing*, 13:1, 3–25.
16. Overton, 'Journeying', p. 5.
17. 'Journeying', p. 5.
18. 'Journeying', p. 3.
19. In *Poems on Several Occasions*, pp. 90–1.
20. Editors of PP as early as Roger Lonsdale have noted the discrepancy between the spelling of her name on the title page and the spelling of the name 'Poynton' in the subscription list.

21. 'The Following Letter by the Author, To her Brother E.P. at Lichfield, After her Arrival at Chester' in *Poems on Several Occasions*, pp. 13–15 (p. 14).
22. 'Extempore Advice, by the Author, to her Brother, when newly appointed Surgeon to a Man of War' in *Poems on Several Occasions*, pp. 48–9.
23. Joseph Spence, though dead in 1768, would have been alive while the subscription list was made. He collected a similarly large subscription list for Thomas Blacklock, the Scottish blind poet.
24. 'Consolatory Reflections, That have Occasionally occurred on that most lamentable Incident, My Loss of Sight' in *Poems on Several Occasions*, pp. 99–105.
25. pp. 13, 14.
26. In the subscription list we find: 'Lister Dighton, Esq: Clifford, Gloucestershire'. Clifford Chambers is 'six miles distant north from Campden, one mile southwest from Stratford upon Avon in Warwickshire, and twenty miles west of Glocester' (Sir R. Atkyns [1768] *The Ancient and Present State of Glocestershire*, 2nd edn [London: numerous publishers], p. 186). The same book also tells us that Clifford-Chambers, which is a parish in upper Tewkesbury, passed from the Raynesford family to the Deighton family after the Civil War.
27. 'The following Letter by the Author to her Brother E.P.', pp. 13–14.
28. Lucy Mason, 'his own god-daughter', received £50 from Lister Dighton in his will, dated 2 December 1805 (*Transactions of the Bristol and Gloucestershire Archaeological Society*, 14, 8, online at: http://discovery.nationalarchives.gov.uk/details/rd/a073336f-af98-4afd-b1e0-a793c24a8c32 [accessed 5 May 2015]).
29. In *Poems on Several Occasions*, pp. 95, 96.
30. 'Extempore Address to the Inhabitants of Warwick', p. 95.
31. 'The following Lines addressed to the Author. By Mr. J.W. Manager of a Company of Comedians in Chester, On perusing some of her Works' in *Poems on Several Occasions*, pp. 8–10 (pp. 8–9).
32. 'A Reply, extempore, to the above' in *Poems on Several Occasions*, pp. 10–11 (p. 10).
33. 'The Following Letter by the Author, To her Brother E.P. at Lichfield', p. 14.
34. 'The following Lines made extempore, on Leaving Biana in Staffordshire, where the Author spent several agreeable months' in *Poems on Several Occasions*, pp. 56–7 (p. 57).
35. In *Poems on Several Occasions*, pp. 66–7.
36. In *Poems on Several Occasions*, pp. 86–7 (p. 86).
37. 'A Journal from Lichfield to Chester' in *Poems by Mrs Pickering*, pp. 35–45.
38. 'The Following Letter by the Author, To her Brother E.P.', p. 15.
39. 'The Following Letter by the Author, To her Brother E.P.', p. 15.
40. In *Poems by Mrs. Pickering*, pp. 9–12, 6–7.
41. In *Poems by Mrs. Pickering*, pp. 20–3, 24–5.
42. In *Poems on Several Occasions*, pp. 33–4.
43. In *Poems by Mrs. Pickering*, pp. 26–9 (p. 27).
44. In *Poems by Mrs. Pickering*, pp. 60–1.
45. In *Poems on Several Occasions*, pp. 34–6.
46. In *Poems on Several Occasions*, pp. 45–6.
47. In *Poems on Several Occasions*, pp. 74–5.
48. In *Poems on Several Occasions*, pp. 31–2 and pp. 32–3.

49. 'A Valentine' in *Poems on Several Occasions*, pp. 24–5 (p. 25).
50. p. 25.
51. p. 25.
52. W. Hay (1754) *Deformity: An Essay* (London: R. and J. Dodsley).
53. 'An Elegy, Extempore, By the Author, On the Countess of Coventry, At the Request of a Lady'; 'Spoken extempore by the Author, walking on Chester Walls with a young Lady, who had just complain'd to her of her disappointment in meeting with no Beaux'; and 'The following Lines by the Author, at the request of a young Lady, to present to a Friend of her's, on his return from Town to a rural Retirement' in *Poems on Several Occasions*, pp. 28–9, 53, 43–5.
54. In *Poems on Several Occasions*, pp. 42–3.

14
'What a Creature is Man'
The Melancholia, Literary Ambition and Manly Fortitude of Robert Burns

Leigh Wetherall Dickson

> What a piece of work is a man! How noble in reason, how infinite in faculty! In form and moving how express and admirable! In action how like an Angel! In apprehension how like a god! The beauty of the world! The paragon of animals! And yet to me, what is this quintessence of dust?[1]

Hamlet's speech to Rosencrantz and Guildenstern paints a picture of humanity's infinite potential only to conclude that all ambitions and achievements are ultimately insignificant and worthless. As Allan Ingram and Stuart Sim have already noted, *Hamlet* is an exploration of how 'Man, with all his advantages, is crippled – by time, by flesh, by motivation, by death and by uncertainty [...]. [T]he human mind would be capable of anything were it not for thinking'.[2] Hamlet's words highlight the point where the ability and desire of 'man' as an individual, in order to elevate himself above the species, intersects with the self-consciousness of mortality. His speech is the articulation of a moment of melancholic introspection that serves to confirm the central place of death even in the midst of a desire for revenge and is, therefore, also an articulation of complete paralysis. Familiar with Shakespeare since childhood, Robert Burns quotes, or rather misquotes, from *Hamlet* throughout his correspondence and this speech clearly resonates with him as he paraphrases Hamlet's exclamation on several occasions. Writing in January 1788 to 'Clarinda', the pen-name of Agnes McLehose, he declares:

> What a creature is man! A little alarm last night and today that I am mortal, has made such a revolution on my spirits! [...] I can no more, Clarinda; I can scare hold up my head[.][3]

To Mrs Dunlop of Dunlop almost two years later, he similarly reflects upon the ever-present spectre of death:

> Lord, what is Man! Today in the luxuriance of health, exulting in the enjoyment of existence; In a few days, perhaps in a few hours, loaded with conscious painful being, counting the tardy pace of the lingering moments. [...] Day follows night, and night comes after day, only to curse him with life that gives no pleasure; & yet the aweful [sic], dark termination of the life, is a something, perhaps a Nothing – at which he recoils with still more horror.[4]

The letters to Clarinda and Mrs Dunlop are Burns's own articulation of moments of paralysis, echoing the sentiment of Hamlet's speech in relation to his own literary ambitions and thoughts about posterity. The letter to Mrs Dunlop goes on to question what kind of afterlife he can expect to enjoy; will he be 'seeing & seen, enjoying and enjoyed' or simply a 'cold stiffened, unconsciously ghastly corse [sic] [...] the prey of unsightly reptiles, & to become in time a trodden clod[?]'[5] Written only a couple of years after his tangible experience of fame when being lionized by the Edinburgh literati, these letters would appear to suggest that Burns fears that he is already fading into obscurity and all his achievements will similarly turn to dust. However, the articulation of his own ambitions, doubts about his own abilities and thoughts about what kind of literary legacy he would leave began before the publication of the first edition of *Poems, Chiefly in the Scottish Dialect* in 1786.

Much has been written about Burns's recurring bouts of melancholia, including by the man himself. Between April 1783 and October 1785 Burns sporadically kept a commonplace book that has been described by its editors as 'the earliest "collected" work he produced, the first vehicle through which he expressed himself'.[6] The commonplace book consists of fragments of poetry and works in progress, critical self-analysis of those works, observations and reflections upon the human character and also records Burns's admiration for other writers of the period, including James Macpherson, Laurence Sterne, Robert Blair, James Thomson and with particular reference to William Shenstone. David Daiches notes that the commonplace book charts the growth of a poet as it is a 'remarkable self-portrait of Burns revelling in sentimental literature [and] constitutes a fascinating record of his mental development from the latter part of the Lochlie period until the end of 1785'.[7] This was a particularly trying period for Burns and the commonplace book records moments of despair that are, in some instances, so paralysing that he feared for his sanity and his life, let alone his literary ambitions. Daiches equates Burns's obvious admiration for sentimental literature with a poetically immature and emotionally battered mind, stating that that the 'influence [...] of the sentimental English models [...] inspired, unfortunately, so much of his earlier works', and, therefore, suggests that the putting aside of the commonplace book in 1785 signals the emergence of the mature Scottish Bard in 1786.[8]

The commonplace book records and recalls periods when Burns suffered from what he named as 'that most dreadful distemper, a Hypochondria, or confirmed Melancholy [...] the recollection of which makes me shudder', and during which he had to 'hang [his] harp on the willow trees'.[9] Robert Crawford observes that during this period Burns composed several 'early English-language poems [that] reflect a concern with the precariousness of existence'.[10] It would appear that it is the sentimental rather than specifically the English element that Daiches objects to, arguing that where the influence can be traced the poems are rendered merely 'imitative and artificial'.[11] Similarly Karen Wilson-Costa's appropriation of Daiches also asserts that Burns 'revelled in sentimental literature and it was this [...] tradition which provided him with a literary pose "in which he could express his feelings of pride, ambition and sensitivity without giving himself away directly"' and, therefore, those elements, tangible in both the commonplace book and *Poems*, smack of lacking authenticity.[12] I want to suggest that, rather than being a literary pose, Burns's admiration for the sentimental provides him with a model for not only expressing his melancholia but also his thoughts about posterity. Therefore, a re-examination of his admiration for, and incorporation of, the sentimental poetry in both the commonplace book and the *Poems* reveals a significant relationship between Burns's literary ambitions and his moments of melancholic paralysis, and begs a closer inspection of what he meant by asking 'what a creature is man'.

Literary ambitions

The contents page of *Poems, Chiefly in the Scottish Dialect* promotes the, as yet, unknown author whose name appears on the title page, as one to be considered with something more than a general interest. One poem is dedicated to a 'brother poet', a second dedicated to 'an old Scotch Bard' (thereby implying that the author is a young bard) and a third is entitled 'On a Scotch Bard gone to the West Indies'. With reference to the latter, although the wider readership may not know the details of Burns's plan, which was subsequently abandoned, to relocate to Jamaica, it is telling that, even though the poem was written at a period when his personal circumstances looked at their most bleak, he still has his eye on the prize by referring to himself as a (if not yet 'the') 'Scotch Bard'. If, by the end, readers were left in any doubt about the aspirations of the author, the final poem is entitled 'A Bard's Epitaph'. The collection is so liberally scattered with the self-referential 'Rob', 'Rab' and 'Robert Burns' in conjunction with 'Bard', 'your Bardship' or the diminutive 'bardie' – the latter a term that Crawford notes as referring to 'at once an ambitious poet of his people in full flight and a snook-cocking belittler of the grandiose tendencies in himself' – that it is impossible not to read 'A Bard's Epitaph' as the last word upon the subject of the author by the author.[13] The preface to *Poems* declares that Burns is unequal 'to the genius of an [Allan] Ramsay, or the glorious dawning of the poor, unfortunate [Robert] Ferguson' as he, Burns, even at the height of his vanity, would never place himself in the same category as 'These two justly admired Scotch Poets'.[14] Ronnie Young suggests that this 'show of authorial modesty before a discerning public' has 'the rhetorical effect of placing the idea of [Burns as] not only their logical successor but also that of the natural genius'.[15] If this self-effacing introduction to the collection is, as Young suggests, a strategy to 'manipulate audience response', then it is one that has been rehearsed in the commonplace book, a document that Crawford has described as being Burns's 'bardic manifesto'.[16] Within the folded sheets of folio paper Burns writes that he is, on the whole, pleased with the 'excellent Ramsay, and the still more excellent Ferguson', but he bemoans the lack of 'any Scotch Poet of any eminence' that can do justice to the landscape inhabited by him, and 'this is a complaint [he] would gladly remedy; but, alas! [He is] far unequal to the task, both in native genius and education'.[17] This modest appraisal of his own worth is set to rights in *Poems*. In 'The Vision', the speaker regrets having wasted his

> [...] youthfu' prime,
> An' done nae-thing,
> But stringing blethers up in rhyme
> For fools to sing.[18]

However, he is then visited by the 'Scottish Muse', 'Coila', who is robed in a mantle of 'greenish hue' that shimmers with 'deep lights and shades'.[19] Coila reveals to the poet the 'well-known-land' of Irvine and Aire, and hails him as 'my own inspired Bard!'[20] In the commonplace book, Burns declares:

> it has often given me many a heart ake [sic] to reflect upon that such glorious old Bards [...] who, very probably, owed all their talents to ~~nature~~ native genius, yet have described the exploits of Heroes, the pangs of Disappointment and the meltings of Love [...] O mortifying to a Bard's vanity, their very names are 'buried amongst the wreck of things which were'.[21]

Here he draws a clear line of Scottish succession that stretches back to the professional poets of medieval Gaelic Bardic culture through to Ramsay and Fergusson, via the 'Scottish Chaucerians' Robert Henryson, William Dunbar and Robert Sempill and James Macpherson's reinvention of the Bardic figure in 'Ossian'.[22] The quotation from Robert Blair's *The Grave* is indicative of Burns's desire not to be 'buried amongst the wreck of things' and to take his place amongst the living poets he admired.

In the preface to *Poems* it is to William Shenstone that Burns turns to for support in order to excuse his boldness for appearing in print, misquoting the work of 'that celebrated poet' when he declares that '"Humility has depressed many a genius to a hermit, but never raised one to fame."'[23] It is also from Shenstone that Burns takes courage in his commonplace book. On the very first page are two quotations: the first is maxim number XLIV from 'On Writing and Books' and the second lines from Elegy I:

> There are numbers in the world, who do not want sense, to make a figure; so much as an opinion of their own abilities, to put them upon recording their observations, and allowing them the same importance which they do to those which appear in print.
>
> > Pleasing when youth is long expir'd to trace,
> > The forms our pencil, or our pen design'd!
> > Such was our youthful air and shape and face!
> > Such the soft image of our youthful mind[.][24]

The first bolsters Burns's claims to literary legitimacy despite his humble origins, while the second appears to anticipate nostalgia for the immature poetic self. Rather than supporting Daiches's notion that Burns's admiration for the English poet is a sign of his immaturity as a poet, it is through Shenstone that he finds expression for his ambitions and thoughts upon posterity. It is of no doubt that Burns intended the commonplace book for eventual public inspection as preceding the quotations from Shenstone is a declaration of intent as to the ultimate purpose of the book:

> Observations, Hints, Songs, Scraps of Poetry &c by Robert Burness [sic], [...] it may be some entertainment to a curious observer of human nature to see how a plough-man thinks, and feels, under the pressure of Love, Ambition, Anxiety and Grief with the likes cares and passions, which, however, diversified by the Modes and Manners of life, operate pretty much alike, I believe, in all the species.[25]

Burns anticipates a future audience as an established poet who, even in obscurity, was capable of addressing universal themes. When contemplating perhaps the largest of them all, the purpose of human life being 'to cultivate an intercourse with that Being, to whom we owe life [...] and to maintain an integrative conduct towards our fellow creatures', he describes himself as 'one who spends the hours & thoughts which the vocations of the day can spare with Ossian, Shakespeare, Thomson, Shenstone, Sterne &c' in order that he be 'a fit [member] for that society of the Pious, and the Good, which reason and revelation teach us to expect beyond the grave'.[26] In a letter written in the same year that the commonplace book was begun, Burns wrote to his former schoolmaster, John Murdoch, stating that his 'favourite authors were of the sentim[ental] kind [...] these are the glorious models after which I endeavour to form my conduct'.[27] 'Coila', in 'The Vision', warns the poet:

> Thous canst not learn, nor I can show,
> To paint with *Thomson's* landscape glow;
> Or wake the bosom-melting throe,
>   With *Shenstone's* art;
> Or pour, with *Gray*, the moving flow,
>   Warm on the heart.[28]

'Halloween', a poem celebrating rural customs, has an epigraph from Oliver Goldsmith's *The Deserted Village* extolling the virtues of 'native charm' over and above 'the gloss of art'.[29] 'The Cotter's Saturday Night', a poem that reflects upon the quiet dignity of domesticity after a week of hard toil that is inspired by Robert Fergusson's 'The Farmer's Ingle', has an epigraph from Thomas Gray's 'Elegy Written in a Country Churchyard' that defends the 'useful toil', 'homely joys, and destiny obscure' against sneering disdain.[30] 'A Bard's Epitaph', as Murray Pittock suggests, 'looks forward to Wordsworth's "Poet's Epitaph"' but it also recalls the epitaph at the end of Gray's 'Elegy' that marks the resting place of the unknown poet.[31] The voice of Gray's graveyard visitor gives way to that of another who celebrates, somewhat paradoxically, 'A Youth to Fortune and Fame unknown'.[32] 'A Bard's Epitaph' similarly contemplates the deceased poet's expectation of future fame, but in such a way that fame is reconnected with the classical connotations of gossip and rumour:

> The poor Inhabitant below
> Was quick to learn and wise to know,
> [...]
> But thoughtless follies laid him low,
> And stain'd his name![33]

'A Bard's Epitaph' surmises that the basis of the poet's posthumous reputation will rest not upon his achievements, as represented by the preceding poems, but upon improprieties beneath the dignity of a national Bard. The poem echoes a sense of regret and shame that can be found in the commonplace book. In September 1783 Burns writes that he is in complete agreement with Adam Smith in that 'remorse is the most painful sentiment' when caused by 'our own follies or crimes', and that to be able to 'bear it up with manly firmness, and at the same time have a proper penitential sense of our misconduct, – is a glorious effort of Self-command'.[34] In *Theory of Moral Sentiments*, Smith writes that remorse is the root cause of the penitent's 'forebodings, of incomprehensible misery [especially when in the presence of] those very judges who he knows have already unanimously condemned him'.[35] Burns's reflections upon remorse, and the underpinning framework of the sentimental poetry in both the commonplace book and *Poems*, connects him to the prevalent mood among his favourite authors: melancholia.

Melancholia

In a much quoted letter, Gilbert Burns writes that 'straits and difficulties', coupled with seeing their father 'growing old [...] [,] broken down with the long-continued fatigues of his life [...] [and] the hard labour and the sorrow of this period [...] [,] was in a great measure the cause of the depression of spirits with which Robert was so often afflicted'.³⁶ Burns's respect for his father can be read in the epitaph composed in the commonplace book, included in *Poems*, which begins 'O ye! who sympathise with Virtue's pains!'³⁷ He acknowledges the dignity of his father's hard labour and the simple pleasures of home and hearth after a hard week in 'The Cotter's Saturday Night', but the epigraph to the poem also makes clear that Burns does not want to follow in his father's footsteps. The worthy Cotter, who 'weary, o'er the moor his course does homeward bend', recalls Gray's ploughman who 'homeward plods his weary way' at the beginning of 'Elegy Written in a Country Churchyard'.³⁸ The epigraph for the poem is also taken from Gray's 'Elegy' and the first line he takes from Gray reads as almost an admonishment to Burns: 'Let not Ambition mock [his] useful toil'. The six months or so preceding Burns's return to the farm at Lochlie were particularly difficult: a marriage proposal had been rejected, which may have contributed to his decision to leave Lochlie and strike out on his own; his father was dying of consumption and was also embroiled in a dispute with the Lochlie farm landlord, David MacLure; and Burns was ill. The farm itself consisted of an unproductive and unprofitable 130 acres of marshland, located in the parish of Tarbolton, to which the family had moved in 1776 and paid a fixed cash rent, regardless of yield. In July 1781 Burns moved to Irvine to learn the trade of flax dressing, a venture that ended in disaster and precipitated his return to Lochlie. During riotous Hogmanay celebrations a candle was knocked over by his partner's wife and the premises burnt to the ground.

While in Irvine, Allan Beveridge notes that Burns consulted physician Charles Fleeming five times in eight days, about what specifically is unclear, but the prescribed treatment included 'powdered cinchona [...] which was held to strengthen the nervous system [and] was considered useful for headaches, hysteric and hypochondriac fits'.³⁹ Burns wrote to his father to give an update as to his slowly improving health but still weak nerves, but also reveals his ambitions for the future and his despair at the very real possibility of them remaining unrealized:

> As for this world, I despair of ever making a figure in it. [...] I foresee that very probably Poverty & Obscurity await me & I am, in some measure prepared and daily preparing to meet and welcome them. [...] [M]y grateful thanks for the many Lessons of Virtue & Piety you have given me – Lessons which were but too much neglected when they were given but which I hope have been remembered ere it is yet too late.⁴⁰

Burns seems to be failing in his attempt to reconcile himself to what appears to be his prescribed station in life. The letter to his father from Irvine has been read as evidence of suicidal despair and Burns does indeed look forward to the inevitable bidding farewell 'to all the pains, & uneasiness & disquietudes of this weary life; for I assure you I am heartily tired of it'.[41] He finds particular comfort in verses from the Book of Revelation that promise a transcendence to a state of pure being, suggesting not suicide but comfort in the thought that there will be an eventual cessation of suffering, struggling and starving, and even the cessation of thought. Burns's desire for existence without thought is a constant refrain throughout his correspondence. Writing to Margaret Chalmers while recuperating from a broken leg, he states that 'there are just two creatures that I would envy, a horse in his wild state [...], or an oyster [...]. The one has not a wish without enjoyment, that other has neither wish nor fear.'[42] To Mrs Dunlop he despairs: 'I am a good deal inclined to think with those who maintain that what are called nervous affections are in fact diseases of the mind – I cannot reason, I cannot think [...]. I am glad you have put me on to transcribing my departed Friend's epitaph – Transcribing saves me the very great trouble of thinking.'[43]

Burns finishes the letter to his father with a postscript that reads: 'my meal is nearly out but I am going to borrow till I get more'.[44] This period of disaster and despair coincides with an immersion into the sentimental poetry and prose of the period, including Henry MacKenzie's *Man of Feeling*, a book Burns 'prize[d] next to the Bible'.[45] David B. Morris writes that the middle of the eighteenth century ushered in 'a new death-centred literature for which the prevailing mood is melancholy'.[46] Similarly John Baker observes:

> The *genre sombre* [...] included various often intertwined strands, the elegiac mode, poetry of loss and mourning, the themes of passing time and of mutability, a heightened awareness of mortality and finitude, the 'Death the Leveller' *topos*, all amplified by the expression of sentiment and sensibility.[47]

Leo Braudy considers the development of the prevailing mood in relation to the desire for fame, suggesting that

> when we note the many works like *Night Thoughts* in the mid-century English 'graveyard' school of poetry, [and] consider the enormous pressure of onrushing death in novels like *Tristram Shandy*, [...] it is

tempting to characterise the latter part of the eighteenth century as
a world in which the waning belief in the afterlife has bred a twin
obsession with posterity and death.[48]

Not only is it tempting to characterize the period as such but the contemplation of the twin obsessions is certainly tangible in the example of Burns, whose favourite authors are named here by Braudy. To Mrs Dunlop, Burns writes: 'Lord, what is man! Today in the luxuriance of health, exulting in the enjoyment of existence; in a few days, perhaps in a few hours, loaded with conscious painful being [...] & yet the aweful dark termination of the life, is a something [...] at which he recoils with still more horror'.[49] Burns does not appear to have completely rejected the notion of an afterlife, as indicated in the letter to his father, but there are moments of uncertainty. Still to Mrs Dunlop he proclaims: 'Jesus Christ [...] I trust thou art not Imposter, & that thy revelation of blissful scenes of existence beyond death and the grave, is not one of many impositions [...] that have been palmed on credulous mankind.'[50]

It is this uncertainty during his darkest moments, when all he can do is think rather than act, that sheds light on Burns's literary ambitions. In the commonplace book, he stridently declares that 'Obscure I am, & obscure I must be, though no young Poet, nor young Soldier's heart ever beat more fondly for fame than mine.'[51] Burns not only wants to become the voice of Scotland in order to record the character and customs of the people, he wants to be remembered for doing it in order to lend meaning to his temporal sufferings. Braudy's observation that 'though the individual may be carried away by death [...] his character could be projected into the future by his work' applies to Burns:

> No matter what their religious or irreligious orientation, eighteenth-century writers faced the identity-destroying power of death by looking beyond their own lives for their justification [...]. [F]ame might be the promise of a spiritual health – on earth, in posterity of both – that would allow him to leave his diseased body behind without regret.[52]

Quoting John Locke in a letter to Agnes McLehose, Burns notes that '"I know you loved me when living [...]. [T]his life affords no solid satisfaction but in the consciousness of having done well, and the hopes of another life"'.[53] He does not want to become one of Gray's unrecorded poor but the very real prospect of that being the case pervades both

Poems and the commonplace. In 'To J[ames] S[mith]', Burns imagines his addressee upbraiding him for daring to aspire to literary heights:

> "There's ither Poets, much your betters
> [...]
> Now moths deform in shapeless tatters,
> Their unknown pages".[54]

In 'The Vision', while the bard cannot compare to the 'unrivall'd Rose' of Gray, Shenstone and Thomson, he is 'the lowly Daisy [who] sweetly blows'.[55] However, the 'lowly Daisy' is subsequently and somewhat ruthlessly mown down in 'To a Mountain Daisy'.[56] A much later abridgment of the commonplace book is prefaced with a tangible sense of disappointment, even after his year of fame:

> On rummaging over some old papers, I lighted on a M.S.S. of my early years, [when] I was placed by Fortune among a class of men to whom my ideas would have been nonsense – I had meant that the book would have lain by me, in the fond hope that, some or other, even after I was no more, my thoughts would fall into the hands of somebody capable of appreciating their value.[57]

What Burns did compose during what he described as his 'lucid intervals' were more prayers than poems; the English poems that Crawford describes as being 'upon the precariousness of existence', as noted above, are all composed during this period. 'Man was made to Mourn. A Dirge', 'Winter, a Dirge' and 'A Prayer on the Prospect of Death' appeared first in the commonplace book and are all pleas for strength to come from elsewhere in the absence of his own in order to weather the storms and resign himself to his fate.

Manly fortitude

James Currie, Burns's first editor and major biographer, cites the 1781 letter to Burns's father as demonstrative of the relationship between 'those depressions of mind, which are perhaps not wholly separable from the sensibility of genius [...] and which indicates a mind conscious of its strength'.[58] Currie's association of melancholy with genius harks back to Aristotelian tradition, but also seems to provide, as Leith Davis observes, 'a commentary which emphasises the unhealthy side of it. The same sensibility which enabled Burns to become the inspired bard also rendered him "liable to inordinate impressions; to fever of body, as well as mind."'[59] Both Burns and Currie connect bodily hypochondriasis with constitutional melancholy. The organs in the abdomen, such as the liver and spleen, were collectively known as the hypochondrias; therefore, melancholy ensued from the failure of a disorder of these organs that in turn disrupted the harmonious working of body and mind. Although Currie promotes the association of philosophical melancholy with native genius, clearly too much feeling can become disabling. What Currie admires as an empathic responsiveness to the world has the potential to turn pathological and render Burns dangerously close to becoming feminized. Though hypochondria is gendered male, it is comparable to female hysteria that resulted from a painfully delicate refinement of feeling and, therefore, for Currie, partly offers an explanation as to why Burns found it difficult to withstand the psychological setbacks. Strength is not a quality Burns would attribute to himself in his darkest moments and his admiration for works such as McKenzie's *Man of Feeling* could be interpreted as an admission of emotional susceptibility. Poor physical health coupled with constitutional melancholia (caused by his despair about having his ambitions unrealized and the effect of financial disasters) contrast unfavourably, at least in Burns's own mind, with his father's stoical endurance in the face of one failing venture after another. The effect of Burns's melancholy upon his perception of himself is powerful. He writes to Mrs Dunlop that he wishes

> that one could resign life as an officer resigns a commission [...]. I am ashamed of all this; for though I do want bravery for the warfare of life, I could wish, like some other soldiers, to have as much fortitude or cunning as to dissemble or conceal my cowardice.[60]

Burns's painful awareness of his lack of 'manly firmness', already alluded to in relation to his contemplation of Adam Smith, is evident throughout letters that date from the same period as the commonplace book and beyond. He writes to Agnes McLehose:

> My favourite feature in Milton's Satan is, his manly fortitude in supporting what cannot be remedied – in short, the wild broken fragments of a noble, exalted mind in ruins [...]. [H]e was a favourite hero of mine.[61]

However, the light-hearted admiration is quickly replaced by despair at his own lack of courage in the light of his hero's own audacious ambitions when he writes, again to McLehose, that 'I have no idea of courage that braves heaven.'[62] To William Nicol, Burns writes in a similar vein:

> I have bought a pocket Milton which I carry perpetually about with me, in order to study the sentiments – the dauntless magnanimity; the intrepid, unyielding independence; the desperate daring, and noble defiance of hardship, in that great personage, Satan.[63]

The presence of the 'Deil' in *Poems*, as Pittock suggests, points to a 'challenging, and politically radical quality' in that Burns, like Lucifer, harboured upstart, albeit poetic, ambitions.[64] The letter to Nicol was written after a visit to Edinburgh and expresses his scorn of the patronizing 'Patricians in Edinburgh' and 'the servility of my plebeian brethren'.[65] The poem was composed late in 1785 or early in 1786, coinciding with the keeping of the commonplace book and his thoughts about posterity. This Devil is of popular superstition and bears no resemblance to Milton's Satan, despite the epigraph from *Paradise Lost* that hails Satan as 'O Prince, O chief of many throned pow'rs / That led th'embattl'd seraphim to war.'[66] Instead, Lucifer is a bogeyman to be summoned by the poet's granny:

> O thou! whatever title suit thee
> Auld Hornie, Satan, Nick, or Clootie
> Wha in yon cavern grim an' sootie
> Clos'd under hatches
> Spairges about the brunstane cootie
> To scaud poor wretches[.][67]

Lucifer has been cut down to size. He is no longer living in the palace of Pandemonium, or a commander of armies and his ambitions have been curtailed, which is a fate that Burns perhaps predicts for himself.

Post-fame

Burns's melancholy fears about remaining obscure turn into melancholic reflection by the time he has acquired his audience. Even when his success proves he is no longer 'the most ungainly awkward being in the parish', he is suspicious of the attention received from the literati both in terms of its sincerity and longevity.[68] Burns writes to Reverend William Greenfield, Professor of Rhetoric and Belles Lettres at Edinburgh University, upon the fleeting nature of fame:

> Never did Saul's armour sit so heavy on David when going to encounter Goliath [sic?] as does the encumbering robe of public notice with which the friendship and patronage of 'some names dear to fame' have invested me. I have long studied myself, and I think I know pretty exactly what ground I occupy, both as a Man, & a Poet [...]. I am willing to believe that my abilities deserved a better fate than the veriest shades of life; [...] and that, – 'When proud Fortune's ebbing tide recedes' – you may bear me witness, when my buble [sic] of fame was at the highest, I stood, unintoxicated, with the inebriating cup in my hand, looking forward, with rueful resolve, to the hastèning time when the stroke of envious Calumny, with all the eagerness of vengeful triumph, should dash it to the ground.[69]

Burns writes to Dr John Moore in a similar vein while preparing to return home after his season as the toast of Edinburgh:

> I have formed many intimacies and friendships here, but I am afraid they are all of too tender a construction to bear carriage a hundred and fifty miles. To the rich, the great, the fashionable, the polite, I have no equivalent to offer; and I am afraid my meteor appearance will by no means entitle me to a settled correspondence with any of you, who are the permanent lights of genius and literature.[70]

In a second commonplace book, begun while in Edinburgh, Burns asserts that 'there are few of the sore evils under the sun give me more uneasiness and chagrin than the comparison how a man of genius nay avowed worth is received every where, with the reception which a meer [sic] ordinary character, decorated with the trappings and futile distinctions of Fortune, meets'.[71] He clearly found it difficult to focus. On his return to Mauchline, Burns writes to James Smith: 'I cannot settle to my mind – Farming the only thing of which I know anything, and Heaven above knows, but little do I understand even of that.'[72] But home is exactly where he belonged according to at least one reviewer of *Poems, Chiefly in the Scottish Dialect*. The *Edinburgh Advertiser* in November 1788 opines that had Burns remained in Edinburgh, not his natural milieu, he would have eventually found himself so far out of his depth that the effects would have been fatal:

> [T]he Ayrshire Bard, is now enjoying the sweets of retirement at his farm. Burns, in thus retiring, has acted wisely. Stephen Duck, the Poetical Thresher, by his ill-advised patrons, was made a parson. The poor man, hurried out of his *proper* element, found himself quite unhappy; became insane; and with his own hands, it is said, ended his life. Burns, with propriety, has resumed the flail – but we hope has not thrown away the quill.[73]

Burns would not have agreed with the description of 'sweet retirements', haunted as he was by the ever-present spectre of back-breaking work and grinding poverty of the kind that saw his father off, with the short-lived nature of fame emphasizing, for him, the futile nature of his achievement. Once again, he turns to his favourite for support and expression of his unsettled but determined state of mind. Writing to Robert Ainslie in January 1789, Burns anticipates the New Year by quoting 'his two favourite passages' from James Thomson's *Alfred: a Masque*:

> tho' repeated [...] ten thousand times, still they rouse my manhood & steel my resolution like Inspiration [...]:–
>
>> 'Hear, Alfred, hero of the State,
>> Thy Genius Heaven's high will declare;
>> The triumph of the truly great
>> Is never, never to despair!
>> Is never to despair!'[74]

Burns turns to Thomson in time of need, but this time in order to bolster his resolve not to succumb to his constitutional melancholia as he prepared to receive 'illiberal abuse and perhaps contemptuous neglect' from an ungrateful world.[75] Taking inspiration from Thomson and Milton's Satan he prepared to defy all – '"Hail horrors! hail, infernal world!"'[76] As J. Walter McGinty observes, Burns would certainly have 'empathized with Satan when the latter said "What reinforcement we may gain from Hope / If not what resolution from despair"'.[77] Burns's ambitions fluctuate between hope and despair, and his melancholia is, as Wilson-Costa notes, often allied with mirth.[78] These alternating states of mind find full expression in the commonplace book, with jaunty reels following immediately in the wake of dirges and elegies.

Burns's desire to be more like the horse or the oyster is to occupy the dead space in between the two where there is neither thought nor conscious action. However, because he is neither equine nor bivalve mollusc, Burns draws upon the literature of sentiment in order to find expression, comfort, support and inspiration and to reconcile himself to being that most complex and contradictory of creatures, man.

Notes

1. W. Shakespeare (2007) *Hamlet* in *William Shakespeare: Complete Works*, J. Bate and E. Rasmussen (eds) (Basingstoke: Macmillan), pp. 165–419, II.ii.284–7.
2. (2011) 'Introduction' in A. Ingram, S. Sim, C. Lawlor, R. Terry, J. Baker and L. Wetherall-Dickson, *Melancholy Experience in Literature of the Long Eighteenth Century: Before Depression, 1660–1800* (Basingstoke: Palgrave Macmillan), pp. 1–24 (p. 7).
3. (1985) 'Letter 182, January 1788' in G. Ross Roy (ed.) *The Letters of Robert Burns; Volume I: 1780–1789*, 2nd edn (Oxford: Clarendon Press), p. 212. All letters will be from Volume I unless otherwise stated.
4. 'Letter 374, December, 1789' in *The Letters*, p. 456.
5. 'Letter 374, December, 1789', p. 456.
6. J. C. Ewing and D. Cook (eds) (1938) *Robert Burns's Commonplace Book 1783–1785, Reproduced in Facsimile* (Glasgow: Gowans and Gray), p. xiii.
7. (1966) *Robert Burns* (London: Andre Deutsch), pp. 70–1.
8. *Robert Burns*, p. 105.
9. Ewing and Cook, *Commonplace Book*, p. 8. The book is divided into two sections: the first is a transcription of the commonplace book by Ewing and Cook and the second comprises of facsimile pages of the book itself. The page numbers in the first part correspond with Burns's own pagination in the second.
10. R. Crawford (May 2011) 'Burns, Robert (1759–1796)' in *Oxford Dictionary of National Biography*, online at: http://www.oxforddnb.com/view/article/4093 [accessed 4 September 2014].
11. *Robert Burns*, p. 140.
12. (2006) 'The Poetry of Robert Burns: A Melancholy not Unallied to Mirth', *Revue Electronique d'Etudes sue le monde Anglophone*, 4:1, 10–15 (p. 12).
13. 'Burns, Robert (1759–1796)', *ODNB* Online.
14. (1786) 'Preface' in *Poems, Chiefly in the Scottish Dialect* (Kilmarnock: John Wilson), pp. iii–vi (p. v).
15. (2008) 'Genius, Men and Manners: Burns and Eighteenth-Century Scottish Criticism', *Scottish Studies Review*, 9:2, 129–47 (p. 132).
16. Young, 'Genius, Men and Manners', p. 132; R. Crawford (2009) *The Bard: Robert Burns, A Biography* (London: Jonathan Cape), p. 198.
17. Ewing and Cook, *Commonplace Book*, p. 36.
18. 'The Vision' in *Poems*, pp. 87–99, lines 21–4.
19. lines 51, 67, and 69.
20. lines 72 and 139.
21. Ewing and Cook, *Commonplace Book*, p. 38.

22. The phrase 'Scottish Chaucerians' is borrowed from David Daiches's survey of Scottish literary tradition in his biography of Burns: see *Robert Burns*, p. 22.
23. 'Preface', p. v. Shenstone actually says 'Humility has depressed many a genius into a hermit; but never yet raised one into a poet of eminence' in W. Shenstone (1765) *The Works in Verse and Prose of William Shenstone*, 2 vols (Edinburgh: Alexander Donaldson), II, p. 10. Neither Burns nor Shenstone are using the term 'depressed' in the modern sense of mental disturbance. Samuel Johnson's dictionary states that 'to depress' is 'to press or thrust down', or 'to let fall; to let down', so the eighteenth-century deployment of the word is as a verb but it is interesting to see how the eighteenth-century application feeds into a later understanding of what it means 'to be depressed'. See (1755) 'To Depress' in *A Dictionary of the English Language*, online at: http://johnsonsdictionaryonline.com/?page_id=7070&i=569 [accessed 5 September 2014].
24. Shenstone, 'On Writing and Books' and 'Elegy I' in *Works in Verse and Prose*, Volume II, pp. 127–50 (pp. 135–6) and Volume I, pp. 13–14 (p. 14), lines 32–6, respectively.
25. Ewing and Cook, *Commonplace Book*, frontispiece.
26. Ewing and Cook, *Commonplace Book*, p. 17.
27. 'Letter 13, January 1783' in *The Letters*, p. 16.
28. lines 247–52.
29. In *Poems*, pp. 101–17, epigraph; O. Goldsmith (1770) *The Deserted Village: A Poem* (London: W. Griffin), p. 14.
30. In *Poems*, pp. 124–37; T. Gray (1969) 'Elegy Written in a Country Church Yard' in R. Lonsdale (ed.) *The Poems of Thomas Gray, William Collins, and Oliver Goldsmith* (London: Longmans), pp. 117–40, lines 29–32.
31. (2008) *Scottish and Irish Romanticism* (Oxford: Oxford University Press), p. 150.
32. Gray, 'Elegy Written in a Country Church Yard', line 118.
33. In *Poems*, pp. 234–5, lines 19–20 and 23–4. In classical mythology Fama (Roman) / Pheme (Greek) is the Goddess of both fame and infamy, and the Latin word *fama* means 'rumour', 'report' or 'tradition' or, more literally, 'what is said'. See P. Hardie (2012) *Rumour and Renown: Representations of Fama in Western Literature* (Cambridge: Cambridge University Press), p. 2.
34. Ewing and Cook, *Commonplace Book*, p. 5.
35. (1759), Part II: 'Of Merit and Demerit': Section II, chapter ii 'Of the sense of justice, of remorse, and of the consciousness of merit' in *Theory of Moral Sentiments* (London: A. Millar; Edinburgh: A. Kincaid and J. Bell), pp. 180–8 (p. 186).
36. Quoted in J. Currie (1838) *The Life of Robert Burns with a Criticism of his Writings* (Edinburgh: William and Robert Chambers), p. 18.
37. Ewing and Cook, *Commonplace Book*, p. 14.
38. Burns, 'The Cotter's Saturday Night', line 18; Gray, 'Elegy Written in a Country Church Yard', line 3.
39. (2014) '"Groaning under the miseries of a diseased nervous System": Robert Burns and Melancholy' in M. Coyer and D. E. Shuttleton (eds) *Scottish Medicine and Literary Culture 1726–1832* (Amsterdam: Rodopi), pp. 145–71 (p. 149). I would like to thank Allan Beveridge for sharing his chapter with me prior to publication.

40. 'Letter 4, December, 1781' in *The Letters*, p. 6.
41. 'Letter 4, December, 1781', p. 7.
42. 'Letter 162, December 1787' in *The Letters*, p. 185.
43. 'Letter 374, December 1789', p. 456.
44. The letter refers to Revelation 7.15–17:

    Therefore are they before the throne of God, and serve his day and night in his temple,
    and he that sitteth on the throne shall dwell among them.
    They shall hunger no more, neither thirst any more; neither shall the sun light on them, or any heat.
    For the Lamb which is in the midst of the throne shall feed them, and shall lead them unto living fountains of waters; and God shall wipe away all the tears from their eyes.

45. 'Letter 13, January 1783', p. 17.
46. (2001) 'A Poetry of Absence' in J. Sitter (ed.) *The Cambridge Companion to Eighteenth-Century Poetry* (Cambridge: Cambridge University Press), pp. 225–48 (p. 234).
47. (2011) '"Strange Contrarys": Figures of Melancholy in Eighteenth-Century Poetry' in *Melancholy Experience in Literature of the Long Eighteenth Century*, pp. 83–113 (p. 101).
48. (1997) *The Frenzy of Renown: Fame and Its History* (New York: Vintage Books), p. 378.
49. 'Letter, 374, December 1789', p. 456.
50. 'Letter, 374, December 1789', p. 456.
51. Ewing and Cook, *Commonplace Book*, p. 36.
52. Braudy, *The Frenzy of Renown*, p. 379.
53. 'Letter 182, January 1788', p. 212.
54. In *Poems*, pp. 69–78, lines 43 and 47–8.
55. lines 204–5.
56. In *Poems*, pp. 170–3.
57. Quoted in Ewing and Cook, *Commonplace Book*, p. ix.
58. *The Life of Robert Burns*, pp. 24–5.
59. (1997) 'James Currie's *Works of Robert Burns*: The Politics of Hypochondriasis', *Studies in Romanticism*, 36, 43–60 (p. 51).
60. 'Letter 184, January 1788' in *The Letters*, p. 215.
61. 'Letter 171, January 1788' in *The Letters*, p. 198.
62. 'Letter 182, January 1788', p. 212.
63. 'Letter 114, June 1787' in *The Letters*, p. 123.
64. *Scottish and Irish Romanticism*, p. 149.
65. 'Letter 114, June 1787', p. 122.
66. Burns, 'Address to The Deil' in *Poems*, pp. 55–61, epigraph; J. Milton (2004) *Paradise Lost*, S. Orgel and J. Goldberg (eds) (Oxford: Oxford University Press), I.128–9.
67. Burns, 'Address to The Deil', lines 1–6.
68. 'Letter 125, August 1787' in *The Letters*, p. 138.
69. 'Letter 66, December 1786' in *The Letters*, p. 73.
70. Burns, 'Letter 97, April 1787' in *The Letters*, p. 107.

71. Manuscript of the second *Commonplace Book 1787–1790*, Robert Burns Birthplace Museum, National Trust of Scotland, Object number 3.6147, p. 2.
72. 'Letter 113, June 1787' in *The Letters*, p. 123.
73. Quoted in I. McIntyre (2009) *Robert Burns: A Life* (London: Constable), p. 233.
74. Burns, 'Letter 295, January 1789' in *The Letters*, pp. 352–3.
75. 'Letter 98, April 1787' in *The Letters*, p. 108.
76. *Paradise Lost*, I.250–1, which Burns quotes in the letter cited above.
77. (2004) 'Milton's Satan and Burns's Auld Nick', *Studies in Scottish Literature* 33:1, 1–14 (p. 5). The internal quotation is from *Paradise Lost*, I.190–1.
78. Wilson-Costa, 'The Poetry of Robert Burns', p. 13.

Bibliography

Primary Sources

A Gentleman of the Navy (1732) *The Beauties of the Universe* (London: J. Roberts).
Addison, J. (1928, repr. 1964) 'Cato' in J. Hampden (ed.) *John Gay's 'The Beggar's Opera' and Other Eighteenth-Century Plays* (London: Dent).
Addison, J. and R. Steele (1965) *The Spectator*, D. F. Bond (ed.), 5 vols (Oxford: Clarendon Press), II, III.
Akenside, M. (1744) *The Pleasures of Imagination* (London: Robert Dodsley).
Arbuthnot, J. (1734) *Gnothi Seauton. Know Your Self* (London: J. Tonson).
Atkyns, R. (1768) *The Ancient and Present State of Glocestershire*, 2nd edn (London: numerous publishers).
Backscheider P. R. and C. E. Ingrassia (eds) (2009) *British Women Poets of the Long Eighteenth Century: An Anthology* (Baltimore: Johns Hopkins University Press).
Baker, H. (1739) 'The Discovery of a Perfect Plant in Semine', *Philosophical Transactions of the Royal Society*, 41, 448–54.
—— ([n.d.] [1734]) *The Universe. A Poem. Intended to Restrain the Pride of Man* (London: T. Worrall).
Bell, S. (1673) *The Legacy of a Dying Mother to her Mourning Children* (London: John Hancock Senior and Junior).
Blackmore, R. (1716) *An Essay upon the Laws of Nature* (London: George Grierson).
—— (1712) *Creation* (London: S. Buckley and J. Tonson).
Blamire, S. (1842) *The Poetical Works of Miss Susanna Blamire, with a Preface, Memoir, and Notes by Patrick Maxwell*, H. Lonsdale (ed.) (Edinburgh: John Menzies).
Bolingbroke, H. St John (1735) *A Dissertation upon Parties; in several letters to Caleb D'Anvers, Esq; dedicated to the Right Honourable Sir Robert Walpole* (London: G. Faulkner).
—— (1740) *The Idea of a Patriot King: With respect to the Constitution of Great Britain. By a person of quality* (London: 'T.C.').
Boyle, R. (1996) *Robert Boyle: A Free Enquiry into the Vulgarly Received Notion of Nature*, E. B. Davis and M. Hunter (eds) (Cambridge: Cambridge University Press).
Bracken, H. (1737) *The Midwife's Companion; or, a Treatise of Midwifery: Wherein the Whole Art is Explained* (London: J. Clarke and J. Shuckburgh).
Brereton, J. (1735) *Merlin, A Poem* (London: Edward Cave).
—— (1744) *Poems on Several Occasions: by Mrs Jane Brereton. With Letters to her Friends And An Account of Her Life* (London: Edward Cave).
Brooke, H. (1735) *Universal Beauty. A Poem* (London: J. Wilcox).
—— (1735) *Universal Beauty. A Poem. Part III* (London: J. Wilcox).
Brooke, H. and C. H. Wilson (1804) *Brookiana* (London: Richard Phillips), II.
Browne, M. (1739) *Essay on the Universe in Poems on Various Subjects. Many Never Printed Before* (London: Edward Cave).
—— (1752) *The Works and Rest of the Creation* (London: A. Millar).

Burges, J. H. (1800) 'John Henry Burges to Richard Llwyd, 11 March 1800', National Library of Wales (NLW) MS 1562 C.

Burney, F. (1846) *The Diary and Letters of Mme d'Arblay*, C. Barrett (ed.), 7 vols (London: Colburn), VII.

—— (1990) *The Early Journals and Letters of Fanny Burney, 1774–1777*, L. Troide (ed.) 5 vols (Oxford: Oxford University Press), II.

Burns, R. *Commonplace Book 1787–1790*, Robert Burns Birthplace Museum, National Trust of Scotland, Object number 3.6147.

—— (1985) *The Letters of Robert Burns; Volume 1: 1780–1789*, G. Ross Roy (ed.) 2nd edn (Oxford: Clarendon Press).

—— (1786) *Poems, Chiefly in the Scottish Dialect* (Kilmarnock: John Wilson).

—— (1938) *Robert Burns's Commonplace Book 1783–1785*, Reproduced in Facsimile, J. C. Ewing and D. Cook (eds) (Glasgow: Gowans and Gray).

Butcher, E. (1805) *An Excursion from Sidmouth to Chester in the Summer of 1803, Part I* (London: C. Whittingham).

Cave Winscom, J (1783) *Poems on Various Subjects, Entertaining, Elegiac and Religious* (Winchester: J. Sadler).

—— (1789) *Poems on Various Subjects: Entertaining, Elegiac, and Religious* (Shrewsbury: T. Wood).

—— (1794) *Poems on Various Subjects: Entertaining, Elegiac, and Religious* (Bristol: N. Biggs).

—— [n.d.] *Prose and Poetry, on Religious, Moral and Entertaining Subjects* (Bristol: George Routh).

Chudleigh, Lady M. (1993) *The Poems and Prose of Mary, Lady Chudleigh*, M. J. M. Ezell (ed.) (New York and Oxford: Oxford University Press).

Cicero (1958) *Orations: Pro Sestio, In Vatinium*, R. Gardner (trans.) (Cambridge, MA: Loeb).

Coleridge, S. T. (1956) *Collected Letters of Samuel Taylor Coleridge, Vol.1*, E. L. Griggs (ed.) (Oxford: Clarendon Press).

Cooper, A. A., Third Earl of Shaftesbury (1999) *Shaftesbury: Characteristics of Men, Manners, Opinions, Times*, L. E. Klein (ed.) (Cambridge: Cambridge University Press).

Cotton, C. (1744) *The Wonders of the Peak*, 2nd edn (Nottingham: [n. pub.]).

Cowper, W (1981) *The Letters and Prose Writings of William Cowper*, J. King and C. Ryskamp (eds), 5 vols (Oxford: Clarendon Press), II.

—— (1980) *The Poems of William Cowper, 1748–1782*, J. D. Baird and C. Ryskamp (eds), 3 vols (Oxford: Clarendon Press), I.

—— (1995) *The Poems of William Cowper*, J. D. Baird and C. Ryskamp (eds), 3 vols (Oxford: Clarendon Press), II.

Dacier, A. (1692) *Miscellany Poems upon Several Occasions* (London: Peter Buck).

Darrell, W. (1704) *A Gentleman Instructed in the Conduct of a Virtuous and Happy Life*, 2nd edn (London: E. Evets).

Denman, T. (1786) *An Essay on Natural Labours* (London: J. Johnson).

Dennis, J. (1701) *The Advancement and Reformation of Modern Poetry* (London: Richard Parker).

—— (1717) *Remarks Upon Mr. Pope's Translation of Homer* (London: E. Curll).

Derham, W. (1713) *Physico-theology: or, a demonstration of the being and attributes of God from His works of creation* (London: W. Innys).

Dryden, J. (1995) *The Poems of John Dryden, Vol. 2, 1682–1685*, P. Hammond (ed.) (London: Longman).

———(2000a) *The Poems of John Dryden, Vol. 3, 1686–1693*, P. Hammond and D. Hopkins (eds) (Harlow: Longman).
——— (2000b) *The Poems of John Dryden, Vol. 4, 1693–1696*, P. Hammond and D. Hopkins (eds) (Harlow: Longman).
——— (2007) *Dryden: Selected Poems*, P. Hammond and D. Hopkins (eds) (Harlow: Pearson Education).
Duck, S. (1737) *The Year of Wonders, Being a Literal and Poetical Translation of an Old Latin Prophecy Found Near Merlin's Cave* (London: J. Johnson).
Edwards, E. (2013) *English-Language Poetry from Wales 1789–1806* (Cardiff: University of Wales Press).
Fairer, D. and C. Gerrard (1999) *Eighteenth-Century Poetry: An Annotated Anthology* (Oxford: Blackwell).
——— (2015) *Eighteenth-Century Poetry: An Annotated Anthology*, 3rd edn (Oxford: Blackwell).
Finch, A. (1987) *Anne Finch: Selected Poems*, D. Thompson (ed.) (Manchester: Fyfield).
Fordyce Mavor, W. (1806) *A Tour in Wales, and through several Counties of England* (London: R. Phillips).
Fortescue, J. (1748) *Nature a Poem; Being an Attempt Towards a Vindication of Providence[...]* (London: M. Cooper).
——— (1747) *Nature, a Poem. Tending to Shew, That Every Part in the Moral World Is, in a Beautiful Variety, Regularly Ordered and Adjusted [...]* (London: M. Cooper).
——— (1750) *Science: An Epistle on It's Decline and Revival [...]* (Oxford: J. Fletcher).
——— (1751) *Science; a Poem, (in a Religious View) on It's Decline and Revival* (Oxford: J. Fletcher).
Fullard, J. (ed.) (1990) *British Women Poets, 1660–1800: An Anthology* (New York: Whitston Publishing Company).
Goldsmith, O. (1966) *Collected Works of Oliver Goldsmith*, A. Friedman (ed.) 5 vols (Oxford: Clarendon Press).
——— (1770) *The Deserted Village, A Poem* (London: W. Griffin).
——— (1774) *History of the Earth and Animated Nature*, 8 vols (London: J. Nourse), I, III, IV, VI, VII.
Grainger, J. (2000) *The Poetics of Empire: A Study of James Grainger's The Sugar Cane*, J. Gilmore (ed.) (London: Athlone Press).
Gray, T. (1969) *The Poems of Thomas Gray, William Collins, and Oliver Goldsmith*, R. Lonsdale (ed.) (London: Longmans).
Grymeston, E. (1604) *Miscelanea. Meditations. Memoratiues* (London: Melch Bradwood).
Gwilym, D. ap (1789) *Barddoniaeth Dafydd ab Gwilym* (Llundain [London]: H. Baldwin).
Hands, E. (1789) *The Death of Amnon. A Poem. With an Appendix: Containing Pastorals, and other Poetical Pieces* (Coventry: N. Rollason).
Hay, W. (1754) *Deformity: An Essay* (London: R. and J. Dodsley).
Heton, T. (1707) *Some Account of the Mines, and the Advantages of them to this Kingdom* (London: W.B. for John Wyat).
Horace (1929) *Horace: Satires, Epistles, Ars Poetica*, H. R. Fairclough (ed.) (Cambridge, MA: Harvard University Press).
—— (1927) *The Odes and Epodes*, revised edition, C. E. Bennett (trans.) (Cambridge, MA: Loeb).

270 Bibliography

———— (1684) *The Odes, Satyrs, and Epistles of Horace Done into English*, T. Creech (trans.) (London: Jacob Tonson).
Horton, Rev. Mr (1750) *Account of the Earthquakes which Happened at Leghorn in Italy, Between the 5th and 16th of January, 1742* (London: E. Withers).
Hughes, J. (1720) *The Ecstasy: An Ode* (London: J. Roberts).
Hutcheson, F. (1972) *An Essay on the Nature and Conduct of the Passions and Affections with Illustrations on the Moral Sense* (Menston, Yorkshire: Scolar Press).
———— (2004) *An Inquiry into the Original of our Ideas of Beauty and Virtue in Two Treatises*, W. Leidhold (ed.) (Indianapolis: Liberty Fund).
Hutton, J. (1781) *A Tour to the Caves, in the Environs of Ingleborough and Settle, in the West-Riding of Yorkshire*, 2nd edn (London: [n. pub.]).
Johnson, S. (1755) *A Dictionary of the English Language* (London: J. & P. Knapton).
———— (1905) *Lives of the English Poets*, G. Birkbeck Hill (ed.) (Oxford: Clarendon Press, 1905), III.
———— (2006) *The Lives of the Most Eminent English Poets; With Critical Observations on their Works*, R. Lonsdale (ed.), 4 vols (Oxford: Clarendon Press), IV.
———— (2000) *Samuel Johnson: The Major Works*, D. Greene (ed.) (Oxford: Oxford University Press).
———— (2010) *The Yale Edition of the Works of Samuel Johnson, Vol. 22*, J. H. Middendorf (ed.) (New Haven and London: Yale University Press).
Jones, M. (1750) *Miscellanies in Prose and Verse* (Oxford: Mr Dodsley, Mr Clements, Mr Frederick).
Joscelin, E. (1624) *The Mother's Legacie to her Unborne Childe* (London: John Haviland).
La Rochefoucauld (1976) *Réflexions ou Sentences et Maximes morales Suivi de Réflexions diverses et des Maximes de Madame de Sablé*, J. Lafond (ed.) (Paris: Gallimard).
Landon, L. E. (1830) *The Poetical Works of L.E.L.* (London: Longman).
Leigh, D. (1616) *The Mothers Blessing* (London: John Budge).
Llwyd, R. (1800) *Beaumaris Bay, A Poem; with Notes, Descriptive and Explanatory* (Chester, J. Fletcher).
———— (1804) *Poems, Tales, Odes, Sonnets, Translations from the British* (Chester: J. Fletcher).
———— (1837) *The Poetical Works of Richard Llwyd, the Bard of Snowdon* (London: Whittaker and Co.).
———— (forthcoming) *Richard Llwyd: Beaumaris Bay and Other Poems*, E. Edwards (ed.) (Nottingham: Trent Editions).
———— (1802) 'Richard Llwyd to William Owen Pughe, 1 February 1802', NLW 13222C, f. 739.
Locke, J. (1979) *An Essay Concerning Human Understanding*, P. H. Nidditch (ed.) (Oxford: Clarendon Press).
———— (1708) *Some Familiar Letters between Mr. Locke, and Several of His Friends* (London: A. and J. Churchill).
Lonsdale, R. (ed.) (1990) *Eighteenth-Century Women Poets: An Oxford Anthology* (Oxford: Oxford University Press).
———— (2003) *The New Oxford Book of Eighteenth-Century Verse* (Oxford: Oxford University Press)
Malthus, T. (1798) *An Essay on the Principle of Population, as it affects the future improvement of society with remarks on the speculations of Mr. Godwin, M. Condorcet, and other writers* (London: J. Johnson).

Manlove, E. (1653) *The Liberties and Customes of the Lead-Mines Within the Wapentake of Wirkswarth in the County of Derby* (London: [n. pub.]).
Manners, R. (1799) *A Review of Poetry* (London: J. Booth).
Mason, J. (1749) *An Essay on the Power of Numbers, and the Principles of Harmony in Poetical Compositions* (London: James Waugh).
Masters, M. (1755) *Familiar Letters and Poems on Several Occasions* (London: D. Henry and R. Cave).
Mears, M. (1797) *The Pupil of Nature* (London: Faulder, Murray and Highly).
Milton, J. (2004) *Paradise Lost*, S. Orgel and J. Goldberg (eds) (Oxford: Oxford University Press).
—— (1968) *The Poems of John Milton*, J. Carey and A. Fowler (eds) (Harlow: Longmans).
Montagu, Lady M. W. (1747) *Six Town Eclogues. With Some Other Poems* (London: M. Cooper).
[Morrice, B.] (1733) *An Essay on the Universe* (London: John Oswold).
Needler, H. (1728) *The Works of Mr. Henry Needler, Consisting of Original Poems, Translations, Essays, and Letters*, 2nd edn (London: J. Watts).
Nihell, E. (1760) *A Treatise on the Art of Midwifery* (London: A. Morley).
O'Keeffe, J. (1797) *The Wicklow Mountains: Or, The Lad of the Hills, a Comic Opera* (Dublin: John Whitworth).
Ovid (1968) *Ovid's Amores*, G. Lee (trans.) (London: John Murray).
Pickering, P. (1794) *Poems by Mrs. Pickering* (Birmingham: E. Piercy).
Plath, S. (2005) *The Bell Jar* (London: Faber and Faber).
Plotinus (1991) *The Enneads*, S. MacKenna (trans.) and J. Dillon (ed.) (Harmondsworth: Penguin).
Pointon, P. (1770) *Poems on Several Occasions* (Birmingham: T. Warren).
Pope, A. (2000) *Alexander Pope: Selected Letters*, H. Erskine-Hill (ed.) (Oxford: Oxford University Press).
—— (1956a) *The Correspondence of Alexander Pope, Vol. II, 1719–1728*, G. Sherburn (ed.) (Oxford: Clarendon Press).
—— (1956b) *The Correspondence of Alexander Pope, Vol. III, 1729–1735*, G. Sherburn (ed.) (Oxford: Clarendon Press).
—— (1956c) *The Correspondence of Alexander Pope, Vol. IV, 1736–44*, G. Sherburn (ed.) (London: Methuen).
—— (1734) *An Essay on Man, Being the First Book of Ethic Epistles, To Henry St. John, L. Bolingbroke* (London: John Wright for Lawton Gilliver), Foxon P852, British Library 1486.d.3.
—— (1743b) *An Essay on Man, Being the First Book of Ethic Epistles. To H. St. John L. Bolingbroke. With the Commentary and Notes of Mr. Warburton* (London: J. and P. Knapton), Foxon P865, British Library C.59.e1.
—— (1984) *The Last and Greatest Art: Some Unpublished Poetical Manuscripts of Alexander Pope*, M. Mack (ed.) (Newark: University of Delaware Press; London and Toronto: Associated University Presses).
—— (1963) *The Poems of Alexander Pope*, J. Butt (ed.) (London: Methuen).
—— (1936) *The Prose Works of Alexander Pope, Vol. I*, N. Ault (ed.) (Oxford: Blackwell).
—— (1939) *The Twickenham Edition of the Poems of Alexander Pope, Vol. I*, E. Audra and Williams (eds) (London: Methuen).
—— (1993) *The Twickenham Edition of the Poems of Alexander Pope, Vol. I*, E. Audra and A. Williams (eds) (London and New York: Routledge).

—— (1962) *The Twickenham Edition of the Poems of Alexander Pope, Vol II*, G. Tillotson (ed.), 3rd edn (London: Methuen).
—— (1950) *The Twickenham Edition of the Poems of Alexander Pope, Vol. III.i*, M. Mack (ed.) (London: Methuen).
—— (1993) *The Twickenham Edition of the Poems of Alexander Pope, Vol. III.i*, M. Mack (ed.) (London and New York: Routledge).
—— (1951) *The Twickenham Edition of the Poems of Alexander Pope, Vol. III.ii*, F. W. Bateson (ed.), 3rd edn (London: Methuen).
—— (1953) *The Twickenham Edition of the Poems of Alexander Pope, Vol. IV*, J. Butt (ed.) (London: Methuen).
—— (1964) *The Twickenham Edition of the Poems of Alexander Pope, Vol. VI*, N. Ault and J. Butt (eds) 1st edn reprinted with minor corrections (London: Methuen).
—— (1735) *The Works of Alexander Pope, Esq; Vol. II* (London: J. Wright for L. Gilliver).
—— (1736) *The Works of Alexander Pope, Esq, Vol. II*, 3rd edn (London: Lawton Gilliver), Griffith 430, British Library C.122.e.31 .
—— (1739) *The Works of Alexander Pope, Esq.; Vol. II. Containing his Epistles, & c.* (London: Robert Dodsley).
—— (1756) *The Works of Alexander Pope*, W. Warburton (ed.), 9 vols (London: A. Millar et al.), III.
Prior, M. (1971) *The Literary Works of Matthew Prior*, H. Bunker Wright and M. K. Spears (eds), 2nd edn, 2 vols (Oxford: Clarendon Press), I.
Rapin, R. (1706) *The Whole Critical Works of Monsieur Rapin in Two Volumes* (London: numerous publishers), II.
Ray, J. (1737) *A Compleat Collection of English Proverbs* (London: J. Hughs).
Read, W. (1818) *The Hill of Caves* (London: Henry Colburn).
Reynolds, J. (1709) *Death's Vision, a Philosophical Sacred Poem* (London: Thomas Varnum and John Osborn).
Richardson, S. (1985) *Clarissa, Or, The History of a Young Lady*, A. Ross (ed.) (Harmondsworth: Penguin).
Sargent, J. (1796) *The Mine: A Dramatic Poem*, 3rd edn (London: T. Cadell, Jun. and W. Davies).
Scafe, J. (1819) *King Coal's Levee, Or Geological Etiquette, with Explanatory Notes. To which is added the Council of the Metals*, 2nd edn (Alnwick: J. Graham).
Seward, A. (1810) *The Poetical Works of Anna Seward; with Extracts from Her Literary Correspondence*, W. Scott (ed.) 3 vols (Edinburgh: James Ballantyne), I.
Seward, W. (1801) *A Tour to Yordes Cave* (Lonsdale: A Foster).
Shakespeare, W. (2006) *Hamlet*, A. Thompson and N. Taylor (eds) (London: Arden Shakespeare).
—— (2007) *William Shakespeare: Complete Works*, J. Bate and E. Rasmussen (eds) (Basingstoke: Macmillan).
Sharp, J. (1999) *The Midwives Book: Or the Whole Art of Midwifry Discovered*, E. Hobby (ed.) (Oxford: Oxford University Press).
Shenstone, W. (1765) *The Works in Verse and Prose of William Shenstone*, 2 vols (Edinburgh: Alexander Donaldson).
Singer Rowe, E. (1737) *Philomela: Or, Poems by Mrs. Elizabeth Singer, [Now Rowe,] Of Frome in Somersetshire*, 2nd edn (London: E. Curll).
Smith, A. (1759) *Theory of Moral Sentiments* (London: A. Millar; Edinburgh: A. Kincaid and J. Bell).

Smith, J. (1755) *The Printer's Grammar* (London: W. Owen and M. Cooper).
Smythson, H. (1781) *The Compleat Family Physician: Or, Universal Medical Repository* (London: Harrison and Co.).
Spenser, E. (2013) *The Shepheardes Calendar* (Cambridge: Cambridge University Press).
Sprat, T. (1667) *The History of the Royal Society of London, for the Improving of Natural Knowledge* (London: J. Martyn).
Sterne, L. (1967) *The Life and Opinions of Tristram Shandy*, G. Petrie (ed.) (Harmondsworth: Penguin).
Swift, J. (1983) *Jonathan Swift: The Complete Poems*, P. Rogers (ed.) (New Haven: Yale University Press).
—— (1948) *Journal to Stella*, H. Williams (ed.), 2 vols (Oxford: Clarendon Press).
—— (1967) *Poetical Works*, H. Davis (ed.) (London: Oxford University Press).
—— (2001) *The Correspondence of Jonathan Swift, D.D.*, D. Woolley (ed.), 4 vols (Frankfurt: Peter Lang), I.
Temple, W. (1680) *Miscellanea* (London: A. M. and R. R. for Edward Gellibrand).
—— (1720) *The Works of Sir William Temple*, 2 vols (London: A. Churchill et al.).
Thomas, E. (1722) *Miscellany Poems on Several Subjects* (London: Thomas Combes).
Thomson, J. (1963) *The Complete Poetical Works of James Thomson*, J. L. Robertson (ed.) (Oxford: Oxford University Press).
—— (1981) *The Seasons*, J. Sambrook (ed.) (Oxford: Clarendon Press).
Tollet, E. (1724) *Poems on Several Occasions: With Anne Boleyn to King Henry VIII. An Epistle* (London: John Clarke).
Watts, G. (1755) *Reflections on Slow and Painful Labours, and Other Subjects in Midwifery* (London: G. Keith).
Wesley, J. (1747) *Primitive Physick: or, an easy and natural method of curing most diseases* (London: Thomas Trye).
Wewitzer, R. (1785) *Songs, Choruses, and Recitative in the Pantomime of the Magic Cavern; Of, Virtue's Triumph* (London: J. Almon).
Wilmot, J. (1999) *The Works of John Wilmot Earl of Rochester*, H. Love (ed.) (Oxford: Oxford University Press).
Yearsley, A. (1796) *The Rural Lyre; A Volume of Poems Dedicated to the Right Honourable the Earl of Bristol, Lord Bishop of Derry* (London: G. G. and J. Robinson).

Secondary Sources

Adams's Weekly Courant (Chester, England), Tuesday, April 10, 1770; Issue 1743.
Adam's Weekly Courant (Chester, England), Tuesday, August 15, 1780; Issue 2479.
Alker, S. and H. F. Nelson (2008) 'Introduction' in S. Alker and H. F. Nelson (eds) *James Hogg and the Literary Marketplace* (Farnham: Ashgate).
Anonymous (1800) *The Antijacobin Review and Magazine [...] From April to August (Inclusive)*, Vol. 6 (London: T. Crowder).
—— (1800) *The British Critic, for January, February, March, April, May, and June*, Vol. 15 (London: F. and C. Rivington).
—— (1800) *The Critical Review; or, Annals of Literature*, Vol. 29 (London: S. Hamilton).

―― (March 1797) *The European Magazine and London Review*, 31, 358.
―― (1800) *The Monthly Review [...] From May to August, inclusive*, M,DCCC, Vol. 32 (London: R. Griffiths).
―― (1786) 'Review of Nature: A poem in six books', *Monthly Review*, 74.
Arnauld, A. (1753) *A General and Rational Grammar*, T. Nugent (trans.) (London: J. Nourse) [Facsimile Reprint (1967) *English Linguistics 1500–1800*, 73, R. C. Alston (ed.) (Menston, Yorkshire: Scholar Press)].
Arthos, J. (1949) *The Language of Natural Description in Eighteenth-Century Poetry* (Ann Arbor: University of Michigan Press).
Ashcroft, B., G. Griffiths and H. Tiffin (1989) *The Empire Writes Back: Theory and Practice in Post-Colonial Literatures* (London: Routledge).
Backscheider, P. R. (2008) *Eighteenth-Century Women Poets and Their Poetry: Inventing Agency, Inventing Genre* (Baltimore: Johns Hopkins University Press).
Baker, J. (2011) '"Strange Contrarys": Figures of Melancholy in Eighteenth-Century Poetry' in A. Ingram, S. Sim, C. Lawlor, R. Terry, J. Baker and L. Wetherall-Dickson (eds) *Melancholy Experience in Literature of the Long Eighteenth Century: Before Depression, 1660–1800* (Basingstoke: Palgrave Macmillan), pp. 83–113.
Barker-Benfield, G. J. (1996) *The Culture of Sensibility: Sex and Society in Eighteenth-Century Britain* (Chicago: University of Chicago Press).
Barnett, L. K. (1981) *Swift's Poetic Worlds* (Toronto: Associated University Presses).
Barrell, J. (2013) *Edward Pugh of Ruthin, 1763–1813[:] 'A Native Artist'* (Cardiff: University of Wales Press).
Batey, M. (1968) 'Nuneham Courtenay; an Oxfordshire 18th-century Deserted Village', *Oxoniensia*, 33, 108–24.
―― (1974) 'Oliver Goldsmith: An Indictment of Landscape Gardening' in P. Willis (ed.) *Furor Hortensis* (Edinburgh: Elysium Press), pp. 57–71.
Bertelsen, L. (1999) *The Nonsense Club: Literature and Popular Culture, 1749–1764* (Oxford: Clarendon Press).
Beveridge, A. (2014) '"Groaning under the miseries of a diseased nervous System": Robert Burns and Melancholy' in M. Coyer and D. E. Shuttleton (eds) *Scottish Medicine and Literary Culture 1726–1832* (Amsterdam: Rodopi), pp. 145–71.
Bohata, K. (2009) '"Unhomely Moments": Reading and Writing Nation in Welsh Female Gothic' in A. Smith and D. Wallace (eds), *The Female Gothic* (Basingstoke: Palgrave Macmillan), pp. 180–95.
Boswell, J. (1964) *Life of Johnson*, G. B. Hill (ed.) and L. F. Powell (rev), 6 vols (Oxford: Clarendon Press), II.
Braudy, L. (1997) *The Frenzy of Renown: Fame and Its History* (New York: Vintage Books).
Brennan, C. (2003) *Angers, Fantasies and Ghostly Fears: Nineteenth-Century Women from Wales and English Language Poetry* (Cardiff: University of Wales Press).
Brower, R. (1959) *Alexander Pope: The Poetry of Allusion* (Oxford: Clarendon Press).
Brown, L. (2010) *Homeless Dogs and Melancholy Apes: Humans and Other Animals in the Modern Literary Imagination* (Ithaca, NY and London: Cornell University Press).
Brunström, C. (2006) 'Leaving the Herd: How Queer was Cowper?', *Journal for Eighteenth-Century Studies*, 29, 157–67.
―― (2004) *William Cowper: Religion, Satire, Society* (Lewisburg: Bucknell).

Burke, T. and J. Goodridge (2010) 'Retrieval and Beyond: Labouring-Class Writing', *Key Words: A Journal of Cultural Materialism*, 8, 8–14.
Christmas, W. J. (2010) 'Genre Matters: Attending to Form and Convention in Eighteenth-Century Labouring-Class Poetry', *Key Words*, 8, 38–45.
Clarke, S. (1956) *The Leibniz-Clarke Correspondence, Together with Extracts from Newton's 'Principia' and 'Opticks'*, H. G. Alexander (ed.) (Manchester: Manchester University Press).
Cocker, M. and R. Mabey (2005) *Birds Britannica* (London: Chatto and Windus).
Colbert, B. (ed.) (2012) *Tourism and Travel Writing in Britain and Ireland* (Basingstoke: Palgrave Macmillan).
Cope, K. L. (forthcoming a) 'Notes from Many Hands: Pierre Lyonnet's Redesign of Friedrich Christian Lesser's Insecto-Theology', *Religion and the Age of Enlightenment*, [6?].
—— (forthcoming b) 'Tea at a Hexagonal Table? Gregarious Insects and the Outer Limits of Eighteenth-Century Sociability' in N. Col and A. Cossic (eds) *Transversales: Sociability in the Enlightenment* (Paris: Le Manuscrit).
Cramp, S. et al. (1977–96) *The Birds of the Western Palearctic*, 9 vols (Oxford: Oxford University Press).
Crawford, R. (2009) *The Bard: Robert Burns, A Biography* (London: Jonathan Cape).
—— (May 2011) 'Burns, Robert (1759–1796)', *Oxford Dictionary of National Biography*, online at: http://www.oxforddnb.com/view/article/4093 [accessed 4 September 2014].
Creaser, W. J. (2004) '"The most mortifying malady": Jonathan Swift's Dizzying World and Dublin's Mentally Ill' in H. J. Real (ed.) *Swift Studies* (Münster: Wilhelm Fink), pp. 27–48.
Crowe, M. J. (1986) *The Extraterrestrial Life Debate, 1750–1900: The Idea of a Plurality of Worlds from Kant to Lowell* (Cambridge: Cambridge University Press).
Crow Jaffe, N. (1981) 'Swift and the "agreeable young Lady, but extremely lean"' in J. Irwin Fischer, D. C. Mell and D. M. Vieth (eds) *Contemporary Studies of Swift's Poetry* (East Brunswick, NJ: Associated University Presses), pp. 149–58.
Currie, J. (1838) *The Life of Robert Burns with a Criticism of his Writings* (Edinburgh: William and Robert Chambers).
Daiches, D. (1966) *Robert Burns* (London: Andre Deutsch).
Davie, D. (1992) 'The Critical Principles of William Cowper' in *Older Masters: Essays and Reflections on English and American Literature* (Manchester: Carcanet).
Davies, R. J. W. (2004) 'Was There a Welsh Enlightenment?' in G. H. Jenkins and K. O. Morgan (eds) *From Medieval to Modern Wales: Historical Essays in Honour of Kenneth O. Morgan and Ralph A. Griffiths* (Cardiff: University of Wales Press), pp. 142–59.
Davis, L. (1997) 'James Currie's Works of Robert Burns: The Politics of Hypochondriasis', *Studies in Romanticism*, 36, 43–60.
Demers, P. (2004) 'Masters, Mary (fl. 1733–1755)', *Oxford Dictionary of National Biography*, online at: www.oxforddnb.com/view/article/18316 [accessed 14 September 2014].
Dobson, M. (8 May 1997) 'Shee Spy', *London Review of Books*, 19:9, online at: http://www.lrb.co.uk/v19/n09/michael-dobson/shee-spy [accessed 5 May 2015].
Doody, M. A. (2010) 'Love in All Its Oddness: The Affections in Women's Private Poetry of the Eighteenth Century', *Huntington Library Quarterly*, 63:4, 491–508.

Dussinger, J. A. (2009) 'Goldsmith, Oliver (1728?–1774)', *Oxford Dictionary of National Biography*, online at: http://www.oxforddnb.com/view/article/10924 [accessed 14 September 2014].
Ehrenpreis, I. (1983) *Swift: The Man, His Works, and The Age*, 3 vols (London: Methuen).
Ehrlich, P. (1968) *The Population Bomb* (New York: Ballantine Books).
Ellenzweig, S. (2008) *The Fringes of Belief: English Literature, Ancient Heresy, and the Politics of Freethinking, 1660–1760* (Stanford: Stanford University Press).
Fabian, B. (1974) 'Pope and Lucretius: Observations on "An Essay on Man"', *The Modern Language Review*, 74, 524–37.
Fairer, D. (2003) *English Poetry of the Eighteenth Century, 1700–1789* (London: Longman).
Foxon, D. (1991) *Pope and the Early Eighteenth-Century Book Trade (The Lyell Lectures, Oxford 1975–1976)*, J. McLaverty (rev. and ed.) (Oxford: Clarendon Press).
Frayling, C. (2009) *Horace Walpole's Cat* (London: Thames & Hudson).
Garrard, G. (2012) *Ecocriticism*, 2nd edn (Abingdon: Routledge).
Gaukroger, S. (2010) *The Collapse of Mechanism and the Rise of Sensibility: Science and the Shaping of Modernity, 1680–1760* (Oxford: Oxford University Press).
Gerrard, C. (2006) *A Companion to Eighteenth-Century Poetry* (Oxford: Blackwell).
—— (1994) *The Patriot Opposition to Walpole. Politics, Poetry, and National Myth, 1725–42* (Oxford: Clarendon Press).
Gibson, M. I. (2004) *From Naming to Saying: The Unity of the Proposition* (Oxford: Blackwell).
Glass, D. V. (1973) *Numbering the People: The Eighteenth-Century Population Controversy and the Development of Census and Vital Statistics in Britain* (Farnborough: D. C. Heath).
Glotfelty, C. (1996) 'Introduction: Literary Studies in an Age of Environmental Crisis' in C. Glotfelty and H. Fromm (eds) *The Ecocriticism Reader: Landmarks in Literary Ecology* (Athens, GA: University of Georgia Press), pp. xv–xxxvii.
Goldgar, B. (1962) 'Pope's Theory of the Passions: The Background of Epistle II of the Essay on Man', *Philological Quarterly*, 41, 730–43.
Gould, S. J. (1987) *Time's Arrow, Time's Cycle: Myth and Metaphor in the Discovery of Geological Time* (Cambridge: Harvard University Press).
Greene, R. (rev. W. R. Jones) (2009) 'Jones, Mary (1707–1778), poet', *Oxford Dictionary of National Biography*, online at: http://www.oxforddnb.com/view/article/37614?docPos=3 [accessed 14 September 2014].
Griffin, D. (1994) *Satire: A Critical Reintroduction* (Lexington: University Press of Kentucky).
Hammond, B. (1984) *Pope and Bolingbroke: A Study of Friendship and Influence* (Columbia: University of Missouri Press).
Hardie, P. (2012) *Rumour and Renown: Representations of* Fama *in Western Literature* (Cambridge: Cambridge University Press).
Holberg, J. B. (2007) *Sirius: Brightest Diamond in the Night Sky* (Berlin and New York and Chichester: Springer).
Hope Nicholson, M. (1959) *Mountain Gloom and Mountain Glory: The Development of the Aesthetics of the Infinite* (Ithaca: Cornell University Press; Oxford: Oxford University Press).
—— (1946) *Newton Demands the Muse: Newton's Opticks and the Eighteenth Century Poets* (Princeton: Princeton University Press).

―――― (1968) *"This Long Disease, My Life": Alexander Pope and the Sciences* (Princeton: Princeton University Press).
Ingram, A. and S. Sim (2011) 'Introduction' in A. Ingram, S. Sim, C. Lawlor, R. Terry, J. Baker and L. Wetherall-Dickson (eds) *Melancholy Experience in Literature of the Long Eighteenth Century: Before Depression, 1660–1800* (Basingstoke: Palgrave Macmillan), pp. 1–24.
Iser, W. (1996) 'The Emergence of a Cross-Cultural Discourse' in S. Budick and W. Iser (eds) *The Translatability of Cultures: Figurations of the Space Between* (Stanford, CA: Stanford University Press), pp. 245–64.
Jackson, N. (2009) 'Rhyme and Reason: Erasmus Darwin's Romanticism', *Modern Language Quarterly*, 70:2, 171–94.
Jarvis, S. (December 1998) 'Prosody as Cognition', *Critical Inquiry*, 40:4, 3–15.
―――― (2007) *Wordsworth's Philosophic Song* (Cambridge: Cambridge University Press).
Johns-Putra, A. (2010) 'Satire and Domesticity in Late Eighteenth-Century Women's Poetry', *Journal for Eighteenth-Century Studies*, 33:1, 67–87.
Jones, E. D. (2013) *Friendship and Allegiance in Eighteenth-Century Literature: The Politics of Private Virtue in the Age of Walpole* (Basingstoke: Palgrave Macmillan).
Jones, G. (2013) 'Early Modern Welsh Nationalism and the British History' in S. Mottram and S. Prescott (eds) *Writing Wales, from the Renaissance to Romanticism* (Aldershot: Ashgate), pp. 21–38.
Juhas, K. (2008) *"I'le to My Self, and to My Muse Be True": Strategies of Self-Authorization in Eighteenth-Century Women Poetry* (Frankfurt am Main and Oxford: Peter Lang).
Karian, S. (2010) *Jonathan Swift in Print and Manuscript* (Cambridge: Cambridge University Press).
Kaul, S. (2000) *Poems of Nation, Anthems of Empire: English Verse in the Long Eighteenth Century* (Charlottesville: University Press of Virginia).
Kerrigan, J. (2008) *Archipelagic English: Literature, History and Politics 1603–1707* (Oxford: Oxford University Press).
Keymer, T. and P. Sabor (2005) *'Pamela' in the Marketplace: Literary Controversy and Print Culture in Eighteenth-Century Britain and Ireland* (Cambridge: Cambridge University Press).
Kidd, C. (2010) 'Wales, the Enlightenment and the New British History', *Welsh History Review*, 25:2, 209–30.
King, H. (2007) *Midwifery, Obstetrics and the Rise of Gynaecology: The Uses of a Sixteenth-Century Compendium* (Aldershot: Ashgate Publishing).
Knowles, E. (2005) *The Oxford Dictionary of Phrase and Fable*, 2nd edn (Oxford: Oxford University Press).
Koselleck, R. (2013) *Vergangene Zeiten: Zur Semantik geschichtlicher Zeiten* (Frankfurt am Main: Suhrkamp).
Land, I. (Spring 2007) 'Tidal Waves: The New Coastal History', *Journal of Social History*, 40:3, 731–43.
Lauren, B. (1975) 'Pope's Epistle to Bolingbroke: Satire from the Vantage of Retirement', *SEL*, 15, 419–30.
Lawlor, C. (2006) 'Poetry and Science' in C. Gerrard (ed.) *A Companion to Eighteenth-Century Poetry* (Oxford: Blackwell), pp. 38–52.
Leranbaum, M. (1977) *Alexander Pope's 'Opus Magnum' 1729–1744* (Oxford: Clarendon Press).

Lutz, A. (1998) 'The Politics of Reception: The Case of Goldsmith's *"The Deserted Village"'*, *Studies in Philology*, 95:2, 174–96.
Lynall, G. (2012) *Swift and Science: The Satire, Politics, and Theology of Natural Knowledge, 1680–1730* (New York: Palgrave Macmillan).
Mack, M. (1982) *Collected in Himself: Essays Critical, Biographical, and Bibliographical on Pope and Some of his Contemporaries* (Newark, NJ: University of Delaware Press).
—— (1969) *The Garden and the City: Retirement and Politics in the Later Poetry of Pope, 1731–1743* (Toronto and London: University of Toronto Press).
Markley, R. (1993) *Fallen Languages: Crises of Representation in Newtonian England, 1660–1740* (Ithaca: Cornell University Press).
Marshall, A. (2013) *The Practice of Satire in England, 1658–1770* (Baltimore: Johns Hopkins University Press).
Martin, P. (1984) *Pursuing Innocent Pleasures: The Gardening World of Alexander Pope* (Hamden, CT: Archon Books).
Mathias, R. (1980/81) 'Poets of Breconshire', *Brycheiniog*, 19, 27–49.
McGinty, J. Walter (2004) 'Milton's Satan and Burns's Auld Nick', *Studies in Scottish Literature*, 33:1, 1–14.
McIntyre, I. (2009) *Robert Burns: A Life* (London: Constable).
McKim, A. E. (2005) 'Making Poetry of Pain: The Headache Poems of Jane Cave Winscom', *Literature and Medicine*, 24:1, 93–108.
McLaverty, J. (2001) *Pope, Print, and Meaning* (Oxford: Oxford University Press).
—— (February 2002) 'Warburton's False Comma: Reason and Virtue in Pope's Essay on Man', *Modern Philology*, 99:3, 379–92.
McMillan, D. (1998) 'Dr Baillie' in R. Cronin (ed.) *1798: The Year of the Lyrical Ballads* (Basingstoke: Macmillan), pp. 68–92.
Mills, R. (2008) 'Thomas, Elizabeth (1675–1731), poet', *Oxford Dictionary of National Biography*, online at: http://www.oxforddnb.com/view/article/27215?docPos=1 [accessed 14 September 2014].
Milne, A. (2010) 'Ecocriticm', *Key Words*, 8, 46–8.
Morris, D. B. (2001) 'A Poetry of Absence' in J. Sitter (ed.) *The Cambridge Companion to Eighteenth-Century Poetry* (Cambridge: Cambridge University Press), pp. 225–48.
Morse, D. (2000) *The Age of Virtue: British Culture from the Restoration to Romanticism* (New York: St. Martin's Press).
Myers, A. C. (ed.) (1975) *The Erdmans Bible Dictionary* (Kampen: J. H. Kok).
[n.a.] (1805) 'Extracted Probate Copy of the Will (2 Dec 1805) of Lister Dighton, Clifford Chambers' *Transactions of the Bristol and Gloucestershire Archaeological Society*, 14, 8, online at: http://discovery.nationalarchives.gov.uk/details/rd/a073336f-af98-4afd-b1e0-a793c24a8c32 [accessed 14 September 2014].
Newey, V. (1982) *Cowper's Poetry: A Critical Study and Reassessment* (Liverpool: Liverpool University Press).
Noonan, G. (1990) *Fixed Stars and Judicial Astrology* (Washington: American Federation of Astrologers).
Nuttall, A. D. (1984) *Pope's 'Essay on Man'* (London: George Allen & Unwin).
Overton, B. (2007) *The Eighteenth-Century Verse Epistle* (Basingstoke: Palgrave Macmillan).
—— (2009) 'Journeying in the Eighteenth-Century British Verse Epistle', *Studies in Travel Writing*, 13:1, 3–25.
—— (ed.) (2001) *A Letter to My Love: Love Poems by Women First Published in the Barbados Gazette, 1731–1737* (Newark, NJ and London: University of Delaware Press and Associated University Presses).

―――― (2012) 'Lord Hervey, Death and Futurity' in M. Hansen and J. Klein (eds) *Great Expectations: Futurity in the Long Eighteenth Century* (Frankfurt am Main: Peter Lang), pp. 141–60.
Paradis, J. (1987) 'Montaigne, Boyle, and the Essay of Experience' in G. Levine and A. Rauch (eds) *One Culture: Essays in Science and Literature* (Madison: University of Wisconsin Press), pp. 59–91.
Passman, D. F. and H. J. Real (2008) 'Barbarism, Witchcraft, and Devil Worship: Cock-and-Bull Stories from Several Remote Nations of the World', *Swift Studies*, 23, 94–110.
Pearson, J. (1999) *Women's Reading in Britain, 1750–1835: A Dangerous Recreation* (Cambridge: Cambridge University Press).
Pitcher, E. W. R. (2004) *The Universal Spectator (London 1728–1746): An Annotated Record of the Literary Contents* (Lewiston, NY; Lampeter: Edwin Mellen Press).
Pittock, M. (2008) *Scottish and Irish Romanticism* (Oxford: Oxford University Press).
Potter, G. R. (1932) 'Henry Baker, F. R. S. (1698-1774)', *Modern Philology*, 29, 301–21.
Powell Jones, W. (1966) *The Rhetoric of Science: A Study of Scientific Ideas and Imagery in Eighteenth-Century English Poetry* (London: Routledge and Kegan Paul).
Prescott, S. (2010) 'Anglophone Welsh Women's Poetry 1750–84' in J. Labbe (ed.) *The History of British Women's Writing, 1750–1830* (Basingstoke: Palgrave Macmillan), pp. 102–24.
Priestman, M. (1983) *Cowper's Task: Structure and Influence* (Cambridge: Cambridge University Press).
Rackham, O. (1986) *The History of the Countryside* (London: J. M. Dent).
Ray, J. (1737) *A Compleat Collection of English Proverbs* (London: J. Hughs).
Rogers, K. (2010) *First Friend: A History of Dogs and Humans* (Bloomington: iUniverse).
Rosa, H. (2012) *Beschleunigung: die Veränderung der Zeitstrukturen in der Moderne* (Frankfurt am Main: Suhrkamp).
Rosenberg, A. (1950) 'The Life and Works of Sir Richard Blackmore' (unpublished PhD thesis, Queen Mary, University of London).
Rudd, N. (1982, c.1966) *The 'Satires' of Horace* (Bristol: Bristol Classical Press).
Rusnock, A. (2002) *Vital Accounts: Quantifying Health and Population in Eighteenth-Century England and France* (Cambridge: Cambridge University Press).
Schneid Lewis, J. (1986) *In the Family Way: Childbearing in the British Aristocracy, 1760–1860* (New Brunswick: Rutgers University Press).
Schürer, N. (2013) 'Jane Cave Winscom: Provincial Poetry and the Metropolitan Connection', *Journal for Eighteenth-Century Studies*, 36:3, 415–31.
Scurr, H. M. (1922) 'Henry Brooke' (unpublished doctoral thesis, University of Minnesota).
Sedgwick, E. (1985) *Between Men: English Literature and Male Homosocial Desire* (New York: Columbia University Press).
Seeber, E. D. (1945) 'Goldsmith's American Tigers', *Modern Language Quarterly*, 6:4, 417–19.
Shklar, J. (1998) 'Poetry and the Political Imagination in Pope's *An Essay on Man*' in S. Hoffmann (ed.) and G. Kateb (foreword) *Political Thought and Political Thinkers* (Chicago: University of Chicago Press), pp. 193–205.

Sitter, John (2001) *The Cambridge Companion to Eighteenth-Century Poetry* (Cambridge: Cambridge University Press).

———. (2011) *The Cambridge Introduction to Eighteenth-Century Poetry* (Cambridge: Cambridge University Press).

Solomon, H. M. (1993) *The Rape of the Text: Reading and Misreading Pope's 'Essay on Man'* (Tuscaloosa and London: The University of Alabama Press).

Spacks, P. M. (2009) *Reading Eighteenth-Century Poetry* (Chichester: Wiley-Blackwell).

Speake, J. (ed.) (2008) *The Oxford Dictionary of Proverbs*, 5th edn (Oxford: Oxford University Press).

Spears, M. (December 1946) 'The Meaning of Matthew Prior's Alma', *ELH*, 13:4, 266–90.

Spence, J. (1966) *Observations, Anecdotes, and Characters of Books and Men*, J. M. Osborn (ed.), 2 vols (Oxford: Clarendon Press), I.

Spencer, J. (1986) *The Rise of the Woman Novelist: From Aphra Behn to Jane Austen* (Oxford: Blackwell).

Stack, F. (1985) *Pope and Horace: Studies in Imitation* (Cambridge: Cambridge University Press).

Stevenson, L. (March 1928) 'Brooke's Universal Beauty and Modern Thought', *PMLA*, 43:1, 198–209.

Tague, I. H. (2008) 'Dead Pets: Satire and Sentiment in British Elegies and Epitaphs for Animals', *Eighteenth-Century Studies*, 41:3, 289–306.

Taylor, C. (1989) *Sources of the Self: The Making of the Modern Identity* (Cambridge, MA: Harvard University Press).

Terry, R. (2005) *Mock-Heroic: Butler to Cowper* (Aldershot and Burlington, VT: Ashgate).

Thomas, K. (2009) *The Ends of Life: Roads to Fulfilment in Early Modern England* (Oxford: Oxford University Press).

Todd, J. (January–April 2000) 'Fatal Fluency: Behn's Fiction and the Restoration Letter', *Eighteenth Century Fiction*, 12:2–3, 417–34.

——— (1996) *The Secret Life of Aphra Behn* (London: Andre Deutsch).

Toone, W. (December 1801) 'Anecdotes of the Author of Beaumaris Bay', *The Monthly Mirror*, 12, 371–2.

Turner, G. L. E. (1974) 'Henry Baker, F.R.S.: Founder of the Bakerian Lecture', *Notes and Records of the Royal Society of London*, 29:1, 53–79.

Wardle, R. M. (1957) *Oliver Goldsmith* (Lawrence: University of Kansas Press).

Watson, A. (2012) *Romantic Marginality: Nation and Empire on the Borders of the Page* (London: Pickering and Chatto).

Webster, R. (2012) '"Health of Soul and Health of Body": The Supernatural Dimensions of Healing in John Wesley' in D. Madden (ed.) *'Inward & Outward Health': John Wesley's Holistic Concept of Medical Science, the Environment and Holy Living* (Eugene: Wipf & Stock), pp. 213–32.

Weinbrot, H. (1978) *Augustus Caesar in Augustan England: The Decline of a Classical Norm* (Princeton, NJ: Princeton University Press).

——— (1979) 'Such as Sir Robert Would Approve? Answers to Pope's Answer from Horace', *Modern Language Studies*, 9, 5–14.

Wendorf, R. (2005) *The Scholar-Librarian: Books, Libraries, and the Visual Arts* (New Castle, DE: Oak Knoll Press; Boston, MA: The Boston Athenaeum), pp. 61–78.

Wilson, C. (2008) *Epicureanism at the Origins of Modernity* (Oxford: Clarendon Press).

―――― (1995) *The Invisible World: Early Modern Philosophy and the Invention of the Microscope* (Princeton, NJ: Princeton University Press).
Wilson-Costa, K. (2006) 'The Poetry of Robert Burns: A Melancholy not Unallied to Mirth', *Revue Electronique d'Etudes sue le monde Anglophone*, 4:1, 10–15.
Wood, N. (Spring 2011) 'Goldsmith's English Malady', *Studies in the Literary Imagination*, 44:1, 63–83.
Woods, R. (2009) *Death before Birth: Fetal Health and Mortality in Historical Perspective* (Oxford: Oxford University Press).
Woolley, J. (2008) 'Swift's "Skinnibonia"' in H. J. Real (ed.) *Reading Swift: Papers from the Fifth Münster Symposium on Jonathan Swift* (Münster: Wilhelm Fink), pp. 309–42.
Wrigley, E. A. and R. S. Schofield (1989) *The Population History of England 1541–1871: A Reconstruction* (Cambridge: Cambridge University Press).
Young, R. (2008) 'Genius, Men and Manners: Burns and Eighteenth-Century Scottish Criticism', *Scottish Studies Review*, 9:2, 129–47.

Websites

A Dictionary of the English Language: http://johnsonsdictionaryonline.com
BibleGateway (Nashville, TN: Harper Collins Christian Publishing): https://www.biblegateway.com
Eighteenth-Century Collections Online: www.gale.com/EighteenthCentury
Oxford Dictionary of National Biography: www.oxforddnb.com
Oxford English Dictionary: www.oed.com

Index

Note: 'n' after a page reference denotes a note number on that page.

Acheson, Lady Anne, 215, 220, 224, 228 *see also* Swift, 'Lady Acheson Weary of the Dean'
Acheson, Sir Arthur, 215, 216, 217, 218
Adams's Weekly Courant, 232
Addison, Joseph, 22, 61 n18, 84, 87, 174
advertisements, 231, 232, 236, 239
advice poetry, 156, 167
ageing, 69, 175, 180, 181, 182–3, 220, 221, 228
agrarianism, 117, 119, 123
Aikin, John, *An Essay on the Application of Natural History to Poetry* (1777), 93
Akenside, Mark, 35, 41, 65, 83, 84, 86
Alker, Sharon, 145–6
ambitions, 77, 97, 173–4, 176, 178, 248, 249, 250, 253, 255, 257, 259, 260, 262
America, 71, 120, 122, 123
 colonization, 71, 122
 Altamaha River, 123, 124
 Georgia, 123, 125–5
 Pennsylvania, 123
 revolutionary wars, 71
 Virginia, 123
Anglesey, 133, 136–8, 139, 143, 146, 147
animals, 41, 50, 71, 93, 94, 102, 128, 181, 192, 193, 201, 202, 248
 bats, 122, 123–4, 128, 219
 bees, 32, 72
 cats, 123, 192, 195, 196, 198, 205 n25
 cougars, 123
 deer, 70, 71
 dogs, 194, 195–6, 200, 203, 205
 earthworms, 32, 92
 frogs, 130

hedgehogs, 128
monkeys, 192, 194
 as pets, 192, 193, 201
porcupines, 128
scorpions, 123
snails, 32
snakes, 45 n36, 123
tigers, 123
Antijacobin Review, 140
Antwerp, 230
Arbuthnot, John, 15, 37
 Gnothi Seauton: Know Your Self (1734), 34–5, 37, 38, 40
Aristotle, 22, 88, 109, 111
Arthos, John, 93, 99 n41
Augustan Age, 4, 12, 22, 76, 77, 103, 104, 106, 107, 109, 114, 115, 191
Austen, Lady Anna, 73–4, 77

Backscheider, Paula R., 2, 6, 156, 173, 188 n21, 189n51, 193, 194, 202–3, 204 n13, 205 n18
Bagot, William, 240
ballads, 65, 112, 141, 147, 164
Baillie, Joanna, 156
Baillie, Matthew (physician), 156
Baker, Henry, 83
 Philosophical Transactions, 91
 The Universal Spectator, 99 n34
 The Universe: A Poem (1734), 89, 91–3, 95, 97
Baker, John, 256
Barbauld, Anna Laetitia, 156, 193
 'Washing Day' (1797), 191
Barber, Mary, 214
 'To a Lady' (1735), 203
Barlow, Thomas, 176
Barnett, Louise K., 217
Barrell, John, 146–7
Batey, Mavis, 119–20
Bathurst, Allen (1st Earl of Bathurst), 18

beauty, 3
  feminine beauty, 166, 180, 182, 191, 244: as animal beauty 196
  masculine beauty, 196
  natural beauty, 31, 33, 40, 41, 42, 83, 88, 122, 248
Behn, Aphra, 230–1
Bell, Susannah, 167
belles lettres, 104, 261
Berkeley, George (Bishop of Cloyne), *Alciphron* (1732), 53
Bethel, Hugh, 18, 20
Beveridge, Allan, 255, 264
Bible, 129, 174, 175, 178, 256
  Authorised Version (1611), 128
  Deuteronomy, 128
  Genesis, 174
  Geneva Bible (1560), 128
  Good News Bible (1966), 129
  Isaiah, 128
  Judges, 178
  Leviticus, 128
  Luke, 175
  New International Version (1973–8), 128
  Revelation, 48, 256
  Song of Songs, 174
  Victorian Revised Version (1881–94), 128
  Zephaniah, 128
birds, 93, 122, 123, 124, 127, 128–9, 130, 132 n25, 139, 193
  bitterns, 125, 127, 128, 129–30
  canaries, 192, 199
  cormorant, 128
  eagles, 93
  grey wagtails, 127
  hawks, 128, 214
  herons, 128, 214, *see also* bitterns
  jack-snipe, 129
  kingfishers, 127
  lapwings, 126, 127, 128, 129, 130, 132 n25
  owls, 128, 219
  pelicans, 128
  plovers, 127
  ravens, 127
  storks, 128
Birmingham Gazette, 236

birth, 6, 39, 155, 156, 157, 158, 159, 161, 162, 163, 164, 165, 167, 169 n2
birth poems, 155, 156, 158, 159, 165, 167, 168, 169
Blackmore, Richard, 83, 86, 87, 89, 94, 97
  An Essay upon the Laws of Nature (1716), 91
  Creation (1712), 83, 84, 85, 86, 89, 90, 96, 98 n19
  Satire upon Wit (1700), 86
Blair, Robert, 249
  'The Grave' (1743), 252
Blake, William, 44, 118
Blamire, Susanna
  'Stoklewath; or The Cumbrian Village' (pub.1842), 174
  'The Bower of Elegance' (pub.1842), 174
Bloomfield, Robert, *The Farmer's Boy* (1800), 13
body (human), 5, 38, 40, 69, 70, 77, 96, 163, 192, 200, 259
  blood, 37, 227
  eyes 32, 106, 115–15, 186, 193, 197, 200, 218, 221, 223, 224, 239, 265 n4; spectacles, 223, 224
  frail bodies, 224, 225
  health, 74, 155, 157, 158, 160, 161, 163, 182, 213, 221, 224, 225, 226, 239, 241, 244, 249, 255, 257, 258, 259
  limbs, 69
  temperature, 220
Boehme, Jacob, 44
Bohata, Kirsti, 148
Boileau, 15, 20
Bolingbroke, 1st Viscount, *see* St. John, Henry
Bonedd y Saint, 142
Bonner and Middleton's Bristol Journal, 158
Bosvil, Mrs. Robert (Biana), 240
Boyle, Richard (3rd Earl of Burlington), 13, 18
Boyle, Robert, 90, 91, 98 n13, 107, 111
  Boyle lectures, 89, 98 n13
Bracken, Henry, 163

Braudy, Leo, 256, 257
Brennan, Catherine, 157
Brereton, Jane, 107, 174
  'Epistle to Mrs Anne Griffiths' (1744), 203
  'Merlin, A Poem' (1735), 107, 108
  'To Mr Thomas Griffith' (pub. 1744), 174
Britain, 3, 120, 124, 128, 137–8
British imperialism, 95
British union, 140
British Critic, 140, 149
British Library, 48, 125
Brooke, Henry, 30, 32, 35, 41, 83, 85, 97
  Gustavus Vasa: the Deliverer of his Country (1739), 30, 45 n3
  Redemption: A Poem (1772), 44
  Universal Beauty (1735), 30, 31, 32, 33, 34, 35, 38, 39, 40, 41, 42, 43, 44, 45 n3, 93–4, 97
Brower, Reuben, 13
Brown, Laura, 194
Browne, Moses, 83, 95
  An Essay on the Universe (1739), 89, 92, 94, 95–6, 97
Brydges, James (1st Duke of Chandos), 13, 19, 22, 25 n6
Buchanan George, *Rerum Scoticarum Historia* (1582), 142
Buffon, Comte de, *see* Leclerc, Georges-Louis
Buissière, Paul, 213
Burlington, 3rd Earl of, *see* Richard Boyle
Burney, Frances, 176
Burns, Gilbert, 254
Burns, Robert, 248, 249, 250, 251, 252, 253, 254, 256, 258–9, 260–3, 264 n23
  'A Bard's Epitaph' (1786), 251, 254
  'A Prayer on the Prospect of Death' (1786), 258
  'Address to the Deil' (1786), 260
  commonplace books, 249, 252, 253, 254, 257, 258, 259, 260, 261, 262, 263 n9
  'Man was made to Mourn. A Dirge' (1786), 258
  Poems, Chiefly in Scottish Dialect (1786), 249, 250, 251, 252, 254, 255, 257–8, 260, 261
  'The Cotter's Saturday Night' (1786), 253, 255
  'The Vision' (1786), 251, 253, 258
  'Winter, a Dirge' (1786), 258
Butler, Samuel, *Hudibras* (1661–77), 111

Camden, William, *Britannia* (1586), 142
Carter, Elizabeth, 189 n51
  'To Miss Hall' (1758), 182–3
cartography, 142
Cato, 24
Catullus, 194, 202
Cave, Jane, *see* Jane Cave Winscom
Cavendish, Margaret (Duchess of Newcastle), 186
Caxton, William, 129
Chandler, Mary, 'A Female Wish' (1733), 177
  'A True Tale' (1744), 177
  'My Wish' (1736), 177
Chandos, 1st Duke of, *see* James Brydges
charity, *see* philanthropy
Chaucer, Geoffrey, 129
Chester Chronicle, 136, 141
Chetwode, John Touchet, 240
Cheyne, George (physician), 161
childbirth, *see* birth
children, 54, 126, 129, 155–9, 168, 169 n2, 171 n43, 177
  child, unborn, 155, 1558, 162, 164–7, 170 n.17
  child mortality 165, 170
  childhood memory, 119
Christianity, 38, 40, 44, 73, 96, 108, 115, 165, 166, 177
Christmas, William J., 148, 149
Chudleigh, Lady Mary, *The Ladies Defence* (1701), 185
Churchill, Charles, 65, 67
Cicero, 19
Clarke, Samuel, 52, 62 n25, 107–8
Cocker, Mark, 129
Coleridge, Samuel Taylor, 96, 111, 113

Collier, Mary, *The Woman's Labour: An Epistle to Mr. Stephen Duck* (1739), 180
Colman, George, 65
colonialism, 71, 122, 123, 136,
  see also postcolonialism
Cooper, Anthony Ashley (3rd Earl of Shaftesbury), 27 n44, 31, 35, 45 n7, 94
  The Moralists (1709), 31
Copernicus, 88
corruption, 23, 24, 58
Cothi, Lewis Glyn, 139, 142
Cotton, Charles, 114, 115
  Wonders of the Peak (1681), 114
courtship poetry, 166, 167, 242
Coventry, Maria (Countess of Coventry), 244
Cowley, Abraham, 86, 90
  'To the Royal Society' (1667), 86, 91
Cowper, William, 'A Poetical Epistle to Lady Austen' (1781), 73–4
  'An Epistle to Robert Lloyd' (1754), 67
  'Conversation' (1782), 72, 75
  'Dissertation on the Modern Ode' (1763), 65
  Poems by William Cowper of the Inner Temple (1782), 71
  'Retirement' (1782), 73
  'Table Talk' (1782), 71
  The Task (1785), 64, 70, 71, 73
  'Written at Bath. On Finding the Heel of a Shoe' (1748), 64
Crawford, Robert, 250, 251, 258
Creech, Thomas, 21, 87
Crisp, Samuel, 176, 177, 188 n4
Cunningham, Alexander *Poemata* (1721), 14
Currie, James, 258, 259

Dacier, André, 22
Daiches, David, 249, 250, 252, 264 n22
D'Arblay, Frances, *see* Frances Burney
Darrell, William, *The Gentleman Instructed* (1704), 165–6
Darwin, Erasmus, 96, 118
  The Botanic Garden (1789), 96
  The Temple of Nature (1803) 96

Davenport, Mr (Rev.), 240
Davie, Donald, 76–7
Davis, Leith, 258
Davy, Humphrey, 96
Defoe, Daniel, 91, 99 n34
Demers, Patricia, 196, 198, 203
demography, 117, 119, 124
  depopulation, 119, 121–2
  migration, 121
  overpopulation, 120
Denman, Thomas, 163
Dennis, John, *The Advancement and Reformation of Modern Poetry* (1701), 86, 87, 88
Derham, William, 32
  Astro-theology (1715), 86
  Physico-theology (1713), 86
Descartes, René, 69, 70
disability, 233, 242, 244, 259
  blindness, 221, 231, 233, 235, 236, 237, 242, 244, 245, 246 n23
  deafness, 91, 224, 225
Dixon, Sarah, 'Cloe to Aminta' (1740), 191
Dobson, Michael, 230, 231
domestic poetry, 191, 202
Donne, John, *Satires*, 12–13
Doody, Margaret, 193
Drury Lane, 30
Dryden, John, 14, 20, 22, 86, 104, 113
  Annus Mirabilis (1667), 111
  'Catullus to Lesbia' (1685), 197
  'Discourse Concerning the Original and Progress of Satire' (1692), 14
  Satires of Decimus Junius Juvenalis (1693), 14
  Sylvae (1685), 15
Dublin, 214, 215, 217
Dublin Philosophical Society, 86
Duck, Stephen, 114, 262
  The Year of Wonders (1737), 114
Dunbar, William, 252
Duncombe, William, 42

earthquakes, 102
ecocriticism, 117, 118, 119, 120, 122
ecology, 117, 118, 123

economy, 40, 103, 118, 121, 130, 142
  microeconomics, 121
Edinburgh, 141, 146, 241, 249, 260, 261
Edinburgh Advertiser, 261
University of Edinburgh, The, 261
education, 1, 14, 202
  literacy, 102
  schools, 21, 67, 136, 221, 240
  self-education, 136
Ehrenpreis, Irvin, 212, 215, 222
Ehrlich, Paul, 120
elegy, 119, 130, 160, 178, 184, 193, 194, 233, 236, 240, 252, 254, 255
  mock-elegy, 192, 194, 195, 198, 199, 201, 202, 203
  pastoral elegy, 120, 122, 130
Eliot, George, *Middlemarch* (1871–2), 185
emotions, 83, 97, 111, 112, 159, 161, 164, 166, 191, 201, 213, 244, 250, 259
  admiration, 3, 32, 51, 64, 66, 67, 76, 77, 90, 140, 168, 186, 197, 222, 223, 249, 250, 259
  anxiety, 12, 95, 144, 157, 163, 164, 167, 212, 226, 253
  disappointment, 66, 180, 247 n53, 252, 258
  fear, 70, 71, 110, 115, 121, 123, 157, 161–2, 163, 164, 165, 176, 177, 178, 179, 180, 183, 213, 225, 228, 249, 250, 260
  grief, 69, 180, 195, 216, 221, 225, 226, 227, 253
  joy, 33, 178, 182, 183, 184, 221, 224
  laughter, 14, 16, 21, 36, 52, 69
  love, 39, 41, 51, 75, 91, 94, 166, 182, 183, 184, 194, 195, 196, 199, 200, 221, 243,4, 252, 253, 257
  misery, 177, 195
  regret, 87, 140, 166, 251, 254
  shame, 16, 21, 179, 221, 223, 254, 259
  sorrow, 184, 254
enclosure, 119,126, 127, 128, 129
England, 71, 87, 121, 133, 142, 143, 157, 212
entertainment, 6, 84, 102, 108, 110, 111, 114, 216, 253
Eusebius, 165–6

Fabian, Bernard, 89
Fairer, David, 2, 4, 194, 205 n25, 234
fame, 68, 69, 90, 156, 173–4, 176, 178, 184, 185, 186, 198, 236, 249, 252, 254, 256, 257, 258, 261, 262, 265 n33
fantasy, 73, 113, 193
femininity, 3, 6, 191–2, 198, 202, 259
Fergusson, Robert, 252
  'The Farmer's Ingle' (1779), 253
Finch, Anne (Countess of Winchilsea), 169, 172 n57, 181
  'Clarinda's Indifference at Parting with her Beauty' (pub. 1713), 180, 82
  'Life's Progress' (1709), 180
  'Petition for an Absolute Retreat' (1713), 175, 178, 186
  'The Hog, the Sheep and Goat, Carrying to a Fair' (1713), 181
  'There's No Tomorrow' (1713), 181
Folklore, 127, 128, 129
Fontenelle, Bernard Le Bouvier de, *Entriens sur la pluralité* (1686), 94
Fortescue, James, 96
Fortescue, William, 18, 19, 26 n27
Fowler, Alastair, 204 n1
Fowler, Joanna, 1
Foxon, David, 56
France, 71, 104
  French Revolution, 177, 183
Francis, Anne, 193
Franklin, Benjamin, 185
friendship, 13, 14, 16, 18, 19, 22, 23, 25 n11, 27 n45, 40, 54, 67, 68, 73, 75, 86, 121, 146, 156, 160, 168, 178,, 182, 183, 184, 193, 194, 213, 214, 215, 217, 222, 225, 227, 233, 234, 235, 238, 239, 243–4, 261
  friendship poetry, 184, 203, 223
fruit, 21, 105, 175, 179
  apples, 174, 75
  figs, 173, 174, 175, 176, 178, 180, 181, 187 *see also* trees; fig trees
  grapes, 175, 181
Fullard, Joyce, 2, 177, 202

Gambol, Robert, *The Beauties of the Universe* (1732), 89
Garlick, Raymond, 143, 144
Garrick, David, 109
Gaukroger, Stephen, 86
genius, 17, 97, 108, 122, 145, 230, 251, 252, 258, 259, 261
Gerrard, Christine, 2, 44 n2, 194
Glanvil, Joseph, 109
Glyn, Guto'r, 142
Glyn, Llywelyn y, *see* Cothi, Lewis Glyn
Goddeus, 202
Goldsmith, Oliver, *An History of the Earth and Animated Nature* (1774), 120, 123, 125, 127, 129, 130
  The Deserted Village (1770),118, 119, 120, 123, 124, 125, 126, 253; Auburn, 119, 120, 122, 124, 125, 126, 130
  'The Revolution in Low Life' (1762), 120
Gower, John, 129
Grainger, James, *The Sugar Cane* (1764), 124
Gray, Thomas, 65, 142, 178, 196, 198, 228, 253, 58
  'Elegy Written in a Country Churchyard' (1751), 254, 255
  'Ode on the Death of a Favourite Cat' (1748), 192, 196–7, 203
Greece, 137
Greenfield, William, 267
Greville, Frances, 181
Grey, Harry, 240, 242
Grosvenor, Constance Gertrude (Duchess of Westminster), 156
Grymeston, Elizabeth, 167
Gwllym, Dafydd ap, 'Yr Haf' ('To Summer'), 138

Hall, Edward, *Chronicle* (1548), 142
Hands, Elizabeth, 'On the Author's Lying-In' (1785), 162
Harcourt, Simon (1st Earl Harcourt), 119, 126
Harley, Mr., 211–12, 213
Harris, Howell, 160
Harris, John, *Astronomical Dialogues* (1719), 94–5
Hawkesworth, John, 212, 214

Hay, William, *Deformity: An Essay* (1754), 244
health, *see under* body, illness
Henryson, Robert, 252
heresy, 19
Herschel, Caroline, 186
Hertford, Countess of, *see* Seymour, Frances
Hervey, John Lord (2nd Baron Hervey), 1
Heton, Thomas, *Some Account of the Mines* (1707), 103
Hiffernan, Paul, *The Heroine of the Cave* (1775), 111
Hobbes, Thomas, 88
Hobby, Elaine, 1
Hogg, James, 145–6
Hogmanay, 255
Holberg, Jay B., 200
Holles, William, 240
Homer, 30, 103, 106
Homer, *The Iliad*, 200
Horace, *Ars Poetica*, 18
  Satires, 12, 17, 21
Horton, Mr. (Rev.), *Account of the Earthquakes* (1742), 113
Hughes, John, 84, 86
Hunter, Anne, 'Song' (1802), 180, 183
  'To my daughter' (1802), 183
Hunter, John (surgeon), 156
Hunter, William (physician), 156
Hutcheson, Francis, 49
  An Essay on the Nature and Conduct of the Passions of the Passions and Affections (1728), 54
Hutton, John, *A Tour to the Caves* (1781), 109
hymns, 3, 31, 95, 96, 159, 162

illness, 161, 191, 215, 225, 226, 227, 232
  fever, 200, 259
  hypochondria, 250, 255, 259
  hysteria, 259
  infirmity, 175, 224
  insanity, 71
  low mood, 244
  melancholia, 96, 174, 181, 184, 228, 248, 249, 250, 254, 256, 258–9, 260, 262

imitation, 11, 12, 17, 20, 199
immortality, 176, 186
industrial revolution, 117
influence, 1, 3, 4, 16, 20, 30, 35, 40, 64–5, 75, 87, 93, 144, 156, 159, 213, 250
Ingram, Allan, 1, 248
Ingrassia, Catherine E., 2, 6, 156, 202–3
insects, 41, 92, 93, 123, 130
Ireland, 30, 119, 126, 129, 142, 225, 226
Iser, Wolfgang, 11, 24

Jaffe, Nora Crow, 218
Jarvis, Simon, 49, 59
Johnson, Esther (Stella), 211, 212, 213, 214, 215, 220, 222, 223, 224, 225, 226, 227
Johnson, Samuel, 41, 43, 65, 67
  'Life of Pope' (1781), 17
  The Vanity of Human Wishes (1749), 109, 182
Johns-Putra, Adeline, 191
Jones, Henry, *The Cave of Idra*, 111
Jones, John, 232, 236
Jones, Mary, 191, 193, 194
  'An Epistle to Lady Bower' (pub. 1750), 178
  'Elegy on a Favourite Dog' (1750), 194, 196, 203
Jonson, Ben, *The Art of Poetry* (1640), 14
Joscelin, Elizabeth, 167
Juvenal, 14, 15

Karian, Stephen, 216, 217, 220
Keats, John, 113
Kelly, Isabella, 156
Kerrigan, John, 142
Killigrew, Anne, 'Upon the Saying that my Verses were made by Another' (1686), 179
King, Helen, 163
King, William (Archbishop of Dublin), 212
Koselleck, Reinhart, 177, 185

Land, Isaac, 143
Landon, Letitia Elizabeth, 'Lines of Life' (1827), 186

laughter, *see* emotions; laughter
Lawlor, Clark, 5
lawyer, 19, 24 n5
  legal training, 67
Leclerc, Georges-Louis, *Histoire naturelle* (1749–89), 123–5
Lehose, Agnes (Clarinda), 248, 249, 257, 259, 260
Leibniz, Gottfried Wilhelm von, 88
Leigh, Dorothy, 167
Leveson, Granville, 240
liberty, 23–4, 96
Lichfield, 234, 235, 236 237, 238, 241
Lipsus, 202
Literary Club, the, 124
literature
  Gothic literature, 147, 148
  maternal guidance literature, 165, 166, 167, 168
  medical literature, 156, 161, 1 63, 164
  national literature, 133, 141, *see* writing
  sentimental literature, 249–50, 254, 256
Lloyd, Robert, 65, 67, 68, 69
Lloyd's Evening Post, 120
Llwyd, Richard
  Beaumaris Bay (1800), 133–48
  Poems (1804), 141
Llŷn Peninsular, 139
Locke, John, 86, 88, 91, 257
  An Essay Concerning Human Understanding (1689), 38
Lockhart, John Gibson, *Peter's Letter to his Kinsfolk* (1819), 146
London, 30, 45 n3, 84, 120, 122, 125, 140, 141, 145, 146, 157, 163
  Tower of London, 123
London Review of Books, 230
Lonsdale, Roger, 2, 3, 4, 5, 156, 157, 193, 196, 202, 232, 245 n20
love, *see* emotions; love
Lucilius, 12, 14, 20, 24
Lucretius, 39, 53, 87, 88, 96
  De Rerum Natura (c.55 BC), 37, 87
Lutz, Alfred, 119
luxury, 24, 95

Lyon, John, 214
Lyttleton, Thomas, 240

Mabey, Richard, 129
Mack, Maynard, 25 n11, 30, 47, 48, 49, 53, 54, 55, 57, 60, 62 n18, 62 n30
Mackenzie, Henry, *The Man of Feeling* (1771), 256, 259
Macpherson, James, 249, 252
Mallet, David, *The Excursion* (1728), 41
Malthus, Thomas, *Essay on the Principle of Population* (1798), 120–1
Manlove, Edward, *The Liberties and Customs of the Lead-Mines* (1653), 104, 105, 106
Manners, Lady Catherine Rebecca, 'A Review of Poetry, Addressed to a Son' (1799), 183
manuscripts, 4, 44 n2, 144–5, 146, 211, 216
  medieval manuscripts, 138, 142
marriage poetry, 242
Marshall, Thomas, 239
masculinity, 3, 192, 254, 259
Masters, Mary, 193, 196, 201, 203
  'A Gentleman having read the foregoing Verses' (1755), 197
  'An Imitation of the foregoing Verses' (1755), 197–8
  Familiar Letters and Poems on Several Occasions (1755), 196
  'Selima's Mistress to Comfort her for the Loss of her Favourite' (1755), 196, 197, 198
Mathias, Roland, 143, 144, 157, 159
McGinty, J. Walter, 262
McKim, A. Elizabeth, 157
McLaverty, James, 49, 62 n25
Mears, Martha, *The Pupil of Nature* (1797), 163
Melancton, 202
Menai Straits, 136, 139
Menai, Lewis, 139
metaphysical poetry, 25, 44, 50
microscopy, 85
midwifery, 163

Milne, Anne, 147
Milton, John, 30, 64, 109, 142, 150 n16
  Paradise Lost (1667), 37, 259–60, 262
Miltonic tradition, 64, 65, 71, 101, 109, 115
mining, 103, 104, 105, 108, 110
Molyneux, William, 86, 87
monarchy, 27 n46, 57, 58
  George I, 25
  George II, 19, 22
  Hanoverian monarchy, 3, 13, 23, 63
  James II, 206 n25
  Queen Anne, 213
  Queen Caroline, 107–8
  William III, 195
Montaigne, Michel de, 90
Monthly Mirror, 144–5
Monthly Review, 97, 140
More, Hannah, 159, 168, 203
  'Epilogue to the Search for Happiness' (1774), 203
Morrice, Bezaleel, *An Essay on the Universe* (1733), 90
Morris, David B., 256
Morse, David, 24
Mount Etna, 18
Mulso, Hester, 'To Stella' (1775), 182

National Archives, 242
natural sciences, 93, 110
  astronomy, 84, 86, 92, 93, 94, 95, 102
  botany, 93, 94, 95, 96, 118, 126
  geology, 93, 101, 102, 111, 113, 114
  hydrology, 118, 126
  mineralogy, 101, 102, 103, 107, 111
  oceanography, 102, 126
  zoology, 93, 118, 126
Needler, Henry, 41–2
Nelson, Holly Faith, 145, 146
Netherlands, the, 71
Newey, Vincent, 71, 73
Newton, Isaac, 84, 88, 89, 91, 107, 186
Nichols, John, *Select Collection of Poems* (1782) 212
Nicholson, Marjorie Hope, 84

Nihell, Elizabeth, 163
Nonsense Club, The, 65, 67
Nuttall, A. D., 40, 50, 53

O'Keefe, John, *Wicklow Mountains* (1797), 110
O'Neill, Henrietta, 'Written on Seeing Her Two Sons at Play' (c.1797), 177
occasional poetry, 191, 203
Opie, Amelia, 184
Ossian, 253
Overton, Bill, 230, 233–4, 235, 241, 245
Ovid, 194, 201, 202

Paget, Henry William, 240
Pascal, Blaise, 29, 53
pastoral, 95, 117, 118, 1119, 120, 122, 130
Pattison, Mark, 54
Pennant, Thomas, 143
philanthropy, 20, 58, 142, 143
Philips, John, *The Splendid Shilling* (1701), 64, 101
Phillips, Katherine, 179
philosophical poetry, 59, 83, 84, 89, 90, 93, 94, 97
Pickering, James, 232–3, 235, 236, 241, 242, 243
Pigot, Robert, 240
Pilkington, Laetitia, 214
Pittock, Murray, 254, 260
Plath, Sylvia, *The Bell Jar* (1963), 173, 174
Pliny the Elder, *Natualis Historia*, 125
Plowden, Edmund, 19
poetry,
 aesthetics, 17, 42, 63, 77, 83, 85, 111, 136, 141, 147, 148
 blank verse, 4, 30, 35, 64, 65, 71, 83, 113
 couplets, 35, 57, 66, 71, 84, 88, 90, 91, 114, 140, 199
 emphasis, 48, 50, 51, 52, 55, 56, 57, 59, 60
 footnotes, 31, 57, 112, 113, 129, 133, 138, 139, 140–1, 142, 143, 144, 146, 147–8, 150 n20, 226
 form, 3, 4, 30, 31, 35, 48, 53, 65, 86, 90, 96, 7, 104, 106, 111, 119, 120
 labouring-class poets, 133, 142, 143, 144, 145, 147, 150 n16
 metre, 112, 115, 159
 octosyllabic poetry, 67, 75
 Pinadric ode, 65, 198
 poetic voice, *see* voice
 rhetoric, 21, 59, 74, 89, 192, 235, 242
 Romantic poetry, 2, 103, 117, 133, 143, 144
 satire, 12–13, 15,19, 20, 21, 22, 26 n27, 71, 73, 75, 85, 86, 189 n47, 201
 verse epistle, 1, 7, 47, 203, 223–4, 235, 236, 237, 238, 239, 241, 242, 244
 versification, 48–9, 51, 57, 65, 88, 102, 121, 140
Pointon, Priscilla, 'A Lady, with whom the Author has resided some time' (1770), 244
 'A Valentine, Extempore' (1770), 233, 243
 'Address to a Bachelor, On a Delicate Occasion' (1770), 233
 'An Elegy, Extempore, By the Author, on the Countess of Coventry' (1770), 244
 'Consolatory Reflections' (1770), 236
 'Elegy by the Author, on the death of her husband' (1794), 232
 'Extempore Address to the Inhabitants of Warwick' (1770), 238
 'Ode to the Memory of Shakespeare' (1770), 238
 'Spoken extempore by the Author, walking on Chester Walls' (1770), 244
 'The following Advice to a gay Bachelor' (1770), 243
 'The following lines by the Author, at the request of a young Lady' (1770), 244
 'To A Friend' (1770), 243

'To Master Jemmy -----, in his 32nd
  Year' (1770), 243
'To Mr. J.P.' (1794), 243
'Valentine, On [a] Leap Year'
  (1794), 242
politics, 3, 12, 13, 14, 16, 18, 23,
  30, 57, 65, 69, 73, 94, 96, 118,
  119, 124–5, 137, 137, 144, 146,
  212, 260
Pope, Alexander; as editor of
  Swift, 220
  An Essay on Criticism (1711), 17,
    46 n18
  An Essay on Man (1734), 13, 18,
    23, 29, 30, 31, 34, 36, 40, 47, 84,
    89, 91
  *Epistle to the Right Honourable
    Richard Earl of Burlington* (1731),
    13, 18 see also Pope; *Of False
    Taste*
  Imitations of Horace (1733–8), 11
  'In Imitation of the Earl of
    Rochester: On Silence' (1712), 39
  Of False Taste (1732), 13, see also
    *Epistle to the Right Honourable
    Richard Earl of Burlington*
  The Dunciad, Variorum (1728), 31
  *The First Epistle of the Second Book of
    Horace, Imitated* (1737), 22
  The Rape of the Lock (1714), 194
  Windsor Forest (1713), 104
  Works (1735), 12, 13, 16, 17, 19, 25
    n6, 48
Port-Royal Grammar, 52
postcolonialism, 136, 144, 146,
  147–8
Powel, David, *The Historie of Cambria*
  (1584), 142–3
Powell Jones, William, 84
Prescott, Sarah, 157, 160
Priestman, Martin, 69
Prior, Matthew, Alma; or, The Progress
  of the Mind (1718), 69–71
  Solomon on the Vanity of the World
    (1718), 65–6, 74
  'The Conversation' (1720), 75
provincial poetry, 141, 143, 157,
  236–7, 238
psychology, 56, 87, 157, 159, 163, 259

publishing, 47, 87, 89, 141, 146, 156,
  157, 158, 160, 168, 211, 217, 228,
  231, 232, 236
Puffin Island, 136, 139
Pugh, Edward, 146–7
Pughe, William Owen, 145

Rackham, Oliver, 118, 131
Radcliffe, John, 213–14
Ramsay, Allan, 251–2
Rapin, René, 'Reflections on Aristotle's
  Treatise on Poesie' (1674), 22
Ray, John, 32, 109
Read, William, *The Hill of Caves*
  (1818), 108–9
readers, 12, 17, 31, 50, 53, 75, 84, 87,
  102, 113, 124, 138, 147, 158, 168,
  197, 234, 245
readerships, 164, 211
religion, 16, 53, 58, 86, 96, 161
  afterlife, 179, 203, 249, 257
  Anglicanism, 54
  Catholicism, 19, 206 n25
  Eden, 37
  free will, 66
  heresy, 19
  Holy Trinity, 67
  Mass, 19
  Methodism; Calvinist Methodism;
    66–7, 159–60; Wesleyan
    Methodism, 159, 160
  predestination, 66
  prophecy, 177, 181, 188 n21
  religious poetry, 64, 67, 157, 162,
    163, 164, 174, 258
reproduction, *see under* birth,
  pregnancy
Reynolds, John, 85, 86, 87, 94
  Death's Vision (1709), 89, 90
Reynolds, Joshua, 120, 121,
  122, 124
Richardson, Samuel, *Clarissa*
  (1748), 175–6
Robinson, Mary 'Ode to My Beloved
  Daughter' (1794), 183
Rogers, Katharine, 205 n25
Rogers, Pat, 214, 223, 224
Romanticism, 2, 77, 103, 113, 117,
  137, 143–4, 146

Rome, 19, 24
Rosa, Hartmut, 184, 185
Rowland, Daniel, 159–60
Royal Society, the, 85, 86, 91, 107

Sackville, Charles (6th Earl of Dorset), 14
Sambrook, James, 31
Sargent, John, *The Mine: A Dramatic Poem* (1796), 111, 112, 113
Scafe, John, *King Coal's Levee, Or Geological Etiquette* (1819), 101, 102, 103
  The Splendid Schist, 101
Schürer, Norbert, 157, 158, 160, 161, 163, 168
Scott, Mary, *The Female Advocate* (1774), 186
Scriblerians, 40
Scribonius, 202
Scurr, Helen Margaret, 35, 41, 44, 85
Sedgwick, Eve Kosofsky, 79 n23
Seeber, Edward D., 123
Sempill, Robert, 252
sensation, 122, 159
  pain, 157, 158, 159, 161, 168, 213, 227, 256
  pleasure, 96, 175, 182
sensibility, 77, 184, 256, 258
Seward, Anna, 159, 236
  'Receipt for a Sweet Jar' (1810), 191
Seward, William, *A Tour to Yordes Cave* (1801), 106, 107, 108,
sexuality, 74, 91, 175, 176, 196
Seymour, Frances (Countess of Hertford and Duchess of Somerset), 94
Shaftesbury, 3rd Earl of, *see* Cooper, Anthony Ashley
Shakespeare, William, 4, 30, 129, 142, 176, 177, 203
  Hamlet, 194, 248
Shelley, Percy Bysshe, 113
Shenstone, William, 249, 253
  'Elegy I' (1765), 252
  'On Writing and Books' (1765), 252
Sherburn, George, 57
Sheridan, Thomas (Rev.), 214, 225, 226
Shklar, Judith, 50

Sidney, Sir Philip, 223
Sim, Stuart, 248
Singer Rowe, Elizabeth, 'To a Friend' (1737), 173
Sitter, John, 2
Smith, Adam, *Theory of Moral Sentiments* (1759), 254, 259
Smith, Charlotte, 174
  'Sonnet Written at the Close of Spring' (1782), 181
  'Sonnet Written in the Church Yard at Middleton in Sussex' (1789), 181
  'Sonnet X: To Mrs. G' (1786), 180
  'Thirty-Eight' (1791), 181–2
Smith, John, *The Printer's Grammar* (1755), 51
Smollett, Tobias, 146
Smythson, Hugh, *The Compleat Family Physician* (1781), 161
Snowdonia, 133, 136, 139, 140, 146
sociability, 50, 72, 94
Solomon, Harry, 89
Somerset, Duchess of, *see* Seymour, Frances
Spacks, Patricia Meyer, 2, 168
Spears, Monroe, 69
Spectator, 84
Speed, John, *Historie of Greate Britaine* (1611), 142
Spence, Joseph, 236
Spencer, Jane, 191
Spenser, Edmund, 4, 108
  The Shepheardes Calendar for Julye (1579), 200
Sprat, Thomas, *History of the Royal Society* (1665), 85, 86
St. James Magazine, 65
St. John, Henry (1st Viscount Bolingbroke), 21, 23, 26 n34, 27, n45, 45 n2, 52
  Dissertation upon Parties (1735), 23
St. Kitts, 124
Stack, Frank, 14, 20
stars, 59, 92, 94, 95, 102, 179, 200, 220
Steele, Anne, 159, 168
Steele, Richard, 84
Sterne, Laurence, 67, 249, 253
  Tristram Shandy (1759–68), 70, 256

Stevenson, Lionel, 44
Stoicism, 21, 22
Stratford upon Avon, 237, 238, 241, 246
subscriptions, 159, 164, 231, 232, 235, 236, 237, 238, 239, 240, 241, 242, 246 n23
suicide, 73, 180, 223
Sutherland-Leveson-Gower, George (2nd Duke of Sutherland), 156
Swift, Jonathan, 'The Power of Time: Written in the Year 1730' (1735), 226
  'Stella's Birth-day, March 13, 1726/7' (1727), 224
  'Birthday Poems', 222, 223, 224, 227, 228
  A Journal to Stella (1766), 211, 212, 213
  A Modest Proposal (1729), 211
  A Tale of a Tub (1704), 211
  'An excellent new Panegyrick on Skinnibonia' (1728), 215
  Cadenus and Vanessa (c.1727), 220, 221, 222, 223, 227, 228
  'Death and Daphne' (1735), 219, 220, 223, 228
  'Holyhead. Sept, 25, 1727' (first pub.1882), 225
  'In Sickness' (1735), 226, 227
  'Lady Acheson Weary of the Dean' (1730), 217, 228
  'Market-Hill' Poems, 215, 216–17, 218, 219, 220
  Miscellanies (1727), 220, 222, 223
  'On Stella's Birthday. Written 1718–19' (1728), 222
  'Stella, March 13' (1765), 227
  'Stella's Birth-day, 1725' (1728), 223
  The Last Volume (1731), 220, 222
  'To Mr Harlyes Surgeon' (1766), 212, 214
  'To Stella on her Birth-day. Written A.D. 1721–2' (1766), 222
  'Verses Made in Swift's Sleep' (first pub. with title 1983), 214
  Works (1735), 219, 220, 222, 226, 228
Sydenham, Thomas (physician), 161

Tague, Ingrid H., 192, 193, 201,
Talbot, Catherine, 'Writ on New-Year's Eve' (1770), 183
Taylor, Charles, 174
telescopy, 85, 92
Terry, Richard, 192, 193, 203, 204 n1, 204 n3
theology, 51, 66, 67, 83, 84–5, 86, 89, 114
  astro-theology, 32
  eschatology, 177
  physic-theology, 32, 86, 93
Thomas, Elizabeth "On Sir J—S—' (1722), 202
  'A Panegyrick. To an Attorney' (1722), 199
  'Canario' (1722), 199, 202
  'In Imitation of Anacreon' (1722), 199
  'Jill. A Pindarick Ode' (1722), 198, 199, 200, 201, 202, 203
  Miscellany Poems (1722), 198
  'The True Effigies on a Certain Squire' (1722), 202
  'To Pulcheria' (1722), 202
  'To the Pious Memory of Mrs. Diana Bridgeman' (1722), 199
  'Apology for the foregoing Ode' (1722), 201
Thomas, Keith, 186
Thomson, James, 30, 31, 32, 35, 40, 41, 42, 44, 94, 109, 113, 146, 148, 249, 253, 258, 262
  'A Hymn' (1730), 31
  Alfred: a Masque (performed 1740), 262
  Summer (1727), 137–7
  The Seasons (1730), 30, 31, 41, 93, 94
  Winter (1726), 31, 41
Thornton, Bonnell, 65
Todd, Janet, 230, 231, 233
Tollet, Elizabeth, 'Hypatia' (1724), 174, 177
Toone, William, 'Anecdotes of Beaumaris Bay' (1801), 145
topography, 142, 147, 148
  topographical poetry, 136, 143, 144, 147, 149

tourism, 106, 114, 137, 141, 146, 149 n6
translation, 11, 14, 21, 22, 24, 32, 87, 114, 128, 129, 139, 188
travel, 96, 102, 115, 137, 141, 143, 234, 235, 241
trees, 41, 42, 124
    fig trees, 173, 174, 175, 178, 179, 181, see also figs
    olive trees, 179
    willow trees, 250
Tuite, Eliza Dorothea, 'Elegy' (1796), 184
    'To A Friend' (1782), 184
typography, 52, 136, 138, 148

Universal Spectator, The, 91, 99 n34
Unwin, Mary, 74
Utrecht, 67, 77, 219

Vanhomrigh, Esther (Vanessa), 214, 220, 224
Venus, 38, 174
Virgil, 15, 16, 30, 103
voice, 1, 2, 3, 4, 11, 13, 21, 62 n25, 74, 136, 137, 138, 141, 143, 145, 156, 174, 179, 182, 186, 197, 200, 211, 217, 220, 228, 240, 254, 257
volcanoes, 18

Walpole, Horace, 196
Walpole, Robert Sir, 16, 18, 19, 24, 30, 44 n2
Walton, Izaak, *The Compleat Angler* (1653), 95
Warburton, William, 19, 48, 49, 52, 53, 57
Warr, Lady Dowager Anne de la, 199, 202
Waterfowl, 127
Watson, Alex, 144
Watts, Giles, 163
Webster, Robert, 164
Weinbrot, Howard, 15, 26 n34
Wendorf, Richard, 53
Wesley, John, 160
    Primitive Physick (1747), 161
Westminster, Duchess of, *see* Grosvenor, Constance

Weston, Joseph, 232
Wewitzer, Ralph, *The Magic Cavern* (1785), 113
Whateley, Mary, 'On the author's Husband' (1794), 203
    'The Vanity of External Accomplishments' (1764), 182
Wheatley, J., 239
Whiston, William, *New Theory of the Earth* (1696), 84
Whitehall, 15, 18
Wilmot, John (Earl of Rochester), 'Satyr Against Reason and Mankind' (1674), 54
    'Upon Nothing' (1679), 39
Wilson, Catherine, 92
Wilson, Richard (artist), 146, 150
Wilson-Costa, Karen, 250, 262
Winscom Jane Cave, birth poems, *see* birth
    'A Poem for Children' (1783), 166
    'An Hymn for a Child' (1783), 159
    'An Hymn for Consecration' (1783), 159
    'Headache' Poems, 157–8
    'My Dear Child' (1786), 155, 156, 158, 164, 165, 166
    'On the Death of Mrs Blake' (1783), 155, 158, 165, 167, 169 n14, 171 n43
    'On the Death of Mrs. Maybery' (1783), 160
    'On the Death of the Rev. Mr. Howell Harris' (1783), 160
    'On the Death of the Rev. Mr. Watkins' (1783), 160
    Poems on Various Subjects (1783), 155, 156, 158, 169
    Prose and Poetry, 161
    'The Head-Ach' (1783), 157
    'To a Young Gentleman much addicted to Detraction' (1794), 166
    'To a Youth, inclinable to Gaiety' (1789), 166
    'To My Child, If a Daughter (1786), 155, 158, 166, 167, 170 n17
    'To My Child, If A Son' (1786), 155, 158, 166, 167

'Written a few Hours before the Birth of a Child' (1786), 155, 157, 158, 159, 161, 162, 164, 165
'Written About a Month after the Birth of the Author's Son' (1789), 155, 158
'Written the first Morning of the Author's Bathing at Teignmouth' (1794), 157
'On the Death of Mr. Whitefield' (1783), 160
Woods, Robert, 162
Woodward, John, 109
Woolley, David, 216
Wordsworth, William, 59, 76, 77, 83, 111
   Lyrical Ballads (1800), 76
   'Poet's Epitaph' (1799), 254
Wortley Montagu, Lady Mary, 176
   Addressed to –' (1749), 179
   'Saturday: The Small-Pox' (1747), 191

Wright, Joseph (of Derby), 103
writing,
   private writing, 6–7, 191, 211, 212, 213, 214, 217, 218, 219, 222, 231, 234, 245
   public writing, 6, 7, 16, 19, 22, 23, 84, 94, 141, 146, 156, 164, 211–12, 213, 214, 217, 219, 222, 251, 253
   women's writing , 5–6, 156, 173, 174, 176, 177, 191, 192, 193–4, 198, 199, 202, 203, 230, 231, 243

Yalden, Mr., 104
Yearsley, Ann, 'To Mira' (1796), 168
Ynys Seriol, *see* Puffin island
Young, Edward, 65, 83
   Night Thoughts (1742–5), 256
Young, Ronnie, 251
youth, 69, 175, 180, 181, 182, 252

Printed and bound by CPI Group (UK) Ltd, Croydon, CR0 4YY